# MARKETING AND CONSUMER IDENTITY IN MULTICULTURAL AMERICA

# MARKETING AND CONSUMER IDENTITY IN MULTICULTURAL AMERICA

## Marye C. Tharp

Sage Publications
*International Educational and Professional Publisher*
Thousand Oaks ▪ London ▪ New Delhi

*For information:*

Sage Publications, Inc.
2455 Teller Road
Thousand Oaks, California 91320
E-mail: order@sagepub.com

Sage Publications Ltd.
6 Bonhill Street
London EC2A 4PU
United Kingdom

Sage Publications India Pvt. Ltd.
M-32 Market
Greater Kailash I
New Delhi 110 048 India

Printed in the United States of America

*Library of Congress Cataloging-in-Publication Data*

Tharp, Marye C.
Marketing and consumer identity in multicultural America / by Marye C. Tharp.
    p. cm.
Includes bibliographical references and index.
  ISBN 0-7619-1102-2 (cloth: alk. paper)
  ISBN 0-7619-1103-0 (pbk.: alk. paper)
1. Target marketing—United States. 2. Market segmentation-United States. 3. Consumers—United States—Attitudes. 4. Multiculturalism—United States. I. Title.
  HF5415.127.T48 2000
  658.8'0089'00973—dc21                          00-010502

01   02   03   04   05   06   10   9   8   7   6   5   4   3   2   1

| | |
|---|---|
| *Acquiring Editor:* | Marquita Flemming |
| *Editorial Assistant:* | MaryAnn Vail |
| *Production Editor:* | Nevair Kabakian |
| *Editorial Assistant:* | Candice Crosetti |
| *Typesetter/Designer:* | Marion Warren/Barbara Burkholder |
| *Indexer:* | Teri Greenberg |
| *Cover Designer:* | Ravi Balasuriya |

*Dedicated to*

Edward W. Cundiff,
teacher, scholar, mentor, friend, and role model,
who showed me how to focus my interests in
people and culture, who risked coauthoring with
an unproven young professor, and who has
supported my scholarly instincts ever since,

*and to*

my mother, Charlese Read Pepper Tharp St. John,
who has always encouraged me to follow my
curiosity, whose love of languages and people I
share, and who gave me a lifelong interest in
cultural similarities and differences.

# Contents

Preface                                                                xi

Acknowledgments                                                       xiii

**1. The Marketing Environment in a Multicultural Society**             1
  Welcome to Multicultural America!                                     1
  Chapter and Book Presentation Plan                                    2
  More Diversity and Celebration of Differences                         3
  Technology Changes the Relative Costs of Mass Versus
    Direct and Interactive Media                                       10
  The Twilight of Mass Markets, Mass Marketing, and
    Market Segmentation                                                13
  Global Basis of Competition                                          15
  What Is a Multicultural Society?                                      21
  A New Philosophy of Marketing: Valuing Consumers
    by Sharing Consumer Values                                         23
  Summary                                                              29

**2. Consumer Identity in a Multicultural Society**      **31**

Consumption as Expression of Social Identity and
    Consumer Values      31

Marketing as Both Economic Exchange and Cultural Medium      34

The Significance of Media Institutions and Representations
    in a Multicultural Society      37

The American View of the Self and Social Identity      40

Mainstream American Culture and Subcultures in
    Multicultural America      47

Consumer Identities as Subcultures      49

Summary      54

**3. Marketing in a Multicultural Environment**      **57**

The Border Mentality and Transmigration      58

Marketing Shift #1: From Long-Term Profitability to
    Shared Interests      61

Marketing Shift #2: From Niche Marketing to Matrix
    Market Planning      64

Marketing Shift #3: From Mass Markets to Mass Choices      70

Marketing Shift #4: From Market Segmentation to
    Market Identification      74

Marketing Shift #5: From Brand Managers to Market
    Specialists      76

Marketing Shift #6: From Mass Communication to
    Consumer Dialogue and Organization Contact Points      77

Marketing Shift #7: From Extensive to Intensive Market
    Information      80

Marketing Strategies for a Multicultural Setting      82

Ethical Dilemmas in Multicultural Marketing      87

Summary      89

**4. Mature Americans: Fastest Growing Subculture**      **91**

Who Are the Mature Americans?      93

The Gulag of Older Americans      94

Economic and Political Strength; Cultural Invisibility      98

Being Old in a Youth-Oriented Society      103

Media Usage: Connections to the World Outside Family      112

Activist Consumers      115

Communication and Shopping Styles of Older Consumers    116
Summary    120

**5. U.S. Latinos: The Largest Ethnic Subculture**    **123**
*Marye C. Tharp With Ernest W. Bromley*

What Does *Hispanic* or *Latino* Mean?    125
Origins of U.S. Latinos    127
Language Use and Acculturation Among U.S. Latinos    129
Size and Shape of the U.S. Hispanic Population    132
Family, Church, and Language as Symbols of Hispanic Values    136
Latino Media Images, Usage, and Availability    144
Search Strategies and Buying Preferences of Latino Consumers    154
Summary    162

**6. African Americans: Ethnic Roots, Cultural Diversity**    **165**
*Jerome D. Williams and Marye C. Tharp*

The Myth of Race, the Reality of Racial Prejudice    165
African American Diversity    170
Ethnic Identity and African American Cultural Values    179
African Americans as Consumers    187
Information Sources and Media Preferences    199
Caveat Marketer    210
Summary    211

**7. Gay Americans: Sexual Orientation as Community Boundary**    **213**
Being Gay or Lesbian in a Straight World: Identity Issues    214
What Is the Demographic Profile of the Gay Market?    217
Gay Geography, Lifestyles, and Politics    221
Diverse Gay Communities, United in Favor of Gay Rights    225
The Media: Importance of Endorsement    226
Marketing Experiences and Response of Gay Consumers    231
Summary    241

**8. Asian Americans: In Search of the American Dream**    **243**
*Satomi Furuichi, Carrie La Ferle, Wei-Na Lee, and Marye C. Tharp*

Asian America: Diversity of Cultures, Resources, and Experiences    244

Continued Traditions                                                    253
Bridging Two Cultures                                                   258
Asian American Sources of Information and Media Patterns                264
Summary                                                                 281

**9. Multicultural Markets and Marketing: Future Directions**          **283**
A Model of the Evolution of Consumer Subcultures
   in the United States                                  284
Evolving Consumer Subcultures in the United States                      289
Marketing Opportunities in Multicultural Settings Outside
   the United States                                     310
Summary                                                                 312

References                                                              315

Index                                                                   361

About the Authors                                                       395

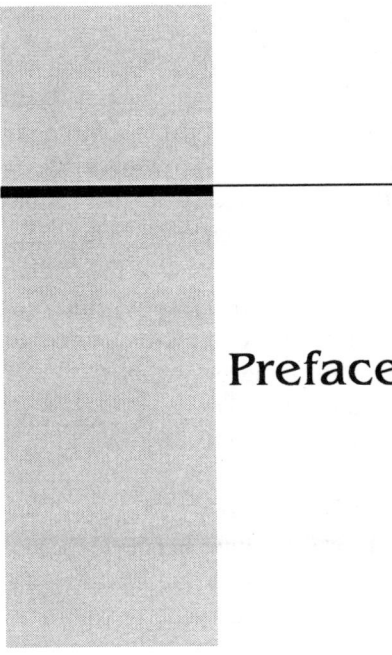

# Preface

The organizing principle of this book is that American consumer identity rests on the values and behaviors we learn from the American subcultures with which we identify. Social identity is fluid and situational; thus, marketers cannot predict individual consumer behavior by knowing the social roles or groups a consumer identifies with. Because there is so much diversity within each of the subcultures that are the focus of this book, not everyone will recognize their subcultures or identify with their descriptions. Two particularly controversial issues should be addressed here to allay the concerns of readers.

First, labeling is a thorny subject: What do members of each group call themselves, and what do they prefer that others call them? Several options could have been used for each subculture: Mature Americans or Senior Citizens, U.S. Hispanics or Latinos, African Americans or Blacks, Gays or Gays and Lesbians, and so forth. *Mature American* was the term most Senior Citizens preferred, so it was used in the chapter title and most frequently within the text, but *Senior Citizen* was also used. In the chapter on U.S. Latinos, that term was used in the title, but the terms *U.S. Hispanics* and *Hispanic Americans* were also used within the chapter to refer to members of this subculture. *Mexican American, Cuban American,* and *Puerto Rican American* were the terms used when discussing members of the Latino subculture from specific countries of origin. The chapter on Asian Americans used the same approach, with *Asian American* used to refer to the group as a whole and *Chinese American, Korean American, Filipino American, Japanese American,* or *Vietnamese American* used for people from those countries of origin. *African American* was the term used most frequently in the chapter about members of that subculture. This term was used, despite the finding that *Black* was a more preferred term among members of the subculture, in order to emphasize ethnicity and not race as a basis of the subculture's distinctive beliefs and values. In the chapter about the Gay market, the terms *Gay, Gays and Lesbians, Gay Americans,* and *Lesbian Americans* were all used. In every chapter, there is a discussion of how members feel about different terms used by and about them.

A second decision had to be made about how to organize the chapters of the book. The choice was made to start with the largest subculture and move successively to smaller ones. This is an arbitrary decision that says nothing about the attractiveness of these subcultures as target markets or markets for particular goods and services. Nor does it reflect anything about the variability within these subcultures. The Mature Market has ethnic, socioeconomic, geographic, age, and health divisions; the African American market has socioeconomic, age, geographic, and value-based diversity. The text of each chapter is where these issues are discussed, and no assumptions should be made about them on the basis of the order of chapters.

# Acknowledgments

This project has benefited from many contributors concerning both ideas and format. I assume total responsibility for their final expression, and any mistakes or omissions are mine alone. At the same time, I would like to recognize these (sometimes unknowing) collaborators.

First, I wish to thank my coauthors in this book, Jerome Williams, Wei-Na Lee, Satomi Furuichi, Carrie La Ferle, and Ernest Bromley. Each of these people signed on to the project despite incredibly busy lives and other professional commitments. Jerome agreed to write a draft of the African American chapter while commuting at various times from University Park, Pennsylvania, to Hong Kong, Singapore, Ann Arbor, Philadelphia and back to University Park again. I truly don't know how he remembered where he was supposed to be, much less that he was able to produce such an insightful review of marketing, communications, and research about African Americans. Wei-Na Lee protested that she didn't have anything new to say about Asian Americans. But the insights from her extensive research background in the media and acculturation behavior of first- and second-generation immigrants, as well as the contributions of her colleagues Satomi Furuichi and Carrie La Ferle, wove together a unique *story* about Asian American consumers. Ernest Bromley has been an overachiever since he was my student. He was determined to do "Hispanic marketing" before there was any such thing. Since 1981, he has made "Hispanic marketing" synonymous with a dynamic company, Bromley Communications, full of talented marketing professionals serving the best companies in the Americas. It is enough to say I now work for him. I thank Ernest for lending the resources of his firm and his experience to the chapter on U.S. Latinos.

For 5 years, I have had numerous research and teaching assistants without whose work this book would have taken many more years. First in a line of people who shared my passion for the project was Liesl Riddle. Liesl took my basic ideas for an outline and developed a format that enriched every part of the book. She interviewed "pioneers" in multicultural America and did exhaustive research on every single subculture discussed here. Her absolute thoroughness in pursuit of fact and citation as well as penetrating abilities to interpret meaning will undoubtedly enrich her career as a sociologist. Eileen Forman helped me brainstorm ideas about how marketing and corporate communications were assuming more meaningful roles in Americans' lives. Esra Sertoglu was plagued by the task of checking my citations and finding secondary data. She was relentless in tracking them down and creative in finding alternate sources of information.

Chang Hoan Cho was the next person I launched into the search for secondary research and case histories. His focus on international marketing and advertising prompted my return to that base of scholarly research in understanding cultural differences. Kim Smith started working for me with no prior interest in multicultural markets in the United States. She did, however, locate a gap in the materials I was asking her to analyze: Why wasn't there anything written about the Internet and cultural differences? With this in mind, she produced a master's thesis that focused on an analysis of cultural content and a test of my ideas about multicultural marketing in Web sites of companies who are major players in marketing to American subcultures. She is now making a career in research and account planning, where her knowledge of subcultures and their behavior are valuable.

Then there's Richard Villarreal de Silva. Our conversations forced me to rethink concepts such as *ethnicity, symbolic ethnicity,* and *multicultural society.* His personal questioning of academic and practitioner definitions of ethnic identity made me realize that I needed to elaborate on what was important to the way consumers see themselves and what they want from the marketplace in a multicultural society. We agree that marketing and media now influence how individuals interpret their own ethnicity as well as reflecting expressions of our ethnicity back to us. His tenacity in seeking realistic and practical theory will direct his own scholarly research. Richard prepared many of the tables based on data from the U.S. Bureau of the Census.

Last but not least, my current assistant, Jaeseok Jeong, who has had the dirtiest job of all: cleaning up all the inconsistencies created by me and prior assistants. Thank goodness he relished these "treasure" hunts.

Along the way, I have subjected many students to my ideas about multicultural markets. In my classes on cross- and multi-cultural marketing and advertising, I have received projects and term papers on topics that have been incorporated into this book. Students in my courses in advertising issues in multicultural markets, multicultural consumer marketing, and international and cross-cultural advertising are too numerous to name; I thank you all as a group for showing me where my logic or examples were weak, as students are wont to do. The research from several master's theses and doctoral dissertations has also been used in this book. I specifically wish to acknowledge Julie Kennemer, Jose Bascaran, Stephanie Hubbard, Dilara Moran, Brian Lee, Kimberly Smith, Rafael Perez, Garland Williams, Carl Brown, Wen-ling Amber Chen, Qin Chen, Brian Hill, Gigi Taylor, JJ Jeong, Tasneem Munjee, Carla Tesak, Lucy Brown Hutton, Viviana Rojas, Jaeseok Jeong, Lucy Brown, and Yolanda Cal.

My colleagues in the Department of Advertising and College of Communication at the University of Texas at Austin have been patient and supportive while my energies have necessarily been focused on this lengthy project. I have enjoyed incredible freedom to develop innovative courses in our curriculum, such as "Advertising and Symbolism," "Advertising Issues in Multicultural Markets," "Multicultural Consumer Marketing," and "The Cultural Marketplace." It was this environment that gave me the freedom to explore the impact of a multicultural society on American consumer behavior.

There have also been colleagues and friends who patiently listened to my ideas, gave me feedback and suggestions, and read and contributed to earlier versions of this manuscript. I appreciate their gifts of time, and I apologize if I have wrongly applied their ideas. This group includes Pat Rose, Marilyn Roberts, Trina Sego, Federico Subvervi, Mimi Drumright, Joel Saegert, Carrie La Ferle, Linda Gerber, Bob Hoover, Adrienne Pulido, Gigi Taylor, Vicente Valjalo, J. Moncada, Angela Kim, Paul Bryan, Amy Niederhauser, Eloise McAllister, and Florence Spalding. This manuscript was reviewed by several anonymous reviewers whose suggestions I have tried to incorporate and for which I believe it is a better, more readable product.

My first editor, Harry Briggs, had the patience of Job and a fisherman's sense of time and place. Without his commitment to the project and confidence in my ability, I could not have finished it. If only I could learn from him how to "waste no energy!" Harry's successor, Marquita Flemming, took his lead and whisked the manuscript through the publication process with record speed and minimal hassle. She has given valuable suggestions for improving the final project.

Last but not least, my family and friends have patiently awaited my return to life "after the book is finished." They have supported me along the way with sympathy, distractions, time and hospitality, pep talks, and the serenity of a Hill Country ranch for writing. Most valuable of all, they convinced me that I could and should finish this book.

# CHAPTER 1

# The Marketing Environment in a Multicultural Society

## WELCOME TO MULTICULTURAL AMERICA!

Welcome to a new America! In multicultural America, your age, address, language and accent, skin color, or shape of eyes, as well as the music you listen to, whom you have sex with, and where you work, are the tools with which American consumers construct, communicate, and change social identity. Rather than lifetime, fixed definitions of ourselves, these self-made, chosen identities are built upon a constantly changing foundation of personal characteristics and behaviors. It is a lifetime project, always in flux, never finalized, but frequently expressed by how we spend our money and time.

In multicultural America, national borders are less important than the distinctions we make between "us" and "them." Chinese Americans are members of the ethnic Chinese diaspora all over the world; at the same time, they are also Americans. Whatever groups we identify with determine our boundaries of community. The purpose of this book is to explain this concept of "chosen" consumer

1

identity and its impact on the marketplace and then to profile different American subcultures as foundations for partnerships with consumers in a multicultural society.

## CHAPTER AND BOOK PRESENTATION PLAN

Marketing and consuming assume more visible, pervasive, and prescriptive roles in a multicultural society. They are powerful influences on how we construct our self-identities, and vice versa. This chapter details the forces that are putting pressure on both consumers and marketers to adapt to a multicultural America. Forces such as increased population diversity, alternative paths toward participation in American mainstream culture, technological innovations in media and marketing, changes in competitive players, and new tools for communicating with consumers are changing the meaning of consumption in our lives. These changes institutionalize an environment in which multiple value systems are in play. These multiple value systems are the basis of a multicultural American society, consisting of various combinations of mainstream and subcultural values.

With this background, the second chapter describes exciting changes in ways Americans construct their self-identities and the effect this has on what consumers want from the marketplace. Consumers want to express who they are and what their values are in the choices they select from our cornucopia of goods and services. These goods and services must continue to satisfy particular economic and performance criteria in addition to signifying compatible values. The third chapter translates the changes in consumer needs and benefits sought to changes needed in how we build marketing programs. With marketing's objective defined as building and maintaining partnerships with culturally compatible consumers, marketing strategy is broadened to include all programs that communicate brand and corporate values or their symbolic associations. The rest of the book is devoted to profiles of American subculture groups that merit investigation as marketing partners for a large number of organizations.

The five subculture groups highlighted in this book are quite different from each other. Three, African Americans, U.S. Latinos, and Asian Americans, are ethnically, racially, and/or culturally grouped. The Mature Market (people over 65 years of age) is grouped according to age; the Gay Market is based on sexual orientation. This book is not "about" ethnic markets alone because that concept does not recognize other groups who share characteristics of subcultures. The influence that factors such as age, geographic region, social class, lifestyle, or their combinations can have on people's buying habits and media choices is substantial. Even more significant, these groups vary in preferred communication styles, value systems, and demographic characteristics. This book emphasizes the characteristics of each group as a *subculture,* starting with a profile of the largest group, Mature Americans (Chapter 4), followed by the soon-to-be-largest *ethnic* group, U.S. Latinos (Chapter 5), then today's largest racial and ethnic group, African Americans (Chapter 6), followed by the increasingly accessible Gay and Lesbian Market (Chapter 7), then another fast-growing ethnic group, Asian Americans (Chapter 8), and last, other groups with potential subculture characteristics in a multicultural America (Chapter 9).

Throughout this book, you will find accounts of successful and not-so-successful attempts to market to these groups. Whether U.S. Latinos, Gay Americans, Disabled Americans, or any other groups are good targets for a particular company or brand can be determined only by a careful study of the potential match between the company, its resources, values, products, and services, and buyers' values, interests, needs, and behaviors. The focus in this book is on opportunities and requirements represented by the subcultures discussed; it is not possible in this context to provide enough data for purposes of marketing plans. This approach encourages marketers to adopt new ways of thinking about consumer needs and marketing activities within a multicultural environment.

## MORE DIVERSITY AND CELEBRATION OF DIFFERENCES

The most significant force causing organizations to rethink how they reach out to American consumers is the increasing diversity of our population. Take a look at some simple demographic statistics that reflect our recent past and foreseeable future. Table 1.1 shows that the percentage of the non-White U.S. population grew from 11.4% in 1960 to 17.5% in 1998. By 2020, the non-White population may include more than 21% of all Americans. Likewise, the proportion of Americans over 65 years of age will rise from fewer than one in eight persons in 1960 to about one in six by 2020. By 2020, Americans over 45 years of age will be 1 of every 2.4 Americans!

The statistics in Table 1.1 also suggest other trends within the increasingly diverse U.S. population. For example, African Americans are increasing their share of the total population, but not as quickly as Asian Americans and U.S. Latinos. By 2010, U.S. Latinos will be the largest ethnic group in the United States.

**TABLE 1.1**  U.S. Population Trends, 1960-2050

| | Total Population (in 1,000s) | | | | |
|---|---|---|---|---|---|
| | 1960 | 1990 | 1998 | 2020 | 2050 |
| | 179,323 | 249,439 | 270,002 | 322,742 | 393,931 |

| | % of Total Population | | | | |
|---|---|---|---|---|---|
| | 1960 | 1990 | 1998 | 2020 | 2050 |
| Non-Latino White population | 88.6 | 83.9 | 82.5 | 79.0 | 74.8 |
| African Americans | 10.5 | 12.3 | 12.8 | 14.0 | 15.4 |
| U.S. Latinos | N/A | 9.0 | 11.0 | 16.3 | 24.5 |
| Asian Americans | N/A | 3.0 | 3.9 | 6.1 | 8.7 |
| Persons over 65 years of age | 12.5 | 12.6 | 12.7 | 16.5 | 20.0 |
| Persons over 45 years of age | 31.1 | 34.8 | 33.9 | 41.1 | 41.8 |
| Persons under 35 years of age | 53.8 | 48.9 | 49.7 | 46.6 | 46.2 |

SOURCE: U.S. Bureau of the Census (1998e).
NOTE: Percentages for each year add to more than 100% because data are shown for ethnic groups as well as age groups. Furthermore, U.S. Latinos can be double-counted as "Whites" and "U.S. Latinos" in the racial categories of the 1990 census.

The large influx of immigrants since 1980 will also continue to expand Asian American numbers. All three of these groups will have a larger presence than they do today.

Even more significant than the population numbers is the increased share of income among ethnic groups and nontraditional households in the United States. U.S. Latinos constituted 8.8% of all individuals with incomes above

$50,000 in 1970 and 14.6% in 1990 (U.S. Bureau of the Census, 1993f). African Americans' share of over $50,000 incomes went from 7.6% to 13.2% for the same years (U.S. Bureau of the Census, 1993d). The Mature Market had over 50% of U.S. disposable income in 1990 (even though their median income was only 56% of median income for other Americans) (Taeuber, 1993). Single-parent, married-without-children, and nonfamily households now outnumber the traditional, nuclear family household. During the 1990s, over 40% of firstborn children were born out of wedlock (Sanders, 1999). Organizations ignore the growing market power of ethnic consumers and new types of households, shown in Table 1.2, at their own peril.

As Table 1.3 shows, age- and ethnic-specific populations vary significantly from city to city and state to state. Marketers can reach these consumers cost-efficiently by concentrating marketing efforts in particular cities or regions (Frey, 1998; Mitchell, 1995). In some ways, the data refute current thinking about how to market to particular subculture groups. For instance, Florida may be a great place for targeting Mature Americans, but Hispanics in either Texas or California constitute a larger total population. A well-planned media effort targeted to U.S. Hispanics in California could cost less and reach more people than one targeted to Mature Americans in Florida. Another surprise might be how broad the diversity of a city like Houston is (Wartzman, 1995) or how concentrated Florida Latinos are in the Miami-Tampa area. It is definitely worth looking at geographic dispersion and demographic predictions together, as shown in Table 1.4; they tell us who and where different subculture groups will be.

Increasing ethnic diversity in the U.S. population is a significant aspect of the market environment. It is not just that there are more and different peoples (Nagourney, 1999). Newcomers to America today are not acculturating or assimilating in ways their predecessors did (Lee, La Ferle, & Tharp, 1998). In earlier times, when many European peoples came here as economic or religious exiles, they adopted as many American customs as they could, as quickly as possible—what they ate, how they dressed or spoke, how they lived, and what they did for fun. Retention of their home cultures or languages and customs had low priority for these immigrants because these interfered with successful adaptation to the American environment (Wartzman, 1995). Figure 1.1 shows the "Melting Pot" versus today's "Salad Bowl" as different ways of explaining how American culture is acquired. In the "salad bowl," immigrants want "to develop a U.S. lifestyle but maintain their language and values" (Teinowitz, 1998, p. S20).

*(text continues on page 9)*

**TABLE 1.2** Population and Household Income Shares for Various U.S. Groups

| | 1960 | | 1990 | | 2020 | |
|---|---|---|---|---|---|---|
| | Population (in 1,000s) | Median Income | Population (in 1,000s) | Median Income | Population (in 1,000s) | Median Income |
| All Americans | 179,323 | $5,620 | 249,439 | $29,943 | 322,742 | N/A |

| | 1960 | | 1990 | | 2020 | |
|---|---|---|---|---|---|---|
| Population Group | % of Population | % of Median Income | % of Population | % of Median Income | % of Population | % of Median Income |
| African Americans | 10.0 | 49.9 | 11.2 | 62.4 | 14.0 | N/A |
| U.S. Hispanics | 4.0 | N/A | 6.4 | 74.6 | 16.3 | N/A |
| Asian Americans | N/A | N/A | 1.6 | 128.4 | 6.1 | N/A |
| Mature Market[a] | 9.2 | 51.5 | 21.9 | 56.3 | 27.4 | N/A |
| Whites | 89.3 | 94.2 | 85.8 | 104.3 | 76.6 | N/A |
| Family households | 83.6 | 100.0 | 75.4 | 119.2 | N/A | N/A |
| Nonfamily households | 19.1 | 60.0 | 29.6 | 59.1 | N/A | N/A |
| Single parents | 12.8 | 52.8[b] | 28.1 | 57.9[b] | N/A | N/A |

SOURCES: U.S. Bureau of the Census (1961, 1992, 1993b, 1998e).

a. For purposes of this table, Mature Market is defined as 65 years of age or older.

b. In 1960 and 1990, single parents were included in two categories: female householders (52.8% of family median income) and male householders (86.5% of family median income). Female householders account for over 80% of all single parent homes.

**TABLE 1.3** Population in Selected Geographic Areas in 1990 (Cities) and 2000 (States)

| City/State | Total Population (in 1,000s) | White Americans (%) | African Americans (%) | U.S Latinos (%) | Asian Americans (%) | Mature Market[a] (%) |
|---|---|---|---|---|---|---|
| California | 35,521 | 78.5 | 7.5 | 32.7 | 13.2 | 10.4 |
| Texas | 20,119 | 84.1 | 12.6 | 29.2 | 2.8 | 10.4 |
| New York | 18,146 | 75.8 | 18.2 | 15.5 | 5.7 | 13.0 |
| Illinois | 12,051 | 80.8 | 15.5 | 10.5 | 3.5 | 12.3 |
| Florida | 15,233 | 82.6 | 15.3 | 15.7 | 1.8 | 18.1 |
| Los Angeles | 14,532 | 64.7 | 8.4 | 32.4 | 9.2 | 9.7 |
| New York City | 18,087 | 70.3 | 18.2 | 15.0 | 4.8 | 13.1 |
| Chicago | 8,066 | 71.6 | 19.1 | 13.0 | 2.5 | 8.0 |
| Miami | 3,193 | 76.5 | 18.5 | 33.1 | 1.3 | 16.6 |
| Dallas | 3,885 | 75.3 | 14.3 | 13.0 | 2.5 | 8.0 |
| Seattle-Tacoma | 2,559 | 86.5 | 4.8 | 2.8 | 6.4 | 10.7 |
| Atlanta | 2,834 | 71.3 | 26.0 | 1.9 | 1.8 | 7.9 |
| Washington, DC | 3,924 | 65.8 | 26.6 | 5.6 | 5.1 | 8.5 |
| Boston | 4,172 | 89.0 | 6.3 | 4.5 | 2.9 | 12.4 |
| Houston | 3,711 | 67.6 | 17.9 | 20.5 | 3.5 | 7.3 |
| Detroit Metro | 4,665 | 76.5 | 20.9 | 1.8 | 1.5 | 11.6 |

SOURCES: U.S. Bureau of the Census (1994a, 1994b).
NOTE: The data for states are based on projected population size in 2000, whereas the data for cities are based on 1990 MSA census data.
a. For purposes of this table, *Mature Market* is defined as 65 years of age or older.

**TABLE 1.4**  Various Groups' Percentage of the Total Population in the Five Largest States, 1960-2020

| City/State | African American | U.S. Latinos | Asian American | Mature Market[a] |
|---|---|---|---|---|
| California | | | | |
| 1960 | 5.6 | N/A | N/A | 8.8 |
| 1990 | 7.4 | 25.8 | 9.6 | 8.2 |
| 1995 | 7.6 | 29.1 | 11.5 | 11.0 |
| 2020 | 8.0 | 36.5 | 20.2 | 13.8 |
| Texas | | | | |
| 1960 | 12.4 | N/A | N/A | 7.8 |
| 1990 | 11.9 | 25.6 | 1.9 | 18.4 |
| 1995 | 12.2 | 27.6 | 2.4 | 10.2 |
| 2020 | 12.6 | 40.3 | 4.2 | 14.2 |
| New York | | | | |
| 1960 | 8.9 | N/A | N/A | 10.1 |
| 1990 | 15.9 | 12.3 | 3.9 | 22.1 |
| 1995 | 17.6 | 14.0 | 4.8 | 13.4 |
| 2020 | 21.1 | 15.9 | 8.1 | 15.8 |
| Illinois | | | | |
| 1960 | 10.3 | N/A | N/A | 10.9 |
| 1990 | 14.8 | 7.9 | 2.5 | 14.5 |
| 1995 | 15.3 | 9.2 | 3.0 | 12.6 |
| 2020 | 18.4 | 15.7 | 6.2 | 15.2 |
| Florida | | | | |
| 1960 | 17.8 | N/A | N/A | 11.2 |
| 1990 | 13.6 | 12.2 | 1.2 | 29.1 |
| 1995 | 14.7 | 13.8 | 1.5 | 18.5 |
| 2020 | 17.9 | 21.5 | 3.0 | 25.6 |

SOURCES: U.S. Bureau of the Census (1961, Tables PC1-6C, 11C, 12C, 15C, 23C, 24C, 34C, 45C, 49C, 50C; 1993b, 1994a).
a. For purposes of this table, *Mature Market* is defined as 65 years of age or older.

MELTING POT

(Natives + Africans + Irish + Chinese + Indians + French + Koreans +
Welsh + Mexicans + Japanese + Russians + Cambodians + Poles + Czechs
+ Vietnamese + All Other Immigrants) + Time and/or Generations =
*American Culture*

SALAD BOWL

*Multicultural American Cultures* $= f$ [Cultural Distance From U.S.
Culture for Immigrants + Other Immigrants and Cultural Influences +
Time and/or Generations + Acculturation Agents (e.g., Schools, Religion,
Family, Media, Government Agencies) + Subculture Values + Unique
Mainstream American Cultural Values]

---

**Figure 1.1.** The Melting Pot Versus the Salad Bowl: Different Acculturation Patterns
in America
SOURCE: The melting pot "formula" is based on the work of Gordon (1964).

Today, it is not necessary for immigrants to rid themselves of their mother
culture before they can find a job, watch TV, or succeed in school. For Latino and
Asian immigrants (over 75% of the total in 1998) ("Indicators of the Century,"
1999), exposure to native-language media in their countries of origin and in the
United States gives a rich, up-close and intimate, if sometimes distorted, vision
of what the United States and "mainstream" American culture are like. What
they see, as newcomers to America, are successful Americans who look like
them and speak their language. In 1998, 10% of all Americans were immigrants
(Escobar, 1999). There are educational opportunities for their children and networks of ethnically owned and ethnically sensitive organizations to patronize.
In response, Americans are becoming more tolerant of alternative lifestyles and
cultures ("The American Character," 1999). In sum, there is a new path for becoming a successful American: By celebrating instead of hiding ethnicity, immigrants can still reach the economic promises of the "American dream"
(Boyce, 1997).

Ethnicity can be both an economic asset (as in set-aside scholarships) and a liability (lower incomes and job discrimination) in the United States today. But
because we celebrate differences to incorporate diversity, the social and political values of ethnic identity are overwhelmingly positive. In a multicultural
America, White males are searching for a positive group image, as are Native,

African, Jewish, Italian, female, Mature, Generation X, and other groups of Americans (Hardy, 1997). Group identity, especially racial or ethnic member- ship, is the social base camp from which newcomers make forays into American culture. Consumers choose to incorporate different aspects of American culture, and by so doing they create a hybrid version of Americanness. In this sense, Mexican American culture is neither Mexican nor American; nor is it on some continuum between the two (Wallendorf & Reilly, 1983). Over time or even gen- erations, there will still be a unique mix of American and Mexican cultural as- pects that constitute Mexican American subculture in the United States. These beliefs and behaviors are the building blocks of multicultural value systems in the United States.

## TECHNOLOGY CHANGES THE RELATIVE COSTS OF MASS VERSUS DIRECT AND INTERACTIVE MEDIA

Ignore the hype about 500 interactive television channels and the Internet as in- formation superhighway. Their significance is that new media offer consumers growing access to an infinite number of information sources at virtually no cost. How will this access change the search strategies and information needs of buy- ers? What strategies are effective for sellers when interactive media permit buy- ers to find "perfect" matches between what they want and what's available? Consumers can "bid" the price they wish to pay for airline tickets, new cars, and just about anything they want. How can companies communicate with large numbers of potential buyers who freely access so many information sources? These are the challenges of communicating with consumers in multicultural America.

Let's look closely at some trends in media that are already changing the ways buyers and sellers communicate with each other. A foundation of modern mar- keting has been the use of mass communication techniques and mass media to reach large numbers of potential buyers. The economies of scale gained by con- tacting larger populations helped to justify the wastefulness and noise of the mass media in reaching a specific audience. Until the 1980s, media planning was not very complicated for a national advertiser such as Procter & Gamble or Chevrolet. Forty-nine percent of all television advertising was seen on the three national networks in 1968 (Rosenthal, 1979). In 1975, 57% of all homes with television were tuned in to network programs; the other sets either were not on or were tuned in to local programs (Rosenthal, 1979). By 1980, *Advertising Age* reported total television advertising as 20.7% of national media expenditures ("1980 Media Expenditures," 1981). In 1993, TV expenditures were still about 21% of the total (*Market Share Reporter,* 1993).

In contrast to increased spending overall in TV, network audiences and advertising continue to lose share as a percentage of total television advertising. In 1970, only 7% of U.S. TV households had cable (Television Digest, 1982); 25 years later, over 65% of homes were cable equipped (Sissors & Summarek, 1987, p. 292). Even radio, newspapers, and magazines, always characterized as more selective media, were available only in print, whereas today they can be delivered online, via satellite, or in a variety of formats to fit the interests of different segments of their audience. Consider this statement at the end of 1998: "In 1965, a product manager at P&G could reach 80% of 18- to 49-year-old women with three 60-second commercials using P&G-controlled programs. Today, it would require at least 97 prime-time commercials to achieve the same result" (Narisetti, 1998, p. S4).

Mass media allowed organizations to reach large audiences, but at substantial expense (Dunn & Lorimar, 1979; McGann & Russell, 1988). Today, few media really reach a "mass" audience. Network TV has a declining share of the television audience (57% for five networks in 1998) as cable (37% of TV audiences in 1998; Roberts, 1999) and syndicated TV programmers offer serious entertainment alternatives and as games and videos account for more of the time consumers spend with their TV sets. Fox, Warner Brothers, and MTV are the networks of under-30 audiences, and CBS appears to program for the Mature Market (Grover, 1998). Whole networks are targeting specific audiences instead of using variety programming to attract different viewers at different times. TV is fast becoming as selective a medium as magazines and radio (Roberts, 1999). The relative costs of reaching consumers by TV are still quite high, and they may even be increasing relative to other media.

Therefore, media planning now emphasizes the percentage of a media audience composed of potential buyers as a more relevant criterion than audience size. Marketers and advertisers look for selected audiences that can be reached with selective media (Shergill, 1993). Because audience demographics were always the basis for placing advertising, this is not a new concept. But today cable and syndicators and independents can reach precisely defined groups with less waste and more price options. In this environment, media planning is a number-crunching science for creating a patchwork of partially overlapping categories of audiences and potential buyers.

TV is no longer the magic mass medium it used to be, nor is it the most effective way to reach smaller audiences. Newer technologies offer superior opportunities for dialogue with potential buyers (Petersen & Rose, 2000; Schonfeld, 1998). Consumer clubs and other in-house databases built around current and past customers can match every persuasive message and promotion to the past responses of each customer on the list. New ways of reaching potential buyers have been springing up wherever new communication technologies find their way to consumers: free high-speed Internet access (DSL), fax machines, rental videos, modems, broadband cable networks, computer bulletin boards, and, of course, company Web sites. These and other online and real-time ways of ordering and purchasing goods and services give buyers and sellers unprecedented access to each other. An individual with desk-top publishing capabilities can communicate with large numbers of customers with a level of sophistication that was once limited to large corporations. Simultaneous language translations (Collette, 1999; Wallich, 1999), on-screen programming, and interactive media approximate interpersonal rather than mass communication within a global market.

With the explosion in communication technology, companies face a myriad of communication opportunities, including consumer and trade promotions, advertising, public relations, employee and stockholder publications, charity and event sponsorships, product placements in media and film, package designs, and executive speeches. E-commerce businesses took in over $3.17 billion during the 1999-2000 holiday season, a small amount of all retail spending but up from zero in 5 years (Stone, 2000). Advertising plays an important role in this package of communications, but other tools can do things that advertising cannot. Product placements in films and sponsorships of events as varied as the Gay Olympics, Calle Ocho in Miami, and the Indianapolis 500 build company and brand awareness in a noncommercial setting. These and other noncommissionable media are part and parcel of a communications program of integrated marketing.

As media have become more fragmented, the source credibility of each medium is once again salient (Hirschman & Thompson, 1997). When TV and radio were new phenomena in American life, they wielded influence over consumer choice by simply advertising a brand in the medium. Media credibility was compounded when coupled with the endorsement of a particular celebrity or well-known person. Newer technologies such as the World Wide Web also have had brief periods as highly credible sources of information. As both marketers and consumers search for shortcuts through the maze of information out there, "where" something was said and "by whom" may be more important than "what" was said.

With the increased variety of ways to communicate with consumers, organizations can devise marketing plans that deliver a more precise match between target audience (people exposed to a medium) and target market (potential buyers of a specific product or service) (Ellis, 1999). They are asking consumers for "permission" to build a dialogue that meets both company and consumer needs for information. The competitive edge of the future will be an organization's ability to interpret and use a "portfolio" of data sources and access to consumers. When information sources are widely accessible and relatively cost-free inputs to marketing decisions, reaching specific customers means customizing message and media.

Another factor that will influence the ways organizations relate to consumers in a multicultural society is the convergence of new technologies for producing, marketing, and consuming goods and services (Bessen, 1994; Bower & Christensen, 1995; Carlson & Goldman, 1994). Robotics in factories and total quality management in service firms allow for "mass" customization of products and services (Schonfeld, 1998). Distribution partnerships and strategic alliances reduce risks by committing organizations to longer-term supplier-buyer relationships. Even radio is becoming a national buy for large and small markets (Tejada, 1999). Computer analysis of customer lists and access to specialized databases help firms build broader and deeper relationships with consumers (White, 2000). A market segment's profitability is directly related to the costs of reaching buyers in the segment. Smaller market niches become profitable when production and/or marketing costs fall, as is occurring with these new methods for producing and marketing.

## THE TWILIGHT OF MASS MARKETS, MASS MARKETING, AND MARKET SEGMENTATION

There has never really been an "average" American, just some statistic like the age, weight, or income of an "average American." Nevertheless, that concept is the philosophical basis of mass marketing, even market segmentation. Until recently, American consumers' needs were treated as if most differences across individuals could be "averaged" without much loss of meaning. In the 1950s and 1960s, if women wanted cars with different features from those available, that was not considered in the marketing programs of car companies. These sellers assumed correctly that women had little influence over the "average" family car-buying decision. For companies wanting a large share of car buyers, it was only cost-efficient to cater to the largest segments among buyers within the American market. Contemporary marketing strategies still assume that sales growth comes from identifying and satisfying an ever-increasing number of consumers.[1]

This idea, that organizations grow by increasing their base of satisfied customers, was implemented in the 1950s and 1960s, when the economy was expanding and consumers were dazzled by product abundance, even flattered by the attentions of competitors intent on their satisfaction. For the first time in history, there were truly mass media that effectively reached national audiences. As competition has intensified, marketing strategies have been continually refined, evolving from mass marketing to an emphasis on segmentation within the national market and then to niche marketing and one-on-one relationship marketing. Market segmentation tactics, introduced in the 1960s, acknowledge the direct link between buyer characteristics and buyer behaviors (Cundiff & Still, 1964, p. 22; Kotler, 1967, p. 65; McCarthy, 1960, pp. 37, 83). But most companies believed, and still do, that reaching different segments requires adjustments in the "marketing mix," varying such tactics as product features, price promotions, media buys, or types of retail outlets.

Why has this philosophy of business growth worked so well, not just in the United States but in many different national markets across the world? The characteristics of the U.S. population in the 1960s shed light on the reasons for success of business strategies directed to the economic interests of the "average" consumer:

- ▶ Ethnic groups (non-Whites) constituted less than 11% of the population and had an even smaller share of disposable income.
- ▶ The average American lived 69 years, and less than 18% of the population was over 55 years of age.
- ▶ There were only three national TV networks, less than 2% of American homes were connected to cable stations, and traditional media (TV, radio, newspapers, and magazines) constituted the majority of all advertising and promotional expenditures.
- ▶ The "American dream" of home ownership and material affluence was accessible if buyers opted for conformity over self-expression; large producers and marketers were beneficiaries of the advantages of economies of scale; meanwhile, the country breezed along with economic growth averaging over 3% a year.
- ▶ Less than 5% of the U.S. gross national product came from international trade or investments; world markets were marginal to the success of domestic marketers.

▶ The driving philosophy of social identity and consumption for most Americans was the "melting pot" ideal (Schwarz, 1995). Fitting in meant sharing in the manna of the most productive economy in the world; visible group differences were relegated to rituals, music, and food.

The United States at the third millenium looks considerably different. We are an increasingly diverse population (Cose, 2000). Consumer preferences and behavior in the marketplace also show more variety. "Averaging" the differences across groups of consumers results in products or services that do not really match the needs of any specific group. In the 1980s, New Coke was a brand designed to appeal to the taste preferences of younger soft-drink consumers but also to maintain the loyalty of Coca-Cola drinkers. When these loyal Coca-Cola drinkers insisted on "real" Coca-Cola, the firm ditched New Coke and substituted an increasing number of niche brands to reach a broader spectrum of soft-drink consumers, a necessary tactic to increase Coca-Cola's share of soft-drink consumers. Figures 1.2a through 1.2c show how Coca-Cola's advertising today tries to appeal to different consumers by using communication styles of the subculture groups (U.S. Hispanics, African Americans, children) with which target consumers identify.

Market segmentation, even relationship marketing techniques, focus only on the relationship of buyer and seller within the marketplace for goods and services. Evidence on the horizon suggests that multicultural Americans judge economic value to be too narrow a commitment. Buying a particular brand or service can be an expression of personal identity as well as an economic decision. Volkswagen offers nostalgia for the idealism of the 1960s to Baby Boomers with the new Beetle's promise: "If you sold your soul in the 80s, here's your chance to buy it back" (Beatty, 1998, p. B6). Marketing efforts themselves are artifacts of our cultural environment as much as they are business propositions. Nike's "Just Do It" slogan speaks to a broad-based belief in America that we can be anything or anyone we choose to become. This is advertising as both "teacher" and "mirror" of cultural values (Englis & Solomon, 1995).

## GLOBAL BASIS OF COMPETITION

National borders are increasingly irrelevant as market boundaries. We are moving inexorably toward a "global village" marketplace within the major trading countries of the world. Exports have grown from about 4% of the gross national product in 1950 to over 10%; imports have expanded from that same percentage

*(text continues on page 19)*

**Figure 1.2a.** Coca-Cola Ads for Different U.S. Subcultures: U.S. Hispanics

**Figure 1.2b.** Coca-Cola Ads for Different U.S. Subcultures: African Americans

**Figure 1.2c.** Coca-Cola Ads for Different U.S. Subcultures: Children

in 1950 to over 11% in 1997 (Darnay, 1998; "U.S. Balance of Payments Accounts," 1997). Globalization has pressured the American economy and our producers to become more productive (Conlin, 1999). Even foreign direct investments in other countries by American businesses account for over 7% of the American gross national product. Our major trading partners for exports and imports in 1950 and 1960 were European; today they include Mexico, Latin America, and Asia at the top of the list. No sector of the American economy or American company is isolated from what happens in other parts of the world in the same industry (Holstein, 1990). The nation-state itself is losing sovereignty as firms become more global and less local in scope (Grunwald, 2000). The interlocking nature of national markets is here to stay.

In the process of becoming more international, national boundaries as parameters of markets become artificial rather than natural barriers (Holstein, 1990). Cultural and behavioral criteria are more useful to firms in grouping potential buyers of products or services. All over the world, sports shoes appeal to people with casual lifestyles, no matter what language they speak; VCRs attract buyers with similar incomes; and even *Time* magazine, CNN, and the *International Herald Tribune* are bought and consumed by people who read English as a first or second language.

The increasingly global basis of competition is also affecting consumer choice. The free-trade environment of the late 20th century lowered the costs of selling products and services across national boundaries. Companies gained competitive advantages and marketing synergies by simultaneously introducing new products and brands across the world (Church, 1997). Because future consumer markets in developed countries are expected to grow at substantially lower rates than in the past, the opportunities for growth continue to be in entry and early penetration of any viable market across the globe. Table 1.5 shows the increasing importance of global markets, as measured by foreign sales as a percentage of total sales, for the top 10 American corporations over the last 20 years.

The ability of firms to compete simultaneously in many different national markets demands skill in understanding and interpreting consumer similarities and differences. This leads to identification and pursuit of consumers whose product-related needs are similar even though their cultures or countries of origin may vary. Such tactics stretch a firm's competitive advantages and strategic positioning. The evolution from national to global markets has created a mandate for a global presence in most large organizations. Yet in the search for marketing partnerships, it is clear that resource limits still force priorities to be

**TABLE 1.5**  Top American Corporations: Percentage of Total Revenues From Foreign
            Sources

|                    | 1980 | | 1990 | | 1995 | | 1999 | |
| --- | --- | --- | --- | --- | --- | --- | --- | --- |
| Company Name       | Rank | % | Rank | % | Rank | % | Rank | % |
| Exxon              | 1  | 72.1 | 1  | 73.2 | 1  | 77.4 | 1  | 80.1 |
| Mobil              | 2  | 60.3 | 4  | 64.7 | 3  | 67.6 | 7  | 58.7 |
| Texaco             | 3  | 67.9 | 8  | 42.3 | 6  | 55.9 | 5  | 79.3 |
| Ford               | 4  | 43.9 | 5  | 33.2 | 5  | 29.6 | 3  | 41.5 |
| Standard Oil-CA    | 5  | 58.4 | ↓  | *    | ↓  | *    | ↓  | *    |
| General Motors     | 6  | 25.3 | 3  | 26.6 | 2  | 28.4 | 4  | 30.8 |
| IBM                | 7  | 53.6 | 2  | 58.9 | 4  | 62.3 | 2  | 56.8 |
| ITT                | 8  | 52.6 | 9  | 43.3 | ↓  | *    | ↓  | *    |
| Gulf Oil           | 9  | 46.4 | ↓  | *    | ↓  | *    | ↓  | *    |
| Engelhard Minerals | 10 | 54.1 | ↓  | *    | ↓  | *    | ↓  | *    |
| Citicorp           | ↓  | *    | 6  | 52.3 | 7  | 62.3 | 8  | 34.4 |
| Du Pont            | ↓  | *    | 7  | 39.8 | ↓  | 42.1 | ↓  | 47.2 |
| Dow Chemical       | ↓  | *    | 10 | 54.1 | ↓  | 50.3 | ↓  | 59.8 |
| Chevron            | ↓  | *    | ↓  | *    | 8  | 42.9 | ↓  | 47.3 |
| Philip Morris      | ↓  | *    | ↓  | *    | 9  | 30.4 | 10 | 34.3 |
| Procter & Gamble   | ↓  | *    | ↓  | *    | 10 | 51.7 | 12 | 48.3 |
| General Electric   | ↓  | *    | ↓  | *    | ↓  | *    | 6  | 31.1 |
| Hewlett-Packard    | ↓  | *    | ↓  | *    | ↓  | *    | 9  | 54.3 |

SOURCES: "The 100 Largest U.S. Multinationals" (1980, 1990, 1995); "Spanning the World"
(1999).
↓ This company was not among the top 10 American corporations in that year.
* Percentage of foreign sales was not included because this company was not among the top 10
corporations that year.

made. This forces marketers to "declare" who they are and who they are not by
which markets they serve and which ones they do not. The marketing program itself differentiates a firm from its competitors. Nichemanship has become the basis for any global or local marketing strategy today.

The internationalization of business activity for large firms has moved the basis of competition from one company's products versus another's to one productive system and its allies versus other systems and their allies. The merger of Time Warner, America On-line, Turner Broadcasting, and Columbia House in 2000 was typical of many joint ventures designed to mine the customer databases of member companies with increasingly convergent marketing efforts (Petersen & Rose, 2000). Content and software are given away on the Internet as "creativity is overtaking capital as the principal elixir of growth" (Petzinger, 2000, p. R31). Many organizations have expanded their marketing efforts to include multiple publics, not just potential buyers, but also competitors, suppliers, regulators, stockholders (48% of Americans) (Conlin, 1999), and the public in general. What makes such strategic alliances work is the perception of shared benefits.

New ideas are also changing the ways companies set goals and manage people. Even staid consulting firms like Price Waterhouse Coopers are considering measuring success by their impact on society and the global environment rather than on the basis of meeting financial goals ("Fire Starters," 1999). These changes in the nature of competition and the declining significance of national borders suggest a concurrent need to redefine what any particular organization's market is: *a group of consumers who have both mutual economic interests and cultural compatibility.*

## WHAT IS A MULTICULTURAL SOCIETY?

So what exactly is a multicultural society? The changes just described in our demographic, media, marketing, technological, and competitive environments are creating the infrastructure of a multicultural society. They trumpet and reinforce competing worldviews and distinctive beliefs. It is the simultaneous influence of multiple value systems that is the substance of a multicultural society.

Subcultures share important characteristics of larger cultural groups. The idea that members of a particular culture have a distinctive worldview is frequently cited (de Mooij, 1998; Hofstede, 1997; Trompenaars & Hampden-Turner, 1998). A culture or subculture's worldview is reflected in that group's beliefs and norms. For example, in collectivistic societies in Africa, Latin America, and Asia, individuals are defined by the groups to which they belong; self-identity is synonymous with group identity (de Mooij, 1998; Hofstede, 1997; Trompenaars & Hampden-Turner, 1998). In contrast, mainstream American culture emphasizes individualism and presupposes the freedom to choose whether group memberships are part of self-identity. Naturally, there is also a difference between how collectivistic and individualistic cultures treat outsiders. In an individualistic culture, there is little difference between outsiders and insiders, but in collectivistic cultures, individuals of different status are treated according to particular rules (Hofstede, 1997, pp. 23-47).

Another belief that distinguishes cultures is the extent to which a society assumes equality or inequality among its members. American culture has the heritage of the assumption that "all men are created equal," whereas African, Latin American, and Asian countries assume inequality and power distance among group members. Yet another norm of cultural systems concerns appropriate roles for men and women. American mainstream culture recognizes fewer differences between men and women or their roles than other contemporary societies (de Mooij, 1998, p. 89).

Other important elements of cultural value systems concern the nature of human beings' relationship to their physical and temporal environments. Some cultures believe that humans are dominated by nature; others (e.g., Asia) cherish an ideal of human beings in harmony with nature; still others see natural resources as belonging to human beings to use as they see fit. Invention and creativity are most carefully nurtured in cultures that believe in taking risks and that place value on what is "new" (American mainstream culture). Other cultures (such as Latin America, Africa, and Asia) foster traditions, rules, and beliefs in determinism as ways to reduce uncertainty and avoid the risks of the unknown. Time, too, has its cultural interpretation: Cultures can be future oriented (United States) or present or past oriented (Asia) and can be monochronic (United States) or polychronic (Asia).

Communication styles are also culture determined (Jandt, 1995, pp. 47-64). As Edward Hall (1984, pp. 85-128) and de Mooij (1998, p. 65) have noted, low-context cultures such as the United States and Scandinavia locate meaning in the verbal aspects of messages between people. They pay less attention to the context within which a message was sent. High-context cultures (e.g., those of Africa, Asia, and Latin America) are keyed in to nuances of facial expression, pace of speech, tone of voice, relationship of speaker and receiver, and all other elements surrounding a verbal message.

It is not just immigrants or ethnic groups in the United States who bring different worldviews to the American mosaic. Different age groups and social classes, disabled Americans, people who identify strongly with the heritage of their geographic region, and even people with different sexual orientations add their own values, beliefs, and norms. The next chapter presents a closer look at what the ideals are of American mainstream culture; in the chapters that profile Mature Americans, U.S. Latinos, African Americans, Gays and Lesbians, and Asian Americans, each group's norms and beliefs are discussed.

In sum, what are valued ideals in one cultural system may be conditions to be avoided in another. The means to a desired end for one group is the end goal itself for other peoples (de Mooij, 1998, p. 96; Rokeach, 1973). As a result, in a multicultural society, behavior is not as clear a guide to a person's identity as are the groups the person identifies with and the values that drive his or her behavior.

Today, most of us experience American life through customized media and marketing institutions that mirror our beliefs and associations. These selective filters introduce and reinforce values, ideals, and symbols of subcultures with which audience members identify. New communities are created from shared experiences, sexual orientation, regional characterization, ethnic identity, or lifestyle. Americans can simultaneously aspire to membership in mainstream America and participate in a subculture that other Americans view as outside the mainstream. This is the appeal of the salad bowl as a model for our multicultural society. Individuals can express the part of themselves that is African American or Gay or teenage or Texan or working class and still belong (or aspire to belong) to mainstream America.

## A NEW PHILOSOPHY OF MARKETING: VALUING CONSUMERS BY SHARING CONSUMER VALUES

The new marketing imperative is to build upon the common interests of these subcultural groups with which consumers identify. The competitive business arena is now a global one, and nimble marketers can quickly match both consumers' tastes and competitor tactics. Media options require precise understanding of the customers that firms want to reach, what their lifestyles are, how particular brands and media fit into their lives, and how and when to reach them. Organizations must abandon the belief in "growth through more satisfied buyers" and learn how to build more satisfying partnerships with the people (sometimes, though not always limited to, buyers) who share overlapping interests.

AT&T is an example of a multicultural marketer within the United States. AT&T has identified subculture groups that its target American consumers identify with and has designed programs that express its shared interests with those groups. Those programs include decisions about philanthropy, financial investments, human resources, and participation in community events, as well as traditional marketing programs. The net results are programs that meet consumers' performance criteria for products and services, as well as reinforcing and expressing their values and identities. AT&T advertising that targets some of these different groups in the United States is shown in Figures 1.3a through 1.3d.

Niche marketing and ethnic marketing have become common strategic alternatives to mass marketing in response to a more intense competitive field and more diverse consumers. To concentrate resources, companies can focus on a limited number of diverse consumer groups and hope to capture a large share of their total demand. But this strategy alone is not enough to hold the loyalty of Americans in a multicultural society.

To succeed today, marketers must build long-term growth from shared interests with consumers. Rather than seeking a larger number of profitable customers, they should aim to acquire customers who are more satisfied because their interests and needs overlap those of the organizations they patronize. This involves using a matrix of marketing decisions in three sequential steps: (a) identifying target consumers and the communities representing their social identities, (b) developing policies that are consistent with these groups' interests, and (c) offering brands and policies that meet the economic and cultural needs of people who identify with those groups.

This is a strategy of growth that links an organization's interests to those of the groups that its desired customers belong to or identify with. Long-term consumer loyalty must be built on a cultural foundation as well as one that satisfies economic value, performance functions, and benefits sought. For an exchange of loyalties to take place, marketing programs should address buyers' social or cultural needs for expressing identity as well as economic interests. A commanding objective of organizations must be finding out how to behave as an authentic member of different American subcultures in order to attract and maintain constituencies among large numbers of consumers.

Greater satisfaction among buyers can evolve from the broader role that a business organization plays in the cultural lives of buyers. Not only is Absolut a tasty brand of vodka, but the social significance of its marketing programs, such as advertising in the Gay press, supporting causes dear to the Gay community, and simply recognizing Gay Americans as a viable market niche, takes the purchase of a bottle of vodka from a strictly economic choice to one that expresses social and even political loyalties in today's America. This cultural partnership between buyers and sellers is a broader based, longer-term, and more profitable relationship than traditional niche marketing. Chapter 3 describes more fully the building blocks of marketer-consumer partnerships on this dual economic-cultural foundation.

(text continues on page 29)

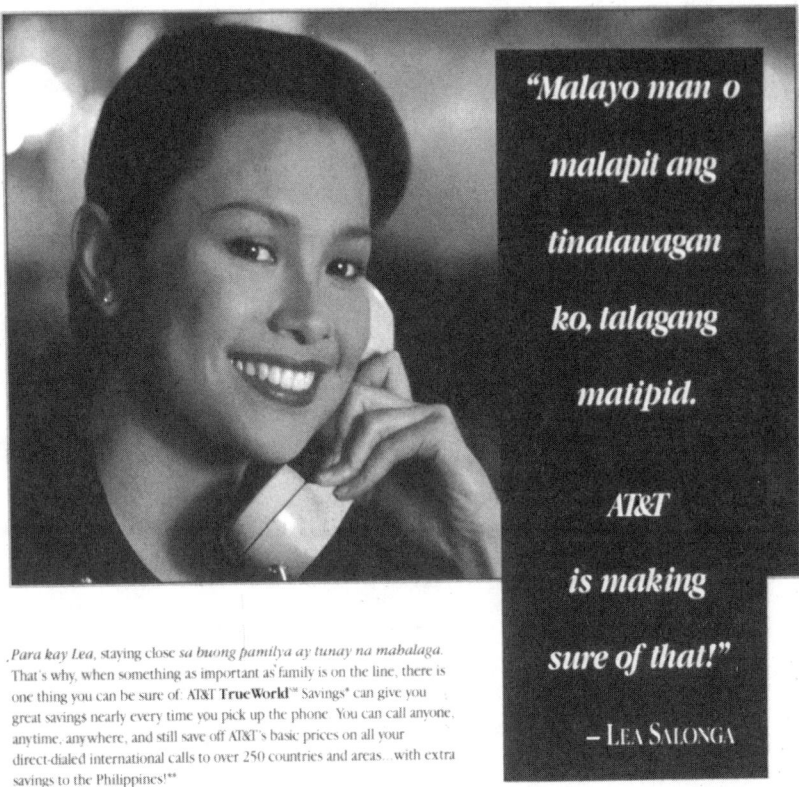

"Malayo man o malapit ang tinatawagan ko, talagang matipid.

AT&T is making sure of that!"

— LEA SALONGA

Para kay Lea, staying close sa buong pamilya ay tunay na mahalaga. That's why, when something as important as family is on the line, there is one thing you can be sure of: AT&T **TrueWorld**℠ Savings* can give you great savings nearly every time you pick up the phone. You can call anyone, anytime, anywhere, and still save off AT&T's basic prices on all your direct-dialed international calls to over 250 countries and areas...with extra savings to the Philippines!**

Umpisa pa lang iyan! The savings are equally exciting on all your direct-dialed, state-to-state calls.† Susundan din kayo ng savings even while you're travelling! Enjoy special discounts on all your AT&T Calling Card calls to and from the U.S., and almost anywhere in the world. Kaya bayaan ninyong AT&T ang mag-asikaso ng lahat ng inyong calling needs, and expect big savings sa inyong mga tawag dito sa Amerika, sa Pilipinas, at sa buong mundo! **Mag-sign up sa madaling panahon!**

Tawagan ang ating AT&T Filipino Customer Service Representatives:

**1 800 FILIPINO, Ext. 222**
(1 800 345-4746)

AT&T Your True Voice.℠
Ang Tunay Na Tinig.

 **AT&T**

*$3 monthly fee applies. Subject to billing availability. **Savings vary by country. Extra savings apply to one selected international country or area. †Savings apply to residential calls not covered by another savings option. Applicable only to calls to calls that appear on the AT&T portion of your home phone bill. Savings on AT&T Calling Card calls to the U.S. apply when you use AT&T USADirect® Service.

© AT&T 1994

**Figure 1.3a.** AT&T Advertising to Consumers in U.S. Subcultures: Target Market, U.S. Filipinos

**Figure 1.3b.** AT&T Advertising to Consumers in U.S. Subcultures: Target Market, U.S. Latinos

## AT&T True Savings. Save 25%.

It's true.

AT&T's simplest way to save 25%.

No circles. No restrictions. No confusion.

Just spend $10 a month and we'll subtract 25% off your AT&T bill for calls to anyone, anytime, anywhere in the USA? Straight up. So call now.

# 1 800-TRUE-ATT

---

**Figure 1.3c.** AT&T Advertising to Consumers in U.S. Subcultures: Target Market, African Americans

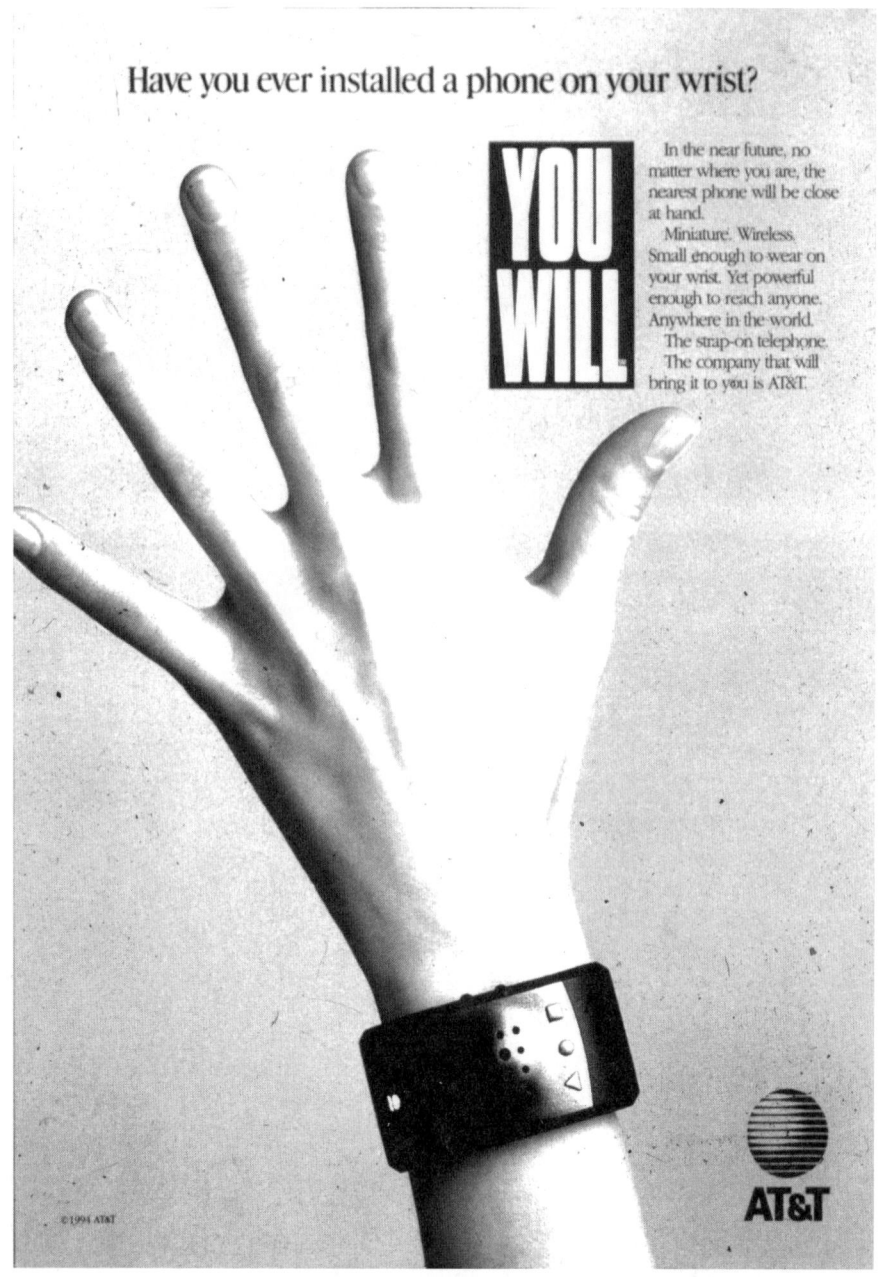

**Figure 1.3d.** AT&T Advertising to Consumers in U.S. Subcultures: Target Market, Generation X

## SUMMARY

Strong forces of change are converting the United States into a truly multicultural society. Our demographic mix includes a growing number of non-Whites and people whose origins are in Latin America and Asia. A larger percentage of our population consists of people over 65 years of age. We describe ourselves as a "salad bowl" rather than a "melting pot," a change of analogy that reflects the growing reliance on expressing individualism in our culture. Our media environment mirrors demographic diversity with an explosion in communication technologies. American life is sliced and diced to best appeal to the values and interests of ever-smaller audiences. Newer media allow dialogue with and message adjustment for individual consumers at plummeting costs.

The competitive advantage of economies of scale is being replaced by the competitive edge of better information portfolios. Market success for competitors large and small relies on the ability to find and attract loyal buyers in a global environment. Consumers feel overwhelmed by information and choices in the marketplace; they choose to support organizations that are members of their communities and that express values similar to their own. In short, cultural compatibility becomes as important a determining attribute for buyers as traditional performance functions and economic benefits.

Though mainstream American culture is not being displaced, its monopolistic hold on the ideals of Americans is. Our demographic, media, marketing, competitive, and technological environments are fields of multiple, sometimes competing value systems. American mainstream culture now competes on a situational basis with the values of subcultures that constitute an important source of identity for Americans. This volatile combination makes it impossible to understand consumer motivations or to predict consumer behavior without insight into how consumers use the marketplace as a cultural medium of expression. The next chapter describes how Americans in a multicultural environment construct social identity and use the marketplace as a cultural medium.

## Note

1. See McCarthy (1960), Kotler (1967), and White (2000). McCarthy and Kotler both emphasize the relationship between size and profitability of a market segment. This cost-benefit trade-off is also the basis of Theodore Levitt's (1983) argument for standardization across national markets.

# CHAPTER 2

# Consumer Identity in a Multicultural Society

## CONSUMPTION AS EXPRESSION OF SOCIAL IDENTITY AND CONSUMER VALUES

The changes detailed in the last chapter are creating a society in which the values of mainstream America are increasingly mixed with those of distinctive subcultures. Individuals no longer have to relinquish their ethnicity or conform to mainstream dictates to participate in the American mosaic. Americans trumpet individuality and, as a result, change the meaning of mainstream American culture itself. We are no longer just the sum of our inherited traits; we are that plus whatever else we choose to be (Walker & Moses, 1996). Because there are few requirements for belonging to a subculture other than what we label ourselves, group labels become less predictive of individual behavior.

Figure 2.1 outlines how the environment detailed in the last chapter affects American consumers' "sense of self." Individuals in a multicultural society draw from multiple value systems in defining their own ideals; in turn, what American consumers want from the marketplace changes. This chapter updates

31

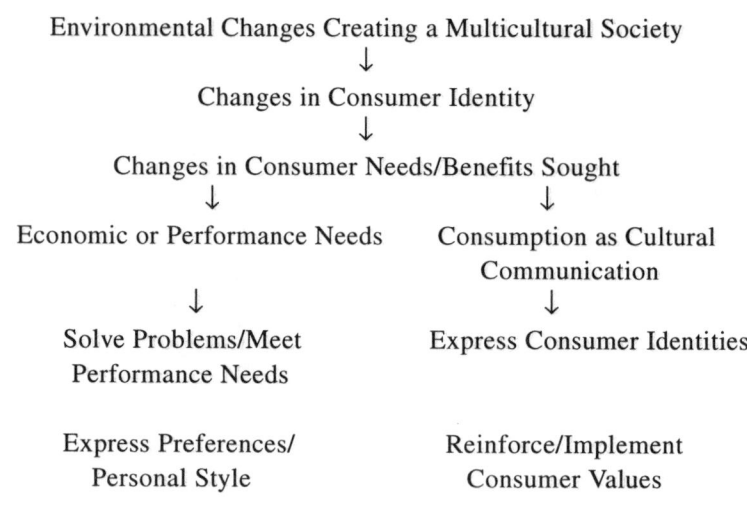

**Figure 2.1.** Consumer Adaptation to a Multicultural Society

our understanding of consumer wants and needs in a multicultural society. Consumption choices are a medium by which consumers compose and communicate their chosen selves to other members of the American mosaic.

Consumer loyalty is undergoing a fundamental change today. Private labels beat national brands for shelf space, retailers choose new products based on push monies available, consumers switch to whatever brand is "on special" and use the Internet to comparison-shop, all because there are no bases other than price and perceived quality to differentiate brands. Psychologists tell us that when attributes of different brands appear equal, new factors become salient to decision makers (Ajzen & Fishbein, 1980).

Consumers are redefining what types of value they seek in the marketplace. Some consumers are loyal to firms that try to reach them in their own language, whether it is MTV-style advertising for Generation X, product labels for the information-intense Mature Market, or designs that favor disabled consumers (Lipman, 1991a; McCarroll, 1993; Moschis, 1994; Roslow & Nicholls, 1996; Rossman, 1994; Woods, 1995a; Zbar, 1996). Corporate policies regarding all kinds of human rights, environmental issues, or civic issues become a new basis on which buyers select one firm's brands and reject another's. Meeting consumers' needs for this kind of information is the central focus of marketing strategy in multicultural America.

Global firms must establish global strategies at the same time that they compete to win loyalty within niche markets. The niche consumers we're seeing today do not behave the way niches used to. Generation X rebels against being a "target market," even though a firm may have taken much care to appeal to their tastes (Mitchell, 1997). Over one third of consumers over 65 have boycotted firms whose marketing communications portray the elderly in ways they consider offensive. The economic exchange is only part of what determines buying preferences.

Value has long been described as the relationship buyers see between quality and price, two marketing variables. Today's American consumers may also consider whether a firm supports the issues that touch their lives or how it treats the groups they identify with. Changing consumer perceptions of value create new sources of competition for customers of many organizations.

The new American consumer "values" other factors in addition to price and product quality. When basic price and quality information is easy to acquire, what else might consumers like to know, or, in other terms, what might they "value"? They might ask, for example, what the company's record is in hiring a diverse workforce. Whoever said that votes in the marketplace must be limited to decisions based on economic criteria alone? The economy is becoming a forum for foreign policy; it may also become an arena for domestic social policy. Consumers are expressing their helplessness to effect political change by saying, "I can't seem to get better schools in my neighborhood by paying taxes or voting, but I can buy from the retailer who provides computers for the school. If they all do that, then I can buy from the store that sponsors the school Halloween carnival."

Relationship marketing is focused on the right problem: how to build a perception of shared interests with particular consumers (Peppers & Rogers, 1993; Rapp & Collins, 1988). Still, its emphasis is on the economic aspects of exchange. Buyers care about what products can do, but they also value what a product or service does within the context of their social and cultural environment (McCracken, 1986). In effect, consumer loyalty is moving from brand to company to identity groups. Consumption is valued in itself as a medium for creating and communicating social identity and expressing consumer values.

Consumer relationships with products and services are quite complex. Some people assign human qualities to brands and their spokesperson icons (e.g., Charlie the Tuna or the Pillsbury Doughboy) (Fournier, 1998). More universal is the use of brands in the negotiation of self-identity. The brand-person relationship is influenced by cohort factors, stage in the family life cycle, and social and family networks, as well as subculture and cultural background. The themes consumers use to define themselves are repeated in their relationships with brands and mirrored in their perceptions of brand personality and symbolism (Aaker, 1997; Belk, 1988; Fournier, 1998; Frank, 1999; Schouten, 1991; Sirgy, 1982; Wattanasuwan, 1998).

## MARKETING AS BOTH ECONOMIC EXCHANGE AND CULTURAL MEDIUM

Socialization into any culture comes from the institutions that teach its norms and values. The role that churches, the family, and government institutions play as socialization agents in America is in decline, while schools, peers, and the media increase their influence but with questionable effects. We belong to fewer community organizations, we spend less time socializing with others, and political participation is at an all-time low (Putnam, 1995). Whether we like it or not, communication media and marketing institutions act as primary socialization agents for whatever we do not learn through personal experience. Media images are the building blocks of contemporary American culture:

> Radio, television, film and the other products of media culture provide materials out of which we forge our very identities, our sense of selfhood; our notion of what it means to be male or female; our sense of class, of ethnicity and race, of nationality, of sexuality, of "us" and "them." Media images help shape our view of the world and our deepest values; what we consider good or bad, positive or negative, moral or evil. Media stories provide the symbols, myths and resources through which we constitute a common culture and through the appropriation of which we insert ourselves into this culture. (Kellner, 1995a, pp. 5-6)

Economic institutions are themselves shaped by their cultural context. Marketing phenomena as diverse as Super Bowl commercials, coupons, price tags, catalogs, home pages on the Internet, magazines, self-service gas stations, brand names, or department stores are cultural artifacts. Malls are remaking themselves into entertainment venues as a way of competing with the more convenient markets online (Ginsburg, 1999). Their economic purpose is to help consumers obtain the goods and services they want, but while performing this role, marketing institutions transmit and reflect cultural values. Even the relative importance of their economic role is determined by the cultural environment in which they exist (McCracken, 1986; Twitchell, 1996).

Sometimes the cultural reflections seen in our marketing phenomena seem like funhouse versions of our values. We see people become frantic over rings around the collar, find true love when they switch to the right brand of toothpaste, or let a passion for Maxwell House coffee lead to other "maybe" passions. These advertising vignettes exaggerate what is true: American culture places importance on cleanliness, physical appearance, and sexual appeal. Able to distinguish such distorted images from personal experience, most Americans would be shocked to realize that this is how we're seen. But for people who know us only through media images, those images are reality.

Recently, a number of writers have pointed to the growing gaps in the way members of different groups think about themselves and their relationships to others in American society (see, e.g., Hughes, 1993; Kotkin, 1992; Schlesinger, 1992). Their refrain is that the lack of feelings of community across groups in the United States is eroding mainstream American culture and our sense of common purpose. Blacks and Whites, Generations X and Y and the baby boomers, the disabled and the Mature Market all seem to want their unique identities recognized and acknowledged as part of the multicultural America we have become. Though we are "American" in terms of national identity, rarely does patriotism drive our behavior in the marketplace. The "splintering" of what we sense to be relevant communities reflects the growing importance of subcultures in defining the American mosaic (Turow, 1997a).

The prominent role of the marketplace within American culture reflects a revolution in our cultural institutions and their roles (Penaloza & Gilly, 1999). If culture includes everything we learn and all human behavior exclusive of instincts, our beliefs, social structure, images of ourselves, and choices of government or economic system all express components of culture and cultural values. But when traditional cultural institutions no longer serve as effective agents of socialization, we look to more accessible subcultures for values, identity, and socialization. We think of ourselves as "hyphenated Americans," changing the first part of the hyphen at whim (Judge, 1997). Depending on what we buy, we can "borrow" cultures, reaffirm our own heritage, or scramble our mix of identities by symbolically putting "salsa on kosher dishes" (Cyr, 1994).

We also find substitutes for permanent markers of identity. Cultural change in a multicultural society is reflected in the more important roles that media and marketers play in people's lives (Leiss, Kline, & Jhally, 1986, pp. 259-297; Turow, 1997a). Programming and advertising in the popular media assume more influential roles as sources of information about what members of different social groups are like. As we spend more time with selective media, social distance increases in the form of shared media and personal experiences across ethnic, age, and lifestyle lines. Media portrayals serve as surrogate personal knowledge of other social groups. This is why stereotyping of ethnic, lifestyle, and age groups in the media has such devastating effects on all of us (Turow, 1997a).

The link between cultural values, what works in the marketplace, and what consumers want is undeniable. That is why this book is about recognizing the cultural role of marketing institutions: Successful marketing strategies must meet both economic and cultural needs of buyers. "The brand is merely a beacon for a set of values in the broad spectrum of choices" (McManus, 1998, p. 6). Marketers have an opportunity to express their firms' cultura l values and to participate in the lives of consumer-partners (Collins & Porras, 1994). An example of the significance of these kinds of marketing efforts is shown in the attitudes of different ethnic groups about ethnic marketing activities in Table 2.1. Ethnic marketing activities recognize the distinctive economic and cultural needs of members of different American subcultures.

The age, lifestyle, ethnicity, regional identity, and other aspects of consumers provide marketers with a platform for building long-term, broad-based relationships with those consumers. This means supporting the media that they consume or the events that they attend, providing the goods and services that recognize the distinctive aspects of their lifestyles, and, in general, speaking the language of a subculture group. Look at the relationship between ethnicity and media consumption patterns shown in Table 2.2. Notice the strong differences in the importance of different media types consumed by members of different ethnic groups. Such patterns may have nothing or everything to do with a particular group's value system, but they establish "group norms" visible to insiders and outsiders alike.

We must acknowledge communications media and marketing institutions as cultural players in multicultural America. By selecting the organizations that a company supports as partners in buying and selling, a firm expresses values that may or may not resonate with those of its intended customers. Whether this assertive cultural role for business organizations is a good or bad phenomenon in our society, it is characteristic of life in postmodern cultures all over the globe (Turow, 1997a, pp. 157-200).

**TABLE 2.1**  Ethnic Group Attitudes About Ethnic Marketing Efforts

| *Ethnic Marketing Effort* *(Attitude Statement)* | *Mean Scores*[a] | | | |
|---|---|---|---|---|
| | *Anglo Americans* | *African Americans* | *Mexican Americans* | *Chinese Americans* |
| Prefer to buy from firms do-ing good in my community* | 3.68 ($N = 279$) | 3.86 ($N = 266$) | 3.94 ($N = 244$) | 2.83 ($N = 243$) |
| Like to buy from firms sponsoring my ethnic festivals/sports events* | 2.79 ($N = 289$) | 3.52 ($N = 287$) | 3.57 ($N = 280$) | 3.34 ($N = 266$) |
| Recommend brands if firm supports my community* | 2.56 ($N = 288$) | 3.49 ($N = 286$) | 3.15 ($N = 280$) | 3.41 ($N = 269$) |
| More likely to buy from firm that supports ethnic businesses* | 2.15 ($N = 290$) | 2.94 ($N = 277$) | 2.77 ($N = 279$) | 2.84 ($N = 269$) |
| Prefer to buy from firms I've heard good things about* | 4.12 ($N = 289$) | 4.35 ($N = 278$) | 4.15 ($N = 264$) | 4.40 ($N = 266$) |

SOURCE: Lee, Tharp, and La Ferle (1999).

NOTE: Methods described in Lee, La Ferle, and Tharp (1999a).

a. 5 = *strongly agree,* 1 = *strongly disagree.*

*$p \leq .05$ for significance of $F$ ratios of group differences, controlling for income, education, and occupation.

# THE SIGNIFICANCE OF MEDIA INSTITUTIONS AND REPRESENTATIONS IN A MULTICULTURAL SOCIETY

The proliferation of ways to reach defined, selective audiences contributes to the diversity of cultural images portrayed in these media. Real social distance between groups is increasing due to our ethic of expressing self-identity via group memberships. The vicarious knowledge of "others" that comes via media images becomes crucial if we are to relate to each other.

In some ways, American mainstream culture has become what the media say it is. Critics argue that we construct our own identities according to scripts for

**TABLE 2.2**  Ethnic Differences in Media Usage

| Medium and Usage | Anglos/ Whites | | African Americans | | U.S. Latinos | | Asian Americans | | Total Pop. |
|---|---|---|---|---|---|---|---|---|---|
| | N | % | N | % | N | % | N | % | N |
| **Time spent watching English-language TV** | | | | | | | | | |
| | 977 | 22.9 | 982 | 23.0 | 1608 | 37.7 | 713 | 16.4 | 4,280 |
| 1-10 hours/ week | 411 | 42.1 | 459 | 46.7 | 914 | 56.8 | 450 | 63.1 | |
| 11-20 hours/ week | 291 | 29.8 | 237 | 24.1 | 350 | 21.7 | 198 | 27.7 | |
| Over 20 hours/ week | 275 | 28.1 | 286 | 29.1 | 344 | 21.4 | 65 | 9.1 | |
| Total | | 100.0 | | 99.9 | | 99.9 | | 99.9 | |
| **Time spent reading English-language newspapers** | | | | | | | | | |
| | 331 | 33.7 | 246 | 25.1 | 147 | 14.9 | 260 | 26.3 | 983 |
| 1-5 hours/ week | 183 | 55.3 | 143 | 58.1 | 81 | 55.1 | 180 | 69.2 | |
| 6-10 hours/ week | 113 | 34.1 | 73 | 29.7 | 55 | 37.4 | 66 | 25.4 | |
| Over 10 hours/ week | 35 | 10.6 | 30 | 12.2 | 11 | 7.5 | 14 | 5.4 | |
| Total | | 100.0 | | 100.0 | | 100.0 | | 100.0 | |

popular programming and that "life movies" tell us how to organize experience (Gabler, 1998). Lifestyles displayed in the media may or may not reflect reality, but they provide the tools consumers use to realize their aspirations (Englis & Solomon, 1993).

It is not just that media themselves have expanded; advertisements have seeped out of the confines of commercial space and have invaded program content (Jacobson & Mazur, 1995; McAllister, 1996). Media vehicles can teach information about the marketplace as well as the roles of different members of American society. In American culture, the media have a preeminent role as cultural teacher (Twitchell, 1996). It is there that high art mixes with folk, modern, and popular arts to become the popular culture of the American mainstream.

**TABLE 2.2** Ethnic Differences in Media Usage (Continued)

| Medium and Usage | Anglos/ Whites | | African Americans | | U.S. Latinos | | Asian Americans | | Total Pop. |
|---|---|---|---|---|---|---|---|---|---|
| | N | % | N | % | N | % | N | % | N |
| **Time spent reading English-language magazines** | | | | | | | | | |
| | 435 | 36.4 | 322 | 26.9 | 207 | 17.3 | 233 | 19.4 | 1,197 |
| 1-5 hours/ week | 322 | 74.1 | 237 | 73.6 | 139 | 67.1 | 189 | 81.1 | |
| 6-10 hours/ week | 81 | 18.6 | 52 | 16.1 | 56 | 27.0 | 34 | 14.6 | |
| Over 10 hours/ week | 32 | 7.3 | 33 | 10.2 | 12 | 5.8 | 10 | 4.3 | |
| Total | | 100.0 | | 99.9 | | 99.9 | | 100.0 | |
| **Time spent listening to English-language radio** | | | | | | | | | |
| | 414 | 32.8 | 343 | 27.2 | 243 | 19.3 | 261 | 20.7 | 1,261 |
| 1-5 hours/ week | 120 | 28.9 | 104 | 30.3 | 84 | 34.5 | 145 | 55.5 | |
| 6-10 hours/ week | 103 | 24.8 | 91 | 26.5 | 84 | 34.5 | 70 | 26.8 | |
| Over 10 hours/ week | 191 | 46.2 | 148 | 43.1 | 75 | 30.9 | 46 | 17.6 | |
| Total | | 99.9 | | 99.9 | | 99.9 | | 99.9 | |

SOURCE: Market Segment Research, Inc. (1994).

Choice of media to consume has become as much a personal statement of identity as a rational search for entertainment and information. A consumer's "media repertoire" describes the variety of media that an individual consumes (Taylor, 1999; Weissman, 1998). This mix communicates the person's associations—aspired, actual, and disavowed—as well as ideals and values this individual uses to interpret and evaluate the rest of the world. The broader the choice a consumer has, the more relevant to that person's multiple identities media choice becomes. For example, the consumption of Spanish-language programming and advertising may reflect a strong Hispanic identity, not because the individual has no other choice, but because a bilingual individual chooses what "speaks to the heart" (Cisneros, 1997; Roslow & Nicholls, 1996).

In all forms of communication, symbols and myths are used to express the abstract concepts of cultural norms and ideals. Media have always used the images and symbols of people outside their target audiences (O'Barr, 1994). African Americans have been shown as uneducated and hedonistic, the disabled as helpless, U.S. Latinos as lazy, Chinese Americans as hard workers, old people as crotchety, Native Americans as savage or noble. If these are the only times or situations in which these people are visible in the media, this denies their diversity and reinforces stereotypes (O'Barr, 1994). In earlier times, these groups had little access to or influence on the media that so disastrously characterized them. Today, the use of cultural symbols and simplistic media representations are not likely to go unnoticed, wherever they appear.

Some groups continue to be less visible than others in American media. There is a gap between the percentage of older Americans in our population and the number of images of them in the media, for example. In contrast, Gays and Lesbians have been more visible than older Americans in program stories and as characters in mainstream programs (Beatty, 1997; N. C. Webster, 1994). As more diversity has been brought into media programs and advertising, the stereotyping of these people in popular culture has begun to diminish (Donovan & Leivers, 1993; Kellner, 1995b). The values and associations of mainstream American culture are mutable over time. The imagery within media is an important instrument of cultural change in a multicultural society.

The act of showing people in the media as members of a particular group acknowledges the significance of that group in American society. Such regard is important to each of the groups discussed in this book. When Wal-Mart uses actors in wheelchairs in their advertising, the benefit is not just more disabled shoppers at Wal-Mart stores but a more active presence for the disabled in American media and popular culture. As media vehicles become more selective yet diverse, even more American subcultures will want to be recognized by the media as full-fledged members of our multicultural society.

## THE AMERICAN VIEW OF THE SELF AND SOCIAL IDENTITY

The American perception of the self is grounded in our individualistic culture. Each person is believed to be a biological and psychological being, as well as a unique member of the social system (Bennett & Stewart, 1991, p. 129). Americans make a strong distinction between ourselves and others, so they find it hard to understand that individuals in more collectivistic cultures may not think they differ much among themselves. Further, Americans' experience of the self is intimately attached to what we "do"—our actions and achievements—rather than by what we know or feel. We reinforce each child's sense of self by offering choice at an early age: Choosing a preferred cereal teaches independent decision making and expression of identity (Bennett & Stewart, 1991, pp. 132-133). Self-actualization is an imperative of the American self, "existing detached from origins and uncommitted to any destiny" (Bennett & Stewart, 1991, p. 143; Sirgy, 1982).

Despite this commitment to a very individually determined sense of self, groups and organizations play an important role in the process of self-definition. Participation in organizations is a venue for trying on values and making allies in support of particular interests. We find ourselves through the people and institutions we relate to. It is thus an irony of American individualism that without the reference point of the groups we identify with or belong to, our self remains incomplete and undefined.

A distinctive characteristic of ethnic identity in multicultural America is that it is "chosen" rather than predetermined. In the American past, race, geographic region, and cultural factors such as language spoken were the foundations of an individual's identity for life. When asked to describe their ethnic identity today, most Americans use labels for themselves that vary with social situation and life stages (Stayman & Deshpande, 1989; Waters, 1990b). Sometimes Americans of different races but of the same age or sexual preference see themselves as more similar to each other than to other members of their race. Because an individual's perceptions of similarity and identification can change when social conditions do, the measurement of "ethnic identity" is complicated (Bosma, Graafsma, Grotevant, & de Levita, 1994). The population groups that a specific consumer *chooses* to identify with are the most accurate predictors of social identity.

Ethnicity is not an important component of social identity for all Americans. White Americans typically do not identify as strongly with their ethnic origins as most African Americans or U.S. Latinos (Alba, 1990). African and Asian Americans or U.S. Latinos who are in the process of establishing their own families are more likely to identify strongly with their cultural or racial heritage than those same people did during teenage years (Waters, 1990b). A person who strongly identifies with an ethnic heritage is more likely to express this behaviorally (Deshpande, Hoyer, & Donthu, 1986). Many individuals also distinguish between public and private behaviors, sometimes reserving expressions of ethnicity for family members and in-home activities (Subervi-Velez, 1986).

Individuals of multiple ethnic origins may choose to identify with some aspects of their heritage over others. This is especially true for groups that are viewed negatively and thus are more distant from the American mainstream. For example, when large numbers of Jewish, Irish, and Italian immigrants came to the United States at the beginning of the 20th century, mainstream Americans did not consider them "White" (Waters, 1990b). It is no surprise, then, that many of them learned to limit their expressions of ethnicity to the home or church. Some Gay and Lesbian Americans choose to stay "in the closet" rather than risk the consequences of rejection from mainstream America. Iranian, German, Japanese, and Iraqi Americans have all found themselves at one time or another belonging to a cultural group with which mainstream America was at war. Thus, some Americans choose not to identify with particular aspects of their heritage.

At the other extreme, some individuals choose to identify "symbolically" with an ethnic heritage about which they know very little (Tharp & Villarreal de Silva, 1998). Situation is a strong influence over the dynamic nature of social identity. Ethnicity may be foremost in considering where to eat with one's parents on one occasion but not on another; it may affect choices of entertainment or food but not clothing. If a person lives where his or her ethnic group is in the majority, ethnicity or race may be less important to identity than it is for those living where their ethnic group is in the minority (Deshpande & Stayman, 1994). In sum, knowing an individual's ethnic heritage is simply not sufficient information for predicting either marketplace behavior or social identity.

The process of identity formation in itself contributes to perceptions of having a common cause with others. As group identity becomes more particular and situational, both self-labeling and labeling by people who are not members of the group become sensitive issues. Although affiliation with groups is how we know where we fit in a multicultural society, we may still not like to be "labeled" by others because we have multiple "social selves." Companies must be especially cautious when using labels: They should not use exclusive labeling in communications to a target group, and even if they use a label in developing and placing messages, they should not place it in the message itself. Instead of making an explicit group appeal, companies should make their affiliations apparent from their philanthropy, their employee policies, and other tools of multicultural marketing.

A firm that builds its own cultural identity from affiliation with one group will be seen as a "niche player," without relevant products/services for other Americans. Further, such strong identification with one group may turn off consumers who only weakly identify with that part of their heritage. Consequently, marketers in a multicultural America must belong to multiple communities simultaneously, always taking the risk that the values of these groups can prompt a firm to support conflicting causes. To be adept at membership in several subcultures, organizations must also learn multiple communication styles.

Self-identity is expressed in the marketplace by adoption of at least some group norms and patterns of communication and behavior. African Americans, Generation X, and Gay and Lesbian consumers are spending more time with media selectively targeted to them. Not only do they prefer media that speak their own language, they also want to shop where they encounter people like themselves (Crockett, 1998). Table 2.3 shows differences in preferred shopping environments and consumption of various product categories across ethnic groups. To determine whether these distinctive behaviors are expressions of social identity or the result of demographic or other influences, more research into consumers' underlying values is needed.

Different age, lifestyle, and ethnic groups are inhabiting increasingly different informational, technological, marketing, and cultural worlds. These differences are reflected in the ways their group members shop, how they find out about goods and services, the values they seek in the marketplace, and the ways they respond to organizations' marketing efforts. In a multicultural America, group identities like Mexican American, Baby Boomer, or Lesbian are essential to personal identity. It is not that ethnic pride is new, it is just that there is a cachet today to "being different" and to being in touch with one's roots. Ethnic origin alone does not explain personal identity, but consumer choices are an arena for expressing ethnicity.

There's nothing new about multiculturalism in U.S. society. What is becoming more frequent is that people express shared and multiple identities by their choices in the marketplace. Buying and owning particular brands are not just expressions of identity; they are part of the process of forming and reinforcing self-identity (Judge, 1997; Kellner, 1995b; Sirgy, 1982). Figure 2.2 shows the relationship between socializing forces such as the family, peers, and the media; the values they transmit; an individual's social self-concept; and the choices the individual makes in the marketplace. This model shows cultural values as the stabilizing force in a fluid social identity, affected by situational influences and

**TABLE 2.3** Ethnic Differences in Product Usage and Store Patronage

| Product Usage or Store Patronage | Anglos/Whites | | African Americans | | U.S. Latinos | | Asian Americans | |
|---|---|---|---|---|---|---|---|---|
| | N | % | N | % | N | % | N | % |
| Types of Electronics Owned (1996) | 157 | 13.6 | 230 | 19.9 | 485 | 41.9 | 285 | 24.6 |
| TV | 145 | 97.0 | 220 | 99.0 | 452 | 99.0 | 273 | 96.0 |
| VCR | 114 | 78.0 | 139 | 78.0 | 357 | 62.0 | 208 | 75.0 |
| Microwave | 128 | 86.0 | 140 | 73.0 | 299 | 57.0 | 221 | 70.0 |
| Camera | 96 | 75.0 | 96 | 60.0 | 277 | 49.0 | 202 | 66.0 |
| Compact disc player | 62 | 34.0 | 56 | 43.0 | 176 | 48.0 | 129 | 52.0 |
| Answering machine | 76 | 48.4 | 84 | 43.0 | 127 | 22.0 | 106 | 43.0 |
| Video game system | 56 | 35.7 | 76 | 36.0 | 193 | 33.0 | 64 | 30.0 |
| Dishwasher | 73 | 46.5 | 39 | 21.0 | 79 | 9.0 | 110 | 21.0 |
| Personal computer | 42 | 26.8 | 40 | 23.0 | 58 | 9.0 | 94 | 41.0 |
| Camcorder | 34 | 21.7 | 28 | 16.0 | 95 | 17.0 | 70 | 25.0 |
| Beeper | 20 | 12.7 | 30 | 31.0 | 57 | 19.0 | 29 | 21.0 |
| Cellular phone | 24 | 15.3 | 24 | 19.0 | 31 | 8.0 | 31 | 19.0 |
| Type of Store Shopped at Most Often (1994) | 204 | 17.1 | 232 | 19.4 | 472 | 39.5 | 286 | 23.9 |
| Dept. store | 146 | 71.6 | 170 | 73.3 | 246 | 52.1 | 221 | 77.3 |
| Discount store | 28 | 13.7 | 20 | 8.6 | 45 | 9.5 | 35 | 12.2 |
| Other mentions | 30 | 14.7 | 42 | 18.1 | 181 | 38.3 | 30 | 10.5 |
| Total | | 100.0 | | 100.0 | | 99.9 | | 100.0 |

*(Continued)*

**TABLE 2.3** Ethnic Differences in Product Usage and Store Patronage (Continued)

| Product Usage or Store Patronage | Anglos/Whites | | African Americans | | U.S. Latinos | | Asian Americans | |
|---|---|---|---|---|---|---|---|---|
| | N | % | N | % | N | % | N | % |
| Store Shopped at Most Often (1994) | 1064 | 20.4 | 1,052 | 20.0 | 2,435 | 40.6 | 1,032 | 19.0 |
| J. C. Penney | 161 | 15.1 | 195 | 18.5 | 452 | 18.5 | 167 | 16.2 |
| Sears | 137 | 12.8 | 229 | 21.7 | 541 | 22.2 | 179 | 17.3 |
| Kmart | 183 | 17.2 | 185 | 17.6 | 514 | 21.1 | 225 | 21.8 |
| Wal-Mart | 299 | 28.1 | 83 | 7.8 | 221 | 9.1 | 49 | 4.7 |
| Other mentions | 284 | 26.7 | 360 | 34.2 | 707 | 29.0 | 412 | 39.9 |
| Total | | 99.9 | | 99.8 | | 99.9 | | 99.9 |
| Hamburger Place in Last 4 Weeks (1996) | 112 | 14.8 | 139 | 19.1 | 355 | 43.2 | 172 | 22.9 |
| McDonald's | 52 | 46.4 | 62 | 44.6 | 166 | 46.7 | 97 | 56.4 |
| Burger King | 29 | 25.9 | 47 | 33.8 | 125 | 35.2 | 54 | 31.4 |
| Wendy's | 11 | 9.8 | 18 | 12.9 | 29 | 8.1 | 11 | 6.4 |
| Other mentions | 20 | 17.8 | 12 | 8.6 | 35 | 9.9 | 10 | 5.8 |
| Total | | 99.9 | | 99.9 | | 99.9 | | 100.0 |

SOURCES: Market Segment Research, Inc. (1994, 1996).

multiple group memberships. Distinctive beliefs, norms, and worldviews under-lie the values of subcultures in multicultural America. Though an individual consumer may not consistently engage in group norms of behavior, his or her values will mirror the ones of groups with which he or she identifies.

Mature Americans can and do feel alienated in a cultural environment that emphasizes youth. The American Association of Retired Persons (AARP), a pioneer in addressing the Mature Market's needs, has been successful by bundling

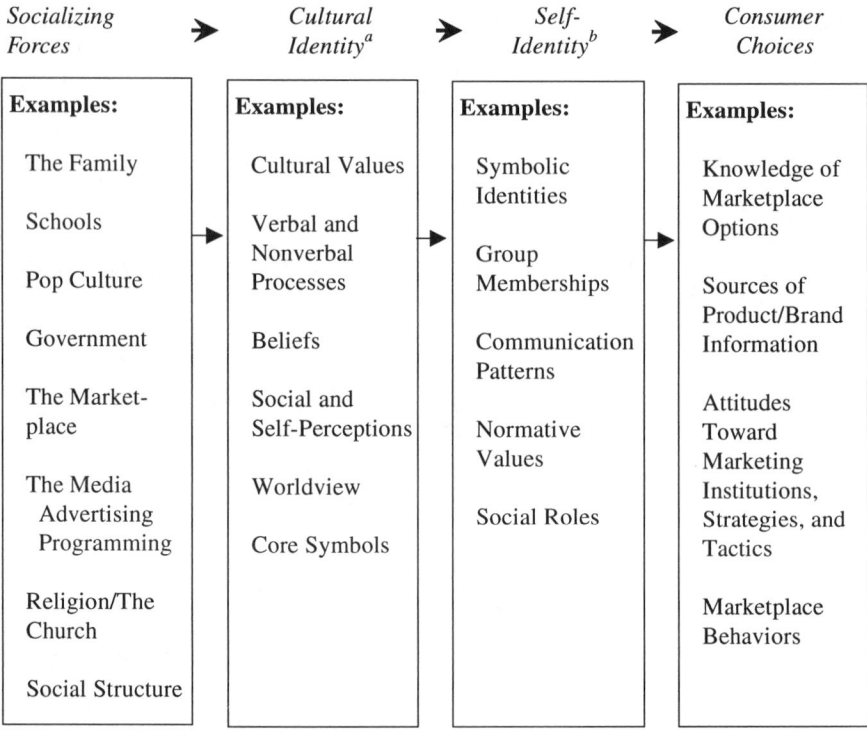

| Socializing Forces → | Cultural Identity[a] → | Self- Identity[b] → | Consumer Choices |
|---|---|---|---|
| **Examples:** | **Examples:** | **Examples:** | **Examples:** |
| The Family | Cultural Values | Symbolic Identities | Knowledge of Marketplace Options |
| Schools | Verbal and Nonverbal Processes | Group Memberships | |
| Pop Culture | | | Sources of Product/Brand Information |
| Government | Beliefs | Communication Patterns | |
| The Market-place | Social and Self-Perceptions | Normative Values | Attitudes Toward Marketing Institutions, Strategies, and Tactics |
| The Media Advertising Programming | Worldview Core Symbols | Social Roles | |
| Religion/The Church | | | Marketplace Behaviors |
| Social Structure | | | |

a. See Collier (1994).
b. See Hecht, Collier, and Ribeau (1993, pp. 1-81).

**Figure 2.2.** A Model of Social Identity and Consumer Choice in Multicultural America

services and marketing strategies that acknowledge the importance of older Americans. The role of marketing efforts in reinforcing group pride indicates another change in the ways we form and maintain social identities. Though the relevance of ethnic, age, or other group memberships may vary by situation, these memberships still affect consumer choices and styles of decision making. Self-identity is validated by social interaction, and there is a tension between the meanings we create for ourselves and what others interpret. Thus, an Asian American consumer may view luxury possessions as symbolic of having achieved the "American dream," whereas others see them as expressions of achievement by a "model minority."

## MAINSTREAM AMERICAN CULTURE AND
## SUBCULTURES IN MULTICULTURAL AMERICA

We learn a system of values via cultural institutions such as our schools, families, government, and of course, the media. These dominant values define mainstream American culture. When compared to cultural beliefs or norms in other countries, "American culture" is unique. Until recently, mainstream American culture had a monopolistic hold on Americans' aspirations and ideals, and it is still a strong, unifying influence. At the same time, some of us are closer or farther away from mainstream American culture, due to our backgrounds and the values we learn from religion, family, or experiences we share with others of our same age or sexual orientation. It is important to understand the substance of mainstream American cultural ideals, for it is against these that we judge ourselves and others.

The importance of individualism in mainstream American culture has already been noted. Yet even among other individualistic countries, the American self is more autonomous. We believe in setting our own goals and pursuing them independently. Our myths suggest that people who work hard can succeed in accomplishing virtually anything they wish (Jandt, 1995, pp. 211-232). We assume that we are all equal, but we encourage conformity to current and so-called modern norms of behavior. We value privacy and development of the "self." We place so much importance on ourselves as individuals that many of us do not see the culture we share with each other (Althen, 1988, pp. 3-34). Our beliefs in equality lead to a general informality in relationships with other people. We are sometimes castigated by foreigners for the superficiality of our initial friendliness, which seems to be universal and not directed to particular persons (Althen, 1988, pp. 90-112).

The emphasis on individualism in mainstream American culture is replicated in the beliefs we have about nature and human nature. Americans tend to see human beings as separate from the natural world and as more valuable (de Mooij, 1998, pp. 42-125; Hofstede, 1997, pp. 109-138; Trompenaars & Hampden-Turner, 1998, pp. 145-160). Thus, the way is paved for us to convert natural resources to our ends. We also have a strong belief in the value of science, rational thinking, and the use of technology to solve problems. The materialism of mainstream American culture is often a topic of critics. It is true that our economic system encourages us to buy and replace things frequently and that we often evaluate people by their material possessions. "Having" experiences, especially unique ones, has taken the place of "owning more" for younger participants in the American mainstream (Ray, 1997).

Our work is important too, for we state more than any other peoples that a "feeling of accomplishment" is the most important aspect we seek in a job (Jandt, 1995, pp. 211-232). We are constantly seeking ways to be more efficient and are particularly open to change, with faith that "newer is better." Discipline and control are important to bringing out our goodness; this is why we are so forgiving—we believe that human beings' fundamental nature is open to change and very much open to "self-improvement" efforts (Althen, 1988, pp. 3-56).

Josh Hammond and James Morrison (1996) recently added to characterizations of mainstream American values. They identified seven forces that they believed define "the national culture of Americans." First is an insistence on choice as the dominant force in all aspects of life. Second is pursuit of impossible dreams that we "make" come true. Our competitiveness leads to an obsession with "bigger and more," as well as an impatience with time, for we seem to want everything "yesterday." The fifth force is our acceptance of mistakes, often due to our sixth value, fixing things up and constantly improvising. Last, we are in "perpetual search of new identities, new ideas, new strategies, and new products, because they provide new choices" (p. 3; see also Lazar, 1994). In contrast to beliefs that there is no such thing as "an American culture," Hammond and Morrison suggested that these forces not only define us but provide the "glue that keeps us together and the common aspirations that drive us forward" (p. 3).

Special attention needs to be given to the communication style endorsed by mainstream American culture. We learn vicariously what subjects to talk about, how to have a conversation, and what parts of a message to pay attention to. The most frequent terms used to describe Americans' styles of interaction are *direct, open,* and *assertive.* Among our preferred topics for discussion with unknown persons are physical surroundings; later, we touch on shared experiences such as favorite entertainments, social lives, or hobbies and jobs. Politics and religion are subjects only for close friends and family. Americans use repartee more than long monologues and use very few conversational rituals such as "Nice to meet you" (Althen, 1988, pp. 22-34). We learn that arguments should be conducted in calm, moderate tones with a minimum of gesturing. Americans can sustain many friendships simultaneously, although often this is at a superficial level of involvement. We give special weight to messages that are "in writing," whereas other cultures value oral speaking or verbal ability. People from high-context cultures pay much more attention to the nonverbal aspects of messages and think Americans are "too talkative, too loud and not sensitive enough" (Althen, 1988, pp. 22-34; Seelye & Seelye-James, 1996).

It is not just the way we talk that distinguishes Americans; when making decisions, we are much more likely to rely on facts and logic than on intuition or experience. We place much weight on rational decision making using an empirical approach. We also value personal experience: Having seen something "with my own eyes" is more reliable than evidence from other people. We distrust emotions if not supported by facts. In the same vein, Americans are more likely to believe "truth" derived from observed facts, whereas people in other cultures are more likely to be swayed by theory and ideas, or even by insights from meditation (Althen, 1988, pp. 22-34; Seelye & Seelye-James, 1996).

The dilemma of a multicultural society is how to interact successfully with so many different rules for behavior. When different value systems are represented by members of different subcultures within one society, it is personally relevant every day to understand cultural differences as a potential source of misunderstandings. Whose rules will dominate is a constant tension in this type of society. This is a good explanation of why mainstream American culture will continue to serve a common ideal, even though its adherents have varying interpretations of what it means and even though the values of mainstream American culture change over time. It is not just that we accept people with different rituals or foods and music as part of the American mosaic; we must also accept their different ways of "being" American.

The increasing recognition of group members with legitimate rights to having their distinctive needs met in American society encourages individuals to identify with specific subcultures. The cultural pride of Native Americans, African Americans, or Mature Americans is both a reaction to past discrimination and a natural by-product of a diverse society (Deshpande & Stayman, 1994; McGuire, McGuire, Child, & Fujioka, 1978; Williams & Qualls, 1989). The recognition of each group's legal rights further strengthens individual members' retention of culturally distinctive patterns of thought and behavior. Though groups activate the legal system to redress discrimination, they also pressure the media to diversify the images they reflect and marketers to meet their needs to express social identity and cultural values.

## CONSUMER IDENTITIES AS SUBCULTURES

The strongest argument for viewing the different groups that consumers identify with as subcultures within a multicultural America is that they represent different values and styles of communication (Englis & Solomon, 1995). The American mainstream is being buffeted by this diversity of values. This in turn opens mainstream American culture to new meanings. To current immigrants, the "American dream" symbolizes "economic opportunity" and "home ownership" rather than political and religious freedom (Boyce, 1997). The distinctive myths, heroes, symbols, group norms, and ideal values of age, ethnic, lifestyle, and other subcultures are familiar and motivating forces. The marketplace is the public venue for making identity and value statements (Oswald, 1999).

Think about your own identity. How do you express your identity—to yourself and to others? Most people first think of the many roles they play: mother, husband, programmer, friend, coach, and so on. These roles, normally associated with specific activities, are significant to the way Americans see themselves, but, like other sources of identity, they fluctuate in importance over time and situation. Thus, they are important but not sufficient in expressing who one is to oneself and to others (Sirgy, 1982).

Table 2.4 suggests other sources of identity that you might not think of at first but that are important at various times to every individual's social self-concept. Our biological heritage of race and sex provides points of comparison to members of the same group and contrasts with other groups. Expressions of ethnicity are a mix of cultural values and norms, along with other factors such as geography, language, or race. An African American's preference for Afrocentric products may be influenced by the environment where that person lives or works as much as by racial or ethnic heritage. Age, physical appearance, disabilities, sexual orientation, and possibly other sources of identity can also express our unique affiliations and value systems.

In addition to the influence of biology and culture on our social selves, geography, age, sexual orientation, occupation, social class, stage in the family life cycle, and education are components of our social identity. Others in our same age group have shared significant experiences that in turn give weight to particular values. The World War II cohort saves money today even though they may have plenty; saving for an uncertain future was a value learned from their experiences of the Depression and World War II.

To summarize, we have multiple sources of identity, some related to the roles we play, some related to our ethnic heritage, and some related to where we live, where we grow up, or who we sleep with. Even the U.S. Bureau of the Census recognizes multiple sources of ethnic and racial identity among Americans (Teinowitz, 1998). People reinforce this social identity by the actions they take. Thus, the products that people buy, the media programs that capture their attention, the hobbies they have, and the services they need should and do reflect their identities. To do successful marketing in a multicultural society, companies

**TABLE 2.4** Consumer Identities in Multicultural America

| Source of Identity | Basis of Community | Examples of Consumer Groups | |
|---|---|---|---|
| Age cohorts | Shared experiences | Teens<br>Baby Boomers<br>Generation X, Y | Children<br>Mature Market<br>Thirtysomethings |
| Gender | Biology and culturally defined roles | Men<br>Boys | Women<br>Girls |
| Geography | Physical proximity and regional differences | Californians<br>Small Town Folks<br>Southerners<br>New Yorkers | Central City<br>  Dwellers<br>Coastal Dwellers<br>Brooklynites<br>Chicagoans |
| Race/physical features | Physical similarities | Blacks<br>Orientals<br>Body Builders<br>The Overweight | Caucasians<br>Tall Americans<br>Blondes |
| Ethnicity/religion | Shared cultural values and/or history | Chinese Americans<br>German Americans<br>Cuban Americans<br>Moslem Americans | African Americans<br>U.S. Latinos<br>Jewish Americans<br>Amish Americans |
| Lifestyle choices/sexual orientation | Shared AIOs[a] and/or behaviors | Single Parents<br>Gays and Lesbians<br>Smokers | Christian Right<br>Condo Owners<br>DINCs[b] |
| Disability | Special Needs or Behaviors | Hearing Impaired<br>Alcoholics<br>Substance Abusers<br>The Obese | Terminally Ill<br>Mobility Impaired<br>Sight Impaired<br>Cancer Survivors |

a. "Attitudes, interests, and opinions."
b. "Double-income, no children" households.

should align themselves with the identities that their customers share. Consumers will buy brands they know and like from the companies they know and like. The increasing importance to consumers of supporting companies that understand and relate to their particular place in the American mosaic creates an unparalleled market opportunity.

Table 2.4 shows different aspects of consumer social identity as the basis of distinctive consumer subcultures. These groups seem to share several qualities that establish their presence as real subcultures in multicultural America. First, each group is distinguishable demographically and behaviorally. That is, group membership may not always be important to or declared by an individual, but consumer distinctions can be made on the basis of media preferences, amount of conformity with group norms, responsiveness to particular forms of communication, or participation in particular communities and events. A person over the age of 65 may not consider him- or herself as part of the Mature Market, but if his or her media habits and personal values mirror those of other Mature Americans, then group norms may be better predictors of behavior than group labels.

Consumers may not agree with the labels used to place them in a group with which they identify, but if a label separates their marketplace behaviors from those of others, it is an effective consumer identity for marketing purposes. Figure 2.3 shows participants at the Calle Ocho celebration in Miami. This event started as a celebration of the Cuban community in Miami, but it has evolved into a gathering of over 1 million Latinos from multiple countries of origin. Each March, the Calle Ocho celebration is a magnet for companies wishing to build brand familiarity among U.S. Hispanics.

Second, each subcultural group is sensitive to marketers who would include too broad a group of people and to ones who draw the lines too narrowly. Should we use the term *U.S. Hispanics* or *U.S. Latinos, Generation X* or *the Free Generation, Disabled Americans* or *Physically Challenged Americans, Senior Citizens* or *the Mature Market, Asian Americans* or *Chinese Americans*? Does the U.S. Hispanic market include only Spanish-dominant Americans or all persons with origins in Hispanic countries? These label issues are important because when a marketer appeals to consumers as members of a group, the marketer has to "group" them with other people—directly or indirectly.

Some consumers will not respond to an organization outside a group's boundaries that is trying to attract their patronage. Consumers can be suspicious of ethnic marketing efforts from firms that do not otherwise "behave" as members of that group would or "should." After Ellen DeGeneres came out on her *Ellen* TV show, loyal viewers vowed to boycott the companies that had withdrawn ads from the "coming out" episode (Beatty, 1997). A marketer can create antagonism by using the language or symbols of a group when the firm is not an estab-

**Figure 2.3.** Calle Ocho Celebration in Miami

lished member of it. Tokenism when marketing to members of a subculture can be devastating to a firm's reputation and destructive to relationships with that subculture community.

A third characteristic of the subcultures in Table 2.4 is significant diversity within each group. Asian Americans include people of multiple races, religions, and languages. U.S. Latinos encompass people from Spain, Mexico, Cuba, El Salvador, and so on; some came to the United States themselves, whereas others' families have been here for generations. "Generation X" lumps all 18- to 29-year-olds together, despite racial, ethnic, educational, and other differences. Generation gaps between first- and second-generation immigrants, or between early and late "Baby Boomers," can be as wide as their differences from other Americans. Marketers who do not understand such diversity run the risk of stereotyping all members of a particular group (Weinstein, 1994).

A fourth dimension that these groups share is a certain amount of geographic concentration. One third of Asian Americans live in California, Gay Americans concentrate in the 25 largest cities, and Florida is a haven for the Mature Market. Though U.S. Latinos from Florida, Illinois, New York, Texas, and California often originate from different parts of Latin America, use different labels for themselves, and speak Spanish and English with very different accents, these five states include a large percentage of all U.S. Latinos.

A fifth attribute of subcultures in multicultural America is their distinctive patterns of media usage. The media remain a potent source for learning about the attitudes and behaviors of different groups. But what chances do MTV viewers have of knowing who Rue McClanahan is if they no longer tune in to "mass" media? What makes age so important in this new America is that American culture changes with time (Smith & Clurman, 1997; Twitchell, 1996). People of similar ages have a community of shared experiences with their cohorts, and people of different ages are products of different American cultures (Meredith & Schewe, 1994). Key events that shaped the worldview and values of American Baby Boomers were the social changes of the 1960s and the Vietnam War. Some shared experiences for Generation X are their experiences as latchkey children and their experiences of divorce and stepfamilies (Holtz, 1995). Generation X was the first age group to add the World Wide Web to their media repertoires for news, whereas Mature Americans remain loyal to television and newspapers. Chinese Americans consume low levels of traditional media, whereas African Americans consume both traditional and nontraditional media at high rates compared to other Americans (Lee, La Ferle, & Tharp, 1999a).

Last, each of these groups has a unique process for making consumption decisions. Asian Americans and U.S. Latinos may give special credence to word of mouth about different products or services; African Americans enjoy shopping and advertising. The Mature Market likes lots of information to be available, even when it results in information overload. Gays and Lesbians prefer to buy from firms that contribute to Gay rights or AIDS projects, so they are influenced by information on corporate giving and human resource policies. Certainly, not all members of these groups respond in such easily predicted ways, but the stronger the consumer's group identity, the more likely he or she is to adopt group norms and patterns of behavior (Leigh & Gabel, 1992).

## SUMMARY

An increasingly diverse society induces individuals to find their identities within the multiple groups, based on age, gender, sexual orientation, race, ethnicity, or geography, to which they belong. Consumers look to media images and goods and services to symbolically express who they are or want to be.

Self-identity has become a constantly changing mix of values, attitudes, and behaviors, making it virtually impossible to predict behavior as a function of group membership alone.

Consumers in a multicultural society have different values, behaviors, and expectations, linked to but not determined by those of their identity groups. Marketers must adapt to this environment by changing the ways organizations set goals and choose tactics. The next chapter discusses new approaches to marketing in a multicultural setting and presents examples and the rationale for these new perspectives.

# CHAPTER 3

# Marketing in a Multicultural Environment

Cultural compatibility is the foundation upon which marketing plans are built in a market of multicultural buyers. This chapter details how to acquire and exercise the skill of moving between subcultures. Shifting identity is natural for consumers in multicultural societies. Teenagers easily switch from an ethnic-influenced world at home to cohort-determined values outside the home. It is more difficult for profit- or goal-driven organizations to express multiple, sometimes conflicting, values and identities (Penaloza & Gilly, 1999). After introducing the concepts of "border mentality" and transmigration, this chapter describes seven paradigm shifts that focus marketing programs on consumer needs in a multicultural setting. It also describes strategy alternatives that organizations can use to build economic and cultural relationships with buyers. The last part of the chapter sheds light on ethical issues in multicultural marketing and the societal effects of target marketing across consumer subcultures (Turow, 1997a, 1997b).

## THE BORDER MENTALITY AND TRANSMIGRATION

"I know what it *costs,* but what does it *mean?*" "I know what it *does,* but what does it *say?*" "I know *who* sells it, but *who else* buys it?" Among consumers, answers to these questions represent two attributes—cultural meaning and group associations—that define the cultural roles played by products and their sellers. To make these an explicit part of brand positioning, organizations must adopt a "border mentality" at every step in the planning process.

People who grow up in more than one culture (such as people who live near the U.S. border with Mexico or children of immigrants) learn naturally to question the cultural context of phenomena. Individuals in multicultural settings learn that what something means is *situational*—its meaning depends on issues such as whether it is said in English, Spanish, or Spanglish; whether it is a message from mainstream media or from a subculture source; and what the characteristics, motivations, and status are of the person(s) who said it. The process of acculturating for immigrants and, for African Americans, the need to accommodate to both their own subculture and mainstream culture, foster the development of a high-context approach to interpreting meaning.[1] All of us use our "border mentalities" on occasion; most of us wouldn't use the same language or tell the same stories with our grandmothers as with our peers.

A multicultural society requires people and organizations to *interpret* cultural meanings and group associations before formulating appropriate communication responses. This "border mentality" is a valuable tool for navigating between and among U.S. subcultures of gender, age, disabilities, sexual orientation, geography, race, and ethnicity (Majors, 1994; Ribeau, Baldwin, & Hecht, 1994; Tannen, 1990). Individuals who find their social identities at the intersections of at least two salient subcultures use their bicultural skills to bridge those worlds. People switch back and forth in expressing identity much more easily than institutions do (Williams & Qualls, 1989). That consumers "reside" simultaneously in multiple cultures presents an opportunity for marketers to participate in the cultural role of the marketplace as a medium for expressing values and identities.

For an organization to cater to both the cultural and economic needs of individuals, it too must use the border mentality in developing marketing programs. Companies must first nurture the border mentality among their decision makers. This perspective requires a "different but equal" attitude about group preferences, as well as appreciation of meaning from multiple perspectives. Furthermore, organizations must become multicultural entities themselves, as deter-mined by their resources, capabilities, and goals.

If products and services express consumer social identities, then marketers must reconstitute marketing plans with defined goals for cultural compatibility. To build strategic alliances and meet consumer needs for economic and cultural expression, brands and their owners must have clear cultural meanings and group associations (Penaloza & Gilly, 1999). Most large organizations have unique resources with which they can build a presence within specific subcul-ture communities using shared ideals, symbols, heroes, myths, rituals, and other sources of cultural meaning (Randazzo, 1995). By mirroring the cultural mean-ings and group associations that reflect situational identities of a desired market, brands can assert their roles as cultural media.

Transmigration is the process whereby organizations, brands, and their deci-sion makers become "fluent" in multiple cultures within the American con-sumer market. Because it is difficult to predict situational influences for a spe-cific consumer or purchasing occasion, organizations and brands must construct *their own cultural identities* and make potential buyers aware of them.

An example of a company that acts as a multicultural entity by supporting particular subculture communities and developing culturally responsive mar-keting programs is Burger King. Burger King "acts" as an authentic member of the U.S. Latino community through a number of communications—coupons handed out at the Calle Ocho festival in Miami, constant advertising in Spanish-language and U.S. Latino-oriented media, and community programs contribut-ing to schools in Hispanic neighborhoods. Burger King hires not only U.S. Lati-nos but also Chinese Americans and African Americans as franchise operators, thereby making itself an "extended" member of those subculture communities also. Such policies communicate Burger King's group associations, position its services within a cultural context, and nurture the border mentality of its manag-ers. Ethnic customers do not eat Whoppers simply because Burger King adver-tises in a familiar language, but if Hispanic consumers of fast-food hamburgers see the major brands as equally attractive, the extra incentive could be a com-pany's participation in ethnic festivals, visibility in ethnic media, or support of relevant causes. Transmigration allows managers at Burger King to tune their marketing programs to subculture community interests and values.

In more general terms than the Burger King example, Figure 3.1 shows how business organizations can adopt the process of transmigration to meet both eco-nomic and cultural needs of consumers. The traditional marketing "mix" (prod-

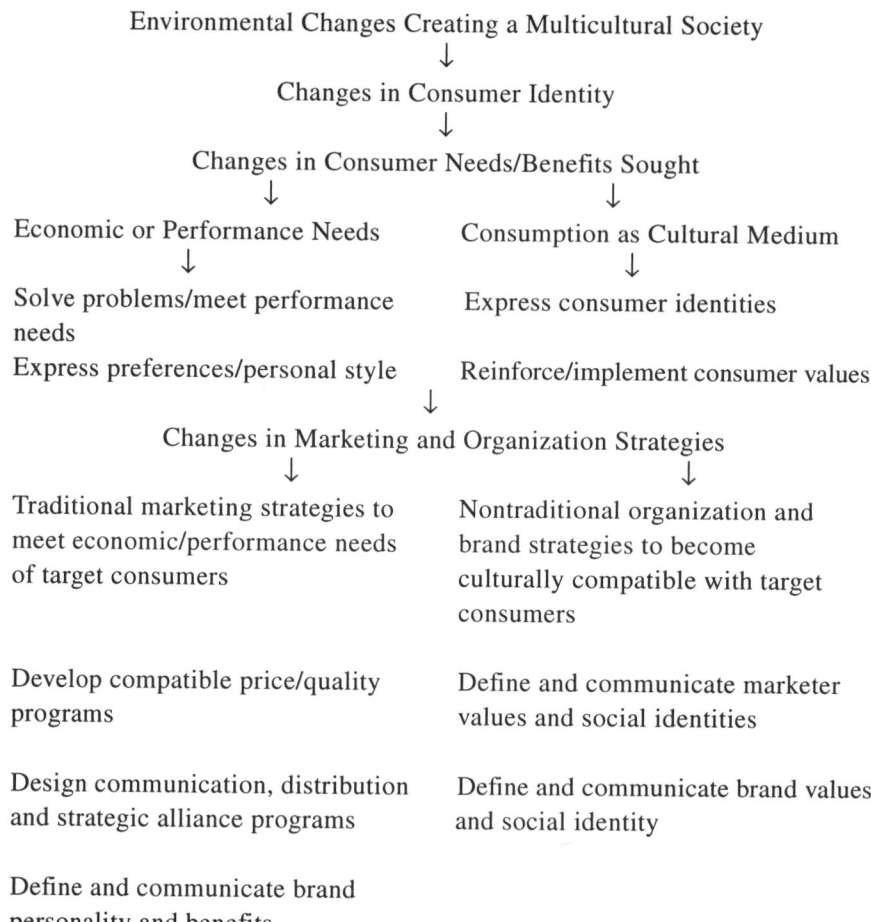

Figure 3.1. Business Transmigration in a Multicultural Society

uct, price, place, and promotions) must be expanded to include other programs and decisions that express clear values and group associations.

The fluidity with which an organization or brand identity moves from one basis to another is a key characteristic of transmigration (called *enculturation* by some authors) (Penaloza & Gilly, 1999). Opinion leaders in multicultural America will be people and organizations who can *communicate with* and *interpret for* more than one subculture group. Many of the ideas in this chapter are not new but suggest the advantages of redefining terms like *market, profits,* and *market share.* That is the border mentality—finding multiple meanings in familiar concepts. It is also good practice for effective communication with consumers who typically identify with multiple subcultures.

## MARKETING SHIFT #1: FROM LONG-TERM PROFITABILITY TO SHARED INTERESTS

Niche marketers design programs that retain loyal buyers by providing price-quality combinations and performance benefits, which motivate a target group of buyers from the larger, potential market. The extra costs of niche marketing efforts are worthwhile (profitable) when a mass-market approach is not effective in securing a large share of the market (see, e.g., Albaum, Strandskov, & Duerr, 1994, pp. 281-291; Harris, 1994; Terpstra & Sarathy, 1997, pp. 195-248). Cultural compatibility programs are left to public relations, human resources, or other interfaces with community groups, as if the consumer's affiliations were not relevant to purchasing decisions. This view of buyer decision making is in direct conflict with recent surveys reporting that three out of four consumers would "switch to a brand associated with a good cause" (Heubusch, 1997). A brand's "market" consists of *buyers who have mutual economic interests and cultural compatibility with the brand and its seller(s).*

Some policies of business organizations may seem peripheral, even unrelated, to buyers' decisions to buy one brand of soft drink over another or to stop at one movie theater and not another. Nevertheless, technology is evolving that gives consumers the ability to search for whatever information they want from a variety of independent sources (David, 1997; Kaufman, 2000; "Shopping for a Cause," 1999). The only perceived difference between two brands of computer, two insurance companies, or two car models may be which groups' media or social causes the brands are associated with. Though automobile companies use their recyclability or low environmental impact as attributes to distinguish their models from those of competitors, the impetus for those policies comes from the executive offices, not their consumers (McGinn, 1998).

A fundamental change has to be made in the ways goals are set and success is measured. Although dollar and volume sales or market share indicate a firm's economic impact, they do not explain its cultural role in consumers' lives. Do current customers believe that a firm whose brands they like and buy contributes to their overall quality of life? If not, their loyalty may not extend beyond the next purchase, especially if a competitor matches the price-quality relationship and then mirrors those buyers' values and affiliations (Collins & Porras, 1994).

This calls for measuring each buyer's belief of "shared interests" with marketers—a missing element in economic models of long-term profitability. An organization's long-term survival comes from its perceived ability to *share customer values,* not its inherently short-term ability to cater to a profitable niche. The marketing costs of attracting new customers are typically higher than the costs of inviting repeat purchases from current customers.[2] It makes sense to retain the loyalty of current customers whenever possible. If a customer's loyalty comes from a brand's perceived cultural compatibility, the *marketer must share the buyer's interests.* This double bond between consumer and marketer is less vulnerable to competitor actions than a relationship based solely on economic criteria.

There is no "best" measure of how well a marketer's actions reflect shared consumer values. The appropriate benchmark will vary for different types of products, firms, and community groups. Table 3.1 shows some ways an organization might incorporate "shared interests" into its estimates of the long-term profitability of a consumer. Some of the measures in the table are in common use: for example, product usage differences across age or ethnic groups, or comparative brand ratings on important attributes. These data may even be purchased on an ongoing basis. Other measures, such as cultural meanings of brand or product use or perceptions of shared interests between particular firms and groups, must be incorporated into the firm's primary research and dialogue with buyers.

An example can show how the concept of shared interests might explain brand preferences and suggest corrective actions. Data on patronage of discount stores for different ethnic groups were shown in the last chapter in Table 2.3. Let us assume that Wal-Mart wants to understand why African Americans seem to prefer Kmart to Wal-Mart. Some focus groups or in-depth interviews with African Americans of different incomes might provide insight into what discount store shopping "means," as well as what attributes appeal to them at Kmart. Let's also assume that the same database indicates that Wal-Mart attracts more Anglo Americans. Is it because Wal-Mart expresses particular values in its marketing strategy and choice of communications media? A values audit of Wal-Mart communications might uncover negative or unintended associations that are meaningful to African Americans. However quantified, perceived cultural compatibility between buyers and sellers is more predictive of long-term loyalty than

**TABLE 3.1** Measures of Shared Interests Between Consumers and Marketers

| *Consumer Perceptions and Behaviors* | *Measures of Shared Interests in the Cultural Domain* |
|---|---|
| Category usage patterns | Product use as expression of group identity |
| | Usage differences across subculture groups |
| | Subculture meanings associated with product use |
| Perception of competitive product differences | Attributes That Consumers Include in Their Perceived Price-Value Ratios |
| | Perceptions of firm and competitors as members of subculture communities |
| | Awareness of firm policies that affect subculture community |
| | Reputations of competitors in subculture community |
| | Comparative brand ratings on cultural criteria |
| | Brand and user image and perceived compatibility with subcultures |
| Brand loyalty and perceived brand value | Importance of price-value ratios in consumer choice |
| | Awareness of targeted marketing efforts |
| | Perception of performance differences across brands on both economic and cultural criteria |
| | Brand preference as expression of group identities |
| | Brand preference as expression of community support |
| Perceptions of organization's cultural identity | Perceptions of corporate aesthetic presence in community |
| | Perceptions of groups/causes supported by corporate philanthropy |
| | Perceptions of corporate human resource policies |
| | Perceptions of corporate environmental impact and policies |

market share, sales growth, or other strictly economic measures (Saporito, 1999).

The American Association of Retired Persons (AARP) informs the Mature Market about social issues of interest via editorial reports on its lobbying efforts in *Modern Maturity*. In the same issue of that magazine, AARP may offer low-interest-rate credit cards, pharmacy by mail, travel planning, and health insurance, among other advertised services. Readers do not distinguish these as product- and non-product-related bits of information. An AARP credit card in the pocket of a Senior Citizen supports an organization that keeps its consumers informed about *relevant* topics. It is a "win-win" economic exchange, but they also share interests and member concerns.

## MARKETING SHIFT #2: FROM NICHE MARKETING TO MATRIX MARKET PLANNING

Matrix market planning is a cost-effective and relationship-driven alternative to both mass and niche marketing. The matrix comes from a strategy of cumulating niches as the means to high market share (Martin & Levine, 1991). To implement matrix market planning, a firm *explores the appropriateness of marketing strategies and tactics for each group whose economic and cultural interests it wishes to share.* The objective is to develop a multifaceted partnership with consumers from different subcultures, interwoven with those buyers' economic and cultural needs (Hample, 1995).

An example of the matrix that McDonald's has built is shown in Table 3.2. For the time being, there is no indication that they have unique corporate strategies or tactics for a presence in the Gay and Lesbian or Asian American communities. Their approach to the Mature Market is to include more Senior Citizens in ads and among personnel. Also, McDonald's communications strive for broader participation in traditional-family households and African American and U.S. Latino communities. Each subculture is supported by a variety of culturally appropriate tactics. Examples of McDonald's advertising targeted to Mature Americans, U.S. Latinos, and African Americans are shown in Figure 3.2. These print advertisements showcase the ability of McDonald's to tailor its communication style at the same time that each ad trumpets the match between McDonald's family environment and the importance of family to consumers from these three different subcultures.

Marketing tactics such as discount pricing, product extensions, consumer premiums, and distribution allowances are activities designed to facilitate exchange. But a partnership with buyers in a multicultural society requires more than tactics leading to an economic transaction. Goya Food Products has a high

*(text continues on page 70)*

**TABLE 3.2** McDonald's Marketing Matrix

| Market Niche | Marketing Strategy | Examples of Niche Tactics |
|---|---|---|
| Mature Market | Adjunct to mainstream | Use of Mature Americans in communications |
| | | Hiring of Mature Americans |
| African Americans | Identification with African American community | Hiring of African American communication firms |
| | | Use of African American targeted media |
| | | Use of African American communication styles |
| | | Use of African Americans in communications |
| | | Support of African American causes, events |
| | | Recruitment of African American franchisees, employees |
| U.S. Latinos | Identification with multiple Latino groups | Use of Spanish-language communications |
| | | Use of Hispanic cultural settings and media |
| | | Use of U.S. Latinos in communications |
| | | Support of Hispanic American causes, events |
| | | Recruitment of U.S. Latino franchisees, employees |
| | | Hiring of Hispanic communications firms |
| | | Use of U.S. Latino targeted media |
| | | Use of U.S. Latino communication styles |
| Gays and Lesbians | No unique strategy | Mainstream marketing mix |
| Asian Americans | No unique strategy | Use of Asian Americans in ads |
| | | Support of Asian American community events |
| | | Use of Asian languages in communications |

*(Continued)*

**TABLE 3.2** McDonald's Marketing Matrix (Continued)

| Market Niche | Marketing Strategy | Examples of Niche Tactics |
|---|---|---|
| Family households | General market strategy: <br> Facility design (playgrounds) <br> Corporate philanthropy <br> (Ronald McDonald Houses) <br> Human resource practices <br> Environmental impact policies | All brand contact points; 4 P's |
| Nonfamily households | No unique strategy | New product development (e.g., Arch Deluxe) <br> Media placements and message design |

NOTE: This table is a summary of information from published sources and interviews with McDonald's corporate personnel. Information does not include franchisee programs in local areas. The table is not intended to be a comprehensive description of McDonald's marketing strategy and tactics for either mainstream American consumers or any of the niche markets listed here. The information has been organized specifically to illustrate how their strategy and tactics vary across subculture groups.

**Figure 3.2a.** McDonald's Ad Targeting the Mature Market

**Figure 3.2b.** McDonald's Ad Targeting U.S. Latinos

**Figure 3.2c.** McDonald's Ad Targeting African Americans

share of canned fruit sales among Latinos in New York, not because its prices or product qualities are necessarily superior to those of Del Monte, but because it is a familiar brand to immigrants from Puerto Rico and Caribbean countries and has strong distribution in the *bodegas* that are preferred shopping outlets among many Hispanic consumers. Wells Fargo Bank's penetration of Chinese American consumers in San Francisco has increased in response to its employment of Mandarin-speaking tellers and support of community events in Chinatown. What matrix market planning does in these cases is suggest a broader mix of marketing tactics in order to provide both an economic and cultural foundation for exchange (Carr-Ruffino, 1996; Schiller, 1989).

## MARKETING SHIFT #3: FROM MASS MARKETS TO MASS CHOICES

> *The brand is merely a beacon for a set of values in the broad spectrum of choices.*
>
> McManus (1998, p. 6)

Product and brand images reinforce consumer self-identity. A buyer's choice of product or technology to meet a specific need is framed within this communicative context (Turow, 1997a). There are as many choices as there are meanings that the consumer wishes to communicate to others (Schonfeld, 1998; Tharp & Scott, 1990). From this buyer's perspective, there are an abundance of "choices" to be made in the marketplace (Narisetti, 1997; Power, 1993; Randazzo, 1995; J. Solomon, 1988; M. R. Solomon, 1988). Diversity of market tastes and marketing tools forces us to expand the materials with which we build strategy. We do not have to build marketing strategy around the cost dimensions of production and delivery if we are able to use other areas of distinctive competence, such as the ability to customize products for our customers (Brody, 1990; Schonfeld, 1998). Firms like Apple Computer have such loyal users that only more innovative products of competitors can lure them away. Pampers uses its database of new mothers to identify needs they have for other Procter & Gamble products. Snapple and Generation X found a match based on marketing "style" rather than product features or price (Caggiano, 1997).

A good illustration of marketplace diversity from the consumer's point of view is the need to quench thirst. There are not just many varieties of soft drinks but also teas, coffees, fruit juices, fruit drinks, beers, wines, liquors, tap water, bottled waters, and carbonated waters. There are infinite numbers of places, quantities, and combinations in which the consumer can acquire any of these drinks. Which one is picked on a specific occasion depends on the nature of the consumer's thirst, his or her perceptions of the different options to meet that need, and *the significance of the choice of drink in expressing identity at that particular moment* (Batra, Myers, & Aaker, 1996, pp. 219-263; Schultz & Barnes, 1995, pp. 3-26, 61-80).

The things people own not only symbolize their group affiliations but also distinguish them from members of other groups. Usage or nonusage of a product category, brand or store choices, frequency of product/brand purchases, and usage occasions can all indicate various aspects of consumer social identity. Thus, they are significant decisions in communicating to other people in a consumption-oriented society (McAllister, 1993; McCarroll, 1993).

Information about users of brands, patrons of stores, and employees of producers is increasingly important to consumers. Such information provides a rationale for how to deal with information and choice overloads—something either is or is not "me" (Englis & Solomon, 1995). All economic criteria being equal, community policies of the company or organization will put one brand in the consumer's basket and keep another one on the shelf. Consumers use the same brands that they believe are used by others in the groups with which they identify. Buyers use information about the cultural meanings of particular brands and products to reduce the number of choices they must make from a marketplace and media cornucopia (Moog, 1990; Randazzo, 1995, p. 173; J. Solomon, 1988).

Integrated marketing communications planning has evolved in companies wishing to maximize synergy from their communication activities (Schultz, Tannenbaum, & Lauterborn, 1994). This approach also offers the opportunity to meet consumer information needs with a consistent message about cultural values and associations. To coordinate IPOs with new product announcements, promotions with advertising, press coverage with innovative advertising campaigns, plant openings with product sales, new CEOs with dealer incentives, and so forth requires marketing managers to act on a broader range of responsibilities (Batra et al., 1996, pp. 71-107; Beard, 1994; Fizdale, 1992).

Integrated plans hinge on the ability to identify all points of contact between the consumer and the brand that affect brand or company perceptions. A joke about the brand on a popular talk show, a story in the tabloid press about someone identified as a brand user, the products next to the brand on store shelves, celebrity endorsers of the brand, a new product design or package, and layoffs at the brand's maker are just a few examples of "contact points." It should be clear that marketers do not control all these points of contact, but the integrated approach brings the broadest array of communication tools into the marketing plan.

Table 3.3 shows marketing contact points as both economic and cultural bases for exchange with buyers. Our traditional marketing tool kit was developed to meet buyers' economic needs for brand-related information. It ensures having the right bundle of attributes and utility for a targeted group of buyers, at the right price, at the right time, and in the right place, and informing buyers about how these attributes match their needs.

We must add to those tactics the tools that help brands (and their sellers) communicate their own subculture affiliations and values. A few examples of decisions that buyers use to evaluate an organization or brand's cultural compatibility are hiring/firing decisions and procedures; geographic location and design of production or service facilities; civic or political activities of a firm and/or its local affiliates; environmental impact of a firm's activities; and participation in social or community events and causes. A compatible community profile in these areas helps to realize cultural partnerships with target buyers.

Table 3.3 contrasts four types of niche marketing strategies in terms of meeting economic and cultural needs of buyers. *Niche marketing* describes marketing programs designed to appeal to one or more segments of a larger market, using the traditional marketing mix. *Relationship marketing* uses the same raw materials (the marketing mix and strategic alliances) to identify and satisfy a broader array of target consumers' economic needs. Marlboro's specially designed merchandise with Marlboro insignias, and experiences such as "smoker-only" travel adventures, are examples of how Marlboro has found goods and services that meet their current customers' needs for other products. This does not necessarily generate a mutually beneficial *cultural* exchange; consumers define the extent of their relationships with the brand and marketers respond, rather than the other way around (McManus, 1998). The appeal of many "dot.com" firms is the data they can mine from their current customers for opportunities to customize and presell other products to them. It is a valuable asset in attracting strategic alliances.

*Ethnic marketing* uses a wider array of marketing tools to capture consumers in targeted subculture groups. Levi's, for example, contributes to ethnic commu-

**TABLE 3.3**  Domain of Marketing Strategy and Consumer Basis of Brand Value

| | Consumer Basis of Brand Value | |
| --- | --- | --- |
| *Domain of Marketing Strategy* | *Economic/Performance Need* | *Cultural Medium of Expression* |
| **Brand Contact Points**  Traditional marketing mix (price, product, distribution, communications) plus strategic alliances | Niche marketing | Relationship marketing |
| **Organization Contact Points**  Traditional marketing mix plus strategic alliances, philanthropy, human resources, corporate aesthetics, environmental impact of organization | Ethnic marketing | Multicultural marketing |

nity organizations and trumpets its diversity commitments in ethnic-directed media as part of its ethnic marketing efforts. Its interests remain focused on an economic basis for exchange, even though it uses cultural compatibility in its marketing mix to capture the attention of U.S. Latino, Asian, and African American consumers (Holland & Gentry, 1999). Support of ethnic media, recognition of ethnic community leaders, and tailored communications maximize a company's access to a subculture group in exchange for goods and services. The organization's other "contact points" (such as Levi's environmental impact or human resource policies) may or may not be compatible with the interests of these subculture communities.

Only *multicultural marketing* formulates strategy to cover all points of contact with external groups and acknowledges the mutual role that consumers and organizations play in each other's economic and cultural lives (Wilkinson & Cheng, 1999). Consumers do react independently to attempts by marketers to persuade them—they frame that information in the context of past marketer efforts and subcultural assumptions about marketing (such as the importance of insiders versus outsiders) and mainstream marketers (Holland & Gentry, 1999). Thus, although not all attempts to accommodate cultural differences generate positive responses, the cumulative effect is to assert economic and cultural roles over the long term.

## MARKETING SHIFT #4: FROM MARKET
## SEGMENTATION TO MARKET IDENTIFICATION

Choosing communities with which to align a firm's values from among the subcultures evolving in American society is fraught with risk. Many subculture
groups are still too small or too diverse to make them profitable market segments
to pursue in the short term. Some groups respond negatively to commercially
motivated offers of cultural alliance (Miller, 1993; Ritchie, 1995, pp. 158-161).
Nevertheless, competitors willing to court buyers by endorsing the groups with
which they identify and by mirroring their values may beat more conservative
organizations to the beachhead of shared allegiance.

Pioneers in multicultural America range from large multinational organizations, such as AT&T, whose efforts benefit from synergy with their international
marketing activities, to smaller organizations such as Overlooked Opinions,
which specializes in research on the Gay Market. However expertise in values,
concerns, and behaviors of subculture groups is acquired, the investment pays
off in increased consumer loyalty and brand preference. Separate research studies of the Mature Market, U.S. Latinos, Gay and Lesbian buyers, African Americans, teenage consumers, and Asian Americans confirm the preference for *culturally compatible* marketers (Berkowitz, 1997; Delener & Neelankavil, 1990;
Domenech Rodriguez, Slater, & Beauvais, 1997; El-Badry, 1994; Heubusch,
1997; Johnson, 1993b; Kahan & Mulryan, 1995; Natale, 1997; Vaillancourt,
1997; Webster, 1992; Weisend, 1997). Buyers cite activities such as share of
voice in specialized media, tailored product designs or advertising messages,
and *support of important issues* as examples of organizations with a presence in
their community (Delener & Neelankavil, 1990; El-Badry, 1994; Heubusch,
1997; Johnson, 1993b; Kahan & Mulryan, 1995; Webster, 1992).

As always, effective market segmentation means marketers must identify the
parameters and characteristics of a distinctive group of buyers before developing appropriate marketing programs (Kotler, 1990, pp. 263-276; McCarthy,
1960, p. 37). In a multicultural society, situational consumer identity results in
subculture groups that are not mutually exclusive. Further, they can defy the rule
for "distinctive behavior" as justification for unique marketing programs
(Cundiff & Still, 1964, p. 22; Kotler, 1967, pp. 65-66). There is as much diversity
of values and behaviors within the Hispanic or Asian or Mature Market as there
is difference among members of the three groups.

Tastes for soft drinks and coffee offer an example of how difficult it can be to
predict marketplace behavior with a superficial understanding of group values.

For over 40 years, coffee consumption has risen and soft drink consumption has declined with increasing age. So, as the Baby Boomers age, we would normally expect their coffee consumption to increase. But because Boomers are a youth-oriented age cohort, they "will continue to consume soft drinks even as they age" (Meredith & Schewe, 1994, p. 22). When we add ethnicity or geography as influences, preferences for coffee versus soft drinks may stray significantly from the norms of an age or ethnic cohort. Market "segments" respond differently to marketing strategies; a buyer within a subculture shares values but not necessarily behaviors with other members of that group.

Many of the old tools for estimating the value of a market segment or its psychographic, demographic, and behavioral characteristics do not work in this context. It is more useful to understand consumer identities and values than to estimate the size of a market segment by the size of an age cohort or ethnic group. Because information technology helps buyers to screen out unwanted information and increases access to *all sources of relevant information,* knowing media habits is not as important as knowing what information filters buyers use (Ellis, 1999; Turow, 1997a, p. 10).

Segmentation in a multicultural setting means identifying the cultural reference points that an organization must reinforce to gain buyer loyalty. Why do bilingual U.S. Latinos feel more positive about firms that advertise in Spanish? The symbolic value of recognizing the place of Hispanics in multicultural America is a better explanation than language skills (Koslow, Shamdasani, & Touchstone, 1994). Such symbolism resonates within a high-context culture where how something is said is as meaningful as what was said (Gudykunst, 1994, pp. 124-129; Gudykunst & Ting-Toomey, 1988, pp. 43-45; Hall, 1976; Jandt, 1995, pp. 201-203; Samovar & Porter, 1991, pp. 232-236). The significance of Spanish-language usage can have political roots among Cuban Americans, whereas it has class connotations among Mexican Americans. Without fluency in such variations of meaning among different Hispanics, the choice to use Spanish-language ads may be made simply on the number of bilinguals in a geographic area.

A much broader array of research tools is needed to uncover the relationships between buyers' social identities and media and marketplace behaviors. Two middle-class teenage African Americans may vary greatly in how strongly each one identifies with teen and African American subcultures. That difference may be critical when each one reaches for a different brand of snack food. We must uncover the relationships between brand choice and user image, consumer group identities, group associations, and cultural meanings (M. R. Solomon,

1988). Qualitative data gathered from focus group discussions, ethnographic observations, cultural studies, semiotic analysis of meaning, in-depth interviewing, and cultural partnering can be paired with quantitative product usage information to find out which product needs and buyer perceptions match an organization's ability to market those benefits.

## MARKETING SHIFT #5: FROM BRAND MANAGERS TO MARKET SPECIALISTS

Planning marketing programs in multicultural markets demands a market-focused organization. Rarely do marketing managers have authority over decisions about corporate philanthropy, corporate architecture, human resources, or even public relations. The typical organizational structure does not support coordinating the many decisions that express a company's cultural identities and affiliations. Most organizations tend to be organized around functional, product, or geographic areas. Marketing planners must overcome this barrier to effective multicultural marketing by asserting their influence in nontraditional areas of authority. Sears' director of Multicultural Marketing says, "You need to have the people who have the expertise, the education, the sensitivity, and the understanding of the marketplace involved in the process from start to finish" (Teinowitz, 1998, p. S6).

Market managers can learn through research and training how different subculture groups vary in norms for the relative importance of price, promotions, product features, services offered, or retail type as a function of cultural values. For example, U.S. Latinos have been cited for their strength of brand commitment and Asian Americans for their reluctance to try new products (Delener & Neelankavil, 1990; Saegert, Hoover, & Tharp Hilger, 1985; Webster, 1992; Wiesendanger, 1993). Some individuals are as likely to patronize a firm that hires a diverse workforce, contributes to relevant causes, or advertises in the person's native language as they are to patronize a company that offers the lowest prices (Wynter, 1996a). Knowledge of subculture norms of behavior, however, is not enough, for cultural values in a multicultural society are constantly in flux, and deviations from group norms are the norm for expressing individualism.

To build this kind of expertise into marketing programs, organizations must position cultural expertise at the point of market planning (Penaloza & Gilly, 1999). An alternative to brand management is market management. Market specialists must have authority to recommend and implement programs that build presence in particular subculture communities and that fit the organization's own cultural heritage and resources.

The most important credentials for market specialists are skills in applying a border mentality and transmigration to the planning process. Market specialists need to understand the ways in which brands and company policies express cultural meanings. That insight is the foundation for marketing program design. It is important to have diversity among the members of an organization's extended community of employees, buyers, and suppliers. Ethnicity, or any other characteristic of decision makers, is not a substitute for expertise in understanding and relating to cultural differences. A better strategy than hiring people based on ethnic origins is to seek out people with experience or training in navigating between cultures or subcultures.

An interesting analogy to market specialization across products and functional areas among marketers is the account planner in integrated marketing communications agencies. The account planner's job is to represent the target audience and its concerns *during the process* of deciding the "what-when-where-how-who-to whom-with what effect" of communication programs (American Account Planning Group, 1997; British Account Planning Group, 1997; Fortini-Campbell, 1992, pp. 159-189). The account planner brings consumer insight into play at each step, ensuring that the communication program and brand are responsive to audience perceptions and anticipated reactions. A market specialist must mimic this by bringing expertise on subculture communities to each interface of the organization with potential buyers and community groups.

## MARKETING SHIFT #6: FROM MASS COMMUNICATION TO CONSUMER DIALOGUE AND ORGANIZATION CONTACT POINTS

The firms that have taken the time to understand, listen to, and speak directly to consumers rise above the cacophony of commercial chatter in our daily lives. To develop economic *and* cultural relationships with buyers requires communication programs that meet buyers' *desires and needs for information*. To make message and media culturally relevant and to break through subculture differences in communication styles and values, managers must listen to their target buyers.

Everything that a company does that affects the image a consumer might have of it or of its products, services, activities, facilities, or personnel becomes a chance to influence what community members think. Any alternatives for communicating with potential buyers should address all of these occasions (Kaufman, 2000). Though many companies plan their communication strategies by identifying brand contact points with consumers, this is too narrow a focus (Fizdale, 1992; Schultz & Barnes, 1995, pp. 6-8). An organization's employees and managers, members of its board of directors, the media it currently uses, past advertising, office locations, and any number of nontraditional communications media may influence the ways this company is perceived by members of a particular subculture. The idea of organization contact points is more appropriate as a cornerstone of communication strategy in multicultural settings.

An excellent example of how an organization's contact points can affect perceptions of cultural compatibility is the case of Freeport-McMoRan, headquartered in New Orleans. Jim Bob Moffett is their colorful CEO. Students at the University of Texas at Austin campus in 1996 protested the naming of a biology building for Mr. Moffett and generated negative press coverage about the environmental impact of his firm's activities in New Guinea. About the same time, another division of Freeport-McMoRan applied for zoning variances for an environmentally friendly residential development in Austin on the Barton Creek watershed. Civic leaders, reacting more to public perceptions of the firm than to the merits or demerits of the project, revoked prior approvals of the zoning variances. Companies like Freeport-McMoRan cannot have the appearance of acting one way in one community and another way in others without injuring public trust and communicating to the public, at best, a confused value system.

A contrast with Freeport-McMoRan's inconsistency across communities is Coors and the steps this company has taken to change and communicate its cultural values and group affiliations to communities within the American public. Until the 1980s, Coors had earned a reputation as a discriminatory employer, and U.S. Latino and African American workers had slapped it with a number of suits. Its beers were not very popular among Hispanic and Black drinkers, to no one's surprise. When Coors announced the 1980s as the "Decade of Hispanics," Hispanics were not the only cynics (Brown, 1990; Green, 1980). Now, after changing its personnel policies, doing almost 20 years of advertising in Spanish and English using cues from the cultural context of Hispanic beer drinkers, and highlighting and financially supporting leaders in Hispanic communities, Coors has a strong identification with issues important to Hispanics. Coors' brands are among the preferred beers of U.S. Latinos (Brown, 1990). There are no corporate secrets from Net surfers in constant search of new and relevant content (Randazzo, 1995).

Many media serve important cultural roles in their users' lives. For example, the image of heavy Internet users is that of surfers—people who jump from site to site in search of information and entertainment. The reality is that millions of people use the medium to meet their needs for "a sense of community" (Hof, Browder, & Elstrom, 1997). A database of customer preferences keeps an organization apprised of changes in its relationship with them but is only the first step to learning about the rationale behind those preferences (Cross, 1992; Ellis, 1999). New information collectors are appearing as intermediaries in the provision of information to buyers (Snider, 1992). CompareNet is one such service on the World Wide Web, which allows its users to make direct comparisons on over 20,000 products (David, 1997). Personalizing content to meet consumer information needs for delivery in customized media is becoming the new "gold standard" for being relevant (Narisetti, 1998).

The constant change in consumer identities sends mixed messages about values, priorities for cultural compatibility, and media (or gatekeepers) for disseminating information. The best way for an organization to maintain dialogue with target buyers and with members of subculture groups is to constantly monitor the perceptions, behaviors, and values of its external publics. This is too expensive for buyers whose loyalty is transaction based rather than founded on shared economic and cultural interests. As marketing authors who emphasize relationship building have pointed out:

> Individual customers teach the company more and more about their preferences and needs, giving the company an immense competitive advantage. The more customers teach the company, the better it becomes at providing exactly what they want—exactly how they want it—and the more difficult it will be for a competitor to entice them away. (Pine, Peppers, & Rogers, 1995, p. 103)

Most firms control outsider access to information about costs, results of performance or safety tests, and other valued information. But buyers can now easily access almost any information about products or companies they want. In the new media environment, buyers acquire whatever information they find relevant and use it as leverage with sellers. In automobile purchasing, consumers are using outside sources on dealers' costs to negotiate how much they are willing to pay. Few Ford dealers would be prepared in the showroom to answer questions about Ford's ethnic hiring policies. They probably will not get to answer a direct question about this because future car buyers will decide if Ford offers them cultural compatibility long before they choose which showrooms to visit. Marketers must anticipate and satisfy buyer interests in both cultural and economic information.

## MARKETING SHIFT #7: FROM EXTENSIVE TO INTENSIVE MARKET INFORMATION

Consumers can be quite sensitive to and unforgiving of token efforts to win their dollar votes (Davidson, 1995). The most important competitive tool in multicultural settings is research and insight into a target group's values, beliefs, attitudes, and behaviors. This information about subculture groups can be acquired by hiring employees and partner organizations with that expertise and by building in knowledge via primary and secondary research. More likely, a strategy of cultural compatibility will require constant qualitative and quantitative research. Competition for consumers in multiple groups will depend on having an information system that is flexible, interactive, and predictive. Just as the experience curve provides economies to early manufacturers, experience in multicultural markets generates information and experience portfolios that are valuable sources of distinctive competence.

Consumer social identity has a strong influence on some purchases but not on others. How simple it would be if there could be a list of products not affected by cultural associations. Unfortunately, cultural meaning is not limited to inherent qualities of products. It results when meaning moves from the product to the consumer's cultural frame of reference (McCracken, 1986; Tharp & Scott, 1990; Twitchell, 1996). As an example of the range of possibilities, Kwanzaa dolls express African American identity, whereas yo-yos seem to reflect no group-specific identity. The Kwanzaa doll might have to find some appeal other than expression of self-identity to attract buyers other than African Americans. For example, the values represented by Kwanzaa customs (e.g., self-determination or loyalty) might be compatible with those of other subculture groups. The yo-yo brand could use tactical moves, such as advertising in ethnic-directed media, to build in cultural associations.

The collection and interpretation of information about the tug of social identities on buyer behavior are valuable competitive tools. Behavioral research among consumer subcultures is a good place to start, for differences in subculture group norms (such as data showing discount store patronage of different ethnic groups) may be significant. Still, product usage data contain no information about what products or stores *signify* to their buyers.

Marketers cannot rely on media to supply the kinds of information needed to plan marketing programs in multicultural settings. Their demographic and lifestyle audience data provide little insight into situation-specific influences over buyers or the roles that a product or medium plays in expressing identity. Nevertheless, increasing competition in media and selectivity on the part of media users are already forcing the media to make finer and finer distinctions across audiences. As a result, they too will be forced to learn more about their viewers in order to sell space or time (Ellis, 1999). In the meantime, a better approach than tracking reach in terms of audience and target demographics is to determine what people who receive communications think about them and how their behavior is affected by these perceptions.

The broader arena of marketing decision making in a multicultural setting requires a supportive information system. This network must focus on acquiring in-depth information about smaller numbers of potential customers, rather than on demographics and lifestyles of a large percentage of all potential buyers. The answers to these types of questions require multiple research methods, a deeper level of interpretation, and a broader range of decision makers.

To uncover the perceptions of brands, as well as brand and product users, among members of different subcultures, requires a shift toward more qualitative methods. Insight into the cultural associations and meanings of particular brands is a more powerful basis for matrix market planning than multidimensional analyses of mega-databases or survey data. The operative term is *insight,* for all research methods are useless without this component. Psychographic information can pinpoint heroes and ideals of a group, but only insight can lead to decisions about whether real or ideal associations are the better basis for brand positioning (Randazzo, 1995, pp. 121-158).

Diversity within groups presents the greatest reason for following up secondary research with detailed qualitative and quantitative analysis. The symbolic meanings of brands vary with the source of a buyer's cultural reference points. Whether a company wishes to strongly identify its brand with one subculture, multiple groups, or a broader swath of buyers depends on the extent of within-group variability in meanings (Leigh & Gabel, 1992). The dilemma of companies like Old Navy or The Gap is to decipher cultural influences and desired affiliations for urban teens who are the opinion leaders for casual fashions. The intersection of urban, ethnic, and age sources of identity for this target market makes it essential to understand what a particular brand signifies about those identities and ideals.

Preferences for timing and format of communications create situations full of cultural significance. What is the relative effectiveness of a product placement in or commercial during the television program *ER* or *Ally McBeal*? How do those compare in communication effectiveness to a story line about the same brand on the same program? Does the effectiveness vary across Baby Boomers or Asian Americans? The question is not only what occasions and formats are most effective but also how they vary across consumer identities.

The collection of intensive market information is hampered by the homogeneity of marketing decision makers. The average copywriter is about 30, and most marketing managers come from middle-class, white-collar backgrounds. Ethnographic research relies more heavily on the interpretive skills of the researcher than on quantitative analysis. The participation of ethnic minorities in marketing positions remains low, and the costs of gaining experience in cultural analysis are high, presenting yet another reason for more diversity in organizations.

Given the complexities of gaining insight into people in different ethnic, age, and/or lifestyle subcultures, marketers must substitute for personal knowledge of those subcultures. The profiles in the next chapters of this book present basic information about the distinctive demographic, value, and behavioral characteristics of five subcultures. This information does not pretend to predict any group's potential for a company or its products and services. It can serve only as a guide to areas where more research is needed as inputs for more detailed marketing planning.

## MARKETING STRATEGIES FOR A MULTICULTURAL SETTING

Recognition of the need to adapt to a changed environment is the first step in implementing a multicultural marketing program. Policies to build in and nurture the border mentality and transmigration expertise are also necessary accommodations to a multicultural setting. Firms can use this expertise to build a strategy of alliances within particular subcultures that match economic opportunities in the market and cultural heritage of the organization. Keep in mind that there are many risks in aligning a firm with different community groups when cultural meaning is in flux, and that it takes both economic and cultural programs to build a partnership with consumers.

There are a number of strategic alternatives in a multicultural market, and none are inherently superior. The best choice depends on factors such as what competitors are doing, the firm's unique resource mix, the size and diversity of needs within a market, and the viable options for approaching a market of multiple subcultures.

One strategy alternative is to make no adaptation of marketing programs to attract buyers as members of subculture groups. This is the way mainstream marketing works in most American consumer goods markets. The hope is that most consumers in a defined target market (of 25- to 34-year-olds, for example) will respond as a homogeneous mass market. There are several situations when this may be the case:

▶ When the brand has an insignificant role in expressing consumer or corporate identity
▶ When a brand has strong yet similar cultural meanings across subcultures
▶ When product usage of a brand does not vary across subculture groups (Kunda, 1994b)
▶ When the brand has unique performance, price, or quality attributes that motivate buyers differentially across subcultures
▶ When the brand complements other products or services in the organization's portfolio and/or does not promise sufficient volume potential on its own

In each of the situations described above, it makes sense to design a marketing strategy that appeals to the broadest group of buyers possible in the American marketplace. Examples of all-inclusive marketing messages are shown in Figure 3.3. They contain a racially mixed group of actors and the cultural message that the product is for everyone, no matter what color.

Many companies are using these techniques to attract buyers from multiple subculture groups. Schick, Pepsi, Fruit of the Loom, Tonka, Hasbro, Federal Express, Xerox, and USAir now include actors of multiple ethnic origins in their ads in general market media ("Hispanic Marketing Wins New Converts," 1988; Wynter, 1993b). This is particularly effective in media such as network television and cable channels with broad audiences. Given the absence of minority representation in both media programming and advertising in the past, this technique captures the attention of ethnic minority consumers, who react positively to seeing people who share their ethnic origins (Green, 1991; Wilkes & Valen-

**Figure 3.3a.** All-Inclusive Marketing Messages in a Multicultural Setting: Head & Shoulders Ad for U.S. General Market

**Figure 3.3b.** All-Inclusive Marketing Messages in a Multicultural Setting: Tommy Hilfiger Ad for U.S. General Market

cia, 1989). They are more likely to see those firms as "good companies to work for," though there is little evidence yet that they are more likely to buy their products (Whittler, 1991; Wynter, 1993b).

A second strategy in multicultural markets involves making tactical changes in the marketing mix: targeted price discounts and promotions, different types of promotions, different intensities of outlets, different models or settings for communications (Wilkes & Valencia, 1989; Whittler, 1991), translation of advertisements into foreign languages, and addition of ethnic minority media to the media mix, to cite a few examples. Procter and Gamble calls this "micro-marketing" and is one of its leading successful practitioners (Schiller, 1989). Miller Brewing Company tried unique ads for black, Hispanic, and Asian consumers in the 1990s but later decided to return to one approach for their target of 21- to 28-year-olds. Of course, it helps that they are reaching an age cohort that already shares many values and attitudes about beer drinking (Melcher, 1997). In contrast, supported by a sophisticated computer tracking system, Target redesigns its store merchandise mixes to satisfy consumer preferences in different ethnic, racial, and lifestyle neighborhoods (Patterson, 1995).

Cosmetics usage varies to a great extent across ethnic and age groups as a function of differing needs and cultural attitudes about makeup. Thus, there is an obvious advantage to be gained by companies in this industry who adjust product mix and communication programs. This is evident in the efforts of Mary Kay and Avon to appeal to African American, U.S. Latino, and Asian American consumers. Both companies' reliance on personal selling has led them to diversify their sales staffs also.

A third alternative for multicultural marketing is redesign of overall marketing strategy, using transmigration and a cultural partnership with consumers from various subculture groups. Cultural expertise can be acquired in-house or via the choice of outside suppliers of specialized services. Ethnic marketing among clients came of age when ethnic specialists appeared on the research and communications scenes in the 1980s (Turow, 1997a, pp. 55-89). The bandwagon really began to roll in the early 1990s, when many mainstream firms placed their ethnic market budgets within ongoing marketing plans rather than on an "experimental" basis. Pacific Bell is one of those firms that set up an Ethnic Markets Group to reach ethnic business owners for phone services (Mehta, 1994a). Anheuser-Busch organized all its ethnic marketing efforts under a Vice President for Emerging Markets, while Procter & Gamble and Levi's put theirs under Vice Presidents for Ethnic Markets. Even general market advertising agencies such as Young and Rubicam and Leo Burnett opened ethnic market divisions.

The strongest platform for multicultural marketing comes from a commitment to use a firm's cultural and economic resources together in consumer marketing. As discussed earlier, it requires an inventory of contact points with external groups, programs of intensive research about the cultural lives of consumers, broad authority for marketing throughout the organization, and adoption of a border mentality about cultural differences. In the case of a mass retailer like Wal-Mart, multicultural marketing may also consist of many inconsistencies in merchandise mix, attention to subculture differences among customers, and roles as cultural agent for its broad base of consumers (Saporito, 1999).

## ETHICAL DILEMMAS IN MULTICULTURAL MARKETING

Today's marketplace is everywhere, anytime, at the touch of a finger. Purchasing decisions are not so different from voting, contributing to causes, or any choices about how to spend limited time, money, or emotional commitment. Naturally, we prefer choices that "mean something" and that support the groups and values in which we believe. The boundaries between the cultural, economic, political, and social parts of our lives are falling. Multicultural marketing asserts a role for businesses (and other organizations) in the cultural lives of consumers. Is this a healthy allocation of responsibilities in our society? What role should these organizations take in changing overall societal values? Should consumers' marketing partners sell information about us to their strategic partners (Wildstrom, 2000)? These are some of the gray areas of multicultural marketing.

At the broadest level of American life, multicultural marketing intends to distinguish members of different subcultures, thus bringing attention to our differences rather than our similarities (Rittenberg & Parthasarathy, 1997). The potential for mistaking group membership for individual preferences is strong. The consequences for signaling social division by images, media, and content chosen to attract ever-smaller groups of consumers are open to speculation. In *Breaking Up America,* Joseph Turow (1997a) expressed the fear that Americans would lose sight of their diversity and "join their own image tribes apart from other image tribes" (p. 199). An irony of the multicultural marketers' recognition of increased American diversity could be loss of our national sense of community.

A major difficulty in implementing multicultural marketing programs is our dependence on and preference for quantitative measures of consumer behavior and/or characteristics. From a client's point of view, for example, the U.S. census is a more objective count of U.S. Latinos in Los Angeles than estimates of English- or Spanish-dominant Hispanics in Los Angeles made by a Hispanic market specialist. Even though a client may recognize the importance of ethnic identity in predicting behavior, product usage data and size of an age or ethnic group have more sway over resource commitments. It is easier (cheaper) to measure how people behave than what they think. Not understanding the complex relationship of consumer identity to what people want and do in the marketplace ignores the intervening importance of cultural values and symbolic affiliations. This omission ignores opportunities to participate at a more significant level in consumers' lives and to be less vulnerable to competitors.

Many proponents of multicultural marketing are among the ethnic market specialists in advertising agencies, research firms, and niche brands. One of their frequent complaints is how little the decision makers that make budget recommendations in large firms know about ongoing changes in our society or the increasing numbers of multicultural consumers. They find that "media planners and buyers often range between the ages of 22 and 26 years old with limited experience in the business and limited life experiences" (Teinowitz, 1998, p. S14). They also believe that stereotypes continue to prejudice deeper understanding of ethnic consumers. African American market specialists have to convince decision makers to buy their expertise by overcoming a perception that African Americans are reached effectively by "general market advertising" on network TV (Teinowitz, 1998, p. S14). Training programs that educate corporate managers are the way to eradicate these misperceptions.

One concern has to do with the qualifications of people in multicultural marketing. Do experts in marketing to consumers in a subculture group have to be members themselves of the subculture? Those who have experience in ethnic marketing say it counts against them with some clients, who discount their rational arguments for more spending: "You're just saying it of course because you're Asian . . . [or African American or Latino] . . . and so you're going to push that" (Teinowitz, 1998, p. S18). At the other end of the spectrum are those people who believe that the only credible expertise is group membership. But without training in cultural analysis and appreciation of the cultural roles brands play, subculture members are often as poorly equipped as anyone else to decipher and translate cultural meaning. Though they may understand the unique worldviews and subtleties of their subculture, they must be able to translate them for other marketing planners.

Participation in subculture communities must be visible to its members. However, extracting an economic quid pro quo can discredit the authenticity of community membership. Uptown cigarettes designed for African American smokers, Dakota smokes for blue-collar women, and the *Reality Bites* movie about Generation X all suffered public backlashes from their "target markets" (Wilson & Gutierrez, 1995, p. 137). The firms marketing these products were seen as exploiting the targeted group. This is a real danger of the narrow focus of ethnic marketing (Hwang, 1999). Marketers who seek only dollar votes ignore the real benefits gained from cultural compatibility in a multicultural environment.

## SUMMARY

Being able to understand cultural differences and adjust to them is an essential skill for both consumers and marketers in a multicultural society. Having a border mentality alerts both groups to cultural differences in meaning without necessarily judging one interpretation as the better one. The term *transmigration* describes the tools an organization can use to build in cultural compatibility with buyers in different subculture groups. These include a broader range of marketing tools and conscious planning for communicative points of contact between the firm and its brands and external publics.

To measure success in a multicultural marketplace, organizations can add perceptions of shared interests to their estimates of consumer long-term profitability. Market planners can start by determining the best strategy and tactics for one subculture niche, then expanding by accumulating market niches among consumers from different subcultures. Meeting the information needs of buyers in a multicultural setting means reformulating how a firm "speaks" from a cultural point of view.

These shifts in emphasis highlight the need for marketing decision makers to take broader responsibility. Market expertise must be acquired, including knowledge of different subcultures and their value systems as well as variability within the subcultures. Authority for marketing must be broad enough to cover areas not traditionally part of the market mix. Planning must originate with market specialists. Communication and information systems must be designed to provide constant input about cultural meaning and consumer perceptions of the firm and its brands.

There is no inherently superior strategy for penetrating consumers in American subcultures. Some companies will decide that their general market strategies are the most cost-efficient way to reach these consumers, whereas other firms may decide to concentrate their resources for a strategy of cultural compatibility within one subculture. The strategy of cultural compatibility with consumers in multiple subcultures requires the brand and its seller(s) to become multicultural entities themselves. Implementing a program of multicultural marketing opens the door to questions such as qualifications of multicultural decision makers and effects on our social and cultural environments.

## Notes

1. For acculturation's effect on cultural meaning, see Penaloza (1994). For the unique styles of communication of African Americans, see Hecht et al. (1993). For discussions of low- versus high-context cultures, see Hall (1976), Jandt (1995, pp. 201-203), Samovar and Porter (1991, pp. 232-236), Gudykunst (1994, pp. 124-129), and Gudykunst and Ting-Toomey (1988, pp. 43-45).

2. A traditional definition of marketing is "the process of planning and executing the conception, pricing, promotion, and distribution of ideas, goods, and services to create exchanges that satisfy individual and organizational goals" (Bennett, 1988, p. 10). Also see Best (1997, pp. 405-406).

# CHAPTER 4

# Mature Americans

## Fastest Growing Subculture

In the not too distant future, the largest number of consumers in the United States will be over 55 years of age. The 1990 census counted 31.1 million Americans over 65 and 52.2 million Americans over 55 years of age; the comparable estimates for 2000 are 35.3 million and 56.9 million, representing more than a 10% increase for both groups within 10 years. By 2010, one of every four Americans will be over 55 years of age (Taeuber, 1993)! In contrast to members of other subcultures discussed later in this book, most Senior Citizens do not choose to represent themselves as "different" from other Americans. Any marketer who labels them or their needs as distinctive finds out quickly the hazards of distinguishing old age in a culture that reveres youth. It is *being old* in a youth-oriented society, not self-identity, that fosters a distinctive subculture for members of the Mature Market.

Older Americans rightly believe they are as "American" as any other people. Over the span of their lives, change has transformed the world around them—the routines and rhythms of daily life; beliefs, heroes, and ideals; how they work, worship, and have fun. Anyone older than 50 in the United States in 2000 was born before widespread use of computers, televisions, VCRs, fast-food restaurants, multiplex theaters, the Internet, fax machines, antibiotics, air conditioning, electric weed trimmers, microwave ovens, digital pagers, and other fixtures of life at the beginning of the 21st century. Seniors may believe younger Americans take these conveniences for granted and have missed important learning experiences. However, on the basis of the reflections they see in the media, it is Senior Citizens themselves who are out of step with "newer is better," the ethos of contemporary America (Hammond & Morrison, 1996).

Age cohorts are people born within a more or less 20-year so-called generation. Americans of each generation tend to retain the tastes and attitudes of their youth throughout life and thus to share an experiential bond (Meredith & Schewe, 1994; Phillips, 1996; Strauss & Howe, 1991). The combination of formative personal experiences and perceived distance from mainstream American life is a significant unifying force for the Mature Market. It is why older Americans constitute a subculture, rather than simply a grouping of people according to age. Mature Americans have distinctive demographic characteristics, visible in where, how, and with whom they choose to live. Furthermore, their economic priorities and resources, relative to Americans in other stages of the family life cycle, shape their product and services needs. Both their values and patterns of behavior have survived radical environmental change.

The particular experiences of their youth are the basis of shared values and cultural symbolism among Senior Citizens. Their worldviews are resistant to forces creating the experience-based value systems of younger Americans. Their media and entertainment tastes, their experience and expectations when interacting with sellers, their knowledge of options for meeting consumer needs, and, in general, their preferences in the marketplace were formed when the marketing infrastructure was very different. Thus, Americans in the Mature Market meet the criteria for a subculture in a multicultural setting—different values, styles of communication, and response to marketing programs.

Trying to convince older persons that they are a unique subculture in America would "set them apart" in a way they might well find offensive. So one of the dilemmas of marketing to the Mature Market is figuring out how to reach them *without distinguishing them* from other Americans. The initial challenge is to decide who is or is not part of the Mature Market. Our government cannot decide; the Labor Department counts people over 55, whereas the Bureau of the Census says it includes only people 65 years or older. The American Association of Retired Persons (AARP) puts everyone 50 years of age or older into its target market, much to the shock of Boomers over 50 who still think of themselves as young. All of us would agree that "typical" 50-, 70-, and 90-year-olds are likely to have different needs and lifestyles. Still, no clear boundaries distinguish members of the Mature Market other than their values, experiences, and for some, unique product needs.

## WHO ARE THE MATURE AMERICANS?

What to call the Mature Market is a challenge that their ambivalence about being old presents to marketers. Because they do not like to be singled out from other Americans, they can react negatively to any age-based label that might be used. In one survey, the two most acceptable names were *Senior Citizen* and *Mature American;* in another one, *Mature* came out first and *Senior Citizen* was third place (Beck, 1990; Brazil, 1998; Donnelly Marketing, 1988). Euphemisms such as "the Golden Years" for age-based labels don't fool anyone, especially older Americans, who dislike marketer embellishment. "Perceived age" is a key component of social identity for Senior Citizens.

Another issue is how to deal with the diversity within a Mature Market, however defined. People of different races, ethnic groups, geographic locations, socioeconomic status, and other personal characteristics are thrown together as if they were a unified group. Special needs of some members of the Mature Market may result in similar consumer choices but may have no relationship to expressing Senior Citizen self-identity. These unique dynamics of economic and cultural meanings confuse marketers who understand the Mature Market only in terms of economic or product needs.

Culturally, Senior Citizens remain invisible, except to their own families. Age discrimination is a common experience of older Americans, even if it is not openly discussed. Older Americans strive to overcome negative stereotypes in the media and workplace, only to find entertainment, popular leisure pursuits, and music also catering to younger audiences (Lee, 1997).

This chapter expands upon these topics. First, several measures are presented for estimating the size and shape of the Mature Market. Next, the values of this age cohort are brought into contrast with those of other Americans. The preferences of Senior Citizens with regard to information sources and expectations of sellers are then outlined. The last section covers responses of Mature Americans to various marketing activities.

## THE GULAG OF OLDER AMERICANS

*Gulag* is a strong but appropriate word to describe metaphorically the situation of older Americans. Alexander Solzhenitsyn (1974) used this term to refer to the enclaves of artists and scientists among political prisoners who were invisible to ordinary Russians and united by the persecution against them. These people were shuttled among hidden prisons designed by USSR officials. Enclaves of older Americans are invisible to other Americans but are tied to each other by exclusion from American public life. Such isolation is a concern of civic leaders; the metaphor accurately describes the virtual absence of older Americans in popular culture.

It is easier to characterize their demographic and economic characteristics than to master the cultural subtleties of the Mature Market for marketing purposes. Table 4.1 shows the size of different age-groups within the Mature Market. For example, at least one half of the over-65 group was younger than 85 years in 1998. As shown in the table, the ranks of older Americans are predominantly White. White men have higher mortality rates after age 85 than older men of other ethnic origins. Women outnumber men for all races and age-groups, even though the proportion varies. Women over 85 tend to be single, whereas older men tend to be married.

The proportion of older Americans in the population has increased markedly over time. In 1900, citizens 65 years of age and older constituted about 4% of the total population. By 1950 this percentage had doubled to 8%, and by 1990 it was 12.5% (Taeuber, 1993, Table 2.1). In 2020 this percentage is likely to rise to 16%, and in 2050 older Americans are predicted to be over 20% of the population, or 79 million people! This could also mean 37 million persons over 85 years of age in 2050 (Stipp, 1999). The actual size of the future Mature Market is a topic of controversy among demographers, who do not agree how mortality rates will affect these numbers (Exeter, 1990).

The future Mature Market will be more diverse than it is today, as ethnic groups increase their percentage of the total population and arrive at old age themselves. African Americans represented about 8% of 1990 consumers aged 65 years or older; in 2050, they will be over 12% of the elderly. The equivalent numbers for persons of Hispanic origin are 3.7% in 1990 and 15.3% in 2050 (Taeuber, 1993).

The fastest growing group among Mature Americans are those in the older age categories (85+). In 1900, there were fewer than 400,000 Americans over 85

**TABLE 4.1** 1998 Mature Market Size and Ethnic Composition

| | *All 65+ Yr.* | *65-74 Yr.* | *75-84 Yr.* | *85-99 Yr.* | *100+ Yr.* |
|---|---|---|---|---|---|
| Men/100 women | 69.7 | 81.1 | 65.7 | 40.0 | 18.9 |
| *Sex* | *N (in 1,000s)* | *N (in 1,000s)* | *N (in 1,000s)* | *N (in 1,000s)* | *N (1,000s)* |
| Men | 14,089 | 8,224 | 4,730 | 1,124 | 10 |
| Women | 20,197 | 10,141 | 7,194 | 2,808 | 53 |
| Total | 34,286 | 18,365 | 11,924 | 3,932 | 63 |

| | *All 65+ Yr.* | *65-74 Yr.* | *75-84 Yr.* | *85+ Yr.* |
|---|---|---|---|---|
| *Race* | *N (in 1,000s)* | *N (in 1,000s)* | *N (in 1,000s)* | *N (in 1,000s)* |
| White Americans | 27,033 | 15,052 | 9,485 | 2,496 |
| African Americans | 2,554 | 1,524 | 786 | 244 |
| Americans of Hispanic origin | 1,516 | 992 | 397 | 127 |
| Native Americans and Asian Americans | 776 | 448 | 286 | 42 |

SOURCE: U.S. Bureau of the Census (1998b).

years of age; by 1990, there were 7 million people over 80, including 4 million over 85 and 1 million over 90. By offering more life-saving medicines and treatments, technology has changed the experience of being old, allowing many of these people to live healthy lives until a few months before they die. Four out of five centenarians are women. In the future, more of the "young old" (55-69 years of age) will be caring for the "old old" (85+).

The aging of our population is not just an American phenomenon. In 1991, 27 countries had over 2 million elderly persons; in 2020, the number of such countries will be 49. Increased life expectancy has brought many changes to the workplace. Pensions, savings, and Social Security payments have made it easier for elderly men and women to retire, but a percentage of this rapidly growing population will have to be supported by the rest of our population for a longer period of time. As a result, many older Americans are both working longer and having a longer retirement. Also, more people are living alone in households for long periods of time, with part-time jobs to preserve Social Security payment eligibility. More Senior Citizens are finding shared housing to be a solution to cost cutting, a way to make friends, and an alternative to living alone (Grimes, 1999).

The geographic dispersion of the Mature Market does not make this group of consumers easy to reach with cost-effective media. The states with the highest *percentages* of Senior Citizens among their population are not the same states with the largest *numbers* of elderly persons. These statistics are shown in Table 4.2. For example, the five states with the highest percentages of elderly among local populations in 1990 were Florida, Pennsylvania, Iowa, Rhode Island, and West Virginia (all over 15%). The five states with the largest numbers of Senior Citizens were California, Florida, New York, Pennsylvania, and Texas. These patterns of concentration are predicted to remain stable at least until 2010. Over 25% of older Americans live in rural areas, but this figure ranges from highs of 64% of all Senior Citizens in Vermont and 57% in North Dakota to lows of 8% in California and 9% in New Jersey (U.S. Bureau of the Census, 1992, pp. CPI-2 to CPI-52). State-by-state variations in size and distributions of the Mature Market population are important for marketers to understand. Table 4.3 shows the cities where the largest numbers of Senior Citizens live.

Researchers have segmented the Mature Market by several demographic classifications. Chronological age has served to introduce the following groupings: the "young old" (55 or 65 to 70 or 75), the "middle-aged old" (71 or 75 to 85), and the "old old" (over 85 years of age) (Mayer, Joyce, Simons, & Cook, 1977). Other firms differentiate the "wellderly" and "illderly," an important determinant of mobility, lifestyle, and product needs. Other criteria that can be valuable in different situations for predicting marketing behavior are race or ethnicity, income or marital status, income source, and nature of the community of residence.

Many marketing researchers have found age-based segmentation approaches to be lacking in prediction capabilities. An alternative is values-based segmentation. Figure 4.1 shows the segments used by three different research groups to help their clients better target buyers within the Mature Market. The presumption of each approach is that lifestyles are more predictive of marketplace behavior than demographic characteristics alone (Gollub, 1989; Moschis, 1996; Wolfe, 1990, pp. 100-132).

**TABLE 4.2** Top Mature Market States (Population 65+ Years)

| Geographic Location | Size of Senior Population (in 1,000s) | | % of Local Population | | % of U.S. Senior Population | |
|---|---|---|---|---|---|---|
| | *2000* | *2010* | *2000* | *2010* | *2000* | *2010* |
| **All Mature Americans** | **35,322** | **40,104** | **12.8** | **13.3** | **100** | **100** |
| **Selected U.S. States** | | | | | | |
| **Top 10 Total:** | 7,368 | 12,740 | | | 20.9 | 31.8 |
| Florida | 2,999 | 3,654 | 19.6 | 21.0 | 8.5 | 9.1 |
| Pennsylvania | 1,913 | 1,904 | 15.6 | 15.3 | 5.4 | 4.7 |
| Missouri | 769 | 837 | 14.1 | 14.5 | 2.2 | 2.1 |
| Arkansas | 383 | 436 | 14.9 | 15.7 | 1.1 | 1.1 |
| Iowa | 439 | 449 | 15.0 | 15.0 | 1.2 | 1.1 |
| Nebraska | 236 | 248 | 13.8 | 13.9 | 0.7 | 0.6 |
| North Dakota | 93 | 93 | 14.5 | 13.7 | 0.3 | 0.2 |
| South Dakota | 108 | 111 | 14.0 | 13.6 | 0.3 | 0.3 |
| Rhode Island | 151 | 153 | 15.1 | 14.8 | 0.4 | 0.4 |
| W. Virginia | 277 | 280 | 15.1 | 15.2 | 0.8 | 0.7 |
| **Other States:** | 16,186 | 18,506 | | | 45.8 | 46.1 |
| California | 3,704 | 4,605 | 10.6 | 11.2 | 10.5 | 11.5 |
| Texas | 2,074 | 2,534 | 10.3 | 11.1 | 5.9 | 6.3 |
| New York | 2,426 | 2,526 | 13.3 | 13.6 | 6.9 | 6.3 |
| Illinois | 1,513 | 1,588 | 12.4 | 12.6 | 4.3 | 4.0 |
| New Jersey | 1,112 | 1,192 | 13.7 | 13.9 | 3.1 | 3.0 |
| Michigan | 1,211 | 1,277 | 12.4 | 12.7 | 3.4 | 3.2 |
| Ohio | 1,547 | 1,619 | 13.5 | 13.9 | 4.4 | 4.0 |
| North Carolina | 998 | 1,200 | 13.1 | 14.4 | 2.8 | 3.0 |
| Georgia | 798 | 998 | 10.5 | 11.7 | 2.3 | 2.5 |
| Virginia | 803 | 967 | 11.4 | 12.5 | 2.3 | 2.4 |

SOURCE: Hobbs (1996, Tables 5-4, 5-7, and 5-8).

**TABLE 4.3**  Top Mature Market Cities (Population 65+ Years)

| Geographic Location | Size of Senior Population (in 1,000s) 1996 | % of Local Population 1996 | % of U.S. Senior Population 1996 |
|---|---|---|---|
| All Mature Americans | 33,867 | 12.8 | 100.0 |
| U.S. adults living in nonmetropolitan areas | 9,303 | 17.4 | 27.5 |
| U.S. adults living in metropolitan areas | 24,404 | 11.5 | 72.1 |
| Top 10 U.S. Cities | 7,660 | | 22.6 |
| New York City | 2,412 | 13.1 | 7.0 |
| Los Angeles | 1,508 | 9.7 | 4.2 |
| Chicago | 955 | 11.3 | 2.7 |
| Philadelphia | 795 | 13.3 | 2.3 |
| Houston | 307 | 7.3 | 0.8 |
| Detroit | 549 | 11.6 | 1.6 |
| San Diego | 290 | 10.9 | 0.8 |
| San Francisco | 729 | 11.0 | 2.0 |
| Baltimore | 289 | 11.7 | 0.8 |
| San Antonio | 149 | 10.2 | 0.4 |

SOURCE: My own estimates, based on 1990 census data (from U.S. Bureau of the Census, 1990), for population 65+ years, plus 1990 to 1996 growth rates for specific cities and metropolitan and nonmetropolitan areas.

# ECONOMIC AND POLITICAL STRENGTH; CULTURAL INVISIBILITY

It is the economic characteristics of Senior Citizens that present the strongest appeal to marketers. Median incomes of most Mature Market households are not significantly higher than median incomes for all Americans, but Mature Ameri-

Three Experiential Stages of Adult Life (Wolfe, 1990, pp. 100-132):

1. Possession Experience Stage (normally ages of young adults):
   - Motivated by self-oriented personality development
   - Provide visible evidence of who they are
   - Building and acquisition experiences as signs of accomplishment
   - Maintenance of self-identity
   - Satisfaction expectations range from mild pleasure to euphoria
   - Examples of peak inanimate objects bought: first car, first home
   - Examples of peak animate objects acquired: first spouse, first baby
2. Catered Experience Stage (normally late 30s+):
   - Purchase of more services, especially for personal, convenience, and entertainment needs
   - Having others do for you can be more exhilarating than acquiring/owning things
   - More opportunity to express individuality
   - Examples of peak catered experiences: season theater tickets, weekend holiday, services of interior decorator, custom-made products
   - More variability in what makes a catered experience a "peak" experience
3. Being Experience Stage (normally 50+):
   - Beginning to confront mortality, development of wisdom and integrity of personality; more tolerance and less stress
   - Seeking experiences that enhance a sense of connectedness and appreciation for life
   - Includes more activities that benefit others and contribute to inner personal growth
   - Aesthetic aspects of services become more important (charm of waiter rather than speed of service)
   - After settling into retirement, new desires to contribute to life around them
   - Family is only one area of importance; other peak experiences might be heading a charity ball, watching a great sunset, mentoring younger people, learning new skills, falling in love, spiritual enrichment

Six Lifestyles and Values Groups of Older Adults (Gollub, 1989):

1. Attainers (9% of 55+ population):
   - Youngest, median age 60

**Figure 4.1.** Values-Based Segmentation of the Mature Market

- Most autonomous, healthy
- Self-indulgent, wealthy, highest incomes of 55+
- Best educated, open to change
2. Adapters (11% of 55+ population):
   - Second-highest incomes and home values
   - Median age 74, tend to be single
   - Aware of needs, seeking information, highly informed
   - Open to change, can be demanding consumers
3. Explorers (22% of 55+ population):
   - Middle incomes, lived 20+ years at current address
   - Rugged individualists, active, forego children's assistance
   - Median age 65
4. Martyrs (26% of 55+ population):
   - Low to moderate incomes
   - Median age 63
   - Inward, denying, closed, uninformed about world
   - Conservative, resistant to change
   - Divorced or single
5. Pragmatists (21% of 55+ population):
   - Moderate or lower incomes
   - Median age of 76, likely to be 70+
   - Middle of the road, cautious but open to change
   - Somewhat outgoing but living alone
   - Moderately demanding
6. Preservers (11% of 55+ population):
   - Low incomes
   - Median age of 78, ¾ over 70
   - Frightened of change, frail, vulnerable
   - Least self-indulgent
   - Living alone or in older adult housing

Life Stages of the Mature Market (Moschis, 1996):

1. Healthy Indulgers (18% of 55+ population):
   - Fewest experiences of major life events (e.g., retirement, chronic illnesses, or widowhood)
   - Most likely to behave like younger consumers
   - Financially well off and settled in careers
   - Major focus: to enjoy life; seek convenience and personal services
   - Market for travel services
   - Interests in reduced-scale, independent housing and security
2. Healthy Hermits (36% of 55+ population):
   - Self-concepts affected by major life events

**Figure 4.1.** *(Continued)*

- Resent isolation but choose to withdraw
- Do not want to behave like "old people"
- Least likely to move; market for remodeling
3. Ailing Outgoers (29% of 55+ population):
    - Positive self-esteem despite major life events or health problems
    - Accepting of "old-age" status
    - Interested in getting the "most out of life," value their independence
    - Major market for health care products and services
    - Place high value on convenience
    - Respond to special attention for special diet needs and whatever makes their shopping tasks easier (e.g., catalog and direct marketing)
4. Frail Recluses (17% of 55+ population):
    - Accepting of "old-age" status
    - Lifestyles reflect physical declines and changing social roles
    - Strong spiritual lives
    - Need services to assist them in maintenance of house and self
    - Large market for health care products and services
    - Earlier Healthy Indulgers, later as Healthy Hermits or Ailing Outgoers

**Figure 4.1.** *(Continued)*

cans' personal wealth and disposable incomes stand out. In the late 1950s, over 35% of the elderly had incomes below poverty levels. In the 1990s, that figure had dropped below 13%. The median net worth of Mature Americans is twice that of all householders. The main sources of this wealth are higher home ownership and interest-earning assets (Taeuber, 1993, Table 2.1). Put another way, it is estimated that Senior Citizens have 75% of all U.S. wealth and 50% of disposable income; in total, the "over 55's" represent a market for over $1 trillion in goods and services each year (Konrad & DeGeorge, 1989)!

The median figures for income and wealth of the elderly obscure wider variance in their economic status than that of any other age-group. Though living standards are higher overall, and Senior Citizens are healthier and better educated than any prior group, many persons do not fit this pattern. This is particularly true for the minority old, women living alone, and Senior Citizens just above poverty levels and not qualified for government aid—16% of people over 65 (Duff, 1995). In African American communities, there is a tradition for families to provide primary care for the elderly rather than to rely on other institutions. Such diverse patterns in the social integration of Senior Citizens make economic status a poor predictor of purchasing power.

Forty million grandparents in the United States spent over $819 per grandchild in 1990 (Tsiantar & Miller, 1991; Walker & Macklin, 1992). Although these people spent more on medical care and drugs than other groups, they also bought 80% of all leisure travel, 25% of all toys, 72% of RV trips, and more than their share of musical instruments, large-size clothing, luxury cars, and small-serving-size foods (Morgan & Levy, 1993, pp. 21-25, 177). Seventy-six percent of the over-55's own their houses outright. Clearly, this group offers marketers significant opportunities.

Another zone of influence for the Mature Market is in political and civic activities. This group has had the highest participation rates in every election over the last 20 years. Their support is important to politicians, and active involvement in the political process is an important part of their values. Such active voices and organized lobbying efforts give Senior Citizens unprecedented access to political decision making (Lonial & Raju, 1993). Almost one half of Americans over 55 are members of AARP, their most vocal advocate. In addition, organizations such as the National Council of Senior Citizens and other lobbying groups represent the interests of older Americans.

Despite the economic and political power of Senior Citizens, they are virtually absent from visible participation in American cultural life (Swayne & Greco, 1987). Though television viewing increases with age, older people constitute less than 8% of all characters in prime time television (Tucker, 1995). The few images there are of older Americans often reinforce negative stereotypes of the old, emphasizing health problems and infirmities associated with aging. In magazines, more recent studies have found more elderly included (about 9% of advertisements), but these were symbolically positioning brands on the basis of their "wisdom" credibility (Ursic, Ursic, & Ursic, 1986). The presence of older people in commercials can associate brands with being "old-fashioned," reliable, having wisdom or authority, and expressing love (Furman, 1985). During the 1990s, the advertising industry lauded several commercials for their positive portrayals of the aged. Clara Peller, who popularized "Where's the Beef?" for Wendy's, acted in one of those campaigns. Ironically, however, the role she played was intensely disliked by actual Senior Citizens. The orientation of most programming toward youth and an emphasis on the pursuit of ideals causes tension and anxiety among the old (Francher, 1973). Ultimately, the virtual absence of older faces in the media contributes to misperceptions that the Mature Market is an insignificant minority.

# BEING OLD IN A
# YOUTH-ORIENTED SOCIETY

Our society confuses the physical aspects of aging with the psychological effects of aging in a youth-oriented society, and this in turn influences the beliefs of older people about what being old means. We associate old age with loss of abilities and attractiveness, and too often with other negatives within American culture (Carr-Ruffino, 1996, pp. 457-496). Such beliefs are barriers to effective communication with the Mature Market and to understanding the needs, both economic and expressive, of older consumers. Table 4.4 shows positive and negative stereotypes about traits of the elderly in American society. Hummert (1994) found many of these to be beliefs of the elderly themselves, as well as old-age associations of other age-groups. Their research uncovered the overwhelmingly negative views of young people about aging and the more complex and ambivalent views of the elderly themselves (p. 165). With copywriters averaging younger than 30 years old, our beliefs about old people reappear as negative images in the media (Goldman, 1993c). Figure 4.2 shows three advertisements targeted to grandparents, each product claiming that it can improve the purchaser's success in the grandparent role. Given the importance to most Senior Citizens of connections to family members, as well as the likely age of the authors, this appeal can be overused in the Mature Market.

A further look at the actual composition of the stereotypes in Table 4.4 suggests the challenge marketers must overcome in building partnerships with members of the Mature Market. First, Senior Citizens themselves believe that many negative qualities are associated with age, but they avoid seeing themselves as having special needs. Even Senior Citizens tend to overestimate the number of older Americans in nursing homes. The actual rate is less than 1 in 20 people over 65, and 1 in 4 over 85 (Treas, 1995). This form of denial forces marketers to search for codes and euphemisms to penetrate Senior Citizen reluctance to discuss special needs.

Second, positive traits (such as "nostalgic," "emotional," "old-fashioned," or "healthy") can be as ill fitting as so-called negative ones ("afraid," "slow thinking," or "ill tempered") to members of the Mature Market. Stereotypes do not accommodate individual variability or unique experiences. Stereotyping is off-putting when treated as norms for how a person *should* behave. However, the association of wisdom with aging creates an opportunity for older Americans to influence younger Americans: "The wisdom of a maturing America promises to be our richest resource" (Ansberry, 2000, p. R57). And showing positive images

*(text continues on page 108)*

**TABLE 4.4**  Stereotypical Beliefs About Older Persons

| Stereotypical Beliefs | Traits | Age Group of Believers |
|---|---|---|
| **Negative** | | |
| Severely impaired | Slow thinking, incompetent, feeble, incoherent, inarticulate, senile | All |
| Despondent | Depressed, sad, hopeless, afraid, neglected, lonely | All |
| Shrew/ curmudgeon | Complaining, ill tempered, bitter, prejudiced, demanding, inflexible, selfish, jealous, stubborn, nosy | All |
| Recluse | Quiet, timid, naive | All |
| Mildly impaired | Tired, fragile, slow moving, dependent | Elderly and middle aged |
| Self-centered | Greedy, miserly, humorless | Elderly and middle aged |
| Elitist | Demanding, prejudiced, wary, snobbish, naive | Elderly |
| Vulnerable | Afraid, worried, victimized, hypochondriac, wary, bored, sedentary, emotionless, miserly | Young |
| **Positive** | | |
| Golden Ager | Lively, adventurous, alert, active, sociable, witty, independent, well informed, skilled, productive, successful, capable, volunteer, well traveled, future oriented, fun loving, curious, healthy, sexual, self-accepting, happy, health conscious, courageous, interesting | All |
| Perfect grandparent | Kind, loving, family oriented, generous, grateful, supportive, understanding, intelligent, wise, knowledgeable, trustworthy | All |
| John Wayne conservative | Patriotic, religious, nostalgic, reminiscent, retired, conservative, emotional, mellow, determined, proud | All |
| Activist | Political, sexual, health conscious, liberal | Elderly |
| Small town neighbor | Emotional, frugal, old-fashioned, quiet, conservative, tough | Elderly |
| Liberal matriarch/ patriarch | Liberal, mellow, wealthy | Middle aged |

SOURCE: Hummert (1994, p. 166).

**Figure 4.2a.** Advertisement Targeted to Grandparents: Radio Shack

**It's easy to be the most popular kid on the block. Again.**

Grandparents who know how to check out the Internet are pretty cool. The IBM Aptiva® L Series makes it simple for kids of any age. With the click of an EZ Button, you can e-mail* family and friends. Visit dinosaur Web sites with your grandchildren. Keep track of your investments. Or search for the cheapest airfares. A feature called voice-enabled Netscape Navigator™ makes it easy to talk your way all over the Internet. Plus, you have access to IBM's service and support to help you along. Call us at 1 800 426-7235, ext. 4207, to find out more.     Solutions for a small planet™  IBM

*Internet access required. Online/telephone charges apply. IBM, Aptiva and Solutions for a small planet are trademarks or registered trademarks of IBM Corporation. All other product or company names are trademarks or registered trademarks of their respective owners. © 1997 IBM Corp.

**Figure 4.2b.** Advertisement Targeted to Grandparents: IBM Aptiva

"Taking care of Sarah has given us a whole new reason to take care of ourselves."

"Holding your first grandchild puts life in a whole new perspective. That's why we drink Ensure."

As an occasional meal or snack, Ensure is a source of complete, balanced nutrition. A great-tasting blend of protein, carbohydrate, vitamins and minerals, Ensure is the supplement doctors recommend #1.

Ensure provides nutrition to help you stay healthy, active and energetic. So help make sure you and the ones you love get good nutrition.

Drink Ensure and drink to your health.

#1 DOCTOR RECOMMENDED SUPPLEMENT

ENSURE. DRINK TO YOUR HEALTH.

**Figure 4.2c.** Advertisement Targeted to Grandparents: Ensure

of the elderly to other old people actually has positive effects on their health ("Positive Images May Help Elderly," 1999).

Third, adoption of a patronizing tone is common among people who are interacting with members of any group about whom they hold stereotypical beliefs (Braithwaite, 1994; Hummert, 1994, pp. 167-180). In a multicultural society, the less we know personally about members of groups, the more likely it is that our communication with them will be inauthentic and distancing. With more social distance, outsiders' tones of voice seem exploitative rather than based on shared interests.

The negative view that Americans of all ages share of being old is best observed in the growing difference between chronological and perceived age as people get older. Most American adults see themselves as 6 to 10 years younger than they actually are; for Senior Citizens, the gap is 15 years (Zola, 1962-1963). Companies like Jockey are finding success by featuring models who are about 15 years younger than their target market (Beck, 1990; Lipman, 1991a). Still, chronological age is simply one measure of how old someone is. An alternative is to separate age into how old someone feels ("feel-age"), how old someone looks ("look-age"), age according to a person's activities ("do-age"), and age corresponding to a person's interests ("interest-age") (Schiffman & Kanuk, 1987, cited in Wolfe, 1990, p. 213).

The best tactic may be to ignore age in communications with Mature consumers and to keep the focus on product benefits. One study of how Senior Citizens felt about offers of "Senior Citizen" discounts identified three types of responses, two of which were negative, for the "young old" (Tepper, 1994). There is a growing list of companies that have made mistakes in approaching the Mature Market. Affinity shampoo for "older hair," 40+ Bran Flakes, and Southwestern Bell's "Silver Pages" were all casualties of an "age" appeal. Being singled out can easily offend this group even when it meets a specific buyer need (Wolfe, 1990, pp. 33-57). Figure 4.3 shows examples of fear and benefit appeals for pain relievers; it is not hard to understand why a positive benefit is more persuasive with Senior Citizens.

What issues *are* important to the age cohorts of Mature Americans? Table 4.5 presents some values of Senior Citizens (the Depression and World War II cohorts), in contrast to those of other age groups in the United States. Different attitudes about the relative importance of saving and consuming show the different worlds of post-World War II cohorts and those born before. Such attitudes

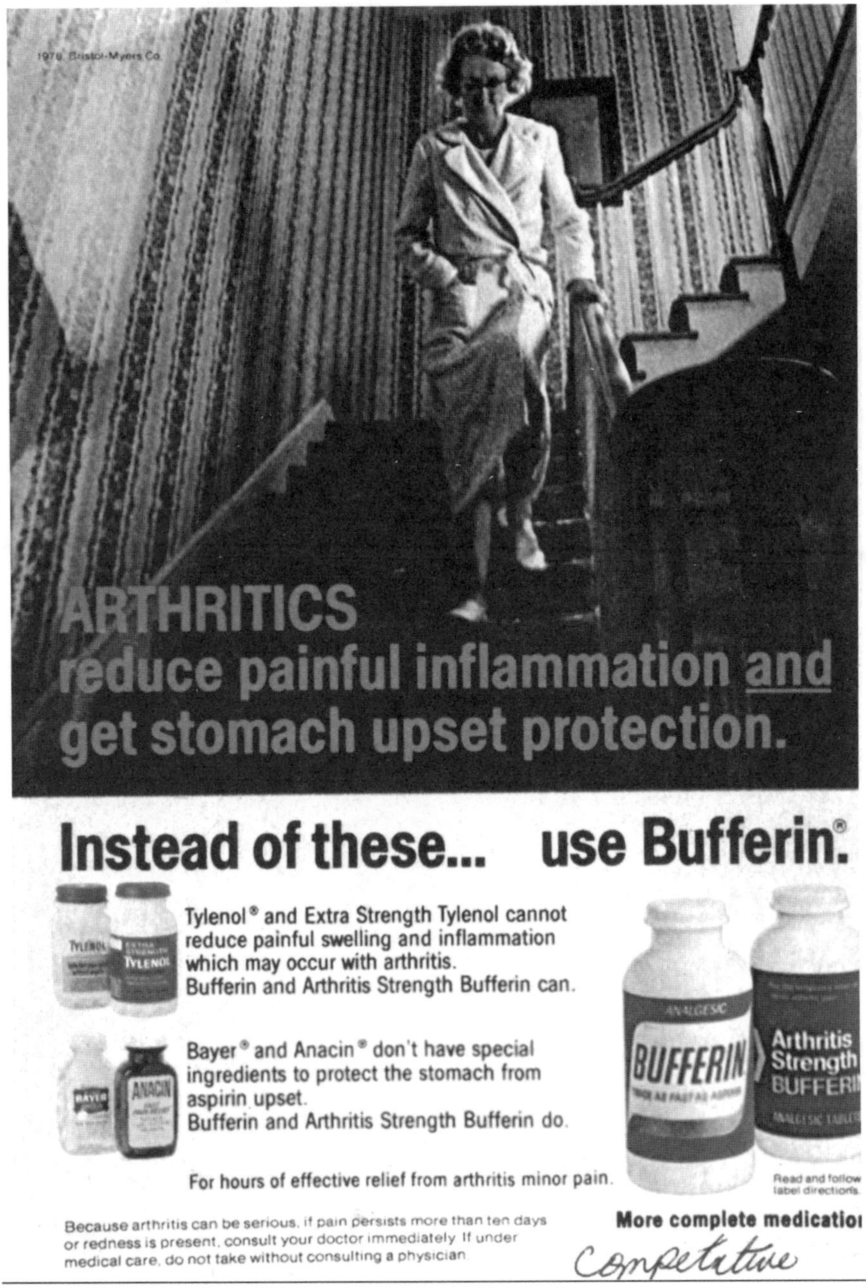

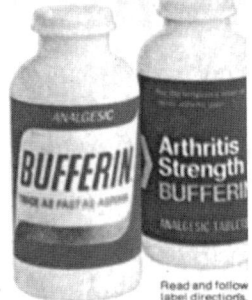

## ARTHRITICS
## reduce painful inflammation and
## get stomach upset protection.

# Instead of these... use Bufferin.

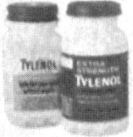

Tylenol® and Extra Strength Tylenol cannot reduce painful swelling and inflammation which may occur with arthritis.
Bufferin and Arthritis Strength Bufferin can.

Bayer® and Anacin® don't have special ingredients to protect the stomach from aspirin upset.
Bufferin and Arthritis Strength Bufferin do.

For hours of effective relief from arthritis minor pain.

Read and follow label directions.

Because arthritis can be serious, if pain persists more than ten days or redness is present, consult your doctor immediately. If under medical care, do not take without consulting a physician

**More complete medication**

*Competitive*

**Figure 4.3a.** Fear Appeal for Health Product

THE MAKERS OF TYLENOL WANT YOU TO KNOW ABOUT...

# ARTHRITIS PAIN RELIEF.

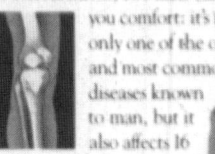 If you're suffering from the pain of osteoarthritis, two facts can bring you comfort: it's not only one of the oldest and most common diseases known to man, but it also affects 16 million other Americans.

### WHAT IS OSTEOARTHRITIS?

Osteoarthritis causes the gradual breakdown of joint tissue, leading to joint pain and stiffness in the hips, knees, feet, and spine. Several factors lead to osteoarthritis, such as heredity, being overweight, and overuse or injury of the joints.

### HOW DO I KNOW IF I HAVE IT?

Osteoarthritis develops gradually, and you'll find that the affected joints hurt most after you've overused them or after long periods of remaining still. Your doctor will be able to diagnose it based on your medical history and a physical examination.

### ARE THERE WAYS TO FEEL BETTER?

Taking care of your joints, by using correct posture and avoiding high-impact exercises, will protect them from stresses and strains. Exercising regularly, on the other hand, will prevent them from becoming stiff and hard to move. Also, don't forget to keep an eye on your weight; the less weight your joints have to carry, the better.

In addition, hot and cold treatments, such as hot baths and cold compresses, are also effective in relieving pain and soreness. Again, be sure to talk to your doctor.

### IS MEDICATING HELPFUL?

Many medications can relieve minor osteoarthritis pain. Doctors know that TYLENOL will do so without irritating your 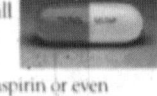 stomach like aspirin or even ibuprofen can.

Above all, don't forget that coping with any disease is difficult. Talk to your family, your doctor, and remember, you're not alone. Sixteen million other people are out there with you.

ARTHRITIS PAIN RELIEF FROM THE NAME YOU TRUST.

©MN-JYC Inc. '91

Use only as directed for occasional arthritis pain.

---

**Figure 4.3b.**  Benefit Appeal for a Health Product

**TABLE 4.5** Different Age Cohort Values of Adults

| | Age Cohort | | | | |
|---|---|---|---|---|---|
| *Cultural Values* | *Depression (1912-1921)* | *World War II (1922-1927)* | *Postwar (1928-1945)* | *Boomers I and II (1946-1954, 1955-1965)* | *Generation X (1966-1976)* |
| Attitudes toward money | Save for a rainy day | Save lots, spend little | Save some, spend some | Spend, spend, borrow, spend | Spend? Save? What? |
| Sex mind-set | Intolerant | Ambivalent | Repressive | Permissive | Confused |
| Favorite music | Big band | Swing | Frank Sinatra Patti Page | Rock and roll | Rap, grunge, retro |
| Worldview | Civic | Adaptive | Adaptive | Idealist | Reactive |
| Youth crisis | Economic/political instability | Depression/war | Conformity | Reverse ideals | Family stability, parents busy |
| Individual and society | Outer fixated, leaders | Conform, arbitrate | Conform, participate | Me-first, nonconformity | Alienated, patchwork selves |
| Materialism | "Being" more important than "owning" | "Being" and "experiencing" most important | "Owning" and "experiencing" both important | "Owning" helps express identity to self and others | "Owning" is key to communicate |
| Activity orientation | Contribute to others | Be productive, contribute | Be productive, enjoy life | Be productive, enjoy life | Work to live, life is outside work |
| Formative issues | Build industrial nation | Immigration, Depression | World War II | Economic boom, civil rights | Information Age, global village |

SOURCES: Adapted from Lifestage Matrix Marketing of Lafayette, CA (cited in Meredith and Schewe, 1994), Phillips (1996), and Wolfe (1990, pp. 33-57,102-129).

Americans, as well as cautious buyers in the marketplace. Their different concept of security, as well as its importance, explains why they have the highest home ownership of American adults, across all income groups.

The importance of connections to others, particularly to family, for Mature Americans is also apparent in this table. Family events and holidays spent with family dominate the social calendars of many Senior Citizens. These are their connections to the larger world of American life, and they fit norms for older Americans in their "Perfect Grandparent" roles (Walker & Macklin, 1992). Family and friends can be important sources of information about products and services for Senior Citizens.

## MEDIA USAGE: CONNECTIONS TO THE WORLD OUTSIDE FAMILY

Mature Americans spend more time with television than any other subculture group in America. Its information value is an important reason, but it is a major entertainment source also. Table 4.6 provides information about the media habits of Senior Citizens as compared to people in their 30s. According to the table, older consumers are more likely to read a daily newspaper and spend more time doing it. They are also more likely to watch TV news. Moschis (1992) has reported that adults over 55 years old spend an average of 40 hours viewing television during the week. About 30% of viewing time is with prime-time programs, but older adults are the largest consumers of daytime television programs (pp. 181-200). Television is the most important medium for reaching older consumers.

Television programmers have yet to capitalize on their most loyal audience of older Americans. Programmers claim that they concentrate on the young as their target audience because that is what their advertisers reward (Thomas & Wolfe, 1995). CBS admits targeting 35- to 49-year-olds but in fact is most successful with the 50- to 64-year-olds (Dychtwald, 1989). Lifetime cable network, CNN, old movie channels, and health programs are popular programs on cable with Mature Americans.

Watching television is the most popular leisure time activity for Senior Citizens, rated higher than walking or driving for pleasure. At the same time, they have the highest readership of newspapers for any age group. The mass media are an extension of social networks that Senior Citizens lose as they age. Media consumption levels are high across all income groups of Senior Citizens, but the

**TABLE 4.6** Media Habits of Senior Citizens as Compared to People in Their 30s

Cable and premium cable television household penetration: 26% of those aged 65+
  years

Radio (primarily morning, AM): 70% of those aged 55+ years listen daily

Internet: 50% of those aged 55+ years claim access; 28% of those aged 55+ years use
  for information purposes

| *Newspaper* *Reading Habits* | *30-39 Yr.* % | *50-59 Yr.* % | *60-69 Yr.* % | *70-79 Yr.* % | *80+ Yr.* % |
|---|---|---|---|---|---|
| Read daily | 49 | 60 | 65 | 71 | 69 |
| Read < 15 min/day | 9 | 11 | 8 | 5 | 8 |
| Read 15-29 min/day | 14 | 14 | 14 | 11 | 10 |
| Read 30-59 min/day | 11 | 17 | 19 | 15 | 17 |
| Read 60 min or more | 5 | 7 | 19 | 23 | 26 |

Percentage of Group Accessing Various Media During an Average Week

| *Medium* | *30-39 Yr.* % | *50-59 Yr.* % | *60-69 Yr.* % | *70-79 Yr.* % | *80+ Yr.* % |
|---|---|---|---|---|---|
| Network television: | | | | | |
|   News programs | 70 | 83 | 85 | 87 | 80 |
|   News magazines | 39 | 51 | 55 | 51 | 53 |
|   Sunday AM news | 9 | 15 | 19 | 19 | 19 |
| Magazines: | | | | | |
|   News-type | 17 | 20 | 17 | 16 | 17 |
|   Personality | 7 | 6 | 6 | 5 | 2 |
|   Business-type | 4 | 4 | 4 | 2 | 5 |
|   Tabloids | 5 | 6 | 8 | 10 | 9 |
|   *Atlantic/Harper's* type | 2 | 3 | 4 | 1 | 4 |
| Books or novels | 39 | 35 | 31 | 35 | 29 |

SOURCES: Data on Internet from C. H. Lee (1996); other data from Moschis (1992, Table 8.2, p. 193).

wealthiest tend toward more print media consumption and think the least of advertising in general (Burnett, 1991). Word of mouth is valued highly as an information source for older consumers. Though older adults claim that they prefer word-of-mouth sources over advertising for making purchase decisions, actually "past experience" is their most reliable source (Burnett & Wilkes, 1986).

A growing number of magazines target the Mature Market. *Modern Maturity,* a publication of AARP, has over 19 million readers; it bans ads for medical devices. Other magazines are *Longevity, Prime Time, Second Wind,* and *Renaissance.* The real success of AARP is in its aggressive direct marketing to over 30 million members. Furthermore, AARP positions itself as *the* spokesperson for a wide variety of issues relevant to Senior Citizens. In exchange, AARP educates older consumers about topics they believe are important, a powerful competitive position. Senior Citizens have been highly responsive to direct marketing appeals via direct mail, telemarketing, and loyal-consumer marketing programs (Moschis, 1992, pp. 246-255; Ostruff, 1989, pp. 249-256). In addition to magazines targeted to the general public, specialty magazines that focus on hobbies and travel are good media for reaching older Americans (Ostruff, 1989, pp. 248-249).

A popular belief is that Senior Citizens are not part of cyberspace. Though they score low on indices of personal computer ownership, television is a medium they already spend time with (Sandberg & Weber, 1997). Thus, Web TV may be the device that finally puts more Web-surfing seniors on-line. Senior Citizens use cyberspace primarily for keeping in touch with family members, monitoring investments, catching the latest news reports, and researching health problems (Sandberg & Weber, 1997). Elderly cybernauts rate the Internet and World Wide Web as their preferred sources of information about products and services in general (C. H. Lee, 1996). In 1999, one study found that older adults spent more time online than any other age-group (Petersen, 1999).

Many older Americans process advertising in different ways than other Americans. For example, they elaborate less when reading print ads but are aggressive information seekers in general. These conflicting patterns suggest that they may think less but more intuitively while processing advertisements and that they have higher needs for cognition overall. Some Mature Americans suffer losses in cognitive processing skills as they age. An example of this is that older Americans have few problems remembering descriptions when given a name but have more trouble remembering names when given descriptions. Research has not yet confirmed this as a deficit in remembering other kinds of proper nouns, such as brand names (Cohen, 1994). Three conditions contribute to positive beliefs about products in response to advertising: actual repetition, perceived repetition, and outside-source attributions (Lawe, Hawkins, & Craik, 1998).

Another preference of Senior Citizens is for less visual and verbal embellishment in product advertising. Losses in visual and hearing acuity accompany the aging process. Older consumers do not process ads as quickly or in the same ways as younger consumers. In earlier studies of time-compressed speech in advertising, college students had higher recall and Senior Citizens had lower recall levels (Stevens, 1982). Such differences in the pace of interpreting television and radio commercials require adaptation. The art and design tastes of Senior Citizens were formed before postmodernism; this is another area for adaptation. It is safe to say the Mature Market responds best to straightforward, engaging copy and simple design in marketing communications. The ads for Radio Shack, the IBM Aptiva, and Ensure in Figure 4.2 illustrate the information-intense, straightforward kind of advertising preferred by older consumers.

## ACTIVIST CONSUMERS

In American society, occupational roles are important to our sense of self. As Mature Americans retire from a lifetime of work, their social identity changes in significant ways. What other people think about them becomes less important, and what they think about themselves becomes more so. Older men especially have to seek other sources of self-esteem to accommodate the loss of work-related expertise and social networks of power (Greene, Adelman, Rizzo, & Friedmann, 1994).

Senior Citizens have the same product needs and criteria as other adults: They buy to replace things they already have, to maintain their lifestyles, to present gifts, and to gain desired experiences (Wolfe, 1990, p. 73). One researcher's position is that Mature adults place different weights on the importance of functional, social reinforcement, and consequential experiences as measures of satisfaction with products and services. Mature consumers take warranties more seriously and dislike ones that are hard to decipher, but otherwise they have the same kinds of expectations about functional performance. They place less importance on a brand's ability to reflect social affiliations, but they wish not to be stigmatized by brands catering to older people's problems. They also value an intangible aspect of satisfaction, whether the consumption experience leads to other pleasing experiences (Wolfe, 1990, pp. 61-76).

These different expectations of sellers get expressed in many ways in the marketplace. Mature Market buyers are skeptical of product claims; in one survey, over 80% claimed products did not work as promised (Moschis, 1988). Furthermore, Senior Citizens communicate their displeasure with products or sellers to people within their social networks; over 75% tell persons in their social networks about marketplace dissatisfactions (Lambert, 1979; Moschis, 1988). But their lack of complaints directly to sellers disguises their dissatisfaction from marketers. Most important to Senior Citizens is being treated with respect by marketers and their employees. Retailers such as Wal-Mart, Kmart, and Target hire older people as "greeters" and offer "value" over "image" to attract Senior Citizens (Underhill, 1996).

Another example of how their expectations can differ from those of other age-groups is their reasons for participating in continuing education programs. Whereas younger people see education as a way to get ahead, older students are likely to be there "for the joy of learning" (Beck, Glick, Gordon, & Picker, 1991; Miller, 1997). Programs can rarely be designed to maximize both groups' expectations. A statistic to remember is that over one third of Senior Citizens claim to have boycotted companies because of the way their ads portrayed older people (Beck, 1990).

## COMMUNICATION AND SHOPPING STYLES OF OLDER CONSUMERS

George Moschis (1996) argued that the "consumer behavior of older Americans has more to do with their outlook on life than their age" (p. 44). Other researchers agree with his premise that Senior Citizens' diverse needs and tastes are shaped by social and psychological changes over a person's life span. Thus, trying to appeal to the Mature Market as a homogeneous group is a strategy destined for limited success. A better approach is to use the experience of major life events, such as chronic illness or loss of mobility, as a basis for identifying buyers with similar market needs and behavior. Moschis's four market segments, based on these criteria, are Healthy Indulgers, Healthy Hermits, Ailing Outgoers, and Frail Recluses. The descriptions of typical members of these groups are contained in Figure 4.1, introduced earlier in this chapter.

Information is important to Mature Americans, but they use it, acquire it, and process it differently from other Americans. Despite negative opinions of advertising in general, the elderly claim that retail advertisements are helpful in shopping. Using media to scan the environment for useful information, they rely more heavily on mass media sources of product information. They also report difficulty with selective attention to details when distractions appear, such as music in commercials. Senior Citizens are more suspicious than younger persons when their favorite cultural icons appear in advertisements ("Sing a Song of Selling," 1999). Preliminary studies reinforce the importance of product-specific claims in ads to influence their beliefs, attitudes, and choice criteria (Lonial & Raju, 1993).

The Mature Market has its own heroes and celebrities, just as other subculture groups in America do. Lauren Bacall, Wilford Brimley, Ray Charles, Lena Horne, Ronald Reagan, Rue McClanahan, Steve Allen, George Burns, and Art Carney have all appeared in ads targeted to older buyers. Combinations of music, images, jokes, and other references that evoke the particular shared experiences of these age cohorts capture the attention of Senior Citizens. These cultural cues must still be paired with other information that these activist consumers seek about product benefits (Phillips, 1996). They particularly dislike communications that focus on the physiological or health care problems of the elderly or ads that show them in isolation from the rest of Americans. Check out Figure 4.4 for a print ad that shows health concern in the context of a better quality of life as payoff.

Many firms are successfully courting the Mature Market today. Senior Citizens account for 80% of all leisure travel, 50% of domestic car purchases, 37% of cosmetics and bath products, 33% of lawn and garden products, and 30% of all prescriptions filled. Branson, Missouri, had over 5.6 million visitors in 1995, the majority of whom were Mature Americans. Kimberly-Clark's experience in bringing incontinence out of the closet by marketing their Depends brand undergarment guards in mass media presages success for the rest of their product line designed for consumers in the Mature Market (Collins, 1994).

One area of particular opportunity for marketers is the growing number of grandparents who are living longer and spending more on their grandchildren. This was estimated to be a $30 billion market in 1998, and it does not yet include the large number of Baby Boomers who are about to enter grandparenthood (Brazil, 1998). One of the reasons for the growth of grandparent expenditures is the larger role that grandparents are taking in their grandchildren's lives. They are not just buying birthday presents; they are paying for tuition and lessons and many other extras that their parents cannot afford. However, they are not being targeted even in traditional gift categories. Toy advertisers spent more than $871 million in 1997, over one half of which was in television. Very few of

Figure 4.4. "Drink Now. Play Later."

**TABLE 4.7**  "Being" Experiences of Interest to Mature Adults

| Sharing Products of Skills With Others | Sharing Wisdom With Others | Entertaining Others | Caring for Others |
|---|---|---|---|
| Composing | Collaborating | Acting | Assisting |
| Creating | Consulting | Arranging | Caring |
| Decorating | Cooperating | Demonstrating | Catering |
| Designing | Educating | Hosting | Counseling |
| Drawing | Influencing | Joking | Curing |
| Fixing | Proposing | Performing | Encouraging |
| Painting | Teaching | Public Speaking | Helping |
| Writing | Training | Singing | Humoring |
| Decorating | | Staging | Nurturing |
| Designing | | Storytelling | Petting |
| Drawing | | | Supporting |
| Fixing | | | Tending |
| Painting | | | |
| Writing | | | |

SOURCE: Adapted from Wonder and Donovan (1984), cited in Wolfe (1990, p. 216).

those dollars were placed in programming that appealed to older Americans (Brazil, 1998).

An important cultural reference point for the Mature Market is their experience of sharing in significant family events (weddings, births, graduations). As a result, intergenerational settings and nostalgia get their attention. Grandparenting may or may not be central to a Senior Citizen's self-concept, but that role persuades more than other appeals (Walker & Macklin, 1992). More than other consumers, they are interested in product features that contribute to their comfort, security, convenience, social interaction, ability to give to others, and independence (Schewe, 1990). The situations in Table 4.7 suggest many settings with particular appeal to Senior Citizens (Wolfe, 1990, p. 216).

The past experiences and fiscal conservatism of Mature Americans make them risk-aversive consumers, looking for strong incentives to try new products. Tactics that reduce perceived risks address the resistance of many older consumers to new products and brands. Many retailers have found in-home trials, money-back guarantees, and 30-day warranties to have special appeal to older consumers. These incentive programs emphasize value, not the age of buyers.

Senior Citizens react strongly to physical features of the shopping environment. Changing a pharmacy from the front to the back of a store, not providing sufficient waiting or sitting areas, and not providing enough employee assistance in specialty stores have been known to chase away loyal Senior clienteles (Underhill, 1996). Losses in problem-solving abilities associated with aging make it more difficult to recall information and encourage older consumers to use "satisficing" rather than more aggressive strategies of information search (Cole & Balasubramanian, 1993). Meeting the information needs of older buyers is rewarded with repeat patronage.

Many older consumers are right to resent the ways they are patronized by firms who are trying to sell them things. Listen to the tone of some comments overheard in the marketing world: "Might damage our brand if younger consumers think we're for old people." "I'd never put an ad for 'seniors' in my book." "Boooring" (Lee, 1997, p. 47). Although the younger ages of advertising and marketing decision makers might explain lack of interest in older consumers, stronger steps must be taken to get communicators in sync with this audience's aspirations, values, and ways of relating. The shortsightedness of these attitudes is appalling given the opportunities in the Mature Market (Russell, 1997; Simons, 1998). Marketers must commit to real learning before they can effectively serve the Mature Market's cultural and economic needs without being viewed as exploiting their community.

## SUMMARY

The fastest growing group of Americans is over 55 years of age and has considerable economic and political clout. At the same time, older Americans live outside mainstream American culture and media, thus forming a distinctive subculture with its own values, beliefs, experiences, and heroes. Age does not distinguish the Mature Market from other consumers as effectively as their particular worldviews, marketplace experiences, and aesthetic and communication preferences. Their experiences of the Great Depression and World War II have had an indelible impact on their saving behavior and willingness to sacrifice for their country. It is these qualities that offer marketers opportunities to build culturally compatible partnerships with Mature Americans.

Among Senior Citizens there is significant diversity. The oldest age-groups are growing fastest, and White Americans are their largest racial/ethnic group. California has the largest number of Mature Americans, but Florida's citizens over 65 represent the largest percentage of local population. Given wide geographic dispersion and a preference for mass media, especially television, the Mature Market is not easy to reach using regional media. Nevertheless, they read more newspapers and respond more positively to direct marketing efforts than consumers of other age-groups.

Perhaps the most important means of gauging the diversity of the Mature Market is the use of segmentation according to lifestyles or life stages. These criteria provide insight into purchasing motivations and interests in particular products and services, as well as the kinds of settings that communicate authenticity to Mature Americans. More than members of other subcultures, Mature Americans are sensitive to stereotyping and age labeling by marketers.

**CHAPTER 5**

# U.S. Latinos

## The Largest Ethnic Subculture

### Marye C. Tharp
### With Ernest W. Bromley

Reyna Gutierrez, 27, lives with her husband, Zeferino, and 2-year-old Hector in Austin, Texas. She cleans the homes of several families and cares for their children; she lived and worked in one family's home for over 5 years. Reyna's sister-in-law, who has two small children of her own, takes care of Hector in her own home while Reyna works with yet another sister-in-law. Reyna claims to speak only Spanish, but she somehow communicates with her English-only employers and enjoys popular English-language TV programs. Her legal status in the United States is questionable, so she is mostly paid in cash. However, her baby is an American citizen, and her husband has the valuable "Green Card," making him a legal resident of the United States. He works for a local construction company. The couple recently purchased a house with a mortgage from a firm willing to count Reyna's cash income toward their eligibility. She has no plans to return to the poor rural area near San Luis Potosi, Mexico, where she was born and lived until age 17.

---

Author's Note: The terms *U.S. Latinos* and *U.S. Hispanics* are used interchangeably in this chapter and do not differ in their intended significance.

Jorge Mas Canosa spoke Spanish eloquently and passionately about a future time in Cuba when there would be democracy again, and when, just possibly, he himself would replace Fidel Castro as Cuban head of state. Over the 30 years that he lived in Florida before his death in 1997, he considered himself "in exile," waiting to return to Havana. However, he didn't let that goal distract him from making money, having amassed a fortune in real estate and investments that allowed him to support his political passions. Few of his family members will move back to Havana when they have the opportunity (Ungar, 1995, pp. 208-213).

Fred Guerra is 42 years old and learning Spanish for the second time in his life. Brought up in Army communities all over the world, Fred spoke Spanish when he was a child with his grandparents, who immigrated to the States from Mexico in the 1930s. Fred's parents hoped he could avoid the discrimination they had felt growing up in California, so they purposefully spoke only English at home. In his new job as copywriter in English for a magazine targeting U.S. Hispanics, he has become aware of the many people like him who are Latino by culture but not fluent in Spanish. Fred is rediscovering his lost bilingualism to be more in accordance with pride in his Latino heritage.

Connie Taylor grew up in Colorado and spent summers in Mexico City with her grandparents and aunts. Her mother married a Texas Anglo and moved to the States before Connie was born. Her mother speaks Spanish when she is with Mexican relatives and in her job as a high school Spanish teacher. Connie has found her niche in the family's tradition as educators by studying for a doctorate in mass communication. In the meantime, she lives in her father's sister's house and visits her aunt daily in a nearby nursing home. Connie can recall her Spanish when it is necessary, but she is not really confident in what she considers her second language. Connie never thinks of herself as U.S. Latino, Hispanic, Mexican American, or any other term she might find on a form. She considers herself "white, of Hispanic origin" but never "Latino."

Each of these persons is Hispanic. Their personal stories emphasize two facets of U.S. Latinos as a subculture. First, as a group, they share some cultural similarities that transcend different countries of origin, races, socioeconomic status, ages, time or generations in the United States, and even languages spoken. The importance of family, pride in ethnic heritage, and retention of the Spanish language are the kinds of values and behaviors that underlie U.S. Latino subculture in the United States. The second characteristic of the individuals above is their diversity. U.S. Latinos are diverse on the basis of race, ethnic identity, acculturation into U.S. mainstream culture, country of origin, and social and educational background. The purpose of this chapter is to describe the ways in which U.S. Latinos are similar to each other and different from other Americans, as well as the ways in which their diversity makes generalizations about U.S. Latinos simplistic. These apparently conflicting characteristics make U.S. Latinos a challenging target for marketers in multicultural America.

The first part of this chapter describes the importance of the choice of label in expressing ethnic identity among U.S. Latinos. Next, recent influences on Hispanic patterns of acculturation are reviewed. The following section presents geographic and demographic characteristics that identify where U.S. Hispanics are and the parameters that frame their social and economic lives. Then the chapter elaborates on cultural values that drive expressions of Hispanic identity in the marketplace and that differ from mainstream American values. This is followed by an introduction to media issues, such as the images of Latinos in mainstream media, media preferences of U.S. Hispanics, and the availability of English- and Spanish-language media vehicles. Last, there is a review of consumer research focusing on Hispanic preferences and behaviors in the marketplace.

## WHAT DOES *HISPANIC* OR *LATINO* MEAN?

The choice of what label to use for this diverse group of Americans is full of significance. If we asked individuals of Hispanic heritage which of the two labels above best expressed how they saw their own ethnic identity, many would answer, "Neither!" The terms *Hispanic* and *Latino* are highly symbolic apart from their ability to distinguish this group from other Americans (Braus, 1993; Marin & Marin, 1991, pp. 18-41; "Quandary Over One Term to Cover Myriad People," 1994). The terms originated with the efforts of mainstream organizations such as U.S. government agencies to classify people of Spanish-speaking origins (Portes & MacLeod, 1996). Nevertheless, they also contain political meanings an individual might or might not claim. A person of Hispanic origin is more likely to see his or her cultural heritage as "dominicano/a," "Cuban American," "Mexican American," "nuyorican," "Chicano/a" and so on, rather than "Hispanic" or "Latino". Most U.S. Latinos experience no conflict in describing themselves one way and filling in a standardized form with another term for mainstream America.

What to call this group of diverse peoples who share key cultural values is also a quick introduction to the multiple facets of Latino ethnicity. Consider the following quotation by Earl Shorris (1992) in his introduction to *Latinos*:

> "Tell them we are not all alike" is good advice, but once that is done, what name should be given to the set of people who share—with many exceptions—a common language, some customs, and some ancestors? . . . There must be one name, a single word that is not objectionable. . . . In 1980 the U.S. Census was on the verge of choosing *Latino* as the correct word when someone said that it sounded too much like *Ladino,* the ancient Castillian now spoken only by descendants of the Spanish Jews who went into exile in the fifteenth century. *Latino* was replaced by *Hispanic* in the census. The battle was joined immediately on all sides. Political, racial, linguistic, and historical arguments were advanced. . . . Geographically, *Hispanic* is preferred in the Southeast and much of Texas. New Yorkers use both *Hispanic* and *Latino.* Chicago, where no nationality has attained a majority, prefers *Latino.* In California, the word *Hispanic* has been barred from the *Los Angeles Times,* in keeping with the strong feelings of people in that community. Some people in New Mexico prefer *Hispano.* Politically, *Hispanic* belongs to the right and some of the center, while *Latino* belongs to the left and the center. Politically active Mexican American women in Los Angeles are fond of asking, "Why *HISpanic*? Why not *HERSpanic*?" Historically, the choice went from *Spanish* or *Spanish-speaking* to *Latin American, Latino,* and *Hispanic.* Economically, Rodolfo Acuna, the historian, is correct when he says that *Hispanic* belongs to the middle class, which seems most pleased by the term. Anglos and people who oppose bilingual education and bilingualism prefer *Hispanic,* which makes sense, since *Hispanic* is an English word meaning "pertaining to ancient Spain."
> (pp. xvi-xvii)

So where does that leave a firm wishing to develop a partnership with Hispanic consumers? Recognizing the possibility that individual persons do not think of their ethnicity in "Hispanic" or "Latino" terms is an important step toward understanding Latino ethnicity. It may be best not to use a label in communications when there is a possibility of stepping into this minefield. The ideal label is the one that a particular Latino prefers, but that is not always easy to determine.

# ORIGINS OF U.S. LATINOS

Different countries of origin are the source of differing political, cultural, and historic traditions among U.S. Latinos. About 63% of U.S. Latinos are of Mexican heritage, 11% are Puerto Rican, 4% are Cuban, and over 14% are from Central and South America (U.S. Bureau of the Census, 1993f). The original motivation to immigrate and the timing and patterns of immigration vary across these groups. For example, economic conditions tend to propel immigration from Mexico and Puerto Rico, but Puerto Ricans have been more likely to return to the island after a period of time living in the continental United States. In contrast, Mexican immigrants have stayed in the United States for generations. In southwestern states, some Hispanics' ancestors were there before the United States moved that far west. Cuban immigrants have been political refugees, and most came to the United States in the early 1960s or 1980s. The relative portion of U.S. Latinos from different countries changes over time because immigration rates respond to external events, such as political unrest in Central America in the 1980s. There are also different rates of fertility among U.S. Hispanic groups (Cuban Americans have the lowest and families of Mexican or Central American heritage the highest).

Table 5.1 shows the total population of each of these groups as well as where they reside in the United States. Cuban Americans dominate the Latinos of southern Florida (about 80% of Latinos there), Puerto Ricans are the majority Latino group in New York (about 58%), and Mexican Americans make up the largest numbers of Latinos in southwestern states (70% of Hispanics in Los Angeles, 90% in San Antonio and Houston). Chicago also has a large percentage of Hispanics originating from Mexico. Members of each country-of-origin group have their strongest identity with other Latinos from the same country of origin. The differing socioeconomic status, physical appearances, and countries of origin are a strong force of diversity within U.S. Latino subculture because their traditions and language preferences vary. Members of established communities assist newer immigrants in adjusting to U.S. lifestyles and work styles, thus perpetuating the concentration of immigrants in particular locales by country of origin.

A simple review of terms used by the U.S. Bureau of the Census also illustrates the confusion, not only about what label to use for U.S. Hispanics but also about counting Latinos. At various times, the following criteria have been used to classify U.S. Hispanics: shared language (Spanish), Spanish surnames, race,

**TABLE 5.1**  U.S. Latino Groups According to Country of Origin

| Country of Origin | Population in 1997 | | U.S. Geographic Locations |
| | N | % | |
| --- | --- | --- | --- |
| Mexico | 18,795,000 | 63.3 | Texas, New Mexico, Arizona, California, Washington, Colorado, Illinois |
| Central America, South America | 4,292,000 | 14.5 | Southern California, New York, New Jersey, southern Florida |
| Puerto Rico | 3,152,000 | 10.6 | New York, California, New Jersey, Florida, Illinois |
| Cuba | 1,258,000 | 4.2 | Southern Florida, western New York, New Jersey |
| Other countries | 2,206,000 | 7.4 | New York, Los Angeles, Miami |
| All U.S. Latinos | 29,703,000 | 100.0[a] | |

SOURCES: U.S. Bureau of the Census (1997a, 1999g).
a. U.S. Latinos constituted 11.1% of the total U.S. population in 1997.

type of ancestors, national origin, and religious traditions. Until the 1940s, "Mexican" was listed as a race on census forms, and from then until the 1970 census, Hispanics were simply counted as "Whites." The 1970 census tried using several criteria simultaneously (Spanish surname, Spanish speaking, parentage) to count U.S. Hispanics. To confuse matters further, during the 1970s the label *Hispanic* was treated as if it referred to a distinctive racial group by other government agencies. As an Uruguayan immigrant said, "I thought I was White until I went to college in the United States and had to choose between 'White,' 'Black,' or 'Hispanic.'" People whose origins trace to Spain but not to Brazil, Portugal, or the Philippines are now included in the counting of U.S. Latinos. The Census Bureau currently uses the term *Hispanic* but recognizes that many people self-identify as "Latino" but not as "Hispanic," and vice versa. These changing definitions of who should be counted among U.S. Latinos contribute to the uncertainty of marketers about the size and cultural unity of the Hispanic market.

# LANGUAGE USE AND ACCULTURATION AMONG U.S. LATINOS

The United States is the fifth largest Spanish-speaking country in the world. Spanish is an important link among U.S. Hispanics to their shared values. Approximately 55% are bilingual in Spanish and English, 25% speak only Spanish, and 20% speak only English (U.S. Bureau of the Census, 1993f). About 75% of Hispanics speak a language other than English at home, and half of those Latinos do not speak English "very well." English fluency varies among groups from different countries of origin (highest among Spaniards and Puerto Ricans), and males tend to be more bilingual than females. Some people speak only Spanish but are "fluent" in mainstream American culture, whereas others find language a barrier to participation in mainstream American institutions. Some Latinos cannot read or write Spanish, whereas others read and write it but are not conversationally fluent.

One of the first questions marketers ask is what language to use in communicating with U.S. Latinos. Relative to past immigrants, U.S. Hispanics tend to acculturate, not assimilate. That suggests that over time or generations, there remain ways in which the Latino subculture is different from mainstream American culture. Retention of Spanish-language fluency is an important signal of Latino heritage and ethnic pride. Therefore, many firms find that Spanish-language usage is an effective way to segment the Latino market.

Several specialists in the Hispanic market have developed schemes for determining the appropriate language mix for their clients. NuStats' Infosource, Market Segment Research, and Bromley Communications have published their measures of Hispanic acculturation shown in Figure 5.1. Other marketers apply "familiarity with or preference for" American and Latino cultures (Berry & Annis, 1986; de la Garza, Newcomb, & Myers, 1995). Bromley Communications' Acculturation Index uses preference for language in various situations to classify Hispanic consumers into three groups. Depending on which Latinos are the best target markets for a client's products, these firms recommend using English, Spanish, or both languages to reach the market (Bromley, 1992). In general, researchers have found differences among Hispanics in amount of acculturation, however measured, to be more meaningful for marketing purposes than cultural variations across Latino countries of origin (Valencia, 1989).

As the four different schemes in Figure 5.1 suggest, there are many different influences on the strength of Hispanic or Latino identity. A further characteristic of Latino identity is that it appears to be both individual and situational (Stayman & Deshpande, 1989; Tharp & Villarreal, 1998). In some environ-

*Market Segment Research, Inc. (1993) Acculturation Measure for Segmenting U.S. Latino Market:*

> *Strong Hispanic cultural identification.* These Hispanics are almost exclusively Spanish speaking. They live in areas more densely Hispanic and are more recent arrivals. They consume the most Spanish-language media and are lower on all socioeconomic indices. Their ties to their countries of origin remain strong, and they maintain a great deal of pride in their culture. Over half (57%) of all Hispanics are in this segment.
>
> *Moderate Hispanic cultural identification.* They live in areas of moderate Hispanic density and they have moderately strong ties to their native culture. They consume moderate amounts of Spanish-language media and have average incomes. One quarter (25%) of Hispanics are in this segment.
>
> *Weak Hispanic cultural identification.* These Hispanics are almost exclusively English speaking. They live in areas less densely Hispanic and they have less strong ties to the Hispanic culture. This group consumes the least amount of Spanish-language media and earns the highest incomes. Only 18% of Hispanics are in this segment.

*Multidimensional Measure of Cultural Identity for Latino Adolescents (de la Garza, Newcomb, & Myers, 1995):*

> *High Level of Bicultural Familiarity.* These individuals negotiate easily in two cultures. They have English and Spanish proficiency as well as positive scores on measures of political activism and social affiliations with Latinos and Anglos. They participate in the cultural traditions from both heritages (Acculturated).
>
> *Low Level of Bicultural Familiarity.* These persons are not comfortable using Spanish. They are the group least politically active and least likely to prefer one ethnic group over another. In general, they are least likely to indicate any strong preferences. Neither Latino nor American cultural traditions are important to their individual identity (Marginal).
>
> *Latino Identification.* They are most comfortable using Spanish, prefer the company of other Latinos, perceive more discrimination in their environment, and are most politically active (Separated).
>
> *American Identification.* These Hispanics prefer English over Spanish and prefer the company of Anglos. They are more likely to have a feminist orientation and less likely than other Hispanics to perceive discrimination in their environment (Assimilated).

---

**Figure 5.1.** Acculturation Measures for Segmenting the U.S. Latino Market

### *Bromley Aguilar and Associates' Acculturation Index Groups (AIGs) (Bromley, 1992):*

*AIG I (Spanish Dominant).* Hispanics who read, write, speak, and think Spanish; about 21% of U.S. Hispanics.

*AIG II (Bilingual/Bicultural).* For practical purposes, this group is divided into two: Half of AIG II persons are considered dominant in Spanish language and culture, whereas the other half are dominant in English language and culture. Together, they make up about 65% of all U.S. Hispanics.

*AIG III (English Dominant).* Hispanics who are most comfortable in English; about 14% of all U.S. Hispanics.

### *NuStats, Inc. Hispanic Assimilation Segmentation (Arce, 1994):*

*Stage 1: Newcomers.* Have spent only a small part of their lives in the United States, less than one fourth of total. Most attitudes and behaviors developed through experiences in country of origin. Low level of assimilation, and consumption of products similar to ones in country of origin. Spanish dominant and, more importantly, Spanish dependent.

*Stage 2: Transitionals.* Have spent one fourth to one half of their lives in the United States. Unique mix of experiences. Have spent most of their youth in the country of origin and their adult life in the United States. Have many characteristics of Newcomers but clearly are advancing along assimilation scale with regard to media preferences and consumer behavior.

*Stage 3: Transplants.* Have spent the greater part of their lives in the United States; at least over half of total. Exhibit characteristics of First-Borns. More comfortable and skillful in using American products and services and English language. Functional in a world that is bilingual and bicultural. They prefer Spanish and maintain their cultural values/attitudes linked to their country of origin more than U.S.-born Hispanics do.

*Stage 4: First-Borns.* U.S. born with one foreign-born parent. First-generation Hispanic; have spent their entire lives exposed to American media, attitudes, behaviors, etc. Heavily influenced by parents' character. Like Transplants, they can function in both worlds. Higher usage of English than Hispanics of the other three stages. Lean more to English.

*Stage 5: Deep Roots.* At least second-generation Hispanic; both parents are from the United States. The vast majority of Hispanics are in this group. Almost all are fully assimilated and English dominant, though not entirely English dependent. The majority maintain strong cultural identification and place a high value on cultural maintenance.

**Figure 5.1.** *(Continued)*

ments, particularly the workplace, many Latinos think and act in the same ways as other Americans (Carr-Ruffino, 1996, pp. 322-366). Latinos living in geographic locations where there are many others of Latino ethnicity tend to identify more strongly as Latino than do Latinos from areas with no local Latino community (Deshpande & Stayman, 1994).

A person's ethnic identity depends first on the individual's knowledge of his or her ethnic background, what the cultural values are, and how ethnicity is expressed (Tharp & Villarreal, 1999). Second, expression of ethnic identity is less prevalent when a group is the target of discrimination or when, for whatever reasons, mainstream culture stereotypes the group (Waters, 1990a). Most important, people may express their ethnicity privately but not outside the home or in public (Subervi, 1994). With all these influences converging upon an individual's sense of self and behavior, there is no uniform way in which Latino ethnicity is expressed. Some observers of U.S. Hispanic styles of consumption have argued that Hispanics have a distinctive expression of their subcultural heritage that represents neither mainstream America nor their culture of origin (Wallendorf & Reilly, 1983). It is a "culture of adaptation," reflecting conflicted feelings about belonging to the U.S. mainstream and being of Latin American origins. Several studies, using different methodologies, suggest that Latino cultural values have combined over time with mainstream U.S. values to create a unique U.S. Latino culture that is unlikely to disappear even when use of Spanish language does (Piirto, 1991a, pp. 198-201; Rueschenberg & Buriel, 1995; Wallendorf & Reilly, 1983). This culture of adaptation is not easy to summarize because so many aspects of identity operate simultaneously and as contradictions that drive U.S. Hispanic behaviors.

## SIZE AND SHAPE OF THE U.S. HISPANIC POPULATION

By 2005, U.S. Latinos are predicted to be the largest minority group in America. This is because they are multiplying and immigrating at high rates. U.S. Hispanics included over 22 million persons of Spanish-speaking Latin American or Caribbean country origins in the 1990 U.S. census; 9 years later, the U.S. Latino population was over 31 million. Now over 11% of the total U.S. population, they are expected to reach 15% by 2020 and to constitute about one in four Americans by 2050. No comparisons of these fast growth rates can be made before 1980 because the U.S. census measured race but not "ethnic" origin. Hispanics are younger and have higher average family sizes and households than most other ethnic groups in the United States; 52% of Latino households have children. About 40% of Latinos were foreign born in 1994, and 37% of the foreign-born people in the United States were Latino, making many Latinos new immigrants to the United States. Growth from both immigration and high fertility rates is expected to continue.

The $279 billion in purchasing power of U.S. Latinos makes them one of the 20 largest consumer markets in the world (Vitucci, 1999). By 2015, Latino purchasing power is expected to exceed $457 billion, and by 2020 it should top $520 billion ("A Robust Economy," 1998; Vitucci, 1999). Their purchasing power today represents 10% of the U.S. consumer market potential. Nevertheless, Hispanic family incomes and education levels are lower than those of Anglo or Asian Americans, and high school dropout rates remain high. Median annual incomes for Hispanic families were $26,178 in 1996 compared to the U.S. median family income of $42,300. Incomes also vary across national origin: For example, the median in 1996 for households of Mexican origin was $23,361, whereas the equivalent was $19,687 for Puerto Rican families and $27,038 for Cuban American households (U.S. Bureau of the Census, 1999g).

Increasing affluence is characteristic of all U.S. Latinos over the last 20 years. By the mid-1990s, 16.2% of all U.S. Hispanic households had incomes of $50,000 or more. From 1990 to 1996, Hispanic buying power increased over 52%, much faster than the U.S. average (Solomon & Johnson, 1995). The highest percentages of affluent Hispanic households are in New Jersey and California, whereas the lowest are in Arizona, Texas, and New Mexico. The increased incomes of U.S. Latinos are correlated with their increasing presence in occupations such as managerial and professional (11.4%), technical, sales, and administrative (16.3%), and services (17.7%). Twenty-four percent of Hispanics with graduate degrees live in California, 15% in Florida, 13% in Texas, and 12% in New York.

The composition of Latinos from different countries of origin varies significantly from city to city. In 1998 in New York, 46% of all Latinos were of Puerto Rican heritage, 15% were Dominican, and 35% were South and Central American. In Miami, 56% of Hispanics were Cuban American, whereas in San Antonio, 92% of Hispanics were of Mexican heritage (Claritas, 1998). Even in one state, the city-to-city variations in Hispanic countries of origin are surprising. During the same year in San Francisco, 68% of all Hispanics were Mexican and 15% Salvadoran; in Fresno, 94% were Mexican; and in Los Angeles, about 80% were Mexican and 14% were Salvadoran (Claritas, 1998). Trends suggest that new immigrants will continue to concentrate in patterns according to country of origin.

U.S. Latinos are concentrated in urban areas (over 90%) and in the geographic areas shown in Table 5.2. Five states have over 74% of all U.S. Latinos: New York, California, Texas, Illinois, and Florida. California and Texas contain 55% of all U.S. Latinos. In these last two states in 2000, over one half of people younger than 18 years were Latino. The geographic concentration of U.S. Latinos makes them easier to reach despite their cultural diversity. Several cities and counties are approaching Hispanic majorities among their populations. Forty-five percent of Dade County residents in Florida are Latino, as are 40% of New York City residents and almost 67% of Los Angeles County residents. Another way of describing these pools of Hispanic concentration is that about 47% of all California Hispanics are in Los Angeles County, 80% of all Illinois Hispanics are in Cook County, and about 69% of Florida Hispanics are in Dade County. Hispanics tend to migrate to established Spanish-speaking communities in the United States, where newcomers are able to conduct their lives largely in Spanish. Thus, further growth of Latinos in these same communities is predicted (Berman, 1994).

In 1999, over 38% of the U.S. Hispanic population was under 20 years of age. In Los Angeles, Latinos represent over 58% of all persons under 20 years of age. Latino youth live in two worlds, one Spanish dominant and traditional and another English dominant and open to change. This dichotomy creates significant diversity within the youth community. Young Latinos value family above all else and look to personal relationships for acceptance and support. At the same time, they want to change their worlds to improve themselves and to be heard (DMB&B, 1997). They often have favorite television shows in both Spanish (*Noticias, Cristina, Sabado Gigante, Lente Loco*) and English (*The Simpsons, The Fresh Prince of Bel-Air, The Jerry Springer Show, Martin, Baywatch*) and listen to music in both English and Spanish (about 70% of 14- to 25-year-old Latinos).

How to best reach Hispanic teens is a question being asked by marketers who note their growing numbers among American consumers. The California Milk Processors Board found that English-language versions of ads for their "Got Milk?" campaign were preferred over Spanish translations, though these same teens expressed tremendous pride in their Hispanic heritage (Wartzman, 1999b). Inner-city Hispanics often share important trend-setting behaviors with African American teens. Thus, some marketers use "urban" marketing tactics to reach them rather than "ethnic" ones. The biculturalism of Hispanic youth as well as their bilingualism provides an advantage over less diverse groups in multicultural America.

**TABLE 5.2** Top U.S. Latino Cities and States

| City or State | Size of U.S. Latino Population (in 1,000s) | % of Local Population | % of U.S. Latino Population |
|---|---|---|---|
| **All U.S. Latinos (1997)** | 29,703 | 11.13 | 100.0 |
| **Selected U.S. Cities (1996)** | | | |
| **Top 10:** | 15,430 | | 54.25 |
| Los Angeles | 5,026 | 32.40 | 17.67 |
| New York | 2,759 | 14.96 | 9.70 |
| Miami | 1,162 | 33.06 | 4.09 |
| San Francisco | 999 | 15.11 | 3.51 |
| Chicago | 909 | 10.79 | 3.20 |
| Houston | 866 | 20.48 | 3.05 |
| San Antonio | 694 | 47.38 | 2.44 |
| Dallas-Ft. Worth | 573 | 13.01 | 2.01 |
| San Diego | 530 | 20.00 | 1.86 |
| El Paso | 476 | 69.60 | 1.67 |
| **Other Cities:** | | | |
| Washington, DC | 236 | 5.60 | <1.0 |
| McAllen, TX | 422 | 85.24 | 1.49 |
| Denver, CO | 257 | 12.08 | <1.0 |
| Brownsville, TX | 257 | 81.73 | <1.0 |
| Fresno, CA | 265 | 34.74 | <1.0 |
| **Selected U.S. States (1997)** | | | |
| **Top 5 Total:** | 21,523 | | 72.5 |
| California | 9,941 | 30.81 | 33.47 |
| Texas | 5,723 | 29.44 | 19.44 |
| New York | 2,570 | 14.17 | 8.65 |
| Florida | 2,105 | 14.37 | 7.10 |
| Illinois | 1,183 | 9.94 | 3.98 |
| **Other States:** | 3,818 | | 12.8 |
| Arizona | 999 | 21.92 | 3.36 |
| New Mexico | 692 | 40.04 | 2.33 |
| Colorado | 556 | 14.29 | 1.87 |
| New Jersey | 959 | 11.91 | 3.23 |
| Nevada | 253 | 15.11 | <1.0 |
| Massachusetts | 359 | 5.86 | 1.21 |

SOURCE: U.S. Bureau of the Census (1999a).

# FAMILY, CHURCH, AND LANGUAGE AS
# SYMBOLS OF HISPANIC VALUES

U.S. Latinos may be becoming English dominant among second and third generations, but certain Latino cultural values remain central for them. The family and the church (primarily the Roman Catholic Church) continue to be the center of U.S. Latino social life and calendars. Spanish retention symbolizes strong Hispanic ethnic identity for individuals.

These three important social institutions anchor many of the values so important to U.S. Latinos. Research on Mexican American families emphasizes the continuing importance of life cycle rituals (e.g., ceremonies relating to birth, marriage, and death) as markers for stages in Latino lives in the United States, regardless of social class (Williams, 1990). The rituals of baptism, confirmation, the *quinceañera,* marriage, and funerals unite family and religion in the expression of ethnicity. Religion is important in these life cycle rituals, but traditions are so rooted in communal and ethnic origins that they operate more as expressions of ethnicity than as religious commitments. The celebration of Posadas at Christmas and the presence of altars in the home for patron saints represent cultural traditions as much as religious fervor.

The Hispanic family differs from the Anglo-American one. For example, men and women play more traditional roles within the family, and many households include extended family members. Children in Latino families are "expected to be dependent for as long as possible, and therefore they are not asked to act independently until they reach maturity" (Hispanic Market Connections, Inc., 1996, p. 2). A "healthy" baby to a Hispanic mom is chubby, has rosy cheeks, wears shoes or socks, and looks at his mother's eyes, not a camera. In the same study, Anglo moms viewed a "healthy" baby as barefoot, dressed in a diaper or light shirt, and looking all around (Padilla, 1999).

"New" traditions in Mexican American culture are distinct from those of Mexico (Williams, 1990, pp. 136-150). A good example is the *quinceañera,* a ceremony that takes place when a girl turns 15 years old. The event celebrates her passage into womanhood, her commitment to Catholicism, and her debut in society. The ritual itself has a Mexican heritage, but it has been adapted to the American Latino environment. A *quinceañera* may or may not have a religious component in Mex-America. Other celebrations like the Day of the Dead and Cinco de Mayo have also found their way onto the U.S. Latino social calendar (Vargas, 1996). Though the extended family may be disappearing from the routines of daily life in Hispanic households, extended family members are still important participants in life cycle rituals of Hispanic families. The fiestas that celebrate these events communicate and reinforce Latino identity. The examples here illustrate Mexican American customs, but all U.S. Latino country-of-origin groups have home country rituals that have been adapted to their U.S. environment.

In many ways, U.S. Latinos are traditional and conservative Americans (Carr-Ruffino, 1996, pp. 322-366; Valencia, 1989; Williams, 1990, pp. 136-150). Table 5.3 contrasts cultural values of U.S. Latinos and those of mainstream America. For the most traditional Hispanics, husbands dominate family decision making for many product categories; care of the home is reserved for female expertise (C. Webster, 1994). The three institutions of family, religion, and language are cultural reference points of contrast with Anglo culture in the United States. For example, the importance of family is linked to the cultural value of personalism—a preference for familiar people and institutions—as well as to the significance of interpersonal relationships in general. Religion, as it is practiced among U.S. Hispanics, reflects an acceptance of hierarchy, the status quo, and a blending of the spiritual, physical, and philosophical with daily life.

Spanish is a high-context language where pronoun use depends on relationships and all nouns have ascribed masculine or feminine gender. These norms for interaction are in place even when U.S. Hispanics may not speak Spanish themselves because they are part of the cultural value system. Figure 5.2 shows advertisements in Spanish for Budweiser and Miller Lite beers. Budweiser, in keeping with its positioning as the "King of Beers" in the United States, uses the respectful *usted* to address Budweiser consumers, whereas Miller appeals to U.S. Hispanics with a more intimate *tu*. Such distinctions in Spanish pronouns for "you" reflect the importance of relative status between source and receiver. A greater appreciation for and sensitivity to status is an important value in the U.S. Hispanic subculture, even for those not fluent in the Spanish language.

Values of U.S. Latinos of many different incomes are more middle class and conservative than those of comparable Anglo Americans (Flores, 1994; Valencia, 1989). Many consumer decisions are undoubtedly affected by their risk-aversive behaviors: a preference for familiar or well-known brands, word of mouth as an important source of product information and endorsement, and a reluctance to complain (Hilger & English, 1978; O'Guinn, Faber, & Imperia, 1986; Pruden & Longman, 1972). Brand "bloc" buying, the informal endorsements of brands by Latino community persons and institutions, is an example of how immigrant consumers reduce perceived risk in the U.S. marketplace

**TABLE 5.3** U.S. Hispanic and Mainstream American Values

| Cultural Values | U.S. Hispanic Subculture | U.S. Mainstream Culture |
|---|---|---|
| **The Family** | | |
| Children | Dependence | Independence |
| Parents | Authoritarian | Egalitarian |
| Family roles | Defined | Diffused |
| Role differentiation | Male dominance/equality | Gender equality |
| **Religion** | | |
| Structure | Hierarchical | Egalitarian |
| Domain | Physical/spiritual/ philosophical/daily | Spiritual |
| Role prescriptions | Defined | Diffused |
| Role differentiation | Male dominant | Gender equality |
| **Language (Spanish vs. English)** | | |
| Structure | Indirect communication | Direct communication |
| Nouns | Feminine or masculine | No assigned genders |
| Verbs/pronouns | Dependent on relationships | Independent of relationships |
| Equivalent meaning | More wordy | Less wordy |
| Speaker's voice | Indirect ("It is thought that . . . ") | Direct ("I think . . . ") |
| Nonverbal use | High context | Low context |
| **Worldviews (Humans and Cosmos)** | | |
| Humans and nature | Humans dominant over nature | Humans dominant over nature |
| Science and technology | Objectivity is ideal, but random events may influence the investigative process | Events have discoverable causes; not random |
| Materialism | Possessions express individual's style and God's will | Possessions are important and a measure of worth/identity |
| **Activity Orientation (Use of Time)** | | |
| Activity and work | Work to live | Live to work |
| Efficiency, practicality | Not so important; longer time horizons | Very important; short-term over long-term goals |
| Progress and change | Traditions are important; more fatalistic | Change is good, new is better than old; future orientation |
| Time orientation | More toward present and past | Time is resource to be managed; linear view, future oriented |

*(Continued)*

**TABLE 5.3** U.S. Hispanic and Mainstream American Values (Continued)

| Cultural Values | U.S. Hispanic Subculture | U.S. Mainstream Culture |
|---|---|---|
| **Human Nature Orientation** | | |
| Goodness | Potential for both good and evil; faith, idealism important | Born evil, potential to be good; self-discipline important |
| Rationality | Lacking objectivity; cannot always be trusted to be fair | Humans act on basis of reason; responsible for actions |
| Mutability | Human nature less subject to change | Human nature can be changed by society; self-improvement |
| **Self-Perceptions (in relation to society)** | | |
| Individualism | Dependence on family and relationships, but individuality in that context; high contact | Independence and individual identity are situational; low contact culture |
| Self-motivation | Destiny determined by circumstances; interdependence with others; opportunism, passion | Set and pursue own goals; competition is good |
| Masculinity versus femininity | Maximum distinctions between sexes | Minimal distinctions between sexes |
| Risk taking | Avoid uncertainty | Take risks |
| **Social Organization** | | |
| Equality | Hierarchy and authority are important; high power distance | Equal opportunity and access for all; more democratic traditions |
| Conformity | Norms of the past; avoidance of uncertainty; simpatia (going along to get along); courtesy | Modern norms and what is "in"; tolerance of deviation |

SOURCES: For U.S. Hispanic subculture values: Carr-Ruffino (1996, pp. 322-366), Kunda (1994a), Valencia (1989). Sources for U.S. mainstream culture: Jandt (1995, pp. 211-234), Hammond and Morrison (1996), Althen (1988), Stewart and Bennett (1991).

(Agins, 1985; Kizilbash & Garman, 1975-1976; L. Lee, 1996; Webster, 1992). U.S. Latinos are optimistic and have high expectations for life improvement in the next 10 years, yet they have low usage of products such as credit cards and financial services in general. These patterns of product usage may have evolved

**Figure 5.2a.** Advertisers Use Different Forms of "You" in Spanish: Bud "Is for You"

**Figure 5.2b.** Advertisers Use Different Forms of "You" in Spanish: "You Too Can Be Part of the 'Lite' Group"

from experiences in Latin American countries of origin, where distrust of those institutions was based on personal experience.

The more traditional gender roles of Latino families mean that females are more immersed in the ethnic culture than males (Flores, 1994, p. 21; Penaloza & Gilly, 1986). They are responsible for passing along Catholic traditions and the Spanish language. Male dominance in decision making is most apparent when an item is expensive. In those cases, more traditional cultural norms and husband decision dominance are apparent among U.S. Latino families, regardless of variations in income, education, or employment status (O'Guinn et al., 1986). Male domination within the family is tempered by economic contributions of the partners, especially among middle- and upper-class households (Flores, 1994, p. 58).

Several researchers believe that being foreign born is more important than country of origin in determining cultural values among U.S. Latinos (Moyerman & Forman, 1992; Valencia, 1989). Those persons who came to the United States as adults have been socialized in their country of origin. If a U.S. Latino came with his or her family to the United States as a child, the individual often acts as the family's translator and bridge to U.S. mainstream culture (Access Worldwide Communications, Inc., 1999). According to the *Hispanic Monitor* (an in-house publication of Market Development, Inc.), these Latinos tend to be "Hopeful Loyalists" or "Recent Seekers" in terms of values and lifestyle. U.S.-born Latinos tend to be "Young Strivers" or "Established Adapters." Persons of second-, third-, and fourth-generation Hispanic heritage vary widely in their adaptation to the U.S. mainstream. In some cases, the public persona is "typically" American, while the individual still expresses cultural values at a subconscious level or in the privacy of the home.

Generation Ñ (pronounced "EN-YE") is made up of Latinos under 35 years of age who are the first and second generations born in the United States. They are not only mainstreaming themselves and their bicultural, bilingual lifestyles but also "Hispanicizing" American mainstream culture. They have their own celebrities and entertainment preferences in the panoply of American arts and pop culture characters (Johnson, 1993a). In American music, fashion, film, television, sports, and the fine arts, the success stories of Hispanics such as Selena Quintanilla of Tejano music fame are becoming visible in mainstream media (Adler & Padgett, 1995). In 1999, several mainstream media vehicles pointed to the so-called crossover of Latino celebrities and the "Hispanization" of American culture (Chambers, Figueroa, Weingert, & Weingarden, 1999; Figueroa, Clemetson, Weingart, Hayden, & Brand, 1999; Haubegger, 1999; Stapinski,

1999a). These persons and trends symbolize the "American dream," bind *aficio-nados* to their country-of-origin roots, and give Latinos their own niche in American popular culture, much as the use of "Spanglish" does. This fusion of cultures is energizing and "Hispanicizing" American pop culture along the way. Salsa is now our favorite condiment!

The symbolic value of Spanish usage cannot be underestimated in the U.S. Latino community. Though the meanings may vary among third-generation Cuban Americans and third-generation Mexican Americans, Spanish is not just the language of the "heart and soul" but also an important part of U.S. Latino identity. The language structure itself expresses emotion and masculinity/femininity in ways that English does not. And, whether speaking English, Spanish, or Spanglish, U.S. Latinos speak more indirectly and are more likely to say what they think someone else wants to hear (de Mooij, 1998; Hofstede, 1984; Samovar & Porter, 1991). Their sensitivity to criticism and frequent use of nonverbal signals to express respect or disgust mean that the language is only one of the ways their communication patterns are distinct from those of Anglo Americans (Carr-Rufino, 1996, pp. 322-366). Several researchers have affirmed the significance of Spanish usage to U.S. Latino preferences for ethnically advertised products and communications (Deshpande et al., 1986; Koslow et al., 1994; Roslow & Nicholls, 1996).

If social relationships and organizations in the U.S. Latino community are more hierarchical than among Anglos, they are also highly personalized. U.S. Latinos prefer doing business with friends or members of their kinship networks. An example of how this attitude affects consumer choice is the positive response of U.S. Latinos to ethnic-directed marketing efforts and higher levels of brand loyalty. An example of how significant just the use of Spanish language can be was the enthusiastic response among U.S. Latinos to Carnival Cruise Lines' Fiesta Marina ship, dedicated to serving the Hispanic marketplace in 18 countries of Latin America as well as the United States. Such consumption preferences are the by-products of strong pride in Latino heritage and Latino contributions as citizens of the United States. This explains such apparent conflicts in behavior as listening to American popular music but relating emotionally to Latin music.

An important aspect of Hispanic culture is viewing interpersonal relationships within the context of an authoritarian social structure (Carr-Rufino, 1996, pp. 322-366). People who are at the top have more power than those at the bottom, but it is important to preserve good relations with all members. *Simpatia* means keeping everyone happy, even when the news may not be so good. That also suggests it is important to just let some things be—it is impossible to predict the future. One phrase that expresses this is "*Si Dios quiere*" ("If God so wills"). Such fatalism also explains the reluctance to set goals and engage in planning (Flores, 1994, p. 38). Fewer Hispanics than Anglos take a shopping list to the supermarket.

There is no typical way "Hispanicness" is expressed, nor is there a pattern for the links between cultural values and marketplace behaviors. The idea of a "typical" physical type for U.S. Latinos is also a myth, for cultural values rather than race are at the heart of U.S. Latinos as consumers. This does not mean there are no prejudices for and against lighter or darker skin, hair color, hair texture, hairiness, and physical size. These physical characteristics vary across Latino country-of-origin groups and thus require specific research when choosing actors or actresses to represent "typical" U.S. Latinos in marketing communications.

## LATINO MEDIA IMAGES, USAGE, AND AVAILABILITY

The Frito Bandito was "a mustachioed Mexican bandit with six-gun, broad sombrero, and a sinister smile who took Fritos corn chips from unsuspecting mothers" (Wilson & Gutierrez, 1995, p. 109). The Frito Bandito was the first Hispanic *visible* in mainstream American advertising. The negative associations he symbolized sparked the first resistance of U.S. Latinos to the ways in which they had been represented, or misrepresented, in American media. Other images in film, literature, comic books, and radio and TV programs have stereotyped Hispanics as lazy (in a sombrero, sleeping at midday beside a cactus), as immigrants unable to speak English properly, as professionals festooned in traditional costumes (Reyes, 1994), and as quick-tempered male lovers and female spitfires like Chiquita banana (Astroff, 1988-1989; Nuiry, 1996; Westerman, 1989; Wilson & Gutierrez, 1995, pp. 161-167).

The damaging effects of these images on all Americans' understanding of Latino culture are inestimable. However, perhaps as significant for Hispanics themselves has been the virtual absence of Hispanic images in mainstream media (Green, 1991; Torres, 1999). Only 1% of 12,000 news stories in 1998 on ABC, NBC, and CBS were about Latinos, and 60% of the Latino-related stories during 4 prior years were focused on crime, immigration, and affirmative action (Torres, 1999). In the absence of images of Hispanics on television, some Latinos "have learned to simply recede into their anonymity" (Doss, 1998).

The growth of Spanish-language media since the 1970s has been nothing short of phenomenal. Television spending at local and national levels exceeded $1 billion in 1999, and radio spending was over $500 million (Dougherty, 1999). All cities with significant populations of Latinos now have multiple Spanish or bilingual television channels, radio stations, and community newspapers. At the same time, mainstream media have learned to court members of the Hispanic market with more culturally sensitive programs in English. The key issues in designing a media program to communicate with Hispanics nationally have become the balance between English- and Spanish-language media and the significant differences in media habits found across geographic locations and age-groups.

Independent researchers claim that advertising in Spanish is 40% more effective in increasing awareness levels than commercials in English among both Spanish-dominant and bilingual viewers of television (Roslow & Nicholls, 1996). Not only is it more persuasive, but Spanish-language advertising increases consumers' perceptions that advertisers are sensitive to Hispanic culture and peoples (Koslow et al., 1994). Table 5.4 lists the major media in both English and Spanish that targeted national Latino audiences in 1999. About 83% of all media advertising for Hispanic audiences went to radio and television (Goodson & Shaver, 1994). Hispanics spend more time with television and radio than general market audiences.

Because spoken Spanish continues to have higher rates of fluency among U.S. Latinos than written Spanish, it is not surprising that radio is such a dynamic medium among Spanish-language media. There is a long tradition in Latin America of radio as a medium for learning how to adapt to a new environment while keeping in touch with immigrant roots (Barbero, 1993). Advertisers spent about $508 million in Spanish-language radio advertising in 1999. The Los Angeles stations of Hispanic Broadcasting alone billed over $71 million in 1999 (Blodau, 1999; Nordholm, 1998). Recent public stock offerings (Radio Unica, a Spanish-language talk-radio network, and Spanish Broadcasting System-SBS, with a $1.6 billion market evaluation; Russell, 1999) and mergers of several multistation firms (such as Tichenor with Heftel, later transformed into Hispanic Broadcasting Corporation) have created truly national reach and audience coverage for both Spanish and bilingual radio (Russell, 1999).

In Los Angeles and San Antonio, the stations with the largest audiences are in Spanish, confirming their effectiveness in covering Latino populations in those cities (Petrozzello, 1996). Among all Hispanics, 83% watch Spanish-language television, 79% listen to Spanish-language radio, and 48% prefer Spanish-

**TABLE 5.4** National Media Vehicles Targeting U.S. Latino Audiences

| Medium and Vehicles | Main Stations or Circulations | Language(s) |
|---|---|---|
| **Television** | | |
| Univision Network (1961-SIN) | 92% of U.S. Hispanic households (16 owned, 23 affiliates) | Spanish |
| Telemundo Network (1987) | 84% of U.S. Hispanic households (43 affiliates) | Spanish |
| Cable TV | Galavision (32% of U.S. Hispanic households), HBO en Espanol, Fox Sports World Espanol (11%), CNN en Espanol, GEMS (11%) | Spanish |
| **Radio (75 Network Stations, 350 Independent)** | | |
| Hispanic Broadcasting Corp. (1940-Tichenor) | NYC, SA, Miami, Chicago, Houston, Harlingen, El Paso (89% of U.S. Hispanic households) | Spanish/bilingual |
| Spanish Broadcasting System (1983) | LA, NYC, Miami, Key Largo | Spanish |
| Radio Unica (Katz) (1962-Lotus) | LA, Oxnard, Chicago, Fresno, Denver (50 stations) | Spanish |
| Lieberman | LA | Spanish |
| El Dorado (1992) | Houston, LA, Dallas | Spanish |
| **Magazines (230 National/Local, 48 Audited)** | | |
| *Hispanic* (1988) | 252,000 | English |

language magazines and newspapers (Yankelovich Partners, 1997). In the 1990s, there was an increase in the use of "Spanglish" and bilingual formats to better reflect the audiences' ways of speaking and relating to mainstream culture. Hispanics are loyal radio listeners, tuning in over 24 hours a week (Yankelovich Partners, 1997).

During the late 1980s, Spanish-language broadcasters complained that the media measurements by Arbitron, Birch, and Nielsen were undercounting His-

**TABLE 5.4** National Media Vehicles Targeting U.S. Latino Audiences (Continued)

| Medium and Vehicles | Main Stations or Circulations | Language(s) |
| --- | --- | --- |
| *Hispanic Business* (1979) | 202,000 | English |
| *Vista* (1985) | 894,000 | Bilingual |
| *People en Espanol* | 201,000 | Spanish |
| *Ser Padres* | 427,000 | Spanish |
| *Nuestra Gente* | 726,000 | Spanish |
| *Latina* | 135,000 | English |
| *Mundo Deportivo* | 32,000 | Spanish |
| *Latin Girl* | 100,000 | English |

**Newspapers (17 Dailies: 400 National/Local, 112 Audited)**

| | | |
| --- | --- | --- |
| *La Opinion* (LA) | 102,000 | Spanish |
| *El Diario-La Prensa* (NY) | 52,000 | Spanish |
| *Noticias del Mundo* (NY) | 32,000 | Spanish |
| *El Nuevo Herald* (Miami) | 102,000 | Spanish |
| *Diario Las Americas* (Miami-1953) | 69,000 | Spanish |

SOURCES: *Hispanic Business* (1999, December, pp. 52-72), Padilla (1994), Veciana-Suarez (1990), Standard Rate and Data Service (1999), Zate (1998a, 1998b).

panic audiences. As a result, there has been a concerted effort to improve audience research methods. Nielsen and Univision joined together in 1992 to develop a system that counts Hispanic audiences in both Spanish- and English-language media. It is now easier for agencies and clients to estimate reach for Hispanic audiences in both languages. Still, only about 2% of U.S. television advertising budgets goes to Spanish-language TV, although the audience constitutes at least 9% of viewers. Table 5.5 shows major Spanish-language or bilingual media in five cities with significant U.S. Latino populations.

**TABLE 5.5**  Spanish-Language Media Vehicles in Major Latino Markets

| Location | Television Stations | Radio Stations | Newspapers |
|---|---|---|---|
| Los Angeles | KMEX-Univision KVES-Telemundo Independents: KVYE, KNET | KLAX-FM, KSSE-FM, KLVE-FM, KBUE-FM, KTNQ, KKHJ, KWKW, KSCA-FM, KXRS-FM, KWIZ, KOXR, KVCA, KKHJ, KRRA, KWRM, KWRN, KXFS, KSZZ, KZLM-FM, KXSB-FM, KUTY, KDIF | La Opinion (1926), El Economico, El Classificado, La Voz, Novedades, Parati, Union Hispana, Nuestro Tiempo (LA Times), Azteca News, Alcancia de Ahorros, Vida Nueva |
| New York | WXTV-Univision WNJU-Telemundo | WSKQ-FM, WXLX, WPAT/FM, WADO, WCUM, WKDM-AM, WJIT-AM | El Diario/La Prensa (1963), El Especial, Noticias del Mundo, El Vocero, Impacto, La Vos Hispana, El Tiempo, Mensaje |
| Miami | WLTV-Univision WSCV-Telemundo WEYS-CBS Telenoticias | WQBA-FM, WQBA, WCMQ-FM, WWFE, WAQI, WKAT, WRTO-FM, WRMA-FM, WAMR-FM, WSUA, WXDJ-FM, WZMQ-FM | El Nuevo Herald (1987), Diario Las Americas (1953) |
| San Antonio | KWEX-Univision WVAW-Telemundo KVDA-Telemundo | KCOR, KEDA, KSAH, KROM-FM, KXTN-FM, KZDC, ZEMU (MX) | La Prensa de San Antonio |
| Chicago | WGBO-Univision WSNS-Telemundo | WOJO-FM, WLEY-FM, WIND, WTAQ, WLXX | El Dia, El Imparcial, La Raza, Exito, Mundo Hispano |

SOURCES: Standard Rate and Data Service (1999), Veciana-Suarez (1990).

There continue to be problems in audience measurement and in researching U.S. Latinos that have not been resolved (Berman, 1994). For example, low telephone ownership, a large number of unlisted numbers, low response rates, and the Latino cultural tendency to please the researcher reduce the reliability of media audience and market research measurements. With mail surveys, researchers must confront illiteracy, especially in English. In addition, it can be difficult to determine a correct dialect of Spanish for interviewing. Personal interviews in Hispanic neighborhoods face a higher number of not-at-homes. Most research firms with experience in Latino communities (Hispanic Market Connections; Market Development Inc.; Strategy Research International; Hispanic & Asian Market Communications Research, Inc.; Market Segment Research; NuStats) have developed methods for improving reliability. Still, it is best to be cautious when interpreting reports about Latino consumers and audiences.[1]

Differences in media habits and language preferences across U.S. cities are important to firms interested in the Hispanic market. For example, San Antonians listen to a lot of Spanish-language radio but prefer English-language television, whereas Los Angeles Latinos watch the most Spanish-language TV and listen to less Spanish radio. Another contrast is between San Antonio and Miami: In San Antonio 80% of the Hispanic population is American born and of Mexican descent, whereas Miami's Hispanic population is 80% foreign born and Cuban American. Miami Hispanics watch more Spanish-language programs, whereas San Antonio Hispanics watch more English television. And younger Hispanics in general listen to more Spanish-language radio than Spanish-language television. American-born Hispanic children can best be reached with English-language television, although there are opportunities for placing advertisements in either language on programs with themes of interest to U.S. Latinos (Katz, 1996; Zbar, 1995b).

Table 5.6 reports consumption of English- and Spanish-language media among U.S. Latinos as a group. The first language learned by Latinos strongly influences their choice of language in media. Spanish-speaking Hispanics spend the most time overall with media and prefer Spanish-language television most. Younger Hispanics spend more time with English TV but find few culturally relevant programs; Fox and MTV Latino have developed programming to fill this void (Fisher, 1995). Telemundo Network, in addition to new firms such as Si-TV, is developing English and Spanglish programs about Latino experiences in the United States (Rodriguez, 1997).

**TABLE 5.6** Media Preferences by Language and Medium

| Medium | Average Daily Media Hours | | | |
|---|---|---|---|---|
| | Hispanics With English First | Hispanics With Spanish First | Bilingual Hispanics | All Hispanics |
| **Total Media Time** | 7.9 | 8.7 | 7.3 | |
| English-language media | 5.9 | 2.5 | 4.4 | |
| Spanish-language media | 2.0 | 6.2 | 2.9 | |
| **Television** | 4.4 | 5.2 | 4.3 | 3.8/4.7[a] |
| English language | 3.4 | 1.4 | 2.3 | |
| Spanish language | 0.9 | 3.6 | 2.0 | |
| **Radio** | 2.9 | 2.9 | 2.8 | 3.6/3.3[a] |
| English language | 1.9 | 0.7 | 2.0 | |
| Spanish language | 0.9 | 2.2 | 0.8 | |
| **Newspapers** | 0.6 | 0.6 | 0.2 | |
| English language | 0.4 | 0.2 | 0.1 | |
| Spanish language | 0.2 | 0.4 | 0.1 | |
| **Magazines** | 1.2 | 1.0 | 0.9 | |
| English language | 1.0 | 0.4 | 0.5 | |
| Spanish language | 0.2 | 0.6 | 0.4 | |

SOURCES: Yankelovich Partners (1994, 1997) and Strategy Research Corporation, cited in Mogelonsky (1995b, p. 21).
a. Numbers refer to hours of English/Spanish media consumption.

Another trend during the 1990s was development of more bilingual and crossover media, affording non-Spanish speakers and non-Hispanics more access to Hispanic-related news and information. CNN's Spanish-language news reports are one example. Spanish-language television programming mirrors Latin American programming more than North American TV. For example, the largest audiences on Univision and Telemundo networks are for shows like *Sabado Gigante, Siempre en Domingo, Noticiero Univision,* and *Primavera.*

*Telenovelas* and game and talk shows dominate the programming that originates from Mexico. Recently there has been more publicity about simulcasting of English-language programs on television. The major Spanish-language networks are also developing new programs set in the United States (Hoeffel, 1994).

The strongest argument for Spanish-language TV advertising is that over three fourths of Hispanics prefer to speak Spanish at home. Florida, New York, and New Jersey have the highest percentages of Latinos speaking Spanish at home—over 85%—whereas Arizona, New Mexico, and Colorado have the lowest percentages. San Antonio and New York are cities where the majority of Latinos consider themselves bilingual (Hispanic Market Connections, Inc., 1995). The introduction of Nielsen's Hispanic Family Panel and better measurement of Spanish-language audiences serve as stimuli for even more advertisers to enter the growing U.S. Latino market. Still, on a station-by-station basis, there can be major conflicts between the survey of audience habits according to the Station Index and the Nielsen Hispanic Family Panel. Recently in New York, the Nielsen Hispanic Family Panel estimated that 54% of Latino households were Spanish dominant, but the survey found that only 28% of Latino homes were Spanish dominant. Univision claims that such discrepancies are worth over $128 million in lost advertising revenues (Wartzman & Flint, 2000).

Spanish-language newspapers have a long history in communities such as Miami, San Antonio, New York, and Los Angeles. More recently, mainstream papers have introduced their own Spanish-language versions. *Nuestro Tiempo* is the *Los Angeles Times*'s Spanish-language medium, and *El Heraldo* is the *Miami Herald*'s entry. There were 507 Spanish-language newspapers in 1997, with over $490 million in advertising revenues (Torres, 1999).

A large majority of U.S. Latinos say they prefer to read in English. In response, most magazines targeting the Hispanic market publish in English. A newspaper insert, *Vista,* was introduced in 1989. *Hispanic* and *Hispanic Business* have been around since the 1970s. *Imagen* was a Spanish-language vehicle targeted to middle- and upper-income U.S. Hispanic women that couldn't attract enough advertisers, but it has been replaced recently by a slate of English magazines targeting U.S. Latinos: *Moderna, Latin Style, Latina,* and *Latin Bride,* for example. Cubans in Miami, with higher education levels overall, are greater readers of both magazines and newspapers than Hispanics from other countries of origin.

The English-language media for U.S. Hispanics are not just mainstream vehicles with the same advertisements and content. Publishers and advertising agencies that place ads in these media for mainstream clients advise them to "picture their products with Latino foods, celebrities, cultural events, community events, and family traditions . . . to adapt the product to make it appear to be a part of the Latino lifestyle in the United States" (Wilson & Gutierrez, 1995, p. 129). Both English- and Spanish-language media are important members of the Latino community in the United States. Although Spanish continues to play an important role in Latino lifestyles, English is becoming the primary language of artistic and intellectual expression (Rodriguez, 1997).

In cities such as Miami, New York, San Antonio, and Los Angeles, yellow page publishers have also found a niche among Spanish-language media. The *Paquinas Amarillas en Espanol de Texas* and Houston's *Spanish Telephone Directory*'s 3,700 advertisers are Hispanic and Anglo-owned firms catering to Hispanic buyers. The use of direct mail in Spanish is also increasing. Hispanics receive fewer mail pieces in general, so there is less clutter in that medium (30 vs. 350 mailings to Anglo homes per year) (Zbar, 1995a). Some marketers have reported that Hispanics respond to direct mail because they feel they aren't "treated with respect in stores" (Wynter, 1995; Zbar, 1995a).

Billboards in heavily Latino neighborhoods also increased their share of advertising in the 1980s and 1990s. Spanish-dominant Hispanics find billboards and radio accessible even with limited literacy skills. Billboards are also a good vehicle for reaching young Hispanics who have low involvement levels while consuming Spanish-language broadcast media (Feuer, 1988). Overall, in 1999 advertisers spent over $1.89 billion in traditional media to reach Hispanic consumers (Dougherty, 1999; Goldsmith, 1996). The 10 largest spenders in the Hispanic market in 1999 were Procter & Gamble ($46.2 million), AT&T ($35 million), MCI ($34 million), Sears, Roebuck ($30 million), McDonald's ($26 million), Anheuser-Busch and Toyota ($20 million each), Kraft Foods and Johnson & Johnson ($17 million each), and Colgate-Palmolive and General Motors ($15 million each) (Zate, 1998a).

The latest medium to enter the Spanish-or-English fray is the World Wide Web. How many U.S. Hispanics are online and where—home, work, or both—are key questions about U.S. Latinos on the Internet. By 1998, over 15% of Latino households were online (with some estimates as high as 36% of Latino homes), and they were purchasing computers in 1998 at twice the rate of the overall population (Romney, 1999). Some analysts call the Internet the "ultimate borderless Hispanic market" and the largest in this hemisphere (Romney, 1999, p. A1). The so-called "digital divide" is between "information-rich"

Americans (Anglos, Asians/Pacific Islanders, those with higher incomes, the better educated, and dual-parent households) and "information-poor" Americans (those who are younger, those with lower incomes and education, certain minorities, and those in rural areas or central cities) (Heines, 1999, p. 16). For example, households with an income of $75,000 or more are at least 20 times more likely to have Internet access than those at the lowest income levels. Hispanic households are one third as likely to have Internet access as Asian/Pacific Islander households and are 40% as likely as Anglo homes (Heines, 1999).

Internet content developed first in response to early users and their terminology (English). In 1999 StarMedia (in Spanish) and Quepasa.com (in both English and Spanish) began targeting U.S. Latinos on the Web. Other contenders in e-commerce ventures targeting U.S. Latinos are Yupi.com, To2.com, Picosito.com, Espanol.com, and Elsitio.com, in addition to general market competitors AOL, Microsoft, and Yahoo! (Hagerty, 1999). Univision joined them in 2000. Loquesea.com is seeking to attract Latino teens from the United States and Latin America with Spanish-language and Spanglish-but-edgy content. The site claimed 100,000 registered users and 15 million page views in early 2000 (Druckerman, 2000). A major barrier that all Web competitors must overcome is the lower number of U.S. Latinos who hold stock portfolios, have credit cards, or seek financial advice (Hagerty, 1999).

The English-Spanish argument continues unabated. Perhaps the best answer to this question depends on which of the country-of-origin, age, or generational groups are the best target market for a firm's products. A recent survey of Spanish speakers at home found that 46% said they were influenced by a Spanish-language television advertisement to make a purchase within the last month, and 23% reported influence from an English-language TV ad (Korzenny, 1997). Whether it is in English or Spanish, programmers should recognize Hispanic lifestyles, leaders, and celebrities within American culture.

Ethnic-oriented media depend on advertising support and thus promote themselves as the best way to reach a group such as U.S. Latinos. This has been a point of criticism by Latino activists who believe that media interest in the community is purely exploitative. The following quote summarizes their position and reflects their ambivalence about advertiser attention to ethnic-minority markets: "Black and Spanish-language media will benefit from the advertising dollars of national corporations only as long as dollars are the most cost-effective way for advertisers to persuade Blacks and Latinos to use their products" (Wilson & Gutierrez, 1995, p. 135).

# SEARCH STRATEGIES AND BUYING
# PREFERENCES OF LATINO CONSUMERS

The symbolic value of buying and owning products to U.S. Latinos is expressed by the following quotation: "The American Dream begins with an education and ends with a good-paying job. Educating oneself and working means money, a home, a car, vacations, entertainment, health care and a secure retirement. The Hispanic Dream should be the same" (Flores, 1994, p. 36). Owning the same kinds of goods and services as other Americans means being "American." With purchasing power exceeding $272 billion in 1999, U.S. Latinos are important consumers in the American market (Zbar, 1996).

Most U.S. Hispanics are proud of their Hispanic heritage but express that at the same time they want to be recognized as Americans. These symbolic roles may seem to be in conflict, but both are at the core of what makes U.S. Hispanic buyer behavior unique. Wallendorf and Reilly (1983) identified a "unique" Hispanic American style of consumption that is a result of adaptation to, rather than acculturation into, mainstream America. An example of two product categories that suggest heavier consumption than would be predicted by a position on a continuum between Latin American and Anglo American preferences are meats and laundry and cleaning products (DRI/McGraw-Hill, 1995; Wallendorf & Nelson, 1986; Wallendorf & Reilly, 1983). Heavy consumption in these categories cannot be explained by assimilation into mainstream America or socioeconomic status. U.S. Hispanics are also heavy consumers of light beer, cosmetics, children's clothing, footwear, fresh fruits and vegetables, food at home, public transportation, and durable goods (Paulin, 1998).

A long history of research suggests that the marketplace is an arena in which Latinos seek cultural reinforcement and familiarity (see, e.g., Kizilbash & Garman, 1975-1976; Longman & Pruden, 1972; Penaloza & Gilly, 1999; Sturdivant, 1969). Procter & Gamble distributes its brands to 7,000 *bodegas* in New York, accounting for one half of groceries bought there by Latinos in New York. Family and friends are major sources of information about stores, products, and brands. Hispanics feel positively in general about advertising and product information, especially when it recognizes their place among American subcultures. As consumers, they may be willing to pay a premium for convenience and ethnic pride. Shopping in *bodegas* or small neighborhood stores, they can get "not just chorizo, but also gossip" (Agins, 1985, p. A1).

Advertising and communications in Spanish have been found to be more persuasive with Hispanics, even when the receivers are bilingual (Faber &

O'Guinn, 1991). However, language is not the only key to a positive attitude about a brand. The cultural nuances of communications must be "Hispanicized" also. A car phone company translated its ads from the Anglo market into Spanish and showed a man relaxing by his pool while he did business on the phone. Anglos got the message that the phone gave them more leisure time; Cuban Americans thought the man in the ad was lazy and missed the key benefit of higher work productivity (Meyer, 1990). Retailers like Sears and Target have found success when they "Hispanicized" their merchandise mixes to become more culturally compatible with store neighborhoods (Steinhauer, 1997).

Figure 5.3 shows a cigarette ad in both English and Spanish. What's interesting is that the ad appears to be a simple translation from English to Spanish, but in fact some meaning is lost, and other associations appear in the Spanish version but not in the English one. In Latin American countries, houses open to the inside and front porches are rare. Thus, there is no tradition of couples relaxing after a meal and sharing a day's events on a front porch swing. The two "cigarette people" in Spanish could even be members of the same sex, for no size or other points of differentiation are made in the photograph. Even the slogan is softer in English ("A moment of pleasure with a 100 mm cigarette") than in Spanish ("The most pleasurable moments are with a 100 mm cigarette").

American and multinational companies increased efforts exponentially during the 1980s and 1990s to compete in the growing Hispanic market. Some of the big spenders today are Procter & Gamble, AT&T, MCI, Sears Roebuck, McDonald's, Anheuser-Busch, Toyota, Kraft Foods, Johnson & Johnson, and Colgate-Palmolive. The largest 50 advertisers in the Hispanic market spent over $545 million in 1999. Total spending in the Hispanic market went from about $150 million in the early 1980s to over $1.89 billion in 1999 (Dougherty, 1999). This figure still represents less than 10% of total U.S. marketing budgets and thus constitutes less on a per capita basis than is spent in general market U.S. advertising. Increasing clutter means that advertisers will have to find other ways to capture the Hispanic buyer's attention and loyalty.

A frequently repeated description of U.S. Latinos is that they tend to be brand loyal. Their preference for well-known brands, familiar within the Hispanic community, is well documented (Saegert et al., 1985; Stankevich, 1998). But recently, cheaper, private-label products have been challenging the major brands' dominant market shares among Hispanics. Yankelovich Hispanic Monitor reported that 79% of the Latinos they surveyed bought store brands in 1995, compared to 65% in 1992 and 42% in 1988 (Kim, 1995).

What may seem confusing illustrates the importance of understanding cultural values rather than product behavior. What seemed to be loyalty to well-known brands may in fact have been lack of information about products in the marketplace and a preference for familiar brands. Goya, a well-known Puerto Rican food processor, had a 65% market share in categories where it competed in New York until U.S. firms like Del Monte began targeting New York Hispanics too. Brand name is important to U.S. Latino shoppers as an indicator of quality, especially in unfamiliar situations and/or product categories (Albonetti & Dominguez, 1989; Faber, O'Guinn, & McCarty, 1987; Fisher, 1993).

Three key tactics have been used to build familiarity with Latino consumers: hiring practices, support of community events and goodwill, and aggressive sales promotions and celebrity advertising. Coca-Cola has used all of these. It has recruited U.S. Latino employees via Latino-targeted media and schools since the early 1980s. It is visible at Hispanic festivals such as Cinco de Mayo in Los Angeles, Puerto Rico Day Parade in New York, Calle Ocho in Miami, and Fiesta in San Antonio. Selena Quintanilla appeared in Coca-Cola advertising in the Southwest, where her Tejano music style was popular among Mexican Americans. Her appeal was limited in New York, Chicago, and Miami, so Coca-Cola added other up-and-coming Latino music stars, put the ads on MTV, and appealed to young Hispanics of all musical tastes.

Advertising that builds awareness of brand names or features is not enough to communicate that the seller is a member of the Latino community family (Penaloza & Gilly, 1999). A fuller complement of communication tools is needed to build a presence in the Hispanic consumer's mind. Sponsoring school programs and events and public service campaigns are other ways to fit into the Latino subculture community. Figure 5.4 shows two examples of integrated marketing programs built from advertising coupled with either sales promotions or philanthropy.

Like immigrants of all nationalities, Hispanics can have trouble finding products they recognize unless marketers include pictures on packages of the product inside and mention its exact location in store aisles within their commercials. New U.S. Latinos use advertising as well as programming in the media to learn how to consume American style (Penaloza, 1994; Wilson & Gutierrez, 1995, pp. 130-131).

A major ploy for capturing the attention of U.S. Latino consumers is the inclusion of Latino celebrities at ethnic events and in marketing communications.

*(text continues on page 161)*

**Figure 5.3a.** Benson & Hedges Print Ad in English: "Sitting & Talking"

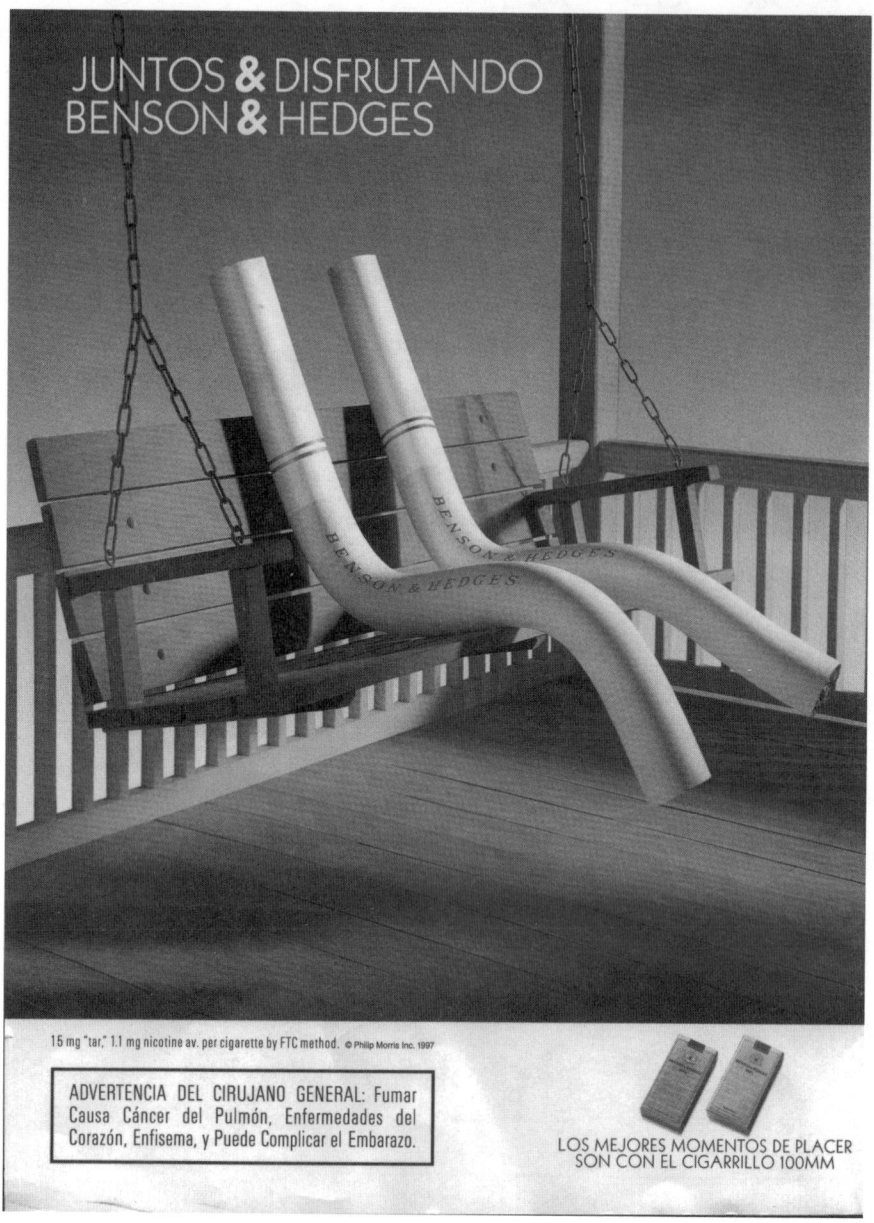

**Figure 5.3b.** Benson & Hedges Print Ad in Spanish: "Juntos & Disfrutando"

The exhibition is made possible by **GOYA** FOODS INC.

**Figure 5.4a.** Supporting the Hispanic Community: Goya Supports Hispanic Arts

**Figure 5.4b.** Supporting the Hispanic Community: Colgate Sponsors a Smile Sweepstakes

Sports figures such as baseball player Roberto Clemente, boxer Roberto Duran, and golfer Nancy Lopez, as well as acting celebrities such as Rita Moreno, Jimmy Smits, Antonio Banderas, Andy Garcia, Edward James Olmos and musicians such as Jennifer Lopez, Enrique Iglesias, Jose Feliciano, Gloria and Emilio Estefan, Ricky Martin, Shakira, Celia Cruz, Los Lobos, Tito Puente, and Marc Anthony, are well-known role models of American success among U.S. Hispanics.

Leisure time in the Hispanic household is frequently spent participating in festivities with family and friends. They may patronize fast-food restaurants and eat ready-made American-style foods, but they are likely to cook from scratch for events with an ethnic theme (Berman, 1994). In this context, event sponsorships have high visibility, just as the use of Hispanic spokespersons defines the seller as an extended member of the Latino community. The patronage of both fast-food restaurants and ethnic festivals shows the variable influence of ethnic identity in product choices across consumption situations.

Two aspects of Hispanic consumer identity affect the strength of subculture influence when making purchase decisions. First, the level of "felt ethnicity" is situational, depending on social dynamics of purchasing and consumption occasions (Stayman & Deshpande, 1989). Second, there is significant variation in Hispanic self-designated ethnicity (Deshpande et al., 1986), suggesting that cultural influence is minimal when persons do not strongly identify as Hispanic. Thus, purchasing decisions for products such as packaged goods in general (analgesics, bar soaps, detergents, toys) may show very little cultural influence, and these have been successfully marketed to U.S. Latinos using mainstream market strategies. But for other categories (or for particular brands within the aforementioned categories), such as soft drinks, beer, or anything that has a strongly regional or local flavor to it, ethnicity can be a stronger influence on brand choice.

In sum, ethnicity as an influence in Hispanic purchasing decisions varies by product or service category, purchase and use situation, socioeconomic background, language preference, language and type of communication medium, individual consumer, and geographic location. In other words, cultural values have a pervasive influence on a person's view of the world, which in turn determines that individual's needs and aspirations. In contrast, a person's ethnic identity may or may not explain preferences for one brand over another or different rates of consumption within particular product categories.

## SUMMARY

The U.S. Hispanic market includes people of many races, countries of origin, economic statuses, degrees and types of language fluency, and levels of acculturation. These differences provide a foundation for exploring effective ways to segment the U.S. Latino market. At the same time, ethnic expression and behavior tend to vary by individual and by situation. In this context, Spanish has a unifying and symbolic value. Other important cultural values are the importance of the family, personalized relationships, and hierarchy, as well as conservative and traditional family roles.

Among this fastest growing ethnic group, over 60% have their origins in Mexico, followed by those from other Central and South American countries, Puerto Rico, the Dominican Republic, and Cuba. U.S. Latinos are concentrated in the South and the Southwest and around major urban areas such as New York and Chicago. This geographic concentration makes for effective reach via Spanish-language and spot media.

Successful marketers understand that such diversity precludes simple rules of thumb when designing communication programs. Language translation may or may not be appropriate to reach a particular Hispanic target market. Early marketers made the well-cited translation mistakes shown in Table 5.7. More subtle but equally disastrous are communications that are not compatible with Hispanic subculture values. Having a presence in Hispanic-oriented media, aggressively using sales promotions, participating in Latino community events, and contributing to social causes of interest to Hispanics have been cited as effective marketing tools for constructing partnerships with Latino consumers.

**TABLE 5.7**  Classic Hispanic Marketing Mistakes

| Product or Company | Mainstream U.S. or Original English Marketing | Hispanic Cultural or Spanish Translation Misfire |
|---|---|---|
| Coors | "Turn it loose" | "Get the runs with . . . " |
| Pet food | "For the cat not wanting to die a ninth death" | Cats only have seven lives in Latin folk culture |
| Telephone | Wife to husband: "Run downstairs to call Maria and tell her we'll be late." | Not typical of husband-wife interaction, nor do guests typically call to say they'll be late. |
| Braniff Airline | "Fly in luxurious leather seats" | "Fly in the nude" |

*(Continued)*

**TABLE 5.7** Classic Hispanic Marketing Mistakes (Continued)

| Product or Company | Mainstream U.S. or Original English Marketing | Hispanic Cultural or Spanish Translation Misfire |
|---|---|---|
| Tropicana Orange Juice | "Orange juice" | "China" or "juice from the Orient" (term used for "orange" is used only in Puerto Rico) |
| Perdue chicken | "It takes a tough man to make a tender chicken." | "It takes a sexually stimulated man to make a chicken affectionate." |
| Cigarette | "Low tar" | "Low asphalt" |
| Borden Ice Cream | "Ice cream" | Nieve ("snow") |
| Adhesive bandages | "For little scratches on a child's leg" | "For coconuts on a child's leg" |
| Miller Lite | "Tastes great, less filling" | "Filling, and less delicious" |
| Budweiser | "The King of Beers" | "The Queen of Beers" (in Spanish, beer is a feminine noun) |
| Pet food | Dog served food in kitchen | Pets more likely to be kept and fed outside |
| NY Lotto | "It's exciting to win." | "It's sexually stimulating to win." |
| Billboard | Chi-cago | Cago means "defecate" in Spanish |
| L'Eggs | Model holding package says: "What L'Eggs!" | The word in Spanish for "eggs" can also mean "testicles." |
| Herculon carpets | Pronunciation: Her-cue-lawn | "Her culon" is bilingual for "her ass" |
| Insecticide | "Kills insects!" | "Kills male genitals!" |
| Candy company | Package: "Over 50 years' experience" | Package: "Contains 50 anuses" (left off the "~" on the n) |
| Food company | "Burrito" | "Burrado" (means "big mistake") |

SOURCES: Westerman (1989), "Hispanic Oriented Ads Lose in the Translation" (1986), Valdes and Sesane (1995, p. 172), Soruco (1990a), Fitch (1987), Oliver (1992), Valencia (1983).

# Note

1. For discussion of research methods, see Morrow (1988), Rodriguez (1990), Saegert and Deiter (1980), Soruco (1990a, 1990b), and Hernandez and Kaufman (1990).

# CHAPTER 6

# African Americans

## Ethnic Roots, Cultural Diversity

Jerome D. Williams
Marye C. Tharp

## THE MYTH OF RACE, THE REALITY OF RACIAL PREJUDICE

### The Myth of Race

It is a shock for many Americans to learn that race is nothing more than a so-cially constructed category, that there is no biological basis for classifying peo-ple according to skin color, body form, or any other physical variations (Fish, 1995). All that we really measure are the differences in how people look and the arbitrary and culturally specific ways that different societies classify physical variability. About 70% of cultural anthropologists and one half of physical an-thropologists reject race as a biological category (Begley, 1995b). Nevertheless,

---

Authors' Note: The terms *African American* and *Black* are used interchangeably in this chapter to improve readability. They have no other intended significance.

the recognition, even legislation, of racial categories has been a central theme in American history.

Americans have historically taken a binary approach toward race, assuming that only two races count and that skin color is the dividing line between them. This belief is rooted in the "one-drop rule," a relic of slavery and segregation that classified people as "Black" if they had one drop of "Black" blood (Morganthau, 1995). The "one-drop rule" has not been applied to any other group, whether Native or Anglo Americans or Chinese or Jewish immigrants. The arbitrariness of this definition of race is expressed by Papa Doc Duvalier's alleged answer to a journalist's question about the racial composition of Haitians. He replied, "We're 99% White of course, since most of us have mixed blood" (Tilove, 1998, p. 53).

Even peoples who seem indisputably "White" have not always been "White" in the United States. In 1924, Congress restricted immigration of so-called "inferior races" from southern and eastern Europe (Italians and Romanians) (Cose, 2000). Over time, Italians, Irish, Jews, and Romanians have all been reclassified as "White." Because Americans are accustomed to classifying anyone with African heritage as "Black," most of us do not question the fact that we treat African Americans differently from other peoples (David, 1991).

The definition of "Black" has not always been so rigid. In the American colonies, free mulattoes were not considered Black. Prior to the Civil War, several Southern states allowed people of mixed Black-White descent to be defined either as White or as something between Black and White. After the war, tolerance for racial ambiguity and mulatto privilege evaporated, and laws were passed that lowered to zero the percentage of "Black" genes a White person could have. Though many of these racial classification statutes no longer exist, the tradition continues. As recently as 1986, the U.S. Supreme Court let stand a lower-court ruling that forced a Louisiana woman with negligible African heritage to be legally defined as Black (Cose, 1995).

What most Americans perceive as racial differences between Blacks and Whites are more likely cultural differences and a different basis of ethnic identity. Whereas U.S. Latinos and Asian Americans see their ethnic and racial origins as separate sources of identity, African Americans are far less likely to make this distinction. And for the majority of Whites of European descent, neither race nor ethnicity is as important to social identity as either one is for other Americans (Alba, 1990). These differences point to why race continues to be perceived, by both members of the group and outsiders, as the distinctive characteristic of African Americans. For many African Americans, the physical characteristics associated with "being Black" are important to ethnic identity and are learned as part of the American "experience" (Wagner & Soberon-Ferrer, 1990). Whether they prefer the label *Black, Black American,* or *African American,* they believe they share the same "race" and heritage of American slavery.

The controversy over the interracial heritage of African Americans is a legacy of laws that made it illegal for Blacks and Whites to marry before the 1960s. Although it was illegal, nearly 75% of African Americans in the 1960s had Euro-American ancestors from sexual unions outside marriage. Today's percentage of "unmixed" African Americans is even smaller. Most African Americans are "probably as far from the pure Negroid type as from the average Caucasoid type" (Carr-Ruffino, 1996, p. 213). In addition, there is a growing number of interracial couples and their offspring. In 1990 (no newer data are available), there were estimated to be over 2 million interracial married couples in the United States, up from only 321,000 in 1970. Of those interracial unions, 20% claimed Black-White heritage and 2% Black and "other race" (Cose, 2000).

In the 2000 census, the Census Bureau recognized our increasing racial diversity (Morganthau, 1995). Earlier census forms required respondents to classify themselves as White; Black; Asian or Pacific Islander; American Indian, Eskimo, or Aleut; or "other." The questionnaires provided a separate Hispanic/Spanish-origin box in addition to the racial categories. The 1990 census generated write-ins for 300 "races," 600 Indian tribes, 70 Hispanic groups, and 75 combinations of multiracial ancestry (Wynter, 1996c). In the 2000 census, forms allowed respondents to check multiple categories for racial background. The expanded categories for race included White, African American, American Indian or Alaskan Native, Asian-Indian, Chinese, Filipino, Japanese, Korean, Vietnamese, "other Asian," Native Hawaiian, Guamanian or Chamorro, Samoan, "other Pacific Islander," and "other race."

The new way races are reported could have a profound impact on marketers who depend on census statistics for target marketing efforts. The child of a mixed African American and Caucasian marriage, who previously would have been reported as either Black or White, will soon have the choice of being reported in an additional category. The potential race classifications jump from 15 to 63 if just two choices are made. Future statistics on race may be more accurate, allowing marketers to gain a better understanding of multiculturalism and the potential for growth among those consumers. The bad news is that the new statistics will be difficult to compare with older databases, especially if many people have made multiple choices in the 2000 census (Teinowitz, 1998).

As more people of mixed racial and ethnic backgrounds start giving equal weight to each of their respective racial and ethnic heritages, it becomes increasingly difficult to place people into discrete racial/ethnic cells—the "Tiger Woods phenomenon." The famous golfer of mixed racial background has refused to classify himself, or let others classify him, as Black, Asian, or any of the racial/ethnic groups represented in his family. Individuals belonging to a particular ethnic or cultural group may not share the common understanding of that group, and they may even identify with another group (Darley & Williams, 2000; Sasao & Sue, 1993).

## The Reality of Racial Prejudice

Even if race is a mythical basis for differences between African Americans and members of other subcultures, it is the touchstone of our experiences with each other as Americans. "Other ethnic groups were never slaves in this country, so there is not the moral tension there. Black and White relations are the true test of whether we as a nation are going to be able to overcome racism" (Shepard, 1997, p. J6).

Racial prejudice is an elusive concept to measure. Early research clearly showed anti-Black attitudes prevalent among Whites until the early 1960s (Katz, 1970). Later surveys have indicated anti-Black prejudice among Whites as less prevalent (Campbell, 1971; Greeley & Sheatsley, 1971; Hyman & Sheatsley, 1956, 1964; Sigelman & Welch, 1984; Smith & Dempsey, 1983; Taylor, Sheatsley, & Greeley, 1978), but many of the traditional items used in racial opinion surveys are highly susceptible to social desirability influences (McConahay, 1986; McConahay, Hardee, & Batts, 1981). What may have changed over time is the social acceptability of *expressing* prejudice rather than actual racial attitudes.

*Ethnocentrism* refers to our natural human tendency to accept those who seem to be like us and reject those who appear dissimilar (Sumner, 1906). Consumer ethnocentrism describes a preference for companies, brands, and/or stores owned by people who are most like ourselves or who have the same national (or ethnic) origins (Shimp & Sharma, 1987). One might expect that African American consumers with strong African American racial and ethnic identity would be more likely to prefer African American-owned businesses. Studies have found that Blacks do tend to reduce their purchases from White retailers during periods of racial strife, but "Buy Black" does not drive the purchasing criteria of most African American consumers under normal circumstances (Gensch & Staelin, 1972; Hills, Granbois, & Patterson, 1973; Petrof, 1963, 1967; Whipple & Neidell, 1971; Williams & Qualls, 1989).

Motivated by a deep belief in the possibility of racial integration, leaders in the 1960s civil rights movement were convinced that racial inequality could be uprooted by changing laws regulating public behavior and social relations. It is a paradox of desegregation that our racial divisions have widened. We cling to stereotyped views that suggest there are racial differences between African Americans and other Americans. In a 1991 survey of racial attitudes among White Americans, 62% said Blacks were more likely to be lazy, 56% said they were violence prone, 53% said they were less intelligent, and 51% thought they were less patriotic (Dirke, 1991). Television news journalists feed racial stereotypes by painting a picture of Black men as violent and threatening toward Whites and Black women as welfare mothers (Entman, 1994). Repetition of social myths, misconceptions, stupidity, and outright bigotry frames how Americans see African Americans (Dates & Pease, 1994).

In recent years, there has been an increase in the number of incidents where members of one ethnic group, as consumers, are engaged in some type of violent confrontation with members of another ethnic group, as store owners. Since the 1970s, these "retail-ethnic" conflicts have occurred in a number of cities where African Americans were the primary customers (e.g., in Detroit with Middle Eastern store owners, in Washington with Chinese merchants, and in Miami with Cuban merchants) (Hatchett, 1988; Smith, 1990). Other incidents have involved African Americans and Asians, particularly Korean store owners in urban communities (Dubin, 1990; Dubin & Clark, 1990; Okazawa-Rey & Wong, 1997; Penaloza & Gilly, 1999).

Williams and Snuggs (1996) found that African Americans believe there is discrimination in the marketplace, whereas White Americans think that race has no impact on services provided. Direct measures of marketplace discrimination have found that all consumers are *not* treated equally (Williams, Qualls, & Grier, 1995; Yinger, 1986). Fewer apartments at higher prices are available to customers of color (Berger, 1992; Donnerstein, Donnerstein, & Koch, 1975; Johnson, Porter, & Mateljan, 1991; Reed, 1991). Discriminatory practices affect every stage of the mortgage loan approval process (Myers & Chan, 1995). Both African Americans and women are quoted higher prices than White males for new automobiles (Ayres & Siegelman, 1995). "Hidden camera" investigations on television newsmagazines such as *Dateline* and *20/20* and articles in the popular press have charged that African Americans wait longer or are denied service at restaurants (Hawkins, 1993; U.S. Attorney General, 1997) and automobile rental agencies ("PA Files Complaint," 1997; Tejada, 1996); African American males are not picked up by taxicab drivers ("Cab Company," 1995); African American females are not granted fitness club memberships ("San Francisco," 1996); and restaurants and other businesses refuse to deliver to sections of towns on the basis of race or class alone ("San Francisco," 1996).

> As young Blacks or Latinos walk into a store, security guards nervously
> shadow them. As they walk toward the cash register and the checkout line,
> White matrons grip their purses tighter. Video cameras record every step until
> the teenagers leave the store. (Marable, 1994, p. 11)

These incidents create dissatisfied customers likely to discontinue patronage and disseminate negative word of mouth. The long-term consequences of disparate treatment of consumer groups can include organized boycotts, negative publicity, and lawsuits. They constitute a substantial drain on managerial resources. Table 6.1 lists a number of incidents and the negative publicity they generated. If it is true that marketers are "not as concerned about the color of a customer's skin as they are the color of his/her money," then such incidents trumpet the need to put that philosophy into action.

## AFRICAN AMERICAN DIVERSITY

### Diverse Heritage and Resources

The term *diaspora* comes from a Greek word that describes the scattering of a group of people with a common background. With regard to African Americans, it refers to the great migrations—voluntary and involuntary—of Africans to other continents. Fifty years ago, most Black Americans were descendants of slaves; today, many African Americans trace their roots more directly to Africa or the Caribbean and Latin America (Palomo, 1996). What may appear to be a culturally unified group is in fact people who share an African heritage but who may come from different countries of origin.

Until recently, few African Americans made distinctions between their ethnic and racial identities. Any known or perceptible African ancestry made a person "Black," with no distinctions for Blacks of African or Caribbean ancestry (Jandt, 1995). Today, 1.7 million Caribbean-origin people identify their race as Black and their ethnic origin as Hispanic. Blacks of recent African heritage dis-

**TABLE 6.1**  Incidents of Racial Prejudice in the Marketplace

A Black man found himself surrounded by sheriff's deputies, pistols in hand, when bank employees called police, thinking he might be a bank robber because he was sitting in his car outside the bank. Actually, he was studying brochures deciding how to invest his savings before entering the bank (Williams & Snuggs, 1996).

In a shopping mall, a security guard stopped two Black teenagers when they tried to leave an upscale store, solely on the basis that they were wearing new shirts. He suspected that they had entered the store and exchanged shirts and were now trying to leave. As it turned out, their father had bought the shirts for them the day before (personal experience of author).

A video store found itself surrounded by police cars after a call was made to stop a robbery in progress. The report was traced to a woman who passed the store and saw a large cardboard cutout of a Black man with a gun drawn as a promotion for a recently released videotape (*Lethal Weapon*). She assumed the person in the cutout was actually a robber and called police (Williams & Snuggs, 1996).

A Black man who was accused of shoplifting and subjected to a strip search along with his 6-year-old son at a New Jersey Bloomingdale's filed a lawsuit against the store and White security guards involved in the incident. On February 10, 1996, Lloyd Morrison was shopping with his son and had already bought him two suits. Morrison left the dressing room to return some pants that didn't fit his son. He was accosted by the security guards, who accused him of taking three pair of pants into the dressing room and only returning two. When Morrison said he didn't know what they were talking about, he was ordered to accompany security under threat of being handcuffed and was taken to a room in the back of the store. After Morrison once again insisted that he hadn't done anything, they demanded that he take off his jacket, his shirt, and ultimately his pants to prove that he wasn't concealing clothes underneath. His son was forced to take his pants off as well (Futterman & Nugest, 1997).

On October 20, 1995, a young African American man shopping at an Eddie Bauer outlet was detained and ordered to remove his Eddie Bauer shirt because he could not produce a receipt. Within 3 months, he and two other teens filed an $85 million suit against Eddie Bauer alleging false imprisonment, defamation, and violations of civil rights. A federal jury eventually found in favor of the young men and awarded the three plaintiffs $1 million. Almost 3 years later, Eddie Bauer management is still appealing the jury's decision (Castaneda & Spinner, 1997).

A series of "Bud Light Spotlight" commercials were to show actual Bud Light drinkers. A Bud Light film crew picked Dugan's, a sports bar in Atlanta, to participate. The owner was delighted to be included, even though the ad would show the interiors without flashing the bar's name. Representatives from Anheuser-Busch discussed including some of Dugan's employees and 350 predominantly African American clientele in the spot. But when the camera crew showed up, they brought about 25 "real" Bud Light consumers, only two of whom were Black. Dugan's no longer serves Bud Light or any other Anheuser-Busch product. "Whoever had the responsibility of setting this up should have been more sensitive" to the bar's regular patrons (Goldman, 1993a, p. B12).

tinguish themselves from Blacks who are the descendants of American slaves. Caribbean and African-origin Blacks have this "double identity" that their African American cohorts do not share. Caribbean-origin Blacks tend to settle in Florida and the Northeast. Now about 20% of all African- and Caribbean-origin Blacks are moving into New York City while other African Americans are moving out (Edmondson, 1996). In Queens, New York, for example, there are apartment buildings, city blocks, and even neighborhoods segregated by African-origin Black, Caribbean-origin Black, and African American residents.

As Table 6.2 indicates, the nation's African American population will almost double over the next five decades. From about 34 million in 2000, African Americans are expected to reach 45 million by 2030 and 54 million by 2050. The African American share of the U.S. population will slowly increase from about 12% today to 14% in 2050 (U.S. Bureau of the Census, 1996). Hispanics will replace Blacks as the largest minority before 2010 because they are growing at a much faster rate, but African American growth is still higher than that of the White population (Fisher, 1996). In 1980, one of five Americans had a minority background (African, Asian, Hispanic, or Native American); in 1990, this figure was one in four, and in 2000, it was one in three (U.S. Bureau of Statistics, 1995).

African American households show other aspects of the diversity in this community. The 1997 median income of $25,050 for African American households was less than that of any other ethnic group. Yet at the same time, the number of poor African Americans in the nation decreased and their real median household income improved (U.S. Bureau of the Census, 1998a, 1998d). Income per household member was $11,998, based on an average household size of 2.75 people. For comparison, the average in White households was $20,093 for 2.58 people, and the estimate for Asian and Pacific Islander households was $18,569 for 3.17 people. The per capita income of African Americans was $12,351 in 1997, compared with $20,425 for Whites, $18,226 for Asian and Pacific Islanders, and $10,773 for Hispanics (U.S. Bureau of the Census, 1998a). By most of these yardsticks, African American disposable income is less than that of other Americans.

There are also great disparities among Black families in terms of resources and structure (McAdoo, 1992). In 1998, there were 8.4 million African American households. About one half of those households had married-couple families, compared to over 80% for Whites of Hispanic and non-Hispanic origins and for Asian households. Some 1.4 million Black children lived with grandparents and 4 million with both parents. Inner-city households are composed of a variety of related and nonrelated residents, whereas suburban Black households mirror their White counterparts and are more likely to contain two parents and children.

**TABLE 6.2** African American Population Growth, 1990-2050

| Year | Total (in 1,000s) | Not of Hispanic Origin | | | | Hispanic Origin[c] |
|---|---|---|---|---|---|---|
| | | White | Black | American Indian[a] | Asian[b] | |
| 1990 | 249,402 | 75.6% | 11.8% | 0.7% | 2.8% | 9.0% |
| 2000 | 274,634 | 71.8% | 12.2% | 0.7% | 3.3% | 11.4% |
| 2010 | 297,716 | 68.0% | 12.6% | 0.8% | 4.8% | 13.8% |
| 2020 | 322,742 | 64.3% | 12.9% | 0.8% | 5.7% | 16.3% |
| 2030 | 346,889 | 60.5% | 13.1% | 0.8% | 6.6% | 18.9% |
| 2040 | 369,980 | 56.7% | 13.3% | 0.9% | 7.5% | 21.7% |
| 2050 | 393,931 | 52.8% | 13.6% | 0.9% | 8.2% | 24.5% |

SOURCE: Adapted from U.S. Bureau of the Census (1996).

a. *American Indian* represents American Indian, Eskimo, and Aleut.

b. *Asian* represents Asian and Pacific Islander.

c. Persons of Hispanic origin may be of any race.

The ratio of Black-to-White median family income varies from 59% for female-headed families to 80% for married-couple families. A White family making more than $50,000 is much more likely to contain a husband making $75,000 and a nonworking wife. In African American families within the same income category, "the husband is likely to be a bus driver earning $32,000, while the wife brings home $28,000 as a teacher or nurse" (Gates, 1992, p. 61). Total African American disposable income rose 54% between 1990 and 1997. Disposable income for the United States as a whole jumped 41%, whereas the African American share rose from 7.5% to 8.2%, for a total of over $469 billion (Wynter, 1997a).

## Diversity Across Class and Residence

The African American community has always had significant diversity and stratification. Social distinctions among slaves were based on where they worked (in the fields or the plantation house) and on the color of their skin (Pinkney, 1969). Early consumer researchers studied low-income Blacks mostly in urban areas and mistakenly generalized the results as representative of all African American consumers (Reid, Stagmaier, & Reid, 1986; Robinson & Rao, 1986; Williams, 1989a). Significant differences across class, geographic location, and age defy the stereotypes about African American consumers that such extrapolations generate. In fashion, J. C. Penney has learned that regional tastes have more influence than ethnicity (Wynter, 1997b).

A central feature of African American economic life since the 1960s has been the simultaneous growth of the middle class and an underclass. Civil rights measures led to upward mobility for many African Americans. The middle class grew dramatically while the really poor tended to get poorer. The middle class began moving up and out to the suburbs, earning more, sending their children to college, and living better. Meanwhile, the underclass began sinking further into intergenerational poverty, with increasing unemployment rates for young men and a dramatic rise in female-headed families. In 1998, about 29% of African Americans lived in the suburbs, whereas 54% lived in central cities, an approximation of the proportionate sizes of the middle class and the poor.

In 1988, about one third of all African American households had incomes of $35,000 or more, compared with 70% of all Euro-American households. However, incomes in the average Black household rose more than six times faster than in White households between 1989 and 1997 (Simons, 1998). Most of this group is still first-generation middle class. They tend to be employees of others rather than owners and managers, and they have relatively little accumulated wealth. One difference between middle-class African Americans and Whites is the likelihood that more relatives of African Americans will come to them for help. Another distinction is that most African Americans lack the resources of people who started life in the middle class (Ellis, 1988; Simons, 1998).

A long-standing if controversial hypothesis is that the more middle class African Americans are, the weaker their ethnic or race commitment (Frazier, 1957, p. 13; Goldsmith, White, & Stith, 1987; Ness & Stith, 1984; Sampson & Milam, 1975). Early studies characterized Black middle-class life as embodying the "worst of Anglo America" and as being representative of a loss of ethnic identity (Dollard, 1937; Drake & Cayton, 1962; Frazier, 1957; Greer & Cobb, 1968; Hare, 1970; Myrdal, 1944). The movement of African Americans into the middle class has been treated as analogous to the assimilation process of immigrants as they become part of the American mainstream over time and generations. Middle-class African Americans are supposedly caught in a dual identity crisis—participate in mainstream America or remain African American—with the result that they do not wholly belong to either group (Cruse, 1967; Woodson, 1933). DuBois (1907) called this the "double consciousness" of being an American and being Black, leading to perpetual conflict between the two social roles. African American consumers who have moved up the socioeconomic ladder may have consumption patterns much like those of their White counterparts, but this does not necessarily mean that they have lost strong ethnic identity (Williams & Qualls, 1989).

At the other end of the scale are increasing numbers of African Americans who are still trapped in poverty. In 1992, 43% of all African American children were living in poverty, most without fathers (Carr-Ruffino, 1996; Thernstrom & Thernstrom, 1997). In the same year, homicide was the leading cause of death for African American males aged 15 to 34, and 23% of men aged 20 to 29 were in prison, on probation, or on parole (Morganthau, 1992). Poor African Americans tend to live in inner cities across the nation and in rural areas of the South. Chicago, home to about 1.4 million Blacks in 2001, is one of America's most segregated places.

Forty-two percent of the inner-city population is African American, whereas 31% is Hispanic and 23% White (Vincenti, 1998). Inner-city households are more likely to consist of a single person or a single parent with children than to be two-parent households. They are also more likely to be headed by either younger adults (under 35 years) or seniors (aged 65 or older). And women are significantly more likely to run inner-city households than men (Mogelonsky, 1998). The median household income in inner cities is no more than 75% of the median for the entire city. The unemployment rate can run 30% or greater. In some locations, the poverty rate is at least 50% greater than the city average (Mogelonsky, 1998).

Though inner-city shoppers may not be as wealthy as people in the suburbs, they do have money to spend—and they spend much of it in their neighborhoods. These 7.7 million households have more than $85 billion to spend each year, and they account for 7% of total retail spending (Vincenti, 1998).

During the 1980s, the great migration of Blacks from the rural South to northern cities slowed to a trickle and then reversed. Now a small stream is flowing in the other direction. Affluent Blacks are finding the good life in southern suburbs, and lower-income Blacks are looking for a better life in the land of their grandparents. The proportion of Blacks living in the South decreased steadily for most of this century, from 90% in 1900 to 53% in 1980, but it is projected to remain at 53% through 2010 (Edmondson, 1996).

Table 6.3 shows the African American share of population across regions and states and in several metropolitan areas. As shown in the table, more than 4 in 10 residents of the Memphis metropolitan area are Black, and more than 3 in 10 residents of the New York metropolitan area are Black (Fisher, 1996). Rich-

**TABLE 6.3**  Top African American Cities and States

| City or State | Size of African American Population (in 1,000s) | % of Local Population | % of African Americans |
|---|---|---|---|
| **All African Americans (1997)** | **33,644** | **12.7** | **100.0** |
| **Selected SMSAs**[a] **(1996)** | | | |
| **Top 10:** | **11,152** | | 33.15 |
| New York | 2,647 | 30.8 | 7.87 |
| Chicago | 1,504 | 19.5 | 4.47 |
| Washington, DC | 1,173 | 25.7 | 3.49 |
| Los Angeles | 1,068 | 11.6 | 3.17 |
| Detroit | 1,016 | 23.4 | 3.02 |
| Philadelphia | 998 | 20.0 | 2.97 |
| Atlanta | 886 | 25.6 | 2.63 |
| Houston | 726 | 19.2 | 2.16 |
| Baltimore | 647 | 25.8 | 1.92 |
| Dallas | 487 | 16.2 | 1.45 |
| **Other U.S. Cities** | | | |
| New Orleans | 472 | 35.7 | 1.40 |
| Miami | 472 | 23.0 | 1.40 |
| Newark | 459 | 23.7 | 1.36 |
| Norfolk/Va. Beach | 453 | 29.2 | 1.35 |
| Memphis | 450 | 41.7 | 1.34 |

a. SMSA stands for Standard Metropolitan Statistical Area

mond-Petersburg, Norfolk-Virginia Beach-Newport News, New Orleans, Baltimore, Atlanta, and Washington DC all have populations that are more than one-fourth Black (Fisher, 1996). Sixty percent of all Blacks in the Midwest live in just six metropolitan areas (Chicago, Detroit, St. Louis, Cleveland, Kansas City, and Milwaukee). In the Northeast, 64% live in New York City, Newark, or Philadelphia. In the West, 46% live in Los Angeles or Oakland (Fisher, 1996).

A growing number of African American households are considered affluent. The number of affluent Black households grew from 338,000 in 1967 to 1.3 million in 1990. Today, about one Black household in eight has an income of $50,000 or more. From 1994 to 1998, the African American share of households with over $100,000 income tripled (Lach, 1999; McLaughlin, 1999). Cities with

**TABLE 6.3**  Top African American Cities and States (Continued)

| City or State | Size of African American Population (in 1,000s) | % of Local Population | % of African Americans |
|---|---|---|---|
| **Selected U.S. States (1997)** | | | |
| **Top 5 Total:** | **12,555** | | **36.47** |
| New York | 3,220 | 17.7 | 9.35 |
| California | 2,456 | 7.5 | 7.13 |
| Texas | 2,430 | 12.3 | 7.06 |
| Florida | 2,268 | 15.2 | 6.59 |
| Georgia | 2,181 | 28.5 | 6.34 |
| **Selected Other States:** | | | **43.67** |
| Illinois | 1,840 | 15.3 | 5.34 |
| North Carolina | 1,665 | 22.1 | 4.84 |
| Maryland | 1,428 | 27.8 | 4.15 |
| Louisiana | 1,407 | 32.2 | 4.09 |
| Michigan | 1,405 | 14.3 | 4.08 |
| Virginia | 1,363 | 20.1 | 3.96 |
| Ohio | 1,290 | 11.5 | 3.75 |
| New Jersey | 1,188 | 14.6 | 3.45 |
| Pennsylvania | 1,166 | 9.7 | 3.39 |
| South Carolina | 1,147 | 29.9 | 3.33 |
| Alabama | 1,132 | 26.0 | 3.29 |

SOURCES: Fisher (1996), U.S. Bureau of the Census (2000).

the largest numbers of African Americans in suburbs include Washington, Atlanta, Los Angeles, Miami, and Philadelphia (O'Hare & Frey, 1992). Affluent Blacks spend heavily on expensive clothing and are more likely to buy a convertible (O'Hare & Frey, 1992).

In most ways, affluent African Americans are like any other affluent consumers. They are likely to be middle aged, married, and relatively well educated and to own their own homes. Like many prosperous Americans, African Americans reach the $50,000-per-year household income threshold by combining the earnings of two or more workers, for only 3% of Black workers make more than $50,000 a year. Also, affluent Blacks are less likely than affluent Whites to be in the very top income bracket, $100,000 or more. This group constitutes 1.1% of Black households, compared to 4.7% of White households. Though affluent Whites are evenly spread across the four major regions of the country, 45% of affluent African Americans live in the South. Most affluent Blacks live in central cities of metropolitan areas, whereas affluent Whites tend to reside in the suburbs. Also, the proportion of affluent Whites living in rural areas (16%) is more than twice the proportion of affluent Blacks in rural areas (7%) (O'Hare, 1992a).

## Diversity Across Generations

*Not every African American person is a basketball player or a thug. . . . Not all black people speak in slang, wear jeans hanging off them [and are] getting high. That's what's portrayed on TV.*
                                                                    Cose, 1997, p. 62

Half of all African Americans, 17 million people, are under 30 years of age. The wedge between African American generations is hip-hop music and lifestyles (Leland & Samuels, 1997). The majority of true hip-hoppers live in inner cities, though not all urban youths embrace the culture. Hordes of suburban kids—both Black and White—follow their inner-city idols in adopting everything from music to clothing and language, reflected also in the licensed sports apparel, baseball caps, oversized jeans, and gangsta rap music found in suburban shopping malls (Fisher, 1996). Although hip-hop got its start in Black America, more than 70% of hip-hop albums are purchased by Whites, and a whole generation of kids—Black, White, Latino, Asian—has grown up immersed in hip-hop (Farley, 1999). Hip-hop and rap now outsell pop and country music (Alexander, 1998).

*Urban* is the term used to refer to this market and lifestyle. Urban gets beyond racial or ethnic divides and brings together a lifestyle of fashion, attitude, street smarts, and music from all backgrounds. It has ethnic roots and uses ethnic imagery but is multiracial—Black, Latino, Asian. *Blaze,* a magazine for the hip-hop movement full of rap music, deejays, break dancing, graffiti, and fashions of baggy clothes and Timberland boots, targets readers of all ethnicities aged 12 to 24 (Alexander, 1998). The hip-hop movement prefers designers and products that don't seem to come from the mainstream, such as FUBU ("For Us, By Us") (Lucas, 1999; Wynter, 1998c).

Hip-hop and rap music and lifestyle genres do not appeal to many older African Americans. If an ad uses an older-oriented artist or a Motown style, for instance, "That's not going to work if the radio station becomes hip hop" (Leland & Samuels, 1997, p. 57). Differences in taste don't just stop at music and fashion. Marketers have found the need to segment this market by age as well as by whether the target group of African American consumers lives in suburbs or central cities.

# ETHNIC IDENTITY AND AFRICAN AMERICAN CULTURAL VALUES

## African Roots

Slavery deprived African American families of attempts to maintain original African culture—its languages and beliefs. Marriages were not recognized. Groups and families were broken up, so languages were lost. Slaves were forced to speak English, to worship in certain ways, and to conform to American beliefs. No other immigrants have met such restrictive laws limiting rights. African American culture has roots in Africa but was constructed in the United States (Jandt, 1995, pp. 329-345). The transfusion of African influences took place despite this broken connection. Not surprisingly, however, many African Americans are unaware of how much their African roots shape contemporary behaviors and attitudes (Palomo, 1996). Figure 6.1 shows an advertising appeal to pride in "African Roots."

Many writers describe African American life and cultural style as holistic, with all parts of a person's thinking, feeling, behaving, and being inextricably connected (Boykin, 1983; Nobles, 1980). Nine areas particularly express African-origin norms. Table 6.4 shows these in contrast to beliefs that dominate other American subcultures. For example, an emphasis on collectivism among U.S. Latinos, Asian Americans, and African Americans contrasts with the individualism of mainstream America. African spirituality and beliefs about expressing emotion are more similar to those of U.S. Latinos than to those of mainstream Americans. Asian and African Americans share attitudes about harmony between humans and their environment and the circularity of time. As mainstream America makes room for more diverse peoples, their cultures of origin are certain to nudge mainstream beliefs in these directions.

A growing number of African Americans insist on viewing the world from an "African-centered" perspective (Early, 1995). Authenticity, "being real," is essential in Afrocentrism. Significant weight is attached to personal qualities such as "telling it like it is," "seeing the good as well as the bad," "sharing," "resil-

**Figure 6.1.** "Take Pride in Your Roots"

**TABLE 6.4**  African-Origin Beliefs Compared With Beliefs of Other American Subcultures

| African-Origin Beliefs | American Mainstream Beliefs | Latin American-Origin Beliefs | Asian-Origin Beliefs |
|---|---|---|---|
| Spirituality: | | | |
| Powers greater than humans exist and are at work | Humans can shape their destiny if God is willing | God shapes our destiny | Mixed |
| Harmony: | | | |
| Humans and their environment are interdependent and connected, as are the parts of their lives | Humans can shape their environment for humanity's betterment | Same as American mainstream | Same as African-origin |
| Movement: | | | |
| A rhythmic orientation to life, manifested in music and dance, behavior and approach | Life and time are linear; progress important | Resist change, rely on traditions | |
| Verve: | | | |
| A preference for tuning in to several stimuli rather than a singular orientation; energy and intensity | Achievement and competition directed; specialized roles; play fair; keep busy | Preserve relationships over achievement; individual style important | Preserve group cohesion; self unimportant |
| Affect: | | | |
| Emotional expressiveness and sensitivity to emotional cues; feelings and cognition integrated | Feeling and thinking are separate | Same as African-origin | Little emotion expressed |

*(Continued)*

**TABLE 6.4** African-Origin Beliefs Compared With Beliefs of Other American Subcultures (Continued)

| African-Origin Beliefs | American Mainstream Beliefs | Latin American-Origin Beliefs | Asian-Origin Beliefs |
|---|---|---|---|
| Communalism: | | | |
| Interdependence of people; a social orientation | Individualistic orientation | Same as African-origin | Same as African-origin |
| Expressive Individualism: | | | |
| Focus on a person's unique style and spontaneity | Mixture of social conformity and individual expression | Social conformity | Social conformity |
| Orality: | | | |
| Importance of information learned and transmitted orally; call and response | Low context, words equal message; direct; superiority of written word | High context, relationship determines style; indirect | Same as Latin-origin |
| Social Time Perspective: | | | |
| Time viewed in terms of the event rather than the clock | Linear concept of time and future orientation | Social time and past orientation | Time is circular and social |

SOURCES: Adapted from Willis (1992), Carr-Ruffino (1996), Hammond and Morrison (1996), de Mooij (1998), Hofstede (1997).

ience," and "distrust of mainstream institutions" within the African American community (Hecht et al., 1993). Assertiveness, speaking up, and expressing emotions are other valued behaviors often misinterpreted as aggression within mainstream society (Carr-Ruffino, 1996, p. 9). Group rituals representing passages from one stage of life to another are also important in Afrocentric life, as seen in the importance of African American funerals and family celebrations of achievements.

## Ethnic Identity and Labels

When individuals identify as members of a particular ethnic group, they typically practice and retain the customs, language, and social views of the group (Devos, 1975). Still, not all individuals within a particular minority culture share all its values and expressions of behaviors; as a result, there may be different degrees of affiliation within the minority culture. For instance, one person may feel a strong identification with African American culture and less affiliation with the American mainstream, whereas a second may have weak ties to African American culture and feel more at home with mainstream American values and beliefs (Whittler, Calantone, & Young, 1991). The most common and yet most direct approach to measuring ethnic identity is a single question, "How strongly do you identify with your racial/ethnic group?" Unfortunately, this does not elicit the dual nature of African American ethnicity. Ironically, those African Americans who feel a strong identification with African American culture prefer African American-dominant ads in racially targeted media, whereas those who do not feel a strong identification prefer Whites in positions of dominance in ads in mainstream media (Green, 1999).

Ethnic identity is part of social identity for both African and European Americans, but it seems to operate very differently in the two groups (Hofman, 1985). Two central dimensions dominate African American identity, one political and the other social/personal. In contrast, Euro-American identity has a more integrated structure based on multiple aspects of social life (Hofman, 1985; Larkey & Hecht, 1991). Higher socioeconomic status is associated with self-perceptions of African Americans that include more "White traits" than "Black traits" (White & Burke, 1987). Racial inequality may not directly affect personal or racial esteem, but it does affect personal efficacy, the belief that one can accomplish goals and be successful (Hughes & Demo, 1989). Other studies show that African Americans have stronger and more positive racial, ethnic, and national identities than European Americans (Hofman, 1985; Larkey & Hecht, 1991;

Smith & Millham, 1979). Perhaps most important, African American self-esteem and strong ethnic identity are positively correlated (Larkey & Hecht, 1991; White & Burke, 1987). In sum, ethnic identity means very different things in mainstream and nonmainstream groups.

The labels used for African American self-identification are revealing of shifts in ethnic consciousness and sensitivity to the sociopolitical milieu (Hecht & Ribeau, 1991; Jackson & Gurin, 1987; Jaynes & Williams, 1989; Lampe, 1982; Smitherman, 1984). Earlier in U.S. history, labels such as *Negro* (from the Latin word *niger*, translated to *negro* in Spanish/Portuguese) and *Black* or *Black American* (the English translation for the Spanish word *negro*) derived from European languages (Fairchild, 1985). The movement from *Negro* to *Black* represented a movement from one European-based language to another but was encouraged by leaders in the community to reflect self-improvement and unity (Carmichael & Hamilton, 1967). The grouping of African Americans and other ethnic groups of color into categories such as "minority," "people of color," or "non-White" are believed by some to connote inferior roles and lesser importance (Dennis, 1994; Gettone, 1981).

No single identity or label is sufficient to describe the variation among African Americans in ethnic identity. Whereas one label or identity may be used by the majority of people or may be used in more situations, other labels reflect the diversity within the group and across situations. Three labels are consistently provided by African Americans to name their ethnic identity: *Black, Black American,* and *African American.* The preference for these labels is as follows: 39% for *Black,* 34% for *African American,* and 10% for *Black American* (Carr-Ruffino, 1996). Those choosing the label *Black* justify their selection by saying it is the right label, is generally accepted, is reflective of their skin color, and is the label they were taught. Those selecting *Black American* explain that the label means being both Black and American and that it expresses both patriotism and ethnic pride. Ethnic heritage is the rationale for those using the label *African American* (Carr-Ruffino, 1996). Though *Black* is still the most frequent self-selected label, its use may be decreasing in favor of the label *African American* (Hecht & Ribeau, 1987, 1991; Hecht, Ribeau, & Alberts, 1989; Jewell, 1985; Lampe, 1982).

Language plays an important role in the shifting nature of ethnic identity (Giles, Bourhis, & Taylor, 1977; Harre, 1989; Tajfel, 1981, 1982; Turner, 1987). Members of language communities maintain linguistic distinctiveness by using a variety of speech and nonverbal markers (e.g., vocabulary, slang, posture, gesture, discourse styles, accent) to create "psycholinguistic distinctiveness" (Giles & Coupland, 1991). African slaves developed a pidgin English to communicate with their masters. They substituted English for West African words but used the basic structure and idiom of their West African language (Smitherman, 1984). Over the years, the pidgin has evolved into Black English or Ebonics.

Social pressures, often subconscious, exist within the African American community to maintain Black English as a form of group identity and a symbol of unity (Carr-Ruffino, 1996; Hecht et al., 1993). Elements of Ebonics may be used by 80% of African Americans, but usage varies significantly in accordance with differences in degree of ethnic identity, social class, gender, age, region, and education level (Jenkins, 1982; Kochman, 1981; Smitherman, 1984). Black English is used less frequently at places of employment than in school and in conversation with family and friends (Williams & Grantham, 1999). Code switching between the language of mainstream America and Black English or Ebonics is often coupled with other communication-style changes in verbal play, nonverbal symbols, and body language.

The development of ethnic pride among African Americans evolves out of a sense of self and personal worth that explicitly takes its reference points from African American history and consciousness (Cross, 1971; Jenkins, 1982; Milliones, 1980; Thomas & Thomas, 1971). The communication style of many African Americans shows how language affirms a sense of identity, as well as an awareness that outsiders do not share that comfort zone of familiar behaviors. Code switching between Black English and that of mainstream America is the most obvious example of African American communication patterns. In addition, Blacks place importance on verbal skills and oral performance ("stylin"), call-response patterns of exchange between speaker and audience, and meaningful nonverbal messages communicated by body language, movement, eye contact, and use of time (Hecht et al., 1993, pp. 82-113).

## Balancing Two Cultures

African Americans grow up a part of, yet apart from, American mainstream society, in it but not of it, included at some levels and excluded at others. This duality is at the heart of their identity struggle and often generates powerful feelings of frustration, anger, and indignation. They must migrate back and forth between African American and Euro-American worlds and find a workable balance between different sets of beliefs as norms for behavior. W. E. B. DuBois expressed the dilemma this creates for African American identity, writing of this double consciousness, this sense of always looking at one's self through the eyes of others, of measuring one's soul by the tape of a world that looks on in bemused contempt and pity. One ever feels his twoness—an American, a Negro; two souls, two thoughts, two unreconciled strivings; two warring ideals in one dark body, whose dogged strength alone keeps it from being torn asunder. . . . The history of the American Negro is the history of this strife—this longing to attain self-conscious manhood, to merge his double self into a better and truer self. . . . He would not Africanize America, for America has too much to teach the world and Africa. He would not bleach his Negro soul in a flood of white Americanism, for he knows that Negro blood has a message for the world. He simply wishes to make it possible for a man to be both a Negro and an American, without being cursed and spit upon. (quoted in Jaynes & Williams, 1989, pp. 1-2)

During the 1960s and early 1970s, scholars assumed that African Americans wanted cultural as well as economic integration. The dominant view was that Blacks bought brands that symbolized their having become "full members" in American society (Bauer & Cunningham, 1970; Bauer, Cunningham, & Wortzel, 1965). Consumption of socially visible goods and services easily serves this signaling purpose, not just for African Americans but for any group that seeks membership in mainstream America. Differences between Black and White consumer behavior were attributed to differences in socioeconomic status rather than cultural differences (Bennett & Kassarjian, 1972; Bullock, 1961a, 1961b). Among lower-income Blacks there was little pressure to conform to mainstream, middle-class standards; for upper-income Blacks, it was important to match accepted, middle-class ideals (Bauer & Cunningham, 1970; Feldman & Star, 1968; Frazier, 1957; Kochman, 1981; Ramirez, 1984; Yovovich, 1982). This thinking is consistent with the assumptions of cultural assimilation: The values and beliefs of an ethnic group are replaced by those of the mainstream.

During the late 1970s and the 1980s, more emphasis was placed on cultural distinctiveness as a foundation for differences in African American and White beliefs. Some African Americans began aggressively substituting their own ethnic alternatives to dominant standards of beauty, behavior, and value. Many beliefs were challenged because they did not express "Black consciousness" (Gibson, 1978).

A third approach considers the adjustments in behavior and beliefs of African Americans from a multicultural perspective (Williams, 1989). Drawing from extensive socialization and life experiences in the two cultures, African Americans synthesize the experience by existing in two cultural worlds, adopting both value systems simultaneously (Ramirez & Castaneda, 1974). This simply means that people who strongly identify as African American will exhibit behavior representative of the African American cultural script in some situations and behavior representative of mainstream culture in others. For example, expenditures for clothing may reflect African heritage, whereas expenditures for food-at-home may reflect European cultural traditions (Wagner & Soberon-Ferrer, 1990). The behavior of a multicultural person refutes any linear view of acculturation (Ellis, McCullough, Wallendorf, & Tan, 1985; Hope & Klonoff, 1996; Valencia, 1985); choice of appropriate behavior depends on the environment and situation.

This discussion of how African Americans adjust to American mainstream life would not be complete without addressing the impact that African Americans have had on mainstream American culture. Music, food, fashion, sports, literature, language, and virtually every sector of American life have been enriched by influences from African American culture. African American and urban trends are a primary source of inspiration for American pop culture:

> We invent a fashion but White guys manufacture the clothes. We play a game, but White guys own the team. We conceive a music, but White guys market the CDs. We create a catch phrase, but White guys make the T-shirts. (Pitts, 1998, p. 9)

Even the way young Blacks talk has been adopted in mainstream America—*Webster's Dictionary* includes words such as *homeboy, dis,* and *gangsta* in newer editions (Chappell, 1995)—and *Wiggers* is a new term referring to Whites who strive to be Black (Kanner, 1994).

# AFRICAN AMERICANS AS CONSUMERS

## The Legacy of Early Marketing Efforts

As the first beneficiaries of efforts to segment demand on the basis of ethnicity, African American consumers draw from a variety of experiences in the marketplace. They have been targeted by both mainstream and African American-owned marketers, often using very different styles of marketing. Their cultural symbols have been mocked and distorted in appeals to other consumers, yet celebrated and embraced by companies seeking African American loyalty (O'Barr, 1994, pp. 107-156). As a result, many African Americans have a heightened sensitivity to interactions in the marketplace. Consumption can be a medium for simultaneously expressing participation in the mainstream and pride in ethnic roots and accomplishments. The marketplace sends messages of both symbolic and social status content.

As early as the 1940s, mainstream marketers developed programs to target African American consumers. In 1946, Pepsi assembled a dozen people on their target marketing team whose job it was to make contacts in Black communities, Black campuses, Elks club meetings, and Black churches. The sympathetic Black press supported Pepsi and in return benefited from the placement of Pepsi advertisements that portrayed Blacks in a positive way. These efforts brought in new customers at a time when Pepsi sales had been falling ("Pepsi Marketers," 1997).

The advertising industry, on the other hand, was extremely cautious in developing ties with the African American community. Even *Ebony* magazine, a publication targeting the African American population, carried advertisements with models with predominantly Caucasian features; only after the 1960s did these ads give way to models with Negroid features and natural "Afro" hairstyles (Dates, 1990). Early marketers represented products such as fast foods, tobacco, and alcohol. It was long after the 1960s that other mainstream advertisers and agencies developed aggressive, proactive, and positive campaigns for African American target audiences. Since the 1980s, the increased economic clout of African American consumers has lured a growing number of ethnic and mainstream marketers. Despite the increased attention to this consumer group, African Americans remain almost invisible in mainstream advertising and communications agencies today (Dates, 1990).

Contemporary marketers must overcome a legacy of earlier mainstream marketers' insults to African Americans. One early print ad showed the kerchief-clad Aunt Jemima smiling at her White masters. Black women were hired to dress up as the traditional "mammies" to cook pancakes at fairs and pose with visitors at Disneyland (Ono, 1994). Greatly exaggerated physical features such as "saucer" lips and "banjo" eyes were used to depict Blacks. Some African American women still remember how upset they were to see the "most negative, pejorative, derogatory features" of Aunt Jemima projected as the prototype of Black women" (Ono, 1994, p. B3). Brand characters such as Aunt Jemima (pancake mix), Uncle Ben (rice), and Rastus (Cream of Wheat) remain constant reminders of what has been acceptable in mainstream society (Kern-Foxworth, 1994).

Terms from other eras have also been defamatory to African Americans. Throughout history, the word *nigger* has been offensive to Blacks. "For Black people the word nigger symbolizes four hundred years of anti-African racism and cultural repression" (Wilson, 1980, p. 16). Yet around the turn of the century it was common to see products bearing the name *nigger* blatantly advertised: Nigger Head canned fruits and vegetables (1905), Nigger Head stove polish (1920), Nigger Head tees (1920), Nigger Head tobacco, and Nigger Head oysters (Kern-Foxworth, 1994).

Quaker Oats continues to distance its marketing efforts from the early Aunt Jemima. In the 1960s, the company changed Aunt Jemima's bandanna into a headband. Then in 1989 the character became slimmer, exchanged her headband for a perm, and put on pearl earrings to reflect a more professional image. Quaker hired Gladys Knight to pitch the pancakes and syrups. Still, "for some consumers, there's no amount of makeover that would sufficiently offset the stereotypes associated with the name and the picture" (Ono, 1994, p. B3; see also Mabry, 1989). The dilemma is what to do about a brand synonymous with quality but considered culturally offensive.

Most marketers try to avoid insensitivity when marketing to African Americans. But decision makers who are unfamiliar with the extent to which African Americans have experienced discrimination, including discrimination in the marketplace, may not be aware of the context in which this group interprets messages from mainstream marketers. Thus, firms without African Americans in key decision-making roles and staff with multicultural training may not anticipate negative reactions from African Americans to certain ads. For example, a controversial United Colors of Benetton print ad featured two young girls, one White and the other Black. The White girl had golden locks and the light appeared to create a halo around her head. The Black girl was not smiling and had her hair shaped into what appeared to be two horns. An angel and devil? Not according to Benetton, who reacted to this interpretation with surprise (Berry, 1996). Walgreen's distributed a flyer during Black History Month that included a coupon for skin lightening cream ("Drug Store Chain," 1997). And a recent ad in *Jet* magazine for Toyota Corolla claimed, "Unlike your last boyfriend, it goes to work in the morning." The negative reactions that the ad generated prompted immediate apologies from *Jet,* Toyota, and Toyota's agency Saatchi & Saatchi ("Toyota Ad," 1999).

One lesson mainstream marketers have yet to learn is how to effectively speak the "language of the target." Mainstream marketers have made many mistakes trying to incorporate the language and behaviors of African Americans into advertising copy. Pringle's rap to a nongreasy chip was "ridiculous and offensive," as was the Fruity Pebbles cereal spot featuring rapper "Barney Rubble" (Kanner, 1994). By not speaking in an authentic voice as an "extended" member of the African American community, these marketers actually increased the perceived cultural distance between them and their African American audience.

Yet another danger in today's marketplace is "urban legends," which are reproduced widely and easily in cyberspace. One such myth, trumpeted around the world by e-mail, was the story of Tommy Hilfiger's appearance on *Oprah* in which he allegedly claimed he didn't want "people of color" to buy his clothes. Now the company is using the Internet as well to assure minority consumers that the story is fiction and that they remain valued customers (McShane, 1998; Wynter, 1993c). Tropical Fantasy, a line of low-priced sodas sold in New York's ethnic neighborhoods, reached sales of $2 million a month until someone started a baseless rumor that the soda was made by the Ku Klux Klan to sterilize Black men (Harris, 1997). Urban legends have always existed, but the Internet grants them an immediate global audience.

## African American Consumer Preferences

African Americans accounted for 8.2% of U.S. consumer spending and more than $450 billion in 1997 ("Black Spending," 1999; Wynter, 1997a). In 1994, African Americans spent more than $7.5 billion on fashions and accessories, $3.4 billion for out-of-home dinners, and $3.5 billion for lunches, the greater part of which was spent in fast-food establishments (Davis, 1994; Goldman, 1993b). It is not by coincidence that the biggest spenders in the African American market are Procter & Gamble, AT&T, Sears, General Motors, MCI, McDonald's, Anheuser-Busch, Philip Morris, Colgate-Palmolive, Ford, J. C. Penney, Quaker Oats, PepsiCo, Burger King, Western Union, MoneyGram, Sprint, Toyota, American Home Products, Honda, Revlon, Coca-Cola, Hallmark, and Miller Brewing. By one estimate, in 1996 about $865 million was spent trying to woo African American consumers, out of a total of $47.3 billion in advertising to all U.S. consumers (Gray, 1997).

Some companies have noted the low median household incomes of African American consumers and decided to not actively pursue them. The nation's 10.2

million African American households spent an average of $23,442 each in 1995, compared to a national average of $32,276, based on the 1995 Consumer Expenditure Survey data. With a spending index of 73, African Americans spend 27% less than the average household. But with faster growing incomes African American spending could approach the national average in a few years ("U.S. Average Household," 1998; Zbar, 1998). Millions of middle-class and upper-class African American households have discretionary money to spend, and the choices they make boost expenditures to above average for numerous goods and services (Fisher, 1996).

In some product categories, African Americans substantially outspend other consumers. For example, though less than 13% of the population, they represented 18% of the nation's 24.2 million pager owners in 1995 (Brownlee, 1996). Some categories (or brands) for which African Americans are a disproportionate share of consumers are Wrigley's chewing gum, beer, presweetened cereals, frozen vegetables, bottled water, cognac, fast foods, nonprescription drugs, instant coffee, baby foods, orange juice, athletic shoes, rice, meat, poultry, fish, eggs, oranges, fresh fruit juice, telephone services, bedroom and infants' furniture, boys' and girls' clothes, women's pants and suits, footwear, new cars, and color TVs. Within the soft-drink industry alone, several products attract a large number of African American and Hispanic consumers. The two groups make up 21% of the U.S. population but account for 40% of lemon-lime sodas drunk and 50% of fruit-flavored (grape and orange) sodas (Mogelonsky, 1996a; Ryan, 1991; Wynter, 1997a).

African American adults care about their appearance and show it in their spending on personal care services. More than 6 in 10 African American households spent something on these services in 1994, including hair styling, massage, and manicures. The average annual household expenditure for personal services among African Americans was $530, 34% more than the U.S. average of $349. African American households spend 41% more on personal care services for women, at $532 a year, and 24% more on services for men, at $212 a year (Fisher, 1996).

The most elusive aspect of African American consumption patterns is whether the differences between African Americans and other consumers are due to cultural or socioeconomic characteristics. Most consumer researchers agree that their consumer behaviors differ, but there is no consensus as to the cause. Some contend that when socioeconomic variables are held constant, the differences are insignificant. Others maintain that there are still behavioral differences attributable to ethnic or cultural differences (Williams, 1989a).

There is also disagreement about what cultural differences communicate about African American values (Alwitt, Qualls, & Williams, 1996). When socioeconomic differences are held constant, do consumption differences indicate a desire to remain culturally distinct, or do they show that African Americans are less concerned with what others think (Robertson, Zielinski, & Ward, 1984)? Given these conflicting explanations, the findings shown in Table 6.5 must be taken with caution. Many misconceptions about African American consumers have been allowed to stand, even though early research focused exclusively on urban and low-income households. That African Americans are "more brand loyal" than other consumers is one such myth. Evidence on their brand loyalty is mixed at best; most findings are based on a limited number of product categories, purchase choices, and survey participants. More research is the only antidote to inaccurate generalizations about African American consumers.

A different approach to variability within the African American market is one taken by many marketers. Profiles of African American consumers and their lifestyles are built and analyzed using values measures such as VALS-2 or LOV (List of Values). These segmentation measures take ethnic or cultural influences into consideration as they translate differences across ethnic groups into beliefs and lifestyle choices. Competence, empathy, belonging, and hedonism are four areas researchers have found that effectively group persons with different overall values in the United States, resulting in segments called Hard-Core Traditionalists, Family Values Boomers, Post Yuppies, and Self-Navigators (Walker & Moses, 1996). The first three groups tend to cross all ethnic groups. The self-navigators are younger (about 50%) and have an approach to living that says, "It's up to me to create my own well-being." They are less likely to invest, and they own lots of credit cards. Interestingly, the Self-Navigators are 80% White, 13% Black, and 7% other.

Tom Burrell found through his agency's focus groups that "status, image and self-enhancement" are priorities for African Americans. This is consistent with other findings that consumers who have the fastest rising incomes are most likely to spend discretionary income on visible signs of success (Brownlee, 1996). As noted earlier, visibly consumed symbols of success are important media for communicating social and economic achievements of African Americans (Fisher, 1996). Consumers who cannot acquire the home they want divert spending to other goods and services that symbolize the "American dream." The opportunity is for businesses that understand this cultural context and can meet those consumers' needs.

In 1995, an estimated 10 million African Americans set the week after Christmas aside for celebrating Kwanzaa, a festival of "family, roots, and community."

**TABLE 6.5** African American Consumer Behaviors

| Consumer Behaviors and Preferences | Study Authors | Findings |
|---|---|---|
| **Brand Attitudes** | | |
| Brand loyalty | Bauer and Cunningham (1970), Bauer, Cunningham, and Wortzel (1965), Wilkes and Valencia (1989), "Less Myth" (1984), "New Survey" (1984) | More loyal than Anglo Americans |
| Well-known/ national brands | Deloitte and Touche (1990) | Prefer well-known brands for major appliances |
| **Retail Preferences** | | |
| Store types | Deloitte and Touche (1990) | Apparel stores for men's clothing; Sears, chains for major appliances |
| Store ownership | Williams and Snuggs (1996) | Negative ratings if no Black owners, but price more important overall |
| Bargaining | Wilkes and Valencia (1989) | Shop for deals more than Anglos |
| Store choice | Deloitte and Touche (1990) | Price and location important for grocery stores; price and selection for children's and women's clothing and shoes; style, selection important for men's clothing |
| Use of coupons | Wilkes and Valencia (1989) | Favorable attitudes |
| **Communication Sources** | | |
| Ethnic media | Nielsen Market Research (2000) | Prefer Black-oriented programs |
| African American models/context | Moore, Williams, and Qualls (1996) | Black models more effective: higher recall, higher credibility |
| Word of mouth | Lee, La Ferle, and Tharp (1999b) | More product and advertising talk |
| Source credibility | Williams and Grantham (1999) | Ethnic media, word of mouth, African American community sources |
| Ethnic advertising | Deloitte and Touche (1990) | Higher response to "Black pride" and messages meeting ethnic needs |

*(Continued)*

**TABLE 6.5**  African American Consumer Behaviors (Continued)

| Consumer Behaviors and Preferences | Study Authors | Findings |
|---|---|---|
| **Attitudes Toward Shopping** | | |
| Entertainment value | Mogelonsky (1998) | High, pleasurable experience |
| Information value | Lee, La Ferle, and Tharp (1999b) | Shopping experience valuable |
| **Price Response** | | |
| Price sensitivity | Mulhern, Williams, and Leone (1998), Wilkes and Valencia (1989) | Price sensitivity varies by product type and brand |

Hallmark has been selling Kwanzaa cards with designs by African American artists as part of its Mahogany line since 1992 (Woodward & Johnson, 1995). An African American-owned publishing company markets 21 styles of Kwanzaa cards and activity books for children. Their Kwanzaa kit comes with a *kinara* and instructions for novices. Some parents even purchase bicycles and Nintendo sets for Kwanzaa gifts. Though some traditionalists disapprove of the commercialization of the festival, it is part of the natural evolution of holiday celebrations (Simpson, 1991; Woodward & Johnson, 1995).

## Effective Marketing Means Giving Back to the Community

It may seem obvious, but treating customers with respect is the first principle of any marketing program targeting African American consumers. The historical marketing depictions of African Americans and incidents of racial prejudice in today's marketplace suggest some of the concerns that African Americans have when entering the marketplace. That sensitivity is at the forefront of their choice of where to shop. "Reasonable pricing" is the No. 1 deciding factor for African American consumers and their White counterparts. The second most important factor for Whites in deciding where to shop is "availability of quality merchandise"; for African Americans, it's "respect" (60%). Being watched or being ignored is a topic that comes up frequently in research and focus groups with African American consumers (Fisher, 1996).

African American consumers also place a higher value on atmosphere. Shopping meets the need for both information gathering and entertainment. It is hard for customers to have a pleasant shopping experience when they feel mistreated. A pleasant store atmosphere ranks fourth among Blacks as a factor in deciding where to shop (Fisher, 1996). Cadillac's programs to attract African American buyers include direct mail, promotional events, and sensitivity training for dealership personnel (Miller, 1994; O'Donnell, 1994).

A commitment must also be made to appropriate product mix and selections for African American tastes. Revlon, Clinique, Prescriptives, and Maybelline have extended their makeup lines with new colors and shadings to capture more of the personal care spending of African Americans (Davis, 1994; Lowe, 1994; Wynter, 1993c, 1996b, 1997b). J. C. Penney added a "Fashion Influences" catalog that featured contemporary, African influenced designs made in the United States. McCall patterns, Spiegel's E-Style clothing catalog, Sears's African Village clothing line, and Ward's in-store specialty boutiques all have used Afrocentric themes to appeal to African American clothing shoppers (Davis, 1994; Edwards, 1996; Wynter, 1994).

Mainstream companies can find it difficult to "fit in" or use the right language when competing with African American-owned firms. Publishers have developed greeting card lines as well as fiction paperbacks that consumers found less authentic than the products of proven ethnic marketers ("Reflections in Black," 1994). Having a "more ethnic" product does not always make African American-owned companies successful. Glory Foods started out selling African American prepared foods, such as greens and other "soul foods." But their marketing research discovered a bigger opportunity in convenient alternatives to mainstream American prepared foods, such as broccoli and asparagus (Ward, 1994).

Having communications with relevant cultural content is another way to tailor marketing programs for African American consumers. When it is done well, African Americans respond positively to the use of Ebonics in advertising to mainstream audiences that include African Americans and other Americans (Williams, 1989b). The so-called "right-on" school of advertising has been known for injecting lexical features of Ebonics into advertising copy. Slang expressions such as *home boys and home girls* are used in the copy for products targeted to African Americans ("Home Boys," 1990). One firm that markets to inner-city African American youth uses street slang to create names and flavors for its potato chips, such as "Chumpies," a commonly used term for "the best of the best," and "Bumpin Barbecue," meaning something "hot and good" (Bush, 1993).

African Americans have been almost invisible in the mainstream media despite their heavy consumption of network and cable television programs. One way to make an impact is to use more inclusive advertising. By placing African American models in ads, putting them in leading roles instead of in the background, using African American celebrities, and using ethnic-oriented media, a message is sent directly to African American consumers that their patronage is wanted. Chrysler sponsored the television premiere of the acclaimed documentary *Hoop Dreams* in hopes of reaching millions of African American teens and their families. The screening was part of a Chrysler-sponsored educational program in schools nationwide. "Programs like this aren't measured by how many cars they sell, but they convey a corporate commitment to things that are important to the African-American community" (Henderson, 1995a, p. B1).

Increasing the visibility of African Americans in the media is an important goal of community leaders. In the past, racially exclusive advertisements communicated a "Blacks-not-welcome-here" message. This was especially true of real estate advertising, where there was the all-too-real experience of discrimination to confirm that interpretation. When African Americans are included in advertising messages, African Americans are not only more likely to pay attention but also more likely to respond to the appeal (Kerin, 1979; Schlinger & Plummer, 1972; Szybillo & Jacoby, 1974; Tolley & Goett, 1971; Williams et al., 1995). The AT&T advertising shown in Figure 6.2 acknowledges the important role that *Ebony* magazine has had in the African American community for over 50 years.

Agencies that either are African American owned or specialize in the African American market have been in business for less than 40 years. Burrell Communications, the Chisholm-Mingo Group, and UniWorld are some of the best known, with clients such as McDonald's, Sears Roebuck, Coca-Cola, and Procter & Gamble. Despite the growing interest in minority markets, African American agencies have not flourished to the extent that their general and Hispanic market counterparts have. According to the 2,000 listings in the *Standard Directory of Advertising Agencies* (National Register, 2000), of the 126 firms specializing exclusively or in part in ethnic markets, 30 reported expertise in dealing with the African American market. These figures show little growth over the 1993 figures of 105 firms and 24 specialists (Woods, 1995b).

For many years, companies have contributed to development of institutions within the African American community. There are many social, political, and

**Figure 6.2.** AT&T Salutes Ebony Magazine

professional associations representing the interests of African Americans, such as the NAACP, the National Urban League, the Rainbow-PUSH Coalition, the United Negro College Fund, and the Congressional Black Caucus Foundation. Other important institutions include churches (the historical centers of social and political life within African American communities), schools, social sororities and fraternal associations, development programs, and even government agencies. There are also a number of professional associations, such as the National Black MBA Association and the National Association of Black Journalists, that are organized around the interests of African American members of those occupations.

Revlon sponsors gospel conventions, choir robes, and the Stellar Awards; product samples are distributed during services, and five Black church groups have even gone into marketing in a joint venture with a White entrepreneur (Branch, 1996; Wynter, 1998b). There is a long tradition of kinship and resource sharing within the African American community, and it is surprisingly tight-knit in many inner cities. There is a real opportunity to match a company's own values with its choice of philanthropic and community-building investments.

One important way in which companies "give back" is the use of African American-owned media and suppliers. African Americans, U.S. Latinos, and Asian Americans generate combined purchasing power over $1 trillion, yet ethnic radio stations, newspapers, and magazines receive a small portion, if any, of advertising budgets targeting those communities (Harper, 1999). PepsiCo is increasing its advertising on Black radio stations and ethnic newspapers to expand its influence in the African American community. AT&T is selling $1 billion in bonds through an offering comanaged by a minority firm, with an additional $200 to $300 million in debt to be managed by "diversity firms" (Harper, 1999).

Yet another way in which companies can assist African American community development is in health and education. Hypertension, diabetes, heart and lung diseases, obesity, and sickle-cell anemia are damaging the health of African Americans. In addition to donations for research in search of cures and treatments for these diseases, some companies are joint-venturing with community institutions to educate consumers. Wrigley is participating in an advocacy program called Health Watch, whose mission is to encourage African, Asian, and Hispanic Americans to use doctors for regular health maintenance instead of as a last resort ("Wrigley Ads," p. B1).

LaVan Hawkins, who plans to have a franchise of over 475 Burger Kings by 2000, uses a full complement of multicultural marketing tools. Some of his franchises are in the roughest neighborhoods of Detroit, Baltimore, and Washington, D.C. He offers patrons banana shakes and Cajun fries in addition to Burger King's regular fast-food fare. He uses klieg lights and neon

[to] light up the restaurants as brightly as baseball stadiums. Hip-hop and R&B pump from their sound systems. Uniformed Nation of Islam guards provide security. African-American flags fly. The familiar orange-and-red logo is there, but this isn't your suburban Burger King . . . Hawkins offers employees stock options and paths to becoming owner-operators. He also makes half-million-dollar grants to church foundations and school programs in nearly every neighborhood where he sets up shop. (Gegax, 1997, p. 57)

The Hawkins philosophy is "to build neighborhoods and self-esteem, not just restaurants" (Gegax, 1997, p. 57).

"Community marketing" is what McDonald's calls its own efforts to participate in African American communities and institutions. McDonald's works with the Better Chance Foundation to offer college and prep school scholarships in underprivileged areas. The company's "Black History Makers of the Future" program highlights 30 African American children and includes them each year in national television advertising. Coors, Mattel, Kraft/General Foods, and Toyota are other marketers that emphasize the successes of African Americans through scholarships to the American Negro College Fund and school and summer meal programs in inner cities (Campanelli, 1991). Dollar General Corporation opens stores near public housing projects in South Carolina, hires residents to work there, then requires them to take literacy training (Edwards, 1996).

## INFORMATION SOURCES AND MEDIA PREFERENCES

### Community Networks: An Oral Tradition

The most trustworthy source of company and product information for African Americans ages 21 to 65 is African American-targeted magazines (87%). Next in trustworthiness is *Consumer Reports* (80%), followed by African American television news coverage. That is a powerful reason to be visible in and respected by those media. In terms of frequency of exposure to company and product information, African Americans cite local television news and African American magazines ("Top Five," 1998). Ethnic and local media offer significant symbolic representation and cost advantages over mainstream media.

What these preferred sources of information reflect is the high credibility given to members and leaders of the African American community. African cultures from which at least some of African American culture is built make greater distinctions between insiders and outsiders, as do the cultures of Latin Americans, Asians, and Mediterranean Europeans (de Mooij, 1998; Hofstede, 1997). Furthermore, there is a long tradition of respect for oral communication in the African American community (Hecht et al., 1993). African Americans talk more with family and friends about products, companies, and advertising than other Americans. For comparison, Chinese Americans engage in little consumer talk, Mexican Americans talk more about advertising than products, and Anglo Americans are more likely to discuss negative product experiences (Lee et al., 1999a; Williams, 1991).

African American celebrities represent another aspect of bias in favor of "insider" sources. There are a large number of African American celebrity endorsers ("Blacks Again Dominate," 1989; "Black Athletes," 1988). Black sports and entertainment personalities dominate annual Q-Ratings, which measure the popularity of certain performers as celebrities—for example, Michael Jackson (Pepsi), Bill Cosby (Jello, Kodak), Michael Jordan (Nike, McDonalds), Ray Charles (Pepsi), and Whitney Houston (Coke) ("Blacks Again Dominate," 1989; "Black Athletes," 1988; Lipman, 1991b). An early study indicated that African American consumers were at least twice as likely as Anglos to rate celebrities as more believable than noncelebrity endorsers. Another researcher reported that celebrity athletes and celebrity entertainers were the most likely advertising spokespersons that would cause African American consumers to buy a product (Hume, 1983; "Survey Measures," 1981; Williams, 1987).

The absence of African Americans in the mainstream media has the effect of giving high visibility to the small number of African American models and actors in those media. Several studies in the early 1990s found that less than 10% of magazine ads contained Blacks; this percentage dropped to only 2.4% when *Ebony* and *Essence* were excluded (Duff, 1993; Green, 1991; Stearns, Unger, & Luebkeman, 1987; Snyder, Freeman, & Condray, 1991; Zinkhan, Qualls, & Biswas, 1990). Representation of African American actors in television advertising varies by product category, with overrepresentation in telephone, liquor/wine/beer, and hair product ads and underrepresentation in tobacco and clothing ads (Stearns et al., 1987; Wilkes & Valencia, 1989). Evidence suggests that African Americans pay more attention to and recall more from ads with African American models (Kerin, 1979; Schlinger & Plummer, 1972; Szybillo & Jacoby, 1974; Tolley & Goett, 1971; Whittler, 1989, 1991; Williams et al., 1995). This attention to model's race is extended to the composition of the entire cast in an ad, for rarely are all-Black casts found in mainstream advertisements (Snyder et al., 1991).

Networking and word-of-mouth communication are the modern-day versions of "oral tradition" (Hecht et al., 1993). African American consumers rely more on in-store displays and word-of-mouth communications from salespeople than other Americans (Alwitt & Donley, 1996). A local barber or beauty shop would not have the same community function for African and European Americans; for African Americans, getting a haircut may be secondary to finding out what is going on in the community. The parents of African American teens are their heroes and sources of product information.[1]

---

## Patterns of Media Use Among African Americans

African Americans have the highest consumption of broadcast media of any ethnic group in the United States. This heavy use of radio and television reflects a preference for entertainment over information technologies (Hoffman, Novak, & Venkatesh, 1997). Table 6.6 shows the average number of hours per week spent with television, radio, and other media for four subculture groups in Houston, Texas. As indicated in the table, African Americans consume English-language media at levels higher than the other three groups, with the exception of newspapers. Ethnic media targeted to African Americans were not measured separately in the study, but they may or may not have been included when African Americans responded to the survey about their media habits. Over the last 40 years, African Americans have made an impact on American popular culture via sports, entertainment, and music, and the media devoted to those activities are television and radio. These media showcase African American success in a mainstream milieu.

With such high consumption of network television, many marketers assume that their messages reach African Americans alongside the general market audience in that medium. But although there is significant crossover, the program tastes of African American and White audiences seem to be moving apart rather than homogenizing. The responses of African Americans to advertisements in mainstream and ethnic media also differ. About 60% of African American consumers reported in a survey that they believe network advertising is designed only for Whites. At the same time, a higher percentage of Black audiences reports paying attention to advertising (Goldman, 1993b).

---

## Television: The Home Entertainment Center

There are dozens of African American-targeted media for promoting goods and services to the African American consumer. Nevertheless, the best medium is network television, a mass medium. Black households watch an average of 73 hours and 30 minutes of television each week, according to March 1994 data from Nielsen Media Research in New York City. That is well above the national average of 48 hours and 25 minutes for all households.

The debate about how best to reach African American audiences on network television hinges on the differences in their program tastes from those of White audiences. There are two crossover audiences of Black and White: viewers aged 12 to 17 and aged 50 plus. Black and White teens like many of the same shows, perhaps because teens share more experiences across ethnic groups (Fisher, 1996). Eleven of the top 20 shows for all viewers aged 12 to 17 are also in the top 20 for Black teens.

Choosing which shows to advertise on can be confusing (Horovitz, 1994). The top 10 rated shows for Black and all U.S. households diverge dramatically; in 1997, only *NFL Monday Night Football* showed up on both lists. Among the top 20 rated shows for both Black and U.S. households as a whole, only the *Monday Night Movie* and *E.R.* were added. African Americans spent 13% more time watching TV during prime time but 90% more time watching TV during late night hours. On the other hand, among daytime audiences, Blacks and Whites seemed to like the same shows (Wynter, 1999a).

Clearly, having an African American performer is more appealing to Black audiences than to Whites (Wynter, 1999c). The top five shows for African American households in 1998 were *New York Undercover, Living Single, The Crew, In the House,* and *The Fresh Prince of Bel-Air.* The top five shows for all households were *E.R., Seinfeld, Friends, Caroline in the City,* and *NFL Monday Night Football.* "Black-oriented" shows had a greater percentage of all-Black ads, ads with African Americans in major roles, and ads depicting Blacks in skilled occupations (Licata & Biswas, 1993).

Television-watching patterns among Blacks and Whites appear to be growing further apart. A new study by BBDO Worldwide found in 1998 that not one of the top 10 rated shows among Black audiences was also among the top 10 in

**TABLE 6.6**  Media Habits of Four Ethnic Groups in Houston, Texas

| Media Activity | Average Hours per Week | | | |
|---|---|---|---|---|
| | *Anglo Americans* | *African Americans* | *Chinese Americans* | *Hispanic Americans* |
| Watching English-language TV | 3.9 | 4.3 | 3.1 | 3.6 |
| Listening to English-language radio | 3.6 | 4.1 | 2.6 | 3.8 |
| Reading English-language newspapers | 2.5 | 2.5 | 2.0 | 2.5 |
| Reading English-language magazines | 2.1 | 2.6 | 2.0 | 2.5 |
| **Total English-language media time** | **12.1** | **13.5** | **9.7** | **12.4** |
| Watching Chinese- or Spanish-language TV | | | 1.6 | 3.6 |
| Listening to Chinese- or Spanish-language radio | | | N/A | 3.9 |
| Reading Chinese- or Spanish-language newspapers | | | 2.0 | 1.9 |
| Reading Chinese- or Spanish-language magazines | | | 1.6 | 2.1 |
| **Total media time** | **12.1** | **13.5** | **14.9** | **23.9** |

overall ratings. Eight years ago, when BBDO commissioned its first study of television viewing among Blacks, 15 of the top 20 shows among Black households also appeared among the top overall shows (Kolbert, 1993). In 1998, *Seinfeld,* the top-rated television show in White households, ranked 50th in African American homes, according to Nielsen Media Research, whereas the comedy *Between Brothers,* No. 1 in Black households, ranked 112th among Whites.

Prime-time television is racially divided in terms of both casts and audiences as the overall television audience dwindles. Networks, under enormous pressure to maximize dwindling profits, have been focusing on sitcoms for the more numerous and generally more affluent White households. Because Whites rarely watch shows, particularly sitcoms, with largely Black casts, the networks broadcast relatively few with Black or integrated casts in the 3-hour block from 8 to 11 P.M. that is the most lucrative and competitive portion of television programming (Sterngold, 1998). The four major networks, ABC, CBS, Fox, and NBC, plus the upstarts WB and UPN, have seen their share of overall viewers reduced to less than 60%. But cable's audience is fragmented by dozens of channels, and the networks still reach the largest audiences by far, making their viewing patterns an important reflection of popular attitudes (Schement, 1997).

Cable television offers more options to meet the growing gap in tastes of different ethnic and age-cohort audiences. African Americans subscribe to premium cable at nearly twice the rate of White households (45% to 26%), and Latino households fall in between (35%). Twenty-two percent of HBO's subscriber base comes from African American households, amounting to 42% of all African American homes (Schement, 1997). African Americans order pay-per-view programs at twice the rates of Whites, with Latinos again in between. Moreover, 70% of African American cable households subscribe to a pay service, compared to about half that for all other households. Subscription to cable services for African American and U.S. Latino households is independent of education or family income. Cable plays a different role in the information environments of African American and Latino households (Mueller & Schement, 1996). If African Americans are seeking to see themselves and their experiences reflected in programming, then subscribing to cable makes sense.

Black Entertainment Television (BET) reaches 59 million households and has 98% penetration of African American households (Alexander, 2000). Many of their award-winning shows highlight important issues in the Black community. BET teamed up Home Shopping Network Inc. to produce a weekly shopping program cohosted by two African American females ("HSN to Debut," 1994). This has given the shopping network access to African American audiences in a high-credibility environment. African Americans and Latinos who have, on the average, less education and family income than Whites participate more in televised home shopping (Schement, 1997).

## Radio: Redefining Black-Oriented Stations as Urban

In 1999, an FCC report concluded that advertisers regularly discriminate against minority-owned stations with large numbers of Black and Hispanic listeners, even when those stations have the largest audiences. Minority-owned stations are paid 29% less per listener than their White counterparts (Harper, 1999; Wickham, 1999). Thus, even though there is a large and loyal audience of African American listeners, the stations that target them are often forced to change their formats to survive.

In the early 1980s, many "soul" stations switched to "urban contemporary" to appeal to general market listeners as well as the African American community. Often listed as the No. 1 AM/FM station in the country, WBLS/WLIB in New York was able to receive top rates for commercials. Most other Black-owned properties, even after switching to the "urban contemporary" format, were unable to obtain top rates for advertising (Dates, 1990, p. 444). In the 1990s, stations that targeted African American listeners followed the path of rock radio and became more narrowly segmented. This meant that the old "urban contemporary" format, which included a wide range of African American-oriented musical styles from rhythm and blues to jazz, gospel, rap, and hip-hop, was replaced by formats that focused on only one or two of those types of music.

Segmentation in African American radio has continued to evolve, but it has quickened in response to the rise of rap and hip-hop. Rap, which has drawn considerable criticism because of its sometimes violent and obscene language, and hip-hop, a dance sound with a funky electronic beat, have become mainstays of the urban contemporary format. As a result, disenfranchised older listeners have fled to talk radio or "lite" jazz or have simply tuned out in favor of tapes or compact discs.

There are approximately 331 African American-oriented music stations in the United States and 129 gospel stations. Of these, 128 stations are now devoted to urban adult contemporary or R&B oldies. According to Arbitron, 71% of all Black radio listeners aged 12 to 24 say they tune in to stations with an "urban" format, a category that includes all forms of contemporary African American-oriented music. For Blacks 25 to 54, urban's share declines to 53.4%. For Blacks 35 to 64, urban's share is 45.1% (Brandes, 1995).

---

## Print Media: The Community Voice and Expression of Style

Black-targeted magazines are the most trustworthy source of company and product information for African American consumers ("Top Five," 1998). A major reason for the trust in African American magazines and other publications is the important role that a few magazines have had in the African American community. *Ebony* magazine has been in business for over 50 years and has specialized in covering topics of special interest to members of the African American community. The association of brands with venerable members of the African American community such as *Black Enterprise, Jet, Essence,* and *Ebony* goes beyond mere exposure numbers (Brown, 1997). It communicates to readers that a brand and its owners understand the importance of African American community institutions.

Several major publishers developed new magazines for African American readers during the 1990s. For example, *Forbes* launched a Black history magazine, *American Legacy,* and Time Warner developed a magazine called *Savoy* (Reilly, 1996). The publisher of *Prevention* magazine teamed up with an African American entrepreneur to produce *Heart & Soul,* a Black women's health magazine (Reilly, 1996; Wynter, 1999d). Even Black Entertainment Television joined the *New York Daily News* in launching a national weekend magazine called *B.E.T. Weekend* for distribution in city dailies and African American newspapers (Reilly, 1996). The new magazines have been cannibalizing some of the older ones, such as *Ebony, Essence, Jet,* and *Black Enterprise,* for readership. Nevertheless, these media offer access to middle- and upper-class African American consumers who are keenly aware of the commitment such advertisers are making to an African American community institution. For example, Motorola, the first pager maker to court African Americans, used *Ebony, Essence,* and *Black Enterprise* to reach African Americans between 21 and 54 years old (Brownlee, 1996).

African American newspapers cover local politics, commerce, and community activities. Most do not have large readerships but represent an opportunity for companies to position themselves within the African American community and can be influential institutions in their own right. A group of 205 African American newspapers is pressuring Procter & Gamble to buy advertisements in its publications. They threaten to urge subscribers to boycott P&G products if the company doesn't comply (Reitman, 1992).

## Billboards: Community Access and Controversy

Outdoor advertising tends to be extremely effective in reaching African American consumers in central cities. Large billboards and smaller posters deliver specific messages to an entire neighborhood and play off the sense of community that is a high priority among African Americans (Campanelli, 1991). Billboards are ubiquitous in cities and can have an effect on children even before they learn to read. Several studies seem to justify the claim that there are more tobacco and alcohol billboards in African American than in White neighborhoods ("Outdoor Cigarette," 1991; Scenic America, 1989; Schooler & Basil, 1989). The American Public Health Association has called on outdoor advertisers to refrain from targeting minority communities with alcohol and tobacco billboards (Gans & Shook, 1994). In contrast, the results of a content analysis of billboards in San Antonio and Detroit indicated that ethnic and Anglo neighborhoods receive similar amounts of tobacco and alcohol advertising (Lee & Callcott, 1992).

The controversy about alcohol and tobacco billboard advertising has caused a continuous decline in outdoor spending in these two categories during the past 10 years. A recent innovation in outdoor advertising has been the increasing use of smaller billboards in African American communities. These ads, most of which feature ads for high-tar and high-nicotine menthol brands, now account for approximately 37% of all billboards in African American communities. Compared to the large highway billboards, the major advantage of these posters is that they can be placed low and close to the street, thus facilitating greater visibility to passersby of all ages (Gans & Shook, 1994).

## The Digital Divide

The Internet is rapidly becoming accepted as a mass medium, and it offers opportunities for both African American entrepreneurs and consumers. At least 5 out of 32 million African Americans had used the Web as of January 2000 (Hoffman et al., 1997). African Americans are already in impressive numbers. Continued development of online content targeted to African Americans is bringing this medium into the African American community of preferred sources of information and entertainment. Some cyberbusinesses claim that the anonymity of the Internet provides an advantage to minority business owners by allowing them to "mask their racial identity" (Crockett, 1998, p. 128).

Penetration of the Internet was over 23% among African Americans in 1998 (Cleland, 1998). African Americans are more technologically savvy than is generally perceived. An informal survey in 1996 indicated that 71% of African American respondents had Internet access at home and that 69% could tap into it at work. Most respondents spent between 1 and 5 hours per week on the Net, primarily conducting research, sending and receiving e-mail, and engaging in educational and newsgroup activities. Forty-two percent of those who completed the survey electronically noted that they had made purchases on the Net (Muhammad, 1996).

Personal computer ownership and use are the penultimate symbols of the information age. Wealthier, more educated people are more likely to own PCs than those in the lowest income groups, and this is true among all ethnic groups. However, there are intriguing exceptions. After college graduates, the group most likely to report using home PCs every day is individuals without a high school diploma. About a third of all Whites (about 32%) are likely to have a PC in the home, as compared to 18% of African Americans and 28% of U.S. Latinos.

These glowing statistics do not address the so-called "digital divide." Technophobia knows no color, but some African Americans have been reluctant to embrace computers. Cyberspace is seen by some as a predominantly White, male domain. Computers also evoke a deep-seated fear, perhaps even paranoia, among African Americans young and old (Marriott, 1995). Though Whites are more likely to have PC access, African Americans are more likely to state they would like to *acquire* access (Marriott, 1995). The factor that best explains home computer access is income (Novak & Hoffman, 1998).

In a classic case of the "chicken or the egg," many Web entrepreneurs do not target African American consumers because demand is not yet sufficient for African American-oriented Web services (Wynter, 1999b). African Americans have different patterns of Internet use from Whites online. Whites are more likely to use the Web to see what's new at their favorite Web sites and to search for product information before purchase. Although both African American and White Web users report searching for product- or service-related information, White Web users are more likely to report searching for nonproduct and noncorporate information and to find Web sites using directories and search engines. One possibility is that, despite a range of sites like Africana.com, NetNoir, BlackVoices.com, Black World Today, the African-American Financial Index, BlackPlanet.com, and Black Entertainment Television, general-purpose search agents may not be an effective way to locate Web content relevant to African American users (Castaneda, 1997; Crockett, 2000; Golden, 2000; Hoffman et al., 1997).

Another explanation for the gap between African Americans and Whites in Web search behavior is insufficient content of interest to African Americans. An article in *Interactive Marketing News* ("Web Marketers," 1997) claimed that "while there are about 10 million sites on the Web, there are fewer than 500 sites targeted to African-Americans" (p. 9). Others, however, note the multicultural diversity of the Web. Skriloff (1997) reported that "there are thousands of Web sites with content to appeal to Hispanics, African Americans, Asian Americans, and other ethnic groups. . . . Many of these sites are ready for prime time with high quality content, graphics, and strategic purpose" (p. 17).

## Direct Mail, Telemarketing, and Nontraditional Media

A type of marketing that works well with the general population but that has not been effective in marketing to African Americans is direct mail. There are over 11 million African American households, but direct-mail marketers have few lists of names to target them. Of the $740 million that corporate marketers spent to woo African American buyers in the early 1990s, less than 0.5% went to direct mail. Marketers complain that they have difficulty identifying purchasers as African American (Campanelli, 1991). At the same time, African Americans are more positive about ordering from catalogs, telemarketers, and direct mail than any other group of American consumers (Lee et al., 1999a).

Black direct-mail entrepreneurs depend heavily on census and zip code information. But because only 30% of Black consumers live in zip codes that are at least 70% Black, direct mail can be a costly hit-or-miss exercise. In Chicago, for example, a newspaper coupon insert was mailed to "occupants" in 450,000 households in zip codes of at least 20% Black residents. "But in my neighborhood, which is 25% Black, I don't get my own product," said the direct mail company (Wynter, 1994, p. B1). Essence By Mail, a fashion catalog for Black women, has built a list of over 500,000 names from over 10 years of mailing, and 80% of their customers live in zip codes that are less than 70% Black. *Essence* magazine used its subscriber lists to begin selling Afrocentric clothing, accessories, and home decorations by mail (Davis, 1994). More recently, direct marketers have refined their lists and increased response rates to between 3% and 10% (Wynter, 1994).

Video games, VCRs, and camcorders constitute add-on equipment for the electronic cottage, especially if there are children in the African American household. In households where videos are played often, 52% have children present; in households that own video cameras, 41% have children present. And even if only 35% of households have children under 18, these statistics indicate lots of video-related activities in homes with children. African American households report more use of video game systems than U.S. Latinos, but they also have high rates of renting videos. The TV set serves as the main game technology in the African American home, and extensive recording of TV programs may represent time shifting in households that stay up late.

Two effective ways to integrate communication programs with the needs of African American community institutions are event sponsorships and philanthropic programs. Wrigley produced a $10 million campaign to encourage minorities to use doctors for regular health maintenance rather than as a last resort. Their partner was Health Watch, a New York advocacy group. McDonald's offers college scholarships to underprivileged Black students and then features the recipients in national television ads. Other companies that have educational programs in African American communities are Toyota, Chrysler, Coors, Mattel, and Burger King (Campanelli, 1991). Many highly respected and well-known Black celebrities are involved with community events that are in turn underwritten by companies whose names share the spotlight with these role models.

## CAVEAT MARKETER

Is racial targeting racist? Of course not. Too many companies ignore cultural differences when they approve advertising messages for their products. They even ignore important ethnic media to ensure reach and a culturally compatible editorial environment. When socially desirable products and marketing strategies are directed at disadvantaged consumers, their efforts are praised ("After Demographic Shift," 1992; "Retailers Target," 1991). However, when targeting involves socially undesirable products or is aimed at consumers who are less knowledgeable, the practice is viewed as unethical or immoral. Some critics argue that poor, elderly, and/or uneducated consumers are vulnerable to specific marketing practices (Freedman, 1991; Korzenny, McClure, & Rzttki, 1990; Moore, Williams, & Qualls, 1996; Scott, Denniston, & Magruder, 1992); other critics focus on their vulnerability to marketing of potential harmful products (Moore et al., 1996).

Since its withdrawal from broadcast advertising in 1971, the tobacco industry has intensified its use of print media advertising and has been one of the heaviest spenders in corporate sponsorships of sports, the arts, and ethnic cultural events. Tobacco companies have increased the use of athletic sponsorships; product placements in movies and cultural events; placements of brand names on clothing or other products; place-based media; contests; and cultural, civic, fashion, and entertainment events. This trend is of particular concern in terms of its impact on African Americans, for African Americans have the lowest success rate in quitting smoking (Stewart & Rice, 1995).

Like tobacco, the alcohol industry has been facing mounting criticism from government agencies, concerned citizens, and the media about the type of advertising that is now targeted toward minority groups. Alcohol companies have long pushed malt liquors toward urban Blacks and Hispanics. Malt liquors contain as much as 50% more alcohol than traditional beer. The advertising of malt liquors is unabashedly aimed at inner-city youth, using themes that allude to the potency of the brew and its association with power, sex, hedonism, and even "a drug-like high" (Freedman, 1991, p. B1; see also Freedman, 1992).

Marketing of legal products such as cigarettes, alcohol, and fast foods has a negative and magnified impact on the health of minorities. Because of this, it will continue to be the subject of criticism by African American and other civic and medical leaders (Moore et al., 1996). Philip Morris and Miller Brewing Company have become major contributors to African American community groups. Whether their philanthropic and community development activities can quiet the criticisms of their products and marketing tactics is yet to be determined.

## SUMMARY

African Americans constitute a subculture of many contrasts: Black African or Caribbean immigrants and mixed-race descendants of slavery; inner-city, non-traditional households stuck in poverty and successful, middle-class families in the suburbs; young consumers of hip-hop, urban lifestyles and affluent professionals with mainstream tastes; persons with little participation in American mainstream institutions and those who aspire to belong and succeed in the mainstream. Generalizations about African American beliefs, attitudes, and behaviors, and even behavioral norms mask these vast differences within the community. Nevertheless, African American consumers appreciate marketers who solicit their patronage and who support African American media and retailers, as well as social and community institutions. The rapid growth of African American incomes during recent decades presents growing opportunities for companies able to understand the paradoxes of African American consumer identity.

## Note

1. Interviews with students of Reagan High School, Austin, TX, conducted by M. Tharp's Advertising 378 class at the University of Texas at Austin, Fall 1999; unpublished report.

# CHAPTER 7

# Gay Americans

## Sexual Orientation as Community Boundary

Gay and Lesbian consumers constitute one of the most interesting and challenging subcultures in multicultural America. Unlike race, age, or even ethnic origin, sexual orientation is not a characteristic easily observed by other people. It is such a personal topic that only in the last 30 years have more than a few individuals publicly recognized themselves and others as "Gay." Persons of alternative sexual orientations share "outsider" status and experience discrimination, even persecution, by other Americans. This has provided the catalyst for organizing Gay communities. The success of these organizations in representing Gay rights in turn has created a basis for Gay pride. Open acknowledgment of being Gay and community groups representing the interests of Gay men and Lesbians are the cornerstones of access to this market.

The existence of a subculture, even a large one, does not necessarily make its members a viable market for partnerships with business and civic organizations. There is no doubt that Gays and Lesbians are a difficult market to understand. There are no Bureau of the Census data to describe the size and growth of the

Gay population. Even people who are Gay disagree about whether a same-sex orientation is a result of genetics or environment. Where do the people who are bisexual fit in? Can marketers reach closeted Gay people or only people who are "out"? These are typical questions firms have when considering a partnership with Gay consumers.

This chapter first describes events central to the self-identity of Gay men and Lesbians in contemporary American society. The emphasis is on how individuals integrate their homosexuality with other aspects of character. The next topic describes the controversy over the size of the Gay and Lesbian populations and the difficulties this creates for marketers. Next, Gay and Lesbian geography is described—the areas of America where Gay men and Lesbians cluster, as well as what Gay-oriented lifestyles and politics are and are not. The chapter then turns to the impact of Gays on American popular culture and media and to sources for reaching Gay and Lesbian consumers. The chapter ends with a discussion of marketing cases in which firms have become identified as members of the extended Gay and Lesbian community. Experiences Gay men and Lesbians have reported that influence their preferences and attitudes about the marketplace are also included.

## BEING GAY OR LESBIAN IN A STRAIGHT WORLD: IDENTITY ISSUES

The distinctive perspective of Americans who prefer same-sex partners is that they are "different"—outside the American mainstream, whatever it might be (Lukenbill, 1995, pp. 103-110). This experience is an essential part of self-identity for most Gay and Lesbian Americans. Their place in the American mosaic of cultures is in this way aligned with that of other subcultures in multicultural America (Costa, 1996, p. xix). For some Gay people, a feeling of being outside the boundary of "typical" Americans is reinforced by real discrimination (Cloud, 1999). For some, it leads to the alternative communities where Gay men or Lesbians constitute a majority. And some Gay persons believe their sexual orientation must always be denied, at least in public (Stewart, 1991). The following quotation expresses the feelings this experience can engender:

> Thus we come to American society, dominated by a white, male, heterosexual, Christian culture. The dominant group expresses its power in and through the control of critical aspects of business, government, home life, education, etc. In

addition, the accompanying ideological system often serves to legitimate and support that control. The material and the ideological work in concert with one another, reinforcing the societal hierarchy and making it seem "natural," "right," both to those in the position of dominance and to many of those who are themselves dominated. The ideology is reinforced, the "correctness" of the inequity re-created, over and over again, through the machinations of culture. . . . One gender, one sexual orientation, one religious affiliation, and one color of skin are seen as mainstream, while all others fall outside this social category. (Costa, 1996, pp. xvii-xviii)

A consequence of socialization with these values can be strong, negative beliefs about gender and sexual aspects of a Gay person's self-identity (Greene, 1994). This identity crisis can be particularly difficult as an individual encounters the usual challenges of adolescence. Gay persons must ultimately decide on a personal strategy for how to relate to mainstream American culture—assimilate (remain "closeted") or separate (declare shared identity with other Gay people). And in between those two extremes are the 30% of men and 15% of women who "do not have an exclusive heterosexual history" but who do not consider themselves to be Gay (Jandt, 1995, p. 356). There is a large difference between these numbers and the much smaller group who identify as Gay persons. Early adolescence is the time when most Gay Americans feel an emergence of a Lesbian/Gay identity, but it is in late adolescence or early adulthood that this identity is consolidated and reinforced. Table 7.1 reports research on typical ages in the development of Gay identity.

Declaring a Gay identity in mainstream society, or "coming out of the closet," has psychological and behavioral dimensions. Though "coming out" may be key for integrating a Gay person's self-concept, it has unknown ramifications. Most stressful is not being able to predict the reactions of family and other significant persons. "Passing for straight" is a common coping strategy to deal with this stress, but there are many variations of behavior along a continuum from "straight" to "Gay" identity. Some people are in touch with their same-sex orientation earlier or later than others, and some choose consciously to deny their sexual orientation at various points in life (D'Augelli, 1994).

A significant risk of "coming out" is the homophobia of other people and an inability to trust the strength of family or friendship bonds to overcome a phobic reaction. Men are more homophobic than women, but all heterosexuals express more prejudice against same-sex orientations when it involves their own gender (Herek, 1994; "Tuaca Targets Lesbians," 1995). The need to accommodate to

**TABLE 7.1**  Identity Issues Among Gay Men and Lesbians

|                                                              | Median Age of Experience for: | |
| --- | --- | --- |
| *Stage of Gay Identity Development*                          | *Gay Men* | *Lesbians* |
| Initial awareness of same-sex affec-tions/erotic feelings    | 12-13     | 14-16      |
| Initial same-sex experience                                  | 14-15     | 20-22      |
| Self-identification as Lesbian or Gay                        | 19-21     | 21-23      |
| Initial same-sex sexual relationship                         | 21-24     | 20-24      |
| Positive Gay or Lesbian identity                             | 22-26     | 24-29      |

SOURCE: Garnets and Kimmel (1991).

this results in much variation in how Gay identity is expressed in lifestyle and group associations.

Due to the hostility Gay people face in the mainstream world, acceptance by and support of family members are extremely important (Cobo-Hanlon, 1999). At the same time, many expect rejection of their homosexuality and feel that family members do not want them to "come out" to other family members. Many Gay people find family warmth only via a chosen and constructed family of friends who accept the whole person. The "extended family" of Gay-friendly organizations extends to churches, media, businesses, professionals, civic and cultural causes, and arts organizations, a perennially Gay-friendly arena.

A primary issue for Gays and Lesbians is which labels they use for themselves and which ones are acceptable for others to use. For example, *Lesbian* and *Gay* are terms used for and by people who have a same-sex orientation. Due to the exclusively sexual connotations of the term *homosexual,* many men prefer to be called Gay, and many women choose *Lesbian. Gay* is acceptable to most men and women of same-sex orientation. *Bisexual* describes those people attracted to both men and women. Outside these terms, most of the slang words for members of this subculture are derogative (*queer, fag, faggot, pansy, dyke, butch,* ad infinitum). Nevertheless, the more offensive terms are sometimes used by both Gay and "straight" people for Gay persons—pejoratively by outsiders and affirmatively by insiders. These labels are also used at times to chastise anyone who doesn't conform to mainstream gender ideals (Greene, 1994; Jandt, 1995, p. 357).

It is important to remember that we depend on self-identification in determining opinions about the labeling issue. Though some Gay people wish to be *respected* as homosexual, many remain afraid of being *labeled* as homosexual. The best solution for marketers may be to use Gay-owned or Gay-friendly media so that labels are irrelevant. A game played between advertisers and consumers is the use of phrases with meanings specific to insiders of Gay culture: "Gayspeak." Examples from advertisements are "Another one coming out," "Show your pride," "We are everywhere," and "Feeling outrageous?" This strategy, used by both mainstream and Gay-oriented advertisers, exemplifies how codes and double meanings can show Gay consumers that an advertised brand or firm understands Gay culture.

Kitzinger (1995) has identified five specific characteristics that result from the experience of being Gay in a straight world. First is a sense of alienation and self-protection, with a tendency to distrust others. Second is a health consciousness and focus on satisfying needs independently. Third, Gay people seek affiliation and want group identity, especially with others "out of the closet." This means seeking communications with and loyalty to those who are friendly to the Gay community. Fourth, Gays generally try new things and want to experience new feelings. Fifth, they try to reduce stress in their lives (Lukenbill, 1995, pp. 106-110).

The endless accommodations within a Gay person's self-concept mean there is no such thing as a single Gay or Lesbian lifestyle. The significance for marketers is that many Gay and Lesbian consumers perceive a community boundary between themselves and the rest of Americans, regardless of other shared identities of age, race, or ethnicity. This perceived separation from mainstream American culture is the foundation of a Gay and Lesbian subculture.

## WHAT IS THE DEMOGRAPHIC PROFILE OF THE GAY MARKET?

There are conflicting estimates of the size of the American Gay population. The 1948 Kinsey study estimated the homosexual population at 10%, and this number was accepted as the "standard" until recently. But in the 1990s, several research studies challenged the 10% estimate. In 1993, the Battelle study (Painton, 1993) reported that only 1% of their male respondents considered themselves exclusively homosexual. The methods of the Battelle study were criticized by Gay activists, who claimed that face-to-face surveys inevitably underestimate the incidence of same-sex relations, which are illegal in many states. Studies in Europe point to a range between 1% and 4%. Lesbians alone were estimated to include about 3 million women in the United States in 1993 (about 1% of the total U.S. population) (Salholz & Glick, 1993).

The Yankelovich study in 1994, perhaps the most "blue chip" firm to study consumer attitudes of Gay people, places the estimate at 6% of the U.S. adult population (Tuller, 1994). Two percent to 10% of the adult population in 1998 (estimated at 178,582,000) means 3.6 to 17.9 million Gay people—too large a range for error for most marketers. Differences in methodology probably account for some of the different findings, depending on whether surveys ask a person to categorize him- or herself or his or her behavior. Many people who have had homosexual experiences do not consider themselves Gay; thus, self-reports tend to be conservative (Jandt, 1995, p. 353; Lukenbill, 1995, p. 51; Penaloza, 1996).

The 2000 population of the United States will include over 180 million adults. On the basis of the discussion above, the Gay and Lesbian population could vary from 3.6 million (2%) to 18 million (10%). Using the Yankelovich calculation of "6% of persons 16 to 65 years of age in the top 25 metropolitan areas," the Gay and Lesbian population in 2000 will include more than the 14 million people they estimated in 1994.

Gay persons tend to congregate in urban and suburban areas of the largest cities in the country (Kahan & Mulryan, 1995). In fact, the Yankelovich study estimated that 27% of the population in cities over 3 million and 34% of the population in cities from 1 to 3 million were Gay. Table 7.2 shows an estimate of the size of the Gay and Lesbian population, using 2%, 6%, and 10% of persons aged 16 to 65, for the top 25 American cities. It is a conservative estimate of the entire market's size (1.5 to 7.7 million), but it is supported by the Yankelovich finding that Gays are highly concentrated in these 25 metropolitan areas (Elliott, 1994a).

Who does the term *Gays and Lesbians* refer to? Certainly, it includes men and women with same-sex orientations. The term customarily covers bisexuals (people attracted to both men and women) as well, though sometimes "and bisexuals" is explicitly added. From a mainstream perspective, Gay men, Lesbians, and bisexual persons tend to be relegated to a single "sexual minorities" category, along with such groups as the transgendered, sadomasochists, fetishists, and pedophiles. Within the Gay and Lesbian community, however, other labels are used in accordance with the sexual behavior in which a person engages.

*Transgendered* is a term that refers to both transsexuals and cross-dressers. It is estimated that over 25,000 Americans have had sex-reassignment surgery. At least 2% of children have "discomfort with their assigned gender and may exper-

**TABLE 7.2** Estimates of Gay and Lesbian Population in the Top 25 U.S. Metropolitan
Areas

| Metropolitan Area | 1998 Adult Population[a] | 2% of Adults | 6% of Adults | 10% of Adults |
|---|---|---|---|---|
| **Estimate of 1998 U.S.** | | | | |
| **Adult Population** | **178,582,000** | **3,571,640** | **10,714,920** | **17,858,200** |
| **Top 25:** | | | | |
| New York | 12,258,867 | 245,177 | 735,532 | 1,225,887 |
| Los Angeles | 10,276,271 | 205,525 | 616,576 | 1,027,627 |
| Chicago | 7,377,275 | 147,546 | 442,637 | 737,728 |
| San Francisco | 4,513,854 | 90,277 | 270,831 | 451,386 |
| Philadelphia | 3,885,962 | 77,719 | 233,158 | 388,596 |
| Detroit | 3,111,639 | 62,232 | 186,698 | 311,164 |
| Dallas | 2,971,673 | 59,434 | 178,300 | 297,167 |
| Washington, DC | 2,943,591 | 58,872 | 176,616 | 294,359 |
| Boston | 2,887,604 | 57,752 | 173,256 | 288,760 |
| Houston | 2,826,974 | 56,540 | 169,619 | 282,697 |
| Atlanta | 2,337,713 | 46,754 | 140,263 | 233,771 |
| Miami | 2,217,565 | 44,351 | 133,054 | 221,757 |
| Seattle | 1,918,978 | 38,380 | 115,139 | 191,898 |
| Cleveland, OH | 1,798,035 | 35,961 | 107,882 | 179,804 |
| San Diego | 1,780,259 | 35,605 | 106,816 | 178,026 |
| Minneapolis | 1,779,287 | 35,586 | 106,757 | 177,929 |
| Phoenix, AZ | 1,666,938 | 33,339 | 100,016 | 166,694 |
| St. Louis, MO | 1,589,804 | 31,796 | 95,388 | 158,980 |
| Denver | 1,442,217 | 28,844 | 86,533 | 144,222 |
| Pittsburgh | 1,409,356 | 28,187 | 84,561 | 140,936 |
| Tampa, FL | 1,324,678 | 26,494 | 79,481 | 132,468 |
| Cincinnati, OH | 1,184,752 | 23,695 | 71,085 | 118,475 |
| Portland, OR | 1,111,965 | 22,239 | 66,718 | 111,197 |
| Kansas City, KA/MO | 1,081,818 | 21,636 | 64,909 | 108,182 |
| Milwaukee, WI | 1,048,000 | 20,960 | 62,880 | 104,800 |
| **Range for size of** | | | | |
| **Gay population** | | | | |
| **in 25 metro areas** | | **1,534,901** | **4,604,705** | **7,674,510** |

SOURCE: U.S. Bureau of the Census (1999d); includes 1990 population for ages 16-64 in MSAs,[b]
plus 1990-1996 MSA estimated growth.
a. Includes only adults 16 to 64 years of age.
b. MSA stands for Metropolitan Statistical Area

iment with gender roles" (Cloud, 1998, p. 48). Neither the transgendered nor other Gay persons use the terms *Gay* and *Lesbian* for effeminate men, "butch" women, hermaphrodites (intersexed persons), or people who engage in alternative sexual practices.

Estimates of the spending power of Gays and Lesbians vary as much as estimates of the size of the population. In 1993, one researcher claimed that Gay spending power was over $500 billion, based on an estimate of 18.5 million Gay people. Even the *Advocate* speculated that there were no more than 5 million people to target in the Gay population. Another researcher estimated Gay spending that year to be $382 billion (Penaloza, 1996). *Business Week* reported that Gay Americans controlled 19% of "spendable income in the United States" (Jandt, 1995, p. 362).

One reason the estimates of spending power for Gays and Lesbians are so unstable is that individual and household incomes of Gays are used interchangeably. The Gay press publicized their readers as having average household incomes almost 70% higher than those of heterosexuals (Alsop, 1999a). However, relying again on the Yankelovich Monitor Survey, their reports estimated household incomes at $37,400 for Gay men as compared to $39,300 for straight men and at $34,800 for Lesbians as compared to $34,400 for straight women. They also found a higher percentage of Gay than heterosexual men with incomes under $25,000 and a higher proportion of Gays and Lesbians than of heterosexuals with incomes above $50,000. Such skewed income distribution suggests that Gay consumers include a smaller middle-income group and larger low- and high-income groups. Ultimately, the Yankelovich study, whose sample reflected the total U.S. population, found no significant differences in the incomes of Gay people and heterosexuals. Myths die hard, and years later the hype about higher Gay incomes is still around (Alsop, 1999a).

One consistency among all studies of the American Gay and Lesbian population is a finding of higher than average education levels. Fourteen percent of Gays and Lesbians attended graduate school, compared to 7% of heterosexuals; 49% have had some college compared to 37% of the "straight" population, according to the Yankelovich study. As for occupations, 56% of Gays/Lesbians were in professional/managerial jobs versus 16% of heterosexuals. They are also more likely to be self-employed and a source of entrepreneurs marketing to fellow members of the Gay community.

With regard to ethnic differences in the Gay and Lesbian population, there are very few sources of information. Nevertheless, testimony to cultural diversity in same-sex orientation is the work by Beverly Greene (1997a). In a study of over

700 Gay and Lesbian African American couples, a significant amount of income, education, and employment diversity was found. Unlike heterosexual couples, there were more Gay couples of mixed ethnicities. Greene also found incomes of male same-sex couples to be statistically higher than incomes of female couples (Peplau, Cochran, & Mays, 1997).

Some Native American tribes have a same-sex tradition of "berdache" couples. Some African societies have "woman marriages," and some Asians recognize male pair bonding (Potgieter, 1997). Nevertheless, Greene suggested that a larger percentage of homosexuals in American ethnic communities remain closeted. An example of why this may be true is the Latino importance given to family and a definition of family that excludes homosexuality (Cobo-Hanlon, 1999). Gender roles in Latino and Asian cultures are tightly defined, and males and females have distinctive role expectations. Disapproval of homosexuality among the Latino community may be more intense than among Anglo Americans (Greene, 1997b). "Coming out" for Asian Americans can be seen as a threat to "the continuation of the family line and a rejection of appropriate roles within the culture as well" (Greene, 1997b, p. 222). African and Native American Gays and Lesbians may also experience fears of the consequences of "coming out" in their respective communities.

The opportunities for marketers who can connect with consumers who prefer same-sex sexual relationships are significant indeed. The demographic profile of the Gay market indicates higher average levels of education, household income, and disposable income, as well as more managerial and professional occupations than other American groups. How great these differences are is in dispute, but they translate to heavy product usage of luxury items such as vacation homes, electronic audiovisual equipment, credit cards, liquor and wine, domestic and foreign travel, and sports and fitness activities. A large percentage of readers of Gay publications report that they are "very likely" to buy the national products advertised there ("Media Kit," 1996). The cities of London and Paris openly appeal to Gay travelers, a segment spending between $17 and $47 billion (Alsop, 1999e).

## GAY GEOGRAPHY, LIFESTYLES, AND POLITICS

An important aspect of Gay and Lesbian life is a strong sense of community, as seen in the growing number of Gay neighborhoods, social groups, publications, redefined "families," and special-interest lobbying efforts. This unifying force has been building a sense of community among Gays since the late 1960s, and it has been fundamental to fighting the AIDS epidemic among members.

Gay neighborhoods satisfy the need to reinforce a Gay person's sense of identity. They serve as a meeting ground for Gay people, and they create physical and psychological safety. Still, most "Gay" neighborhoods are predominantly "Gay male" (Alsop, 1999d; Jay & Young, 1979, p. 796). One of the most important reasons for the congregation of Gay people in urban areas is the greater acceptance of alternative lifestyles. A participant in an earlier study expressed his feelings about Gay neighborhoods this way:

> The topic is integration versus ghetto. I prefer integration even though it's tougher. First of all, the ghetto makes you forget what society is really like, and you lose the motivation to push for change. Second, if everyone is in the ghetto, who will be the positive gay model for young people trying to come to grips with their identities in cowtown? (Jay & Young, 1979, p. 798)

The following are cited as neighborhoods with high concentrations of Gay population: New York's Greenwich Village, SoHo, Brooklyn Heights, Park Slope, and Chelsea; San Francisco's Haight-Ashbury and Castro; Boston's South End and Back Bay; Houston's Montrose and Heights; Chicago's Lincoln Park and New Town; Los Angeles's West Hollywood and Silverlake. In addition there are concentrations of Gay-owned property in Fire Island, New York; Provincetown, Massachusetts; South Beach, Key West, and Pensacola, Florida; Laguna Beach and Palm Springs, California; Takoma Park, Maryland, outside Washington; and Royal Oak, Michigan, outside Detroit.

As far as distribution across the United States, 25% of Gay persons live in the South, 21% in the northeastern states, 32% in the north central states, and 22% in the West (Lukenbill, 1995, p. 99; Sears, 1990). Over 27% are to be found in cities with over 3 million people, and 60% live in metropolitan areas with 1 million or more people. These numbers compare to 18% of heterosexuals in cities with over 3 million people and 45% of heterosexuals in cities with over 1 million people. Urban neighborhoods such as Park Slope in Brooklyn and Oakland in San Francisco are cited as popular neighborhoods for Lesbians. There is a growing presence of Gay people in smaller cities and suburbs. The movement out of predominantly Gay neighborhoods is a result of increasing tolerance and the desire to achieve the same American "dream house" that non-Gays prize (Kahan & Mulryan, 1995).

The Gay bar is frequently the first public experience for a Gay person (Majors, 1994). Gay-owned and Gay-friendly businesses, especially Gay bookstores and Gay publications, are important members of the community. Other important organizations include groups formed among computer chat rooms and social and political organizations. Religious groups such as Dignity, Integrity, and the Metropolitan Community Church are active supporters of their Gay congregations. The Metropolitan Church is a long-standing member of the Gay and Lesbian community that was established in 1968; recently it included over 200 congregations in the United States and 300 worldwide. One of its most worthwhile endeavors is bringing a sense of personal dignity to thousands of Gay Christians (McNeill, 1988, p. 181).

More Lesbians are likely to live in rural and suburban areas than are Gay men. Lesbians are almost as likely to be mothers as are heterosexual females (67% compared to 72%). This is a likely explanation for why they prefer suburban areas more than Gay men do. About 22% of Lesbians have children under 18 years of age in their homes (Alsop, 1999d), whereas only 15% of Gay men do. Sixty percent of Lesbians and 40% of Gay men are in long-term committed relationships (Blumenfeld, 1988, p. 374; Jandt, 1995, p. 365). Contrary to their stereotypes among mainstream Americans, 70% of Gay men and 80% of Lesbians have always been monogamous.

Many Gay people speak of a Gay or Lesbian "sensibility or culture, something beyond the mere question of same-sex sexual acts" (Jay & Young, 1979, p. 763). Is there such a thing as a Gay lifestyle? Early studies confirmed that homosexual relationships are more similar to than different from heterosexual ones (Walters, 1992, p. 14). At the same time, there is more role flexibility. Same-sex couples are less likely to internalize stereotypical gender roles (Walters, 1992, p. 14). Redefinition of the "family" and the important role of Gay-identity organizations have created an extensive network of community for Gays and Lesbians. Success in fighting AIDS has been due in part to the access that these community organizations have to members of the Gay and Lesbian subculture. Table 7.3 lists national nonprofit and political organizations in the Gay community.

Typically, urban Gays and Lesbians have an outgoing life. They actively seek out new experiences, especially in shopping, food, and entertainment. Stress is a major issue in the lives of Gay men and Lesbians. Whether traveling or at home, security is important. A strong friendship network is an important antidote for this perceived stress, as are, on occasion, other forms of tranquilizers. For a small minority of the subculture, drug use is a serious hazard, just as it is for

**TABLE 7.3** Significant Nonprofit and Political Organizations in the Gay Community

| Organization Name | Brief Description of Purpose or Activities | Address Online |
|---|---|---|
| Human Rights Campaign | Largest Lesbian and Gay political organization | www.hrcusa.org |
| GLAAD (Gay and Lesbian Alliance) | Promotes fair, accurate, and inclusive representation of individuals and events | www.glaad.org/ |
| Queer Nation | Aggressive Gay and Lesbian organization: "We're Here, We're Queer, Get Used to It!" | Www.altculture.com/ aentries/q/queerxnati. html |
| ACT-UP (AIDS Coalition to Unleash Power) | Direct-action protest to focus concerted efforts on finding an AIDS cure | www.altculture.com/ aentries/a/actxup.html |
| NGLTF (National Gay and Lesbian Task Force) | Progressive civil rights group with grassroots organizations and advocacy | www.ngltf.org |
| CUAV (Community United Against Violence) | Addresses and prevents hate violence directed at Lesbians, Gay men, transgendered persons, and bisexuals | www.xq.com/cuav/ |
| DQ (Digital Queers) | Dedicated to promoting use of computer technology among activist groups | www.dq.org.dq/ |
| Qworld | Features interactive forums, online publications | www.qworld.org |
| Lesbigay Directory at IGC | Nonprofit online service provider, assists activist groups to make use of Internet technology | www.igc.apc.org/lbg/ |
| ACLU Gay and Lesbian Rights | Information about Gay rights issues | www.aclu.org/issues/gay |
| National Lesbian and Gay Health Association | Organization in Washington, DC, dedicated solely to Gay health and health care | www.serve.com/nlgha/ |
| Gay.com Network | Online chat network, 2,000 affiliate sites, news, info, and matchmaking | www.gay.com or www.gay.net |

heterosexuals. Many Gay persons are avid consumers of fashion and fitness products. As several Gay people have said, "It's a life, not a lifestyle." Yet it's not *one particular* life: "The gay subgroup encompasses as great a variety of appearance and behavior as does the nongay segment of the population" (Lukenbill, 1995, p. 101; see also Jandt, 1995).

Several authors cite the importance of clothes, symbols, and language as important markers of Gay identity (Altman, 1987; Kates, 1998; Meyer, 1994). An example of the relevance of "style" in communicating a Gay aesthetic is Gay male parody in the form of camp. Camp is a highly dramatic style in fashion or design that exaggerates, is outrageous, and otherwise celebrates the banal. Meyer (1994) claimed that camp is a critique of society and a vehicle of social mobility for Gay men. One form of camp involves idolizing female stars such as Bette Davis, Mae West, and Bette Midler and making a parody of these strong, sexually aggressive women succeeding in a patriarchal world. There continues to be censorship of Gay themes in art, in theater, and even on the Internet. A number of symbols serve as markers of Gay identity, such as the rainbow, the color lavender, a pink triangle, the number 338, and the Greek sign for lambda.

## DIVERSE GAY COMMUNITIES, UNITED IN FAVOR OF GAY RIGHTS

In the "nature versus nurture" debate over the "cause" of homosexuality, recent evidence suggests that both contribute (Begley, 1995a; Thompson, 1995). Many Gay people feel their same-sex preferences to be as innate as skin or hair color. This argument has significant political implications because legal protection might be extended to Gays to prevent discrimination, just as it has been used to combat racial and gender discrimination (Thompson, 1995). About 60% of transgendered persons claim to have been assaulted. Attacks on all Gay people made frequent headlines in the late 1990s. In several states, it is illegal for Gay people to adopt children or serve as foster parents. Such differences in the rights of Gay people versus other Americans are a motivation behind political activism in the Gay community. Still, less than one third of Gay persons have actively participated in such causes (Jay & Young, 1979, pp. 740-778).

The Gay civil rights movement had its origins in the 1950s. During that time, homosexuals looked inward, seeking tolerance and understanding from outsiders. During the 1960s, the movement focused on debates about how to proceed within mainstream society. The first "bill of rights" was proposed in 1961 by the

Mattachine Society of Washington. The next major advance was recognition by the American Psychiatric Association that homosexuality was not a mental illness. During the 1970s and more in the 1980s, the Gay press focused on the "coming-out" process and its importance to self-respect. In this regard, the Gay media have played an important role in educating Gay people about how to deal with Gay issues. The Gay Liberation Movement has been committed to changing attitudes, improving communication and community among Gay people, and combating stereotypes in mainstream society.

Gay activism today centers on equal rights and the freedom to be visible in the mainstream world (Stewart, 1991). To that end, over 1 million people participated in the Gay Rights parade in 1994 in New York, celebrating 25 years of activism since the Stonewall riots of 1969. Another group seeking recognition of their rights are Gay and Lesbian teenagers; their advocacy groups are the Gay-Lesbian-Straight Education Network and Gay-Straight Alliances. Partially due to increasing visibility in the media, the 1990s saw a national rise in hate crimes against Gay people, already the most frequent victims of hate crime according to the U.S. Justice Department (Jandt, 1995, p. 359). Legal recognition of Gay marriages is yet another issue driving the fight for rights among Gay and Lesbian groups. This is a means by which they can press for domestic partnership programs and benefits such as health and life insurance and leaves for paternity or maternity illness and bereavement.

As more people have "come out of the closet," Gay and Lesbian leaders have encouraged others in the community to support the organizations that contribute to Gay and Lesbian causes. This has made it less risky for mainstream organizations that target the Gay market. Mainstream firms such as Absolut Vodka, Benetton, Hiram Walker, American Airlines, Virgin Atlantic Airways, Coors, and Philip Morris jumped into the Gay market in the early 1990s by supporting nonprofit organizations in the Gay community and maintaining a presence in Gay media.

## THE MEDIA: IMPORTANCE OF ENDORSEMENT

Gay-oriented media have a long history. The *Advocate* started as an underground newsletter in 1967 that supported Gay issues (Saveri, 1995). It continues to be one of the few national media by which Gays can become informed about political issues. Each issue of the *Advocate* has a section called "The Advocate

Report: Front Page" that highlights recent cases affecting Gay rights. It is also a venue for mainstream politicians to communicate their support of Gay issues without the spotlight that the mainstream press would put on the politician's position. In the March 31, 1998, issue of the *Advocate,* there was a "viewpoint" by Vice President Al Gore (1998) that went unpublicized in mainstream media.

The *Advocate's* readers claim that they spend about 74 minutes on each issue and that each copy has at least 2 readers. More than 80% claim not to read other national Gay and Lesbian magazines. The most important statistic is the 86% of its readers "likely to purchase products or services advertised in the *Advocate.*" Other interesting statistics from their media kit are the following: 45% of readers used editorial/advertising information when choosing travel/leisure activities; 43% mentioned to others advertised products or services; and 36% purchased advertised products or services.

In the 1990s, a number of new national magazines were introduced to Gay readers: *Out, Ten Percent, Girlfriends, Genre, POZ,* and *Deneuve* (now *Curve*) are examples. These publications are slicker and more upscale than the earlier Gay press. The transformation hasn't been easy. The publisher of *Genre* discovered one reason the magazine wasn't selling well at first: Gay readers were still looking for it in the back, "where they always look" (Mathews, 1992, p. 62). In 1996, *Genre* had 44,000 paid subscribers. The *Advocate* was hit hard by the newer competitors. In 1993, the *Advocate* had over 125,000 national circulation; in 1994, circulation dropped to 68,000. The paper now sticks to news issues and lets *Out, Genre,* and *Curve* showcase Gay lifestyles. At the local level, there are over 100 Gay newspapers and magazines in the United States.

In 1994, it was estimated that no more than $50 million was spent by national advertisers in all Gay-oriented media (Levine, 1995). The Gay media focus on editorial content of interest to members of the Gay community. For example, movies account for 6% of editorial coverage, theater 5%, and the arts 23%. Seventy-two percent of Gay men and women attended a movie in the past year, and 71% went to live theater (compared to 21% of the American population). Gays were five times more likely than the general population to attend classical music concerts and four times more likely to see a dance performance. Although only 3% of articles in the Gay press concern bars, clubs, and restaurants, they generate 23% of the advertising (Klein, 1998; Mulryan/Nash, 1997). Gay men are seen as "fashion conscious and trend setting" by other Americans too (Jandt, 1995, p. 362).

Print has been the mainstay of Gay-oriented media, but that is no longer the only way to reach Gay and Lesbian consumers. More than 90% of Gay men and

82% of Lesbian women report reading magazines and books as hobbies. Top non-Gay magazines among Gay readers are *Newsweek, Time, People, National Geographic, Gentleman's Quarterly, New Yorker, Smithsonian, Vanity Fair, Men's Health,* and *Consumer Reports.* Gay men report a preference for reading nonfiction, whereas Lesbians read more fiction. Several cities have Gay-oriented radio and television stations. Two Gay television networks are available by cable or direct satellite broadcasts.

There is also a long history of direct marketing to Gay consumers, and there are higher than average response rates within the Gay community. Over 90% of *Advocate* readers claimed to have ordered merchandise by mail or phone in the last 12 months; 84% said they had ordered from a catalog in the last 12 months. Not only is there a high response rate among Gay consumers to direct marketers, but they buy more frequently and spend more money per purchase (average = $483). Catalogs are estimated to reach about 1 million Gay and Lesbian households. Shocking Gray's list alone claimed over 130,000 names and 3% response rates. Readers of Gay media have a higher than average index on renting cars, foreign travel, and hotel and resort stays, and over 50% are enrolled in frequent flyer programs. Other important and traditional media in the Gay community are the numerous city and national directories, such as the Gayellow Pages (Renaissance House), that list Gay-owned or Gay-friendly professionals, accommodations, bars, events, organization meeting places, and social groups.

The Internet has become second only to print media as the most used channel of communication for members of the Gay community. There are innumerable Gay-oriented personal Web pages, and companies are listed that seek business from the Gay community. The Internet may be the only place where the so-called "openly closeted" ("out" online only) Gay population can be reached (Bank, 1999). An analysis of the Web pages of the top mainstream advertisers in the Gay market concluded that those firms were communicating information about their products as well as their policies of interest to Gay consumers (Smith, 1998). As e-commerce becomes more widespread among marketers, Gay and Lesbian consumers are sure to explore its appeal. A 1999 study found that Gay people spent more money online than the general population, and Gay.com, PlanetOut, Gay Financial Network, and Online Partners were the first gay businesses to capture the attention of venture capitalists (Bank, 1999). Table 7.4 lists the major Gay-oriented media.

Another way to reach Gay consumers is via mainstream programs and entertainment that include Gay characters and themes. Recent films with Gay characters include *Billy's Hollywood Screen Kiss, As Good as It Gets, My Best Friend's*

**TABLE 7.4** Specialized Media for Gay and Lesbian Audiences

| | |
|---|---|
| **Gay Television Networks**<br>　Gay Entertainment Television<br>　Q Network<br>　Gay Cable Network<br>**Gay Radio**<br>　WINS-AM, NYC<br>　WBAI (Gay-oriented show)<br>　WFNX, Boston<br>**Gay Magazines**<br>　*Advocate*<br>　*Genre*<br>　*Out* (100,000 reported circulation)<br>　*10 Percent* (75,000 reported circulation)<br>　*Victory! The National Gay Entrepreneur*<br>　*Magazine*<br>　*POZ*<br>　*Plus Voice* (Chicago)<br>　*DSN* (*Diseased Pariah News*)<br>　*Art & Understanding*<br>　*Our World*<br>　*Frontiers*<br>　*Urge*<br>　*On Our Backs*<br>　*Deneuve* (changed name to *Curve* in 1998)<br>　*Outweek*<br>　*Puhleeze* | **Gay Television Programs**<br>　*Party Talk*<br>　*Inside Out*<br>　*Mokostyle*<br>　*Forward and Out*<br>**Gay Mailing Lists**<br>　Strubco of New York<br>　Body Politic (Toronto)<br>**Gay Newspapers—National**<br>　*QW*<br>　*Next News*<br>　National Gay Newspaper<br>　Guild<br>**Gay-Oriented Catalogs**<br>　Shocking Gray<br>　M2M<br>　Made in Gay America<br>　Proud Enterprises<br>　Direct Male<br>　TZABACO<br>　In the Company of Women<br>　Best Sellers Club<br>**Publishers of Gay Literature**<br>　Viking/Penguin Press<br>　Publishing Triangle |

*Wedding, The Opposite of Sex, Love and Death on Long Island, Love Is the Devil, Longtime Companion, The Crying Game, Philadelphia, The Birdcage, In and Out, Gods and Monsters,* and *High Art.* Popular television programs such as *Roseanne, Northern Exposure, Will and Grace,* and *Melrose Place* have included Gay characters (Poniewozik, 1999). Likewise, well-known Gay endorsers such as Greg Louganis, Martina Navratilova, k.d. lang, Anne Heche, and Ellen DeGeneres can reach both Gay and mainstream consumers simultaneously.

Images of Gay people in mainstream media have come a long way in the 1990s. Gay people must overcome mainstream America's fears that homosexuality is a threat to society. Long-held stereotypes describe them in terms such as *perverted, abnormal, mentally ill,* and *maladjusted.* In research studies, Gay women are described as less attractive or feminine than straight women. The connection of homosexuality with AIDS and the legitimate fears of all Americans of catching what seemed to be an incurable disease have melded into an intense homophobia among some Americans. The "bathhouse" images of the early 1980s did not help Gays gain respectability. A *Life* magazine article in 1964 described the homosexual lifestyle as "obsessive, sadistic, screaming, lewd, aggressive, emotionally unstable, furtive, hazardous, lonely, lazy, luxury-loving, sponging, unwanted, utterly dependent, compulsive" (Winter, 1975, pp. 103-111). The lack of a clear, "scientific" explanation for same-sex preferences, compounded with a natural fear of the "different," is translated into a judgment that Gays are "morally irresponsible" by people who have different behavioral norms.

Though it may seem that mainstream media images have until recently mostly worked against the acceptance of Gays and Lesbians in American mainstream society, they have also given Gays and Lesbians a very visible place in our popular culture. There is a shared language code that some scholars call "Gayspeak." Though its secret codes continue to change, it is in use in youth-centered "urban slang" as well as in mainstream media (Jandt, 1995, p. 360; Lukenbill, 1995, pp. 7-16). The episode of the popular television show *Ellen* in which Ellen "came out" was the highest-rated show that year on the ABC network, with an average rating of 30. Volkswagen kept its "Drivers Wanted" ads on Ellen for the "coming-out" episode, whereas other big car advertisers (e.g., Chrysler, GM, and Ford) and Wendy's opted out of the episode. The reaction among Gay viewers was immediate: 18% of planned viewers said they would be more likely to buy from advertisers who stayed with the show and 17% said they'd be less likely to buy from advertisers who deserted it (Beatty, 1997).

The mainstream media have more recently publicized a number of alternative sexual practices and presented them as just "another wacky lifestyle choice" (Lukenbill, 1995, p. 17; Marin, 1997-1998). S&M (sadism and masochism) was the theme behind a Manhattan restaurant, La Nouvelle Justine. And S&M references were all over advertising for Gucci, a Janet Jackson album, and scenes in *Deconstructing Harry,* a Woody Allen movie of the late 1990s. Cross-dressing celebrities like Ru Paul and Divine have been mimicked by cross-dressing basketball star Dennis Rodman. These references to alternative sexual behaviors lose some of their power to shock as they become part of mainstream popular culture.

In the mid-1990s, Hartford Insurance targeted Gay consumers via Gay media but also through mainstream newspapers and outdoor transit and billboards. The campaign for "Diverse Household Auto Insurance" was first introduced by ads in *Out* and the *Advocate* and then was rolled out to selective urban markets. The ad paired various combinations of blue and pink cars with a tag line of "Commitment. Bring It On." The fine print offered 25% discounts to Gay, Lesbian, and "even . . . heterosexual couples" (Petrecca & Arndorfer, 1998, p. 12). An example of the print ad is shown in Figure 7.1. The playful use of colors is an example of the "double meanings" that Gay consumers can read into mainstream media messages. Encoding mainstream messages with "double entendres" and "Gayspeak" is an excellent tactic for capturing the attention of Gay consumers of mainstream media.

Although community events are not a "medium" in the traditional sense, for the Gay market they have proven an economical way to establish a firm as a supporter of the Gay and Lesbian community. In 1994, the Gay Games IV hosted 11,000 competitors from 44 countries, and companies paid over $4 million to be associated with the games, political events, and rallies. Some of the companies represented were AT&T, Continental Airlines, Hiram Walker distillers, Naya bottled water, and Miller Brewing. The producers expected revenues of at least $2.5 million from ticket sales and a contribution of $111 million to the local economy, the same amount as the U.S. Open tennis tournament. More recently, Anheuser-Busch created an ad with a Bud Light bottle in studded black leather straps and cap to publicize the Folsom Street Fair, billed as "the world's biggest leather event" (Alsop, 1999b). Specialized events have also been created by marketers. For example, the Wyndham Hotel in Palm Springs, CA, has hosted the "White Party," "One Night in Rio," and "A Country Affair" at "Dinah Shore" weekends (the same timing as the Nabisco Dinah Shore LPGA Golf Tournament). This is a "circuit party" for Lesbians, with many repeat customers. The "Lina Shore Golf Classic" is a golf tournament for Lesbians held since 1988 (Ocamb, 1998). Schwab's $40,000 sponsorship of the 19th San Francisco Gay and Lesbian Film Festival brought in over $10 million in new accounts before Schwab had even mailed out a brochure to participants (Levine, 1995). And in 1995, the exhibition *In a Different Light* at the University Art Museum of Berkeley focused exclusively on Gay and Lesbian artists.

## MARKETING EXPERIENCES AND RESPONSE OF GAY CONSUMERS

It is helpful to note the similarities between the Gay and Lesbian and immigrant markets. Like immigrants, Gay people are "birds of a feather." They stick to-

**Figure 7.1.** Hartford Insurance Advertisement for "Diversified Household Auto Insurance" Service

gether, support each other, and vote for each other. Like immigrants, they often start their own businesses because it is difficult to find appropriate employment within the mainstream community. Like immigrants, they are proud of their distinctiveness but fear being branded as different. In addition, Gay men and Lesbians exhibit all the characteristics of an immigrant tribe. They have distinctive mores and fashions, language, signs, symbols, gathering places, and enclaves. If Gays are like immigrants, "marketers who study them must think like anthropologists" (Kahan & Mulryan, 1995, p. 42).

Reading the Gay and Lesbian consumer means understanding the ironies recognized by the last paragraph. Gay consumers want to be full-fledged members of the American mosaic, able to express an individuality that includes their homosexuality. They may have some unique tastes and behaviors, but they do not want to be branded as outsiders or set apart (Bowes, 1996, p. 221; Freitas, Kaiser, & Hammidi, 1996). This paradox creates a fine line for marketers to walk in recognizing members of the Gay subculture without threatening members of mainstream society who are likely to compose the majority of their customers. Outdated stereotypes of Lesbians continue to keep mainstream companies out of media such as *Curve* and in denial of the market's potential (Alsop, 1999d).

Penaloza (1996) has outlined four alternatives for companies that want to attract Gay and Lesbian consumers. The first option is to redirect a general market campaign to Gay/Lesbian media. Without incurring the additional costs of producing distinctive marketing communications for Gay and Lesbian consumers, many organizations can position themselves as members of the extended Gay and Lesbian community.

As noted earlier, Gay consumers have a high awareness of mainstream companies that advertise in Gay-oriented media. In addition, they often prefer to buy from companies that have a visible presence in the Gay community. Miller Lite has been the "beer of choice for Lesbians" partly because Miller has been aggressively advertising in Gay magazines for over 10 years (Chase, 1997). In product categories like casual clothes, there are few differences in the tastes of Gay and heterosexual consumers (Rudd, 1996). An example of the "standardized message, targeted media" approach to Gay consumers is the Saab campaign placed in Gay-oriented print media using general market advertisements that read, "Peel off your inhibitions. Find your own road."

A second alternative is to use messages featuring only men or women together to invite Gay/Lesbian identification. American Express used this kind of ambiguity when it introduced "Checks for Two." The ads showed two male or two female names in the fine print. The advertisements were placed in both mainstream and Gay media, doubling the exposure to Gay consumers. A 1992 Kmart ad showed two men shopping for Father's Day presents, with one considering a saw and the other reminding him that his father didn't have a fireplace, though "we do." Gay men thought they were being targeted, but Kmart claimed that was not the case ("Tuaca Targets Lesbians," 1995). In 1999, Philip Morris added a second man to a couple in the mainstream version of a Parliament ad when it was featured in Gay magazines (Alsop, 1999c). Figure 7.2 shows another version of this kind of message. It is a Benson & Hedges advertisement using "cigarette people," and it was placed in both Gay and mainstream media. The "cigarette people" have no obvious genders.

Yet a third option is to develop a separate marketing communications campaign with distinct and identifiable appeals to members of the Lesbian/Gay subculture. An example is the ad that Kenneth Cole put together, featuring pink and black shoelaces in the shape of a triangle. The copy read, "Shoes shouldn't have to stay in the closet either." Gay media are sprinkled with firms using Gay symbols like the rainbow, the pink triangle, 338, and the Greek sign for lambda. Advertisements using these symbols, placed in Gay-oriented media, or even integrated communications programs incorporating Gay-oriented events, support of Gay-oriented causes, and other Gay-friendly corporate policies, may draw the ire of some mainstream consumers. But more and more firms are willing to take that risk (Kates, 1999). IKEA gained a tremendous amount of publicity within mainstream media when it used an ad openly targeting Gay men in the mainstream media. Their ads showed two men shopping for furniture.

The fourth approach is to use "Gayspeak" coding, such as Miller Lite's "Pour on the Pride" (Clark, 1991, cited in Freitas et al., 1996, pp. 89-90). This kind of appeal is easily tied in with other elements of an integrated communications campaign within the Gay community subculture (Alsop, 1999c). AT&T used lavender envelopes in a Gay-targeted direct mail campaign. A number of mainstream marketers create a high-profile presence at events such as circuit parties for Lesbians, exclusively Gay male travel cruises, or the Gay Games while keeping their messages in mainstream media low-key. For example, Saturn had a two-page layout that ran in mainstream media, showing a female engineer in a tuxedo. There were no references to gender or sexual orientation, but they believed Lesbians would identify with the woman. The campaign was followed up by support of a variety of Gay-friendly events. Subaru quietly put personalized plates with "SENA LVR" and "P-TOWNIE" and the logo of the Human Rights campaign on the bumpers of cars in its advertising. A spokesperson said, "It's clever and not offensive, and if you're in-the-know, you chuckle" (Alsop, 1999c, p. B1). Halloween's popularity in Gay subculture has become a mainstream

**Figure 7.2.** Benson & Hedges "Peace and Quiet" Advertisement in Gay-Oriented Medium

event for heterosexual adults as well, making it a major "Gayspeak" opportunity (Kates, 1999; Zonana, 1992). Both Figures 7.3a and 7.3b illustrate the use of "Gayspeak" and send a message of the affiliation and acceptance that many Gay consumers seek.

Whatever overall strategy a company chooses to use, other authors suggest that a corporate policy of nondiscrimination should be in place first (Baker & Judge, 1996). That step alone places an organization among pioneers in sharing values with members of the Gay market. Lukenbill (1995, pp. 134-135) suggested that the next move should be to publicize and contribute to organizations that defend Gay and Lesbian individuality. The goodwill generated by such gestures is believed to cost little and to go a long way with Gay consumers.

Lukenbill (1995) also recommended that the specific needs of Gay consumers living in "straight" society set priorities for communication messages: Focus on individuality, meet their needs for association, provide solutions for their desires to experience life's diversity, and help alleviate stress by promoting understanding rather than skepticism and mistrust of companies (pp. 134-135). Using the symbols of Gay culture such as the pink triangle without a long history of presence and support in the Gay community is dangerous. If a firm is committed to diversity, every ad does not have to have a "Gay spin"; its messages just have to show diversity.

Table 7.5 suggests several ways to segment the Gay and Lesbian consumer market. Having a clear target within the Gay and Lesbian market helps keep the diversity of the group within focus. For example, Gay people who came of age "before Stonewall" (before 1969) are less likely to be "out of the closet." They are more likely to have lived "closeted" and to have been part of traditional family structures conforming to heterosexual expectations. They are hesitant participants in the Gay pride movement (Kates, 1998, pp. 82-92). They are unlikely to participate in activities that endanger their invisibility in the mainstream; in fact, products help them "pass" for being "straight." As a result, this group would prefer a low profile and a "less is more" message.

In contrast, younger, affluent Gay men and Lesbians are spending over $17 billion a year on travel, much of it to destinations or events where there are others like them (Drummond, 1995). The VP for Marketing at Carillon Importers has described young, affluent, and "out" Gay consumers as "a very socially mobile, active, affluent, aspirational segment of the population. They opt for the finer things in life" (Wolk, 1992, p. 2). This perhaps explains their heavy consumption of luxury items such as vacation homes, electronic equipment, credit cards, liquor and wine, and sports and fitness activities. In general, Gay consumers re-

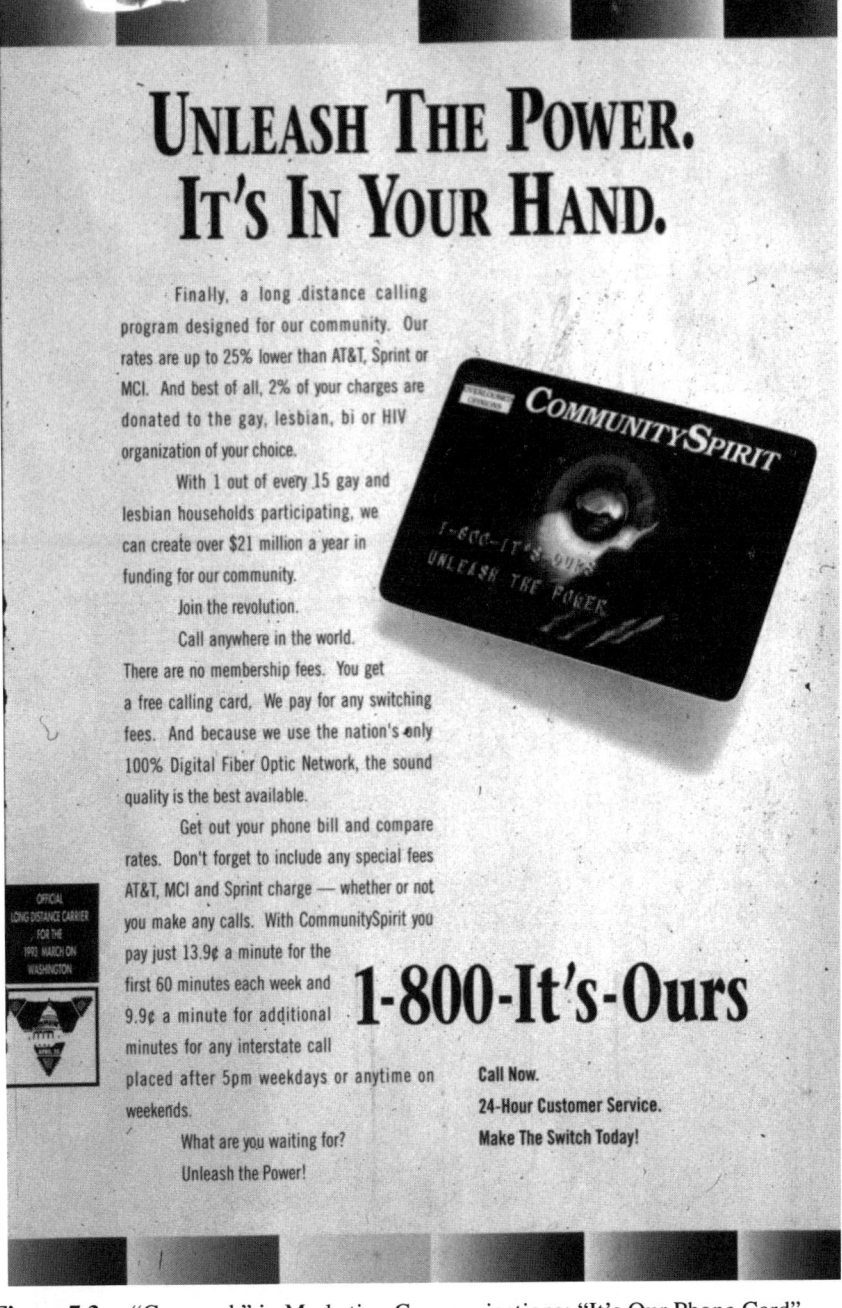

**Figure 7.3a.** "Gayspeak" in Marketing Communications: "It's Our Phone Card"

**Figure 7.3b.** "Gayspeak" in Marketing Communications: "We Are Everywhere"

**TABLE 7.5**  Segmentation Within the Gay and Lesbian Population

| *Basis of Segmentation* | *Examples of Different Groups* |
| --- | --- |
| Sex of consumer | Gay men<br>Lesbian women |
| Age of consumer | Teens to early 20s (before coming out)<br>20s-40s: cohort most affected by AIDS<br>50s plus: came of age before AIDS |
| Household of consumer | One-person household<br>DINCs (double income, no children)<br>Double income, children present in household |
| Income of consumer | Under $25,000<br>$25,000-50,000<br>Over $50,000 |
| Technical literacy | Active online consumers<br>Technology-literate consumers, not currently online<br>Non-technology-literate consumers |
| Neighborhood of consumer | Gay-oriented or gay-tolerant neighborhood<br>Gay persons in top 25 cities<br>Gay persons in suburban or rural areas |
| Sexual Orientation | Homosexual<br>Bisexual<br>Transgendered<br>Other sexual orientations |

portedly spend more than heterosexuals with the same income, and they are more brand and fashion conscious (Lukenbill, 1995, pp. 35-36).

A number of companies have specialized in catering to the Gay market during the 1990s. Some examples of firms and their products are Community Marketing (travel); Pink, Inc. (personal checks); Everyday Feelings (specialized greeting cards); APP Community Pharmacy (prescription drugs by mail order); Don't Panic Designs! Inc. (gay-theme T-shirts); Community Spirit (calling cards); Alyson Publications Inc. (books); and Medagenics Inc. (nutritional supplements for people with HIV or cancer). Also, there are several affinity credit cards such as the Rainbow Visa (Hirsch, 1995). Patronizing these and other Gay-friendly businesses is a way Gay men and Lesbians have gained political and economic clout (Warren, 1995). The lists of Gay-friendly businesses have been instrumental in facilitating a "buy Gay" movement. Research and communications firms such as Prime Access, Spare Parts, WinMark, Overlooked Opinions, Direct Male, Mulryan/Nash, aka Communications, and Rivendell Marketing have helped mainstream companies become adept at communicating with Gay consumers (Alsop, 1999a; Penaloza, 1996, p. 27). The lists of direct marketers, such as one labeled "AIDS-Involved Households," are needed for penetrating the significant variety of consumers within the Gay market (interview with Howard Buford, Prime Access, Inc., September 11, 1999; see also Alsop, 1999a; Cox, 1994).

Several studies assert that clothing and appearance styles are important tools for signaling membership in the Gay subculture (Freitas et al., 1996). Furthermore, aesthetic differences in homosexual and heterosexual men suggest that Gay men are most likely to be influenced by other Gay men, especially those in urban areas with higher incomes. Gay men as trendsetters also influence heterosexual male consumers in areas of style and taste (Rudd, 1996, p. 111).

Lesbians and Gay men have years of experience in the mainstream marketplace, where they have not always been well received. As a result, Gay-friendly retailers, hospitality providers, and professional service providers have a unique opportunity to meet their need not to receive discriminatory or rude treatment (Jones, 1996; Walters & Curran, 1996). Growth in the patronage of Gay professionals and service firms has been supported by a growing number of local Gay-friendly business directories (Lukenbill, 1995, p. 171; Warren, 1995). Services that concern household finances or retirement plans and wills are particular areas where Gay providers may be preferred over strangers.

Mainstream marketers continue to be reluctant to overtly target Gays and Lesbians. IKEA and its agency Deutsch received hate mail after their ads aired on television (Elliott, 1994b). Norwegian Cruise Lines' Gay cruise with 915 men was once denied docking privileges in the Cayman Islands. Visa was a target of the "Religious Right" for having contributed $10,000 to the Gay Games (Penaloza, 1996, p. 35). Some mainstream firms choose "after 10 p.m. time slots" because there are less likely to be protesters tuned in at that time. The Gay Day at Disney World was a quiet event that had grown to 60,000 strong, with an estimated $2.4 million in admission tickets, when this event and Disney's domestic partner benefits policy became the target of boycotts among the Christian Right. Ultimately, Disney, seeing intense competition for employees, decided it had to offer a variety of incentives that were Gay-friendly (Gill, 1998). Other companies believe that "alternative lifestyles have become part of mainstream America" (Saveri, 1995, p. 38). Even with this kind of leadership, interest in the Gay and Lesbian market seems to ebb and flow, but it responds more to opportunity than threat.

As members of the Gay subculture become more tolerated by members of mainstream America, how will that affect Gay consumers and their preferences in the marketplace? Some marketers fear that as more Gay people "come out," they will merge into the general market and lose their interest in companies and their products who are now reaching them with Gay-specific strategies. Some young professionals refuse to use their sexual orientation as a "personal calling card" and have rejected Gay affinity cards and merchandise (Gutierrez, 1996).

## SUMMARY

The willingness of consumers to identify as Gay or Lesbian has made it more practical to target this community. The integration of homosexuality within an individual consumer's self-concept is a key step in openness to and preference for Gay-friendly marketers. Because the Gay population is not counted by independent sources such as the U.S. Bureau of the Census, there is significant uncertainty over the size of the Gay population and important characteristics such as income, spending patterns and volume, and growth. But despite the lack of reliable statistics, mainstream and Gay-owned companies alike have increased efforts to attract and retain Gay and Lesbian consumers. Long-standing Gay magazines as well as newer media options such as the Internet, Gay television networks, multiple directories listing Gay-friendly businesses, and direct marketing lists of Gay consumers are major avenues for reaching Gay consumers.

The Gay subculture has its own language of signs and symbols, called "Gayspeak," which is visible in Gay media and in play as part of American popular culture in mainstream media. The growing unity of the Gay community is due to discrimination from outside and to organizations within that represent Gay interests to mainstream society. Gay consumers are loyal to organizations that not only recognize members of the Gay subculture but also support the values and policies important to them.

# CHAPTER 8

# Asian Americans

## In Search of the American Dream

Satomi Furuichi

Carrie La Ferle

Wei-Na Lee

Marye C. Tharp

The term *Asian American* describes a mix of peoples whose origins are in countries around the Pacific Rim. As an identity, it is as meaningful as *European American,* which is to say that it is useful for comparison with other *Americans* but does not express vast internal differences or ways that individuals see their heritage. Asian Americans are accustomed to filling in forms with the designation *Asian American,* and they easily use this identity to compare themselves to other Americans; thus, the label is acceptable. At the same time, virtually no Asian American family socializes children into "Asian" customs and traditions; there are only Japanese, Chinese, Korean, Vietnamese, or Filipino traditions, for example.

This distinction is an important one for marketers for several reasons. First, grouping consumers with Pacific Rim origins is a convenient way to gain insight into their general marketplace preferences and behaviors, but it is not the avenue for reaching them as consumers. There are still different languages and ethnic-oriented media that must be taken into consideration when developing communications programs that target Asian American consumers. Second, the different languages and communities within Asian America are significant enough that marketers must decide if the cost of trying to reach all Asian Americans justifies the effort. Few economies of scale are possible if an overall strategy must be implemented by messages in various languages and media. Third, as discussed in this chapter, the "chameleon" behavior of many Asian American consumers creates a marketing dilemma in choosing between a special communications effort and a campaign targeted to a broader group of mainstream Americans. Factors such as whether a product or its purchase reflects status and belonging or is the subject of substantial consumer word of mouth may be more important than consumer ethnicity in reaching Asian American consumers. And perhaps most important, there are very few examples of successful marketing efforts that have tried more than one approach with Asian American consumers, and even fewer rules for identifying a superior strategy.

## ASIAN AMERICA: DIVERSITY OF CULTURES, RESOURCES, AND EXPERIENCES

### Shared Experience as 20th-Century Immigrants

The growth in our Asian American population has been due primarily to changes in American immigration policy and conflicts in Southeast Asia. Waves of immigration from China and Japan in the 19th century were reduced to a trickle by strict quotas set forth early in the 20th century that gave priority to European immigrants. A 1965 change in immigration laws in effect reopened migration from the Pacific Rim. The 1965 law allowed members of families already living in the United States and professionals with needed skills, education, and knowledge to seek legal residency. Using these family and professional quotas, a great number of Chinese, Koreans, Filipinos, and Asian Indians began migrating to the United States.

U.S. involvement in the Vietnam War resulted in an influx of refugees from Vietnam, Laos, and Cambodia. The Southeast Asian refugees came after 1975 when the war ended for the United States, and another large wave arrived after the Refugee Act of 1980. In less than 40 years, the Asian American population has been transformed from one composed of a limited number of cultures and countries of origin to one that represents significant diversity. In 1970, 96% of Asian Americans were Chinese, Japanese, or Filipino, and most of their families had immigrated to the United States from the 1850s to the 1930s. In the 1990s, however, these groups accounted for about 54% of Asian Americans. As a point of comparison, whereas only 8% of Asian Americans were from Southeast Asia in 1980, persons from Vietnam, Cambodia, and Laos accounted for 40% of Asian American immigrants by 1989 (O'Hare & Felt, 1991, p. 4).

Table 8.1 shows the size and country-of-origin composition of the Asian American population from 1970 until 2020. The table shows that Japanese Americans have declined from over 40% in 1970 to less than 12% of Asian Americans in 1990. Vietnamese and Asian Indians were not even counted in the 1970 census, yet Asian Indians jumped to over 10% of the 1990 Asian American population. Table 8.1 includes U.S. census projections of the Asian American population from 2000 to 2020, showing growth from about 11.2 to 19.6 million persons (U.S. Bureau of the Census, 1996). Given the radical change in the composition of Asian Americans in the last 30 years, the share for different countries of origin should continue to fluctuate over the next 20 years. The table shows conservative projections of country-of-origin shares for 2000 to 2020, on the basis of their 1990 share of Asian Americans.

Annual growth of 4% per year during the 1990s made Asian Americans the fastest growing ethnic group in the United States. Asian Americans increased by 98% between 1980 and 1989, resulting in over 6.9 million persons and 2.8% of the U.S. population (Carino, 1996; Weiss, 1973). At over 11 million today, the Asian American population almost doubled in the 1990s and now accounts for about 4% of the U.S. population. By 2050, Asian Americans may account for 10% of the U.S. population. The contributions of five American groups, including Asian Americans, to expected growth in the American population from 1990 to 2050 are shown in Table 8.2.

The recent, large increases in our Asian American population signify a large number of foreign-born Asians, currently about two thirds of Asian America. Undoubtedly, native- and foreign-born Asian immigrants have drastically different American experiences. Native-born Asian Americans, who may be the second, third, or fourth generation of Asians who immigrated before 1965, have been raised in American culture and may affiliate more strongly with other mainstream Americans than with new immigrants from their same country of origin (Min, 1995; Takaki, 1993; Ungar, 1995). Although their physical appearances may be similar, the strength of their ethnic identity and relationships to other Americans can be very different.

**TABLE 8.1**  Asian American Population Trends, 1970-2020

| Population Characteristics (in 1,000s) | 1970 | 1980 | 1990 | 2000 | 2010 | 2020 |
|---|---|---|---|---|---|---|
| Total U.S. population | 203,302 | 226,542 | 248,709 | 274,634 | 297,716 | 322,742 |
| Total U.S. Asian population | 1,357 | 3,726 | 7,273 | 11,245 | 15,265 | 19,651 |
| Asian % of U.S. population | 0.6 | 1.6 | 2.9 | 4.1 | 5.1 | 6.0 |
| Chinese (in 1,000s) | 432 | 812 | 1,645 | 2,541[a] | 3,450[a] | 4,441[a] |
| % of Asian total | 31.8 | 21.7 | 22.6 | 22.6 | 22.6 | 22.6 |
| Filipino (in 1,000s) | 337 | 782 | 1,407 | 2,170[a] | 2,946[a] | 3,793[a] |
| % of Asian total | 24.8 | 20.9 | 19.3 | 19.3 | 19.3 | 19.3 |
| Japanese (in 1,000s) | 588 | 716 | 848 | 1,304[a] | 1,771[a] | 2,280[a] |
| % of Asian total | 43.3 | 19.2 | 11.6 | 11.6 | 11.6 | 11.6 |
| Korean (in 1,000s) | 70 | 357 | 799 | 1,226[a] | 1,664[a] | 2,142[a] |
| % of Asian total | 5.1 | 9.5 | 10.9 | 10.9 | 10.9 | 10.9 |
| Vietnamese (in 1,000s) | N/A | N/A | 615 | 945[a] | 1,282[a] | 1,651[a] |
| % of Asian total | | | 8.4 | 8.4 | 8.4 | 8.4 |
| Asian Indian (in 1,000s) | N/A | 387 | 815 | 1,259[a] | 1,710[a] | 2,201[a] |
| % of Asian total | | 10.3 | 11.2 | 11.2 | 11.2 | 11.2 |
| Other Asian[b] (in 1,000s) | | 426 | 1,145 | 1,203[a] | 1,633[a] | 2,103[a] |
| % of Asian total | N/A | 11.4 | 10.7 | 10.7 | 10.7 | 10.7 |

SOURCES: Data for the years 1970, 1980, and 1990 are from U.S. Bureau of the Census (1995). Data for the years 2000, 2010, and 2020 are from U.S. Bureau of the Census (1996).
a. My own estimates, based on each group's 1990 percentage of the Asian population, from U.S. Bureau of the Census (1995).
b. Total of Hawaiian, Samoan, Guamanian, and "Other Asian and Pacific Islander."

In contrast with the pattern of the late 20th century, the foreign-born segment of the Asian American population is expected to decline from 66% to 50% in

**TABLE 8.2** Comparative Population Growth of American Ethnic Groups, 1990-2050

| | *% of U.S. Population Growth* | | | | | |
|---|---|---|---|---|---|---|
| | *Asian American* | *White American* | *African American* | *Native American* | *U.S. Hispanic* | *Total* |
| 1990-1994 | 12.8 | 37.0 | 16.6 | 1.0 | 32.7 | 100.1[a] |
| 1995-1999 | 15.2 | 29.6 | 16.7 | 1.0 | 37.5 | 100.0 |
| 2000-2004 | 16.5 | 24.2 | 16.9 | 1.1 | 41.3 | 100.0 |
| 2005-2009 | 16.6 | 22.0 | 16.9 | 1.2 | 43.3 | 100.0 |
| 2010-2019 | 16.6 | 20.2 | 16.3 | 1.1 | 46.0 | 100.2[a] |
| 2020-2029 | 18.4 | 10.8 | 16.2 | 1.2 | 53.5 | 100.1[a] |
| 2030-2039 | 20.0 | —[a] | 17.0 | 1.4 | 63.2 | 101.6[a] |
| 2040-2049 | 20.1 | —[a] | 17.4 | 1.4 | 68.2 | 107.1[a] |

SOURCE: U.S. Bureau of the Census (1996).
a. Percentages do not add to 100% because of the declining size of the "White non-Hispanic" population in these years.

the next decade (U.S. Bureau of the Census, 1996). More native-born Asian Americans will lower the average age of Asian Americans and increase their exposure to American socialization agents in school and media. We can expect continued changes in their core values, ethnic identities, and marketplace needs and behaviors.

If immigrants are considered to be "Generation 1.0" and native-born Americans are "Generation 2.0," what is "Generation 1.5"? This label is used for foreign-born Americans who immigrate before adulthood. Age of immigration is inversely related to English-language proficiency and closely correlated to acculturation to American culture (Wu, 1997, pp. 143-144). In other words, younger immigrants have better English acquisition and better adjustment to and understanding of American culture. Highly acculturated individuals behave more like mainstream Americans than persons from their home countries (Berry, 1980). Children who grow up in immigrant households often play an important role as family "change agents," adapting to life in America. Their acculturation tends to be higher than that of their parents (Hamers & Blanc, 1989; Hitch, 1983). At the same time, members of Generation 1.5 do not have the same components of self-identity as native-born Americans from the same country of origin. Generation 1.5's identity reflects stronger ties to their country of origin and its cultural norms.

## Differences Among the "Model Minority"

The ancestry of Asian Americans includes Asian Indians, Pakistanis, Chinese, Filipinos, Japanese, Koreans, Malaysians, Thai, Vietnamese, Cambodians, Laotians, Indonesians, Guamanians, and subculture groups such as the Hmong of Vietnam, Laos, and Cambodia. The U.S. Bureau of the Census currently lists 16 categories of Asian and Pacific Islanders. The people of these countries of origin have different languages, religions, cultural histories, traditions, and values. To think that Chinese are no different from Koreans because they are all Asian Americans ignores important cultural and historical differences among these countries, as well as their different histories in the United States.

The Japanese, being the eldest of the Asian American populations, are significantly different from the Hmong, who are among the most recent Asian immigrants. These differences are reflected in their levels of education, English proficiency, and per capita incomes. Although education is highly valued among most Asian Americans, actual educational attainment tends to differ greatly among the subgroups. About 88% of Japanese Americans have at least a high school education, compared to only 31% of Hmong Americans. Japanese Americans had per capita incomes three times the incomes of the Hmong (Sakamoto & Furuichi, 1997). These differences across cultural groups within Asian America lead to what appear to be contradictory statistics. For example, median household income is higher for Asian Americans than for non-Hispanic Whites, but at the same time the poverty rate of Asian Americans is higher (15%) than the rate for all Americans. The Hmong's 62% family poverty rate is a dramatic contrast to the 3% family poverty rate among Japanese Americans (U.S. Bureau of the Census, 1993c, Table X). In 1997, Indian Americans had the highest average incomes ($30,985), and Korean Americans were next ($25,823), with Chinese-origin households close behind at $24,438. On the other end, Vietnamese Americans and Filipino Americans had average incomes of $14,191 and $15,373 respectively (Thomas, 2000).

Tables 8.3 and 8.4 shed more light on education and income levels of Asian Americans as compared to those of other Americans. Almost 15% of Asian

**TABLE 8.3** 1997 Education Levels of White, African, and Asian Americans

| Educational Attainment | White Americans[a] | | African Americans | | Asian Americans/ Pacific Islanders | |
|---|---|---|---|---|---|---|
| Population (in 1,000s) (25 years+) | No. 144,058 | % 100.0 | No. 19,072 | % 100.0 | No. 6,107 | % 100.0 |
| High school | 48,860 | 33.9 | 6,835 | 35.8 | 1,416 | 23.2 |
| Associate degree | | | | | | |
| Occupational | 5,603 | 3.9 | 653 | 3.4 | 200 | 3.3 |
| Academic | 5,012 | 3.5 | 619 | 3.2 | 214 | 3.5 |
| Bachelor's degree | 23,771 | 16.5 | 1,817 | 9.5 | 1,665 | 27.3 |
| Master's degree | 7,943 | 5.5 | 567 | 3.0 | 578 | 9.5 |
| Professional degree | 2,170 | 1.5 | 85 | 0.4 | 190 | 3.1 |
| Doctorate degree | 1,547 | 1.1 | 65 | 0.3 | 143 | 2.3 |
| Total | 94,906 | 65.9 | 10,641 | 55.6 | 4,406 | 72.2 |

SOURCE: U.S. Bureau of the Census (1997b).
a. Not including persons of Hispanic origin.

**TABLE 8.4** Proportions of Families at Various Median Family Income Levels, by Race, 1997

| | All Races (70,880 Families) | Asian (2,381 Families) | White[a] (52,871 Families) |
|---|---|---|---|
| $24,999 and below | 25.6 | 20.1 | 20.3 |
| $25,000 to $34,999 | 12.8 | 9.8 | 12.4 |
| $35,000 to $49,999 | 17.4 | 17.8 | 17.7 |
| $50,000 and over | 44.2 | 52.2 | 49.6 |
| Total | 100.0 | 99.9 | 100.0 |
| Median income | $44,570 | $51,850 | $49,640 |

SOURCE: U.S. Bureau of the Census (1999e).
a. Does not include persons of Hispanic origin.

Americans had a graduate or professional degree in 1997, compared to 8.1% of White non-Hispanic Americans and 3.7% of African Americans. Over 42% of Asian Americans had completed college, whereas less than 25% of White non-Hispanic Americans and 13% of African Americans held at least a bachelor's degree. Asian Americans place high value on education, and these statistics show it. Incomes are higher too in Asian America. The median family income for all Americans in 1997 was $44,570, and for White non-Hispanic Americans it was $49,640. Asian Americans had the highest median income of any group, at $51,850. High education and income levels not only have attracted marketers to Asian American consumers but also are the basis for their description as the "model minority."

High growth, high education, and high incomes make Asian Americans a desirable market. However, as noted above, not all Asian Americans are currently in "model minority" status. They are a bimodal mix of extremely successful and well-educated "bananas" (a derogatory term used among Asian Americans for those who are trying too hard to fit into mainstream America) and a large undereducated group of recent immigrants (sometimes called "FOBs," for "fresh off the boat," by other Asian Americans) (Taylor & Stern, 1997). Furthermore, Asian Americans face a formidable "glass ceiling": They occupy less than .02% of all corporate directorships and average lower median salaries than college-educated White Americans (Ragaza, 1999). Asian Americans of different countries of origin and foreign versus native born have different consumer and socialization needs. Even within each cultural group, there are differences in religion, language, and economic background. Some Asian American consumers must be thought of, looked at, and talked to in different ways.

## The Important Role of Community in Asian America

Asian immigrants prefer to live near friends and family members. That has created concentrations of Asian American population on the West Coast and in gateway cities like San Francisco, Honolulu, New York, Seattle, and Los Angeles. Whereas 21% of all Americans live in the West, 54% of Asian Americans live there (Lee, 1998). Table 8.5 shows the top Asian American cities, counties, and states in the United States. The extreme concentration of Asian Americans makes them easy to reach, even though they constitute a small population and may speak multiple languages. For example, over 77% of all Asian Americans live in just 10 states, and over 26% live in just five U.S. counties.

**TABLE 8.5** Top Asian American Cities, Counties, and States

| City, County, or State | Size of Total Population (in 1,000s) | Asian % of Local U.S. Population | % of U.S. Total Asian Population |
|---|---|---|---|
| **All Asian Americans (1998)** | **10,507** | **3.88** | **100** |
| **Selected States (1998)** | | | |
| **Top 10 Asian American States** | **8,173** | | **77.77** |
| California | 3,938 | 12.00 | 37.50 |
| New York | 995 | 5.47 | 9.46 |
| Hawaii | 757 | 6.34 | 7.20 |
| Texas | 556 | 2.81 | 5.29 |
| New Jersey | 453 | 5.57 | 4.31 |
| Illinois | 403 | 3.34 | 3.83 |
| Washington | 330 | 5.80 | 3.14 |
| Florida | 271 | 1.81 | 2.57 |
| Virginia | 247 | 3.63 | 2.35 |
| Massachusetts | 223 | 3.62 | 2.12 |
| **Smallest Asian American States** | **33.1** | | **.0029** |
| Maine | 8.9 | .72 | .0008 |
| North Dakota | 5.3 | .83 | .0005 |
| Montana | 5.3 | .60 | .0005 |
| Vermont | 4.9 | .82 | .0004 |
| South Dakota | 4.7 | .64 | .0004 |
| Wyoming | 4.0 | .83 | .0003 |
| **Selected Cities (1992)** | **1,477** | **14.03** | |
| New York, NY | 513 | 6.9 | 4.88 |
| Los Angeles, CA | 342 | 9.5 | 3.25 |
| Honolulu CDP, HI | 258 | 65.1 | 2.45 |
| San Francisco, CA | 211 | 28.2 | 2.00 |
| San Jose, CA | 153 | 17.7 | 1.45 |
| **Selected Counties (1997)** | **2,818** | | **26.79** |
| Los Angeles County, CA | 1,200 | 13.32 | 11.42 |
| Honolulu County, HI | 566 | 64.88 | 5.38 |
| Orange County, CA | 361 | 13.27 | 3.43 |
| Santa Clara County, CA | 359 | 21.87 | 3.41 |
| Queens County, NY | 332 | 16.62 | 3.15 |

SOURCES: Data for all Asian Americans from U.S. Bureau of the Census (1999c). Data for states from U.S. Bureau of the Census (1999f). Data for cities from U.S. Bureau of the Census (1998c). Data for counties from U.S. Bureau of the Census (1999b).

The desire to live in preestablished Asian American communities points to the importance of community in Asian American life. Ethnic enclaves with nicknames such as "Chinatown," "Little Korea," or "Little Saigon" exist in most cities with large Asian American populations. These communities not only provide services, housing, and jobs; they symbolize cultural unity and provide a physical center for cultural rituals. Bilinguals in these ethnic neighborhoods assist new immigrants in their transition to American life. Most acculturated Asian Americans live in suburbs today, but they continue a preference for ethnic institutions as varied as churches; legal, medical, and other professional services; grocery stores; and language tutors (O'Hare, Frey, & Fost, 1994). Most Asian suburbanites live in western states, in communities like Daly City (Filipino), Walnut, San Marino, San Gabriel, Pasadena (Indian Americans), Westminster (Vietnamese), and Monterey Park (Chinese) in California.

It is not by accident that Japanese, Chinese, and Filipinos are the majority of Asians who live in Hawaii, California, and Washington State, for these were the locations where earlier immigrants established ethnic neighborhoods. Newer immigrants such as the Chinese, Koreans, Indians, and Vietnamese have large populations in Massachusetts, New York, northern New Jersey, and Texas. Asian American-focused media and merchandise are easier to find in these areas. These institutions have the dual roles of continuing country-of-origin lifestyles and cultural traditions and facilitating adjustment to American life. Gateway cities for Asian immigrants continue to be in the central metropolitan statistical areas of Los Angeles, New York, San Francisco, Washington, D.C., and Chicago (Frey, 1998). Eight of the top 10 Asian-majority suburbs are on the Pacific Rim, but it is in the heart of America that the most recent growth of the Asian American population is taking place (Edmondson, 1997a; O'Hare et al., 1994).

Another expression of the importance of community in Asian American life is the concentration of persons from one country of origin in particular professions or businesses. For example, over 80% of Korean Americans own their own businesses; the Korean-American Grocers Association alone represents 17,000 businesses worth over $13 million in yearly sales (Wong, 1997, p. 25). Indian Americans are found disproportionately in engineering and high technology. Vietnamese Americans are found in agriculture, fishing, and personal services. Typically, small business ownership is a way to make best use of available resources such as family labor; the children of these small business owners often become professionals (Glenn, 1983; Sanders & Nee, 1996).

The household is an important unit of consumer decision making and link to the greater Asian American and mainstream communities. The Asian American household also affirms the important roles of community and family in Asian America. Asian Americans, especially foreign-borns, are more likely than non-Hispanic White Americans to live in extended-family households. Consequently, the average Asian American household is larger than the average U.S. family of 3.8 persons. As Table 8.6 shows, Asian households contain both more married couples and nonfamily households. Several unrelated couples, extended-family members, and multiple generations or single persons may live together to save money in an Asian American household. Fewer Asian Americans than White or African Americans live alone.

## CONTINUED TRADITIONS

*"Someday you will see," said my mother. "It is in your blood, waiting to be let go."*
                                    Amy Tan, *The Joy Luck Club* (1989, p. 267)

## Confucian Influences on Asian American Values

Despite diverse languages, customs, and religions, there are some values that most Asian Americans share. Many East Asian cultures have their roots in the doctrines of Confucianism. Confucianism is a system of subordination of the son to the father, the younger to the elder, the wife to the husband, and the subject to the throne. It is an overarching system that governs all relationships within family and society (Park & Cho, 1995; Wong, 1997, p. 69). Confucianism also presents a form of strict conservatism that can make the adoption of innovations a slow process. Risk taking increases the chance of "losing face," and thriftiness is taught as the norm (Wong, 1997, p. 83). This conservatism is aptly reflected in Asian Americans' money management. Asian Americans typically have preferred to save rather than to invest in stocks. Investment in land is considered the best way to secure wealth because "land is the last thing to change." This deeply ingrained Confucian code of manners, social relations, and outlook is a major influence over the ways Asian Americans think and act.

**TABLE 8.6** Household Types for Different Ethnic Groups in 1997

| | White American[a] | | African American | | Asian American | |
|---|---|---|---|---|---|---|
| | No. | % | No. | % | No. | % |
| Total households | 85,059 | 100.0 | 12,109 | 100.0 | 2,998 | 100.0 |
| Married couples | | | | | | |
| With children | 21,914 | 25.8 | 1,974 | 16.3 | 1,032 | 34.4 |
| Without children | 25,736 | 30.3 | 1,877 | 15.5 | 731 | 24.4 |
| Other families | | | | | | |
| With children | 6,322 | 7.4 | 2,913 | 24.1 | 171 | 5.7 |
| Without children | 4,962 | 5.8 | 1,692 | 14.0 | 312 | 10.4 |
| People living alone | 21,513 | 25.3 | 3,126 | 25.8 | 560 | 18.7 |
| Other nonfamily households | 4,612 | 5.4 | 528 | 4.4 | 191 | 6.4 |

SOURCE: U.S. Bureau of the Census (1999e).
a. Does not include persons of Hispanic origin.

Table 8.7 includes some translations of Confucian sayings that describe Confucian views of the world. They are contrasted in the table with "lessons" from American sayings. It is interesting how differently strangers are treated in Eastern and Western cultures. Asians tend to treat strangers by the rule "Enemies until friends," whereas Americans "never met a stranger." The strong "insider" bias of Asians prescribes different codes of behavior for friends and family than for persons unknown. A by-product of this cultural norm is the Asian consumer preference for well-known companies and brands (de Mooij, 1998; Lee & Tse, 1994; Mueller, 1996). "Time heals all (wounds)" and "Time is money" are cultural sayings in both Asian and American cultures, but "Time is money" provides insight into how much emphasis we Americans place on action and efficiency, whereas "Time heals all" best reflects the Asian valuing of deliberation and contemplation over action. Another interesting difference in cultural teachings is apparent in sayings about individualism: "The nail that sticks up gets knocked down" as opposed to "Do your own thing" and "Be all you can be."

Confucian beliefs provide a layer of similarity to the diverse cultures of Asian America. At the same time, there are widespread differences in religious tradi-

**TABLE 8.7** Cultural Lessons in Asian and American Sayings

| Subject of Cultural Lesson | Asian Saying[a] | Mainstream American Saying |
|---|---|---|
| Virtues | A good heart always gives a little extra. (CH) | God helps those who help themselves. |
| | Wealth is a treasure for a lifetime, wisdom a treasure for all time. (J) | He who dies with the most toys wins. |
| Time | Time is a healer. (K) | Time is money. |
| | Time opens every door to him who waits. (CH) | A rolling stone gathers no moss. |
| Relationships with others | Enemies until friends. (CH) | All men are created equal. |
| | The nail that sticks up gets knocked down. (K) | Do your own thing! |
| | Everyone has fate bound about his neck. (J) | Be all you can be! |
| | A wise man has long ears and a short tongue. (J) | A squeaky wheel gets the grease. |
| | Once a word is out, the swiftest horse cannot overtake it. (CH) | Let's get right to the point. |
| | Fair without, fair within; foul without, foul within. (K) | You can't judge a book by its cover. |
| | The face belies the heart. (J) | Beauty is as beauty does. |
| Age/wisdom | Of the five blessings, long life is the greatest. (J) | There's no fool like an old fool. |
| | Ignore an old man's advice and one day be a beggar. (CH) | |
| Success | Hide yourself in a pot, yet you will never escape your fate. (K) | If at first you don't succeed, try, try again. Where there's a will there's a way. |
| | When the melon is ripe, it will drop of itself. (CH) | Take the bull by the horns. |
| | Ice does not freeze on the busy spinning wheel. (K) | Busy hands are happy hands. |
| Family | Treat every old man as thy father. (J) | Blood is thicker than water. |
| | Silk clothing warms even a cousin. (K) | You made your own bed, now lie in it. |

SOURCES: Ha (1970), Young-chol (1991), de Mooij (1998), Althen (1988), Stewart and Bennett (1991).
a. CH = Chinese, K = Korean, J = Japanese.

tions among peoples of Asia and Asian America. The Philippines is predominantly Roman Catholic; India is majority Hindu; Pakistan and Malaysia are Moslem; Thailand, Nepal, and Tibet are Buddhist; Japan has Shinto, among other religions; and China, Vietnam, and Korea have Buddhist and Christian traditions. What is most significant is the effects of these differences on Asian American acculturation to mainstream America. Those Asian Americans who are practitioners of Eastern religions are more likely to continue those traditions and to retain strong ethnic identity and affiliation with their country-of-origin culture. Those who convert to Christianity more quickly identify as mainstream Americans and are more likely to intermarry (Montero, 1980; O'Brien & Fugita, 1991; Shinagawa & Pang, 1996).

The presence of a close-knit community promotes Asian American ethnic cohesion. The ethnic residential and business communities where new immigrants gather create social interactions that help the residents financially and psychologically. They create community networks for people who share the same interests through churches, schools, and local clubs. What strengthens these family and community ties is the Asian orientation toward collectivism and promotion of social harmony (Locke, 1992; O'Hare, 1992b). The group-centered behavior of Asians is in direct contrast to American individualism. Asian Americans take responsibility as a group; the basic human unit is not "me" but "us." It is not "my family" or "my house"; instead, it is "our family" and "our house." Asians are not really comfortable being identified as individuals. Western cultures penalize those who do not conform to social norms with guilt, whereas Asian cultures emphasize the shame of not meeting others' expectations.

## The Special Role of the Family

Another important and basic Asian value is the emphasis on family. Asian Americans tend to live in traditional, two-parent families (Lee, 1998; O'Hare & Felt, 1991). Rates of divorce and single motherhood among Asian Americans are the lowest among all racial groups in the United States. What this shows is the value that Asian Americans place on maintaining the traditional family structure. Respect for authority and for the elderly is an important value common to all Asian ethnic groups. In Asian culture, a hierarchy based on age dictates interpersonal relations. In social relations, younger individuals must be polite to the elderly, either men or women. In business relations as well, those who are new in a company or who are younger should show respect and be humble. In general, elders are highly respected because they are believed to be "wiser." Asian American family members sometimes feel more obligated to work in family-owned businesses than free to pursue their own dreams in other careers (Jacob, 1993).

Children and parents remain close in traditional Asian American families. As a consequence, parents exert significant influence on their children in many areas, especially education. Many Asian parents make the decision to immigrate to the United States in hopes not only of economic gain but also of educational opportunities for their children. Some Asian Americans, especially those who lack transferable skills, realize that better education for their children comes with the price of low-pay, low-status jobs for them. Stories about parents paying their children's college tuition in full so that the children can concentrate on studying, or about mothers coming to cook during exam periods, are familiar among college-age Asian American students (Tuan, 1998). Family-oriented decision making is also apparent in consumer decisions: Individuals may choose to buy what is good for the family rather than what is good for themselves. Metropolitan Life Insurance Company's ad that said, "Your Metropolitan program is your children's security blanket," successfully captured the family/children orientation of Asian Americans.

## Generational Differences in Asian America

As Asian American parents devote their lives to their children, Asian American youth are obligated to excel in school and to be successful in the workplace (Wu, 1997, p. 140). Stereotypes of Asian Americans as science oriented and study-manic have their roots in the high expectations of Asian American parents (Taylor & Stern, 1997). Plenty of Asian American parents expect their children to attend Ivy League schools and prefer that they become doctors or engineers (Tuan, 1998; Ungar, 1995; Wysocki, 1997). According to the Asian American work ethic, high socioeconomic status is a respectable and worthwhile achievement goal. It is believed that anyone can achieve high status as long as he or she spends longer hours and more energy either studying or working. There are plenty of role models within the Asian American community to support this belief.

The Asian American orientation toward high academic achievement has led mainstream Americans to perceive Asian Americans as a "model minority." This is unfortunate because that image can be detrimental to Asian Americans as a group. It gives policy-makers the excuse to neglect disadvantaged populations within Asian America. It also fails to acknowledge the extra hurdles of prejudice or discrimination that Asian Americans and all other racial minorities must overcome. Most important, it places pressure on individual Asian Americans to conform to expectations that ignore individual differences in interests and talents (Taylor & Stern, 1997).

Another example of strong ties between parents and children is the close supervision of the young by adult members of the family. The rate of teen pregnancy among Asian Americans is 6%, compared to 10% for Anglo Americans and 23% for African Americans. Such low rates of teen pregnancy and single motherhood have positive effects on individuals' later economic status. The social relations of adolescents often come into conflict with the expectations and wishes of Asian American parents. East Asians have such strong ethnic identity that they are reluctant for their children to date people of other ethnicities. In the case of South Asian families, emphasis is placed on marrying not only within the same race or ethnic group but also within the same religion and class. Immigrant parents today more frequently accept their U.S.-born children's choices to marry outside their ethnicity (Tuan, 1998).

In the 1960s and the 1970s, marrying Caucasian was a trend among East Asian women, in reaction to the repeal of laws forbidding interracial marriages and the subsequent rush of movies with romances between Caucasian heroes and Asian women. A large number of intermarriages during the 1960s showed the desire of second-generation Asian American women to assimilate at the time (Fong & Yung, 1995-1996; McAdoo, 1993; Takaki, 1993). More recently, there has been a resurgence of ethnic pride and identity among Asian American youth. Marriage within the same heritage is again in vogue. In the 1960s, Asian culture was embarrassing to the second generation. In the 1990s, the new generations are proud of their Asian background and traditions (Kibria, 1997; Shinagawa & Pang, 1996; Wysocki, 1997).

## BRIDGING TWO CULTURES

### Adjusting to American Life

Due to unique customs, history, and language, each ethnic group of Asian Americans has formed its own community support organizations. Chinese, Japanese, Koreans, Indians, and Vietnamese have their own networks and leaders.

The older generation of Chinese and Japanese Americans have started to lose co-hesion and to marry outside their country of origin. A recent influence on Asian America has been violence against them that does not discriminate between groups of Asian Americans. Asian Americans themselves have started to realize that ethnic differences within Asian America do not matter to outsiders in main-stream America or other ethnic groups. In many instances, these differences are neither recognized by nor considered significant to other Americans, who some-times do not distinguish between Asians and Asian Americans and who cannot recognize members of different country-of-origin groups (Espiritu, 1992; Tuan, 1998; Yeh & Huang, 1996). Violence against Asian Americans first surfaced in the 1980s, when a Chinese American man was killed by ex-auto workers who blamed their loss of jobs on Japanese auto imports. This case awakened Asian American willingness to cooperate, for it sent a message to move beyond ethnic boundaries and unite as "Asian Americans." Still a small group relative to other ethnic groups in the United States, Asian Americans, by joining forces, are gain-ing better access to political and economic resources.

Espiritu (1992) called the move toward creating Asian American organiza-tions outside country-of-origin boundaries "Asian American pan-ethnicity" (pp. 1-18). Some Asian American leaders advocate forming Asian American pan-ethnic organizations to promote cultural awareness and pride, but other Asian Americans want to be treated the same as Caucasians and accepted as "nonhyphenated" Americans. This struggle embodies Asian Americans' dual desire to become bona fide members of the mainstream and to simultaneously maintain their cultural heritage (Min, 1995; Takaki, 1993; Tuan, 1998; Wysocki, 1997).

Few persons actually call themselves "Asian American." One study found that 70% of Vietnamese use the term *Vietnamese* to identify themselves, whereas 6% use *Vietnamese Americans;* in contrast, 26% of Japanese Ameri-cans use the term *Japanese* and 41% use the term *Japanese American.* Among Chinese Americans, the preferences are 62% for *Chinese* and 11% for *Chinese American,* and Korean American self-designations are 71% *Korean* and 23% *Korean American* (Wong, 1997, author's note).

*Acculturation* describes the process whereby persons outside mainstream American society learn about American culture. Acculturation may include learning English and adjusting behaviors to the American lifestyle and manner-isms. Typically, an acculturating individual feels excitement over the newness of the culture and later moves into culture shock (Brown, 1994). The accultura-tion experience brings an infusion of more and more new values and norms, which in turn foster conflicts within an individual's self-image and shake his or her sense of security. Cultural stress follows culture shock and may motivate activities to find solutions to the ensuing self-image crisis. Discrepancies between self-image, attitudes, and behaviors are likely to continue until the individual reaches a comfortable accommodation to American ways. For some immigrants, the last adjustment is only experienced by the second generation.

The drive and self-confidence of individuals who have remade themselves by learning and then playing new roles in a new country are rooted in the pride of having successfully bridged two cultures (Brown, 1994). Asian Americans deal with acculturation from a practical and survival orientation. In essence, nothing fundamental changes (Lee, 1993; L. Lee, 1996; Matsuoka, 1990). Success comes from playing new roles confidently, not from changing into a new person. This is the so-called "chameleon" behavior of Asian Americans, although studies of situational ethnicity with other ethnic groups suggest that it is shared by other ethnic immigrants (Nahm, 1997; Stayman & Deshpande, 1989). Being able to switch back and forth between roles in an ethnic culture and the American mainstream culture is another example of the "cultural transmigration" discussed in Chapter 3.

A majority of Asian Americans express a desire to be part of the mainstream while retaining their unique cultural heritage. The concept of role switching is a departure from the theory of role transition and assimilation, where changes are considered permanent and unidirectional (Gergen & Gibbs, 1966; Oberg, 1960). In role switching, depending on the situation, persons, and tasks to be performed, Asian Americans can switch between obligations in the Asian American community and obligations as employees in mainstream American institutions (Yanagisako, 1985, pp. 250-251). Table 8.8 compares Asian beliefs to those of the American mainstream and other American subcultures. The table presents Asian American values as more like the worldviews dominant in other American subcultures than those of mainstream society. With increasing diversity, American mainstream beliefs are likely to evolve in the direction of Asian ones.

Until recently, the desire to become part of American society has meant peaceful coexistence with the rest of Americans. The strong support of cultural ties and heritage is reflected in continued celebration of holidays such as the Chinese Lunar New Year, Moon Festivals, and the Japanese Bon Festival. Cultural origins are also honored by requesting American assistance for home countries. There is again a preference for marrying other Asian Americans (Shinagawa & Pang, 1996). Attitudes still vary across country-of-origin groups;

**TABLE 8.8** Comparison of the Dominant Cultural Values in American Subcultures

| Cultural Value | American Mainstream Subculture | Asian American Subculture | African American Subculture | U.S. Latino Subculture |
|---|---|---|---|---|
| Personal identity | Individualistic | Collectivistic, family important | Both | Both |
| Expressiveness | High but objective | Low, subjective | High | High, subjective |
| Male-female roles | Overlap | Distinctive | Overlap | Distinctive |
| Competition as key to success | Important | Not as important | Not as important | Not as important |
| Role of social networks | Not as important | Very important | Somewhat important | Very important |
| Power distance | Low | High | Medium | High |
| Uncertainty avoidance | Low | High | Medium | High |
| Communication style | Direct | Indirect | Both | Indirect |
| Relationship to nature | Humans dominant | Humans and nature in harmony | Humans and nature in harmony | Humans dominant |
| Universal rules of behavior | Yes | No, depends on relationships | No | No |
| Use of time | Present, future | Past, cyclical | Cyclical | Past, present |

SOURCES: Trompenaars and Hampden-Turner (1998), Hofstede (1984), Kluckhohn and Strodtbeck (1960), Hall (1959).

Asian Indian Americans of Generations 1.5 and 2.0 "may feel more American than Indian. . . . They may listen to American pop music and watch American movies, but they are also comfortable with the popular music and movies of India" (Mogelonsky, 1995a, p. 38).

Acculturation to American life can be more difficult and take longer for some Asian Americans. English-speaking peoples from Pacific Rim countries have an advantage over non-English-speaking immigrants. Parents sometimes encourage their children's fluency in English because it is critical to success in America; at the same time, they do not always force their children to become fluent in the home country language. "ABCs" (American-born Chinese) may find themselves "between two cultures," not fitting into either particularly well. They can't speak with or understand their grandparents, and American friends don't understand their dedication to pleasing their parents (Lee, 1992, p. x).

## Asian Influences on Mainstream America

Asian Americans have been almost invisible in mainstream American popular culture compared to other American ethnic groups (Cintron, 1991; Martindale, 1997; Taylor & Lee, 1994). Asian Americans in the media are typically portrayed as "foreigners." When Asians have appeared in movies and other pop culture venues, Asian women have been presented as passive, oversexualized, exotic, and humble, or as treacherous and evil. Asian men have been stereotyped as incompetent, asexual beings, as supremely wise, or as martial arts experts (Lee, 1991; Spigner, 1994). Stereotypes of Asians who appear in popular culture vehicles are generalized by other Americans and applied to the Asian American population (Hamamoto, 1992; L. L. Wang, 1998).

Stereotyping of Asian Americans has also occurred in advertisements that reinforce simplistic views of Asian Americans. Asian Americans are most often shown in the background of ads and as endorsers of high-technology products. Asian American women are virtually absent (Graves, 1996; Taylor & Stern, 1997). Asian American actors or models in mainstream television programs or magazines are still limited. Mainstream magazine and television advertisements show hardly any Asians in major selling roles for products (Graves, 1996). Few Asian models, especially Asian American women, are shown in social and home settings or in ads for nontechnical products (Bowen & Schmid, 1997; Taylor, Lee, & Stern, 1995; Taylor & Stern, 1997). Even in marriage and family textbooks and journals, Asian Americans receive little coverage compared to their proportion of the American population (Bean & Crane, 1996; Shaw-Taylor & Benokraitis, 1995).

During the 1990s, this pattern began to change. Asian Americans were seen in a greater variety of roles and began chipping away at stereotypical portrayals. Amy Tan's (1989) best-selling novel *The Joy Luck Club* became a major movie success. Margaret Cho, a Korean American comedian, briefly starred in a prime-time television show, *All American Girl.* Asian Americans Matsuda, Vivienne Tam, Anna Sui, and Josie Natori are counted among the hottest fashion designers.

Imported movies, games, cuisines, and pop culture phenomena from the Pacific Rim, including Tamagotchi pets and Pokémon collecting, have made "Asian" influence a trendsetter in American popular culture (Yang, Gan, Hong, & Staff of *A Magazine,* 1997). Sumo wrestling is now covered in mainstream media and underwritten by Canadian Airlines ("First Event," 1999-2000). Asian American entrepreneurs such as James Chu of Viewsonic, Sabeer Bhatia of Hotmail, Vinod Khosla of Sun, Frank Lin of Trident, and Andrew Yang of Yahoo! are role models as high-profile founders of booming high-technology firms and e-commerce ventures. They contribute to a perception of Asian Americans as major architects of the information economy (Takahashi, 1998; Thurm, 1999; Wysocki, 1997).

## Communication Styles of Asian Americans

An important skill in successfully moving between Asian and mainstream culture is the ability to adjust communication style. Mainstream Americans use direct and informal communications and rely on written and verbal parts of message content to decipher intended meaning. At the other extreme, Asian cultures value relationships over communication efficiency, and *how* something is said is as full of meaning as *what* is said (Althen, 1988; de Mooij, 1998; Stewart & Bennett, 1991).

The cultural contexts of communication in mainstream and Asian America are significantly different. High-context cultures, such as those of Asia, Latin America, the Middle East, and eastern and southern Europe, value indirect communication. It is considered good manners to be implicit and ambiguous. A message's meaning depends on the relationships between sender and receiver, what effects the message might have on those relationships, and whether the message is oral or written. Message interpretation in Asian America depends on decoding its context and an overriding need to maintain harmony (Wong, 1997, p. 178). Low-context cultures such as those of mainstream America and northern and western Europe emphasize direct communication.

Mainstream Americans engage in less ritual interaction (such as "How are you?" and "Hope to see you again") than members of Asian cultures, who place high value on gift giving, exchange of business cards, inquiries about family members or their health, and other ritualistic communication behaviors (Morrison, Conaway, & Border, 1995; Trompenaars & Hampden-Turner, 1998). Mainstream Americans see a person who insists on too much ritual as "too shy," "too polite," or unwilling to disclose. Asians and Asian Americans place more importance on not "losing face" and are reluctant to volunteer personal opinions when the consequences are unclear.

Bilingual Asian Americans face many communication dilemmas. First, many concepts do not translate from one language to another. Second, bilinguals may find it difficult to behave as other Americans do when actions come into conflict with Asian American cultural norms. Asian American students can be less assertive team members and less verbal overall than their mainstream counterparts. Third, because much of culture is unconscious behavioral programming, Asian Americans misinterpret more communications, experience more discomfort, and frequently find themselves isolated from the important social networks of American organizations (McAdoo, 1993; Tuan, 1998).

Second-, third-, and fourth-generation Asian Americans who speak only English may use language in an "Asian" way—being more indirect and less assertive and participating less (Althen, 1988, pp. 21-35). Awkward and uncomfortable communications between Asian and other Americans affirm the impression that Asian Americans do not want informal contact. These children of immigrants find themselves considered "different" even when they otherwise fit into mainstream America because of the legacy of Asian communication norms.

## ASIAN AMERICAN SOURCES OF INFORMATION AND MEDIA PATTERNS

### Source Credibility and the Asian American Community Network

On a scale from low to high social and psychological distance, many Asian Americans recognize a hierarchy from insiders to outsiders: family, friends from the same village or region in the same country of origin, acquaintances from the same country of origin, individuals from other Asian countries, other immigrants/minorities, and Anglo Americans. This hierarchy mirrors movement from most to least credible sources of information. From this perspective, Asian American endorsers are effective in communications because they have higher source credibility than any other experts (Burton, 1993; Lee & Tse, 1994; N. Wang, 1998). In Figure 8.1, Michael Chang is shown in association with the Discover card. His status as a world champion, despite his youth, and his consistent dedication are key themes in the copy. The copy also recognizes him rather than having him endorse the card so that he will appear more modest, making his qualities more compatible with the values of Asian America.

Word-of-mouth marketing is the most cost-effective, productive method of getting the word out in Asian communities. Asian and Asian American families are "networks within themselves" (Wong, 1997, p. 99). Several researchers have verified the importance of word-of-mouth communication, advice from friends, and face-to-face personal selling in the Asian American community (Schmid, 1995). In a study examining information sources used for financial decisions, Asian Americans were found to seek personal advice from friends and relatives and other word-of-mouth sources; other American investors gave more weight to mass media. Marketers should consider reaching Asian Americans through these community network channels and other grassroots, face-to-face, and personal approaches. These sources have the high credibility that comes with being insiders in Asian American communities. A trustworthy relationship is rated by Asian American consumers as more persuasive than a sales pitch based on brand attributes (de Mooij, 1998).

The preference of Asian Americans for "insider" sources of communication creates bias against non-Asian American persons or companies. Americans define people by the jobs they have, whereas Asians measure people by the relationships they have with them (Althen, 1988, pp. 3-35). Prejudice against companies not part of Asian American community networks is elastic and depends on the parties involved (de Mooij, 1998; L. Lee, 1996). A Japanese American may be the "insider" source for a Chinese American in an organization with no other Asian Americans, but he may be the "outsider" in his Chinese-dominant church congregation. Figure 8.2 shows Pat Morita, a Japanese American, as the "Colgate Wisdom Tooth." This advertisement was not well received by other Asian American consumers, who were left wondering why a Japanese American was in the role as endorser. More careful choice of endorsers can position a company or brand within the Asian American insider network (N. Wang, 1998).

A major obstacle in accessing Asian American community networks is the low incidence of product- and advertising-related word-of-mouth communica-

**Figure 8.1.** Michael Chang in Discover Card Print Advertisement

# SHOULD ONE FIGHT TARTAR? OR PLAQUE?

## YES. –The Colgate Wisdom Tooth

*Like many things in life, your mouth has natural enemies continually causing it trouble. Two of them are tartar and plaque.*

*Tartar is crusty, and can make your teeth ugly and yellow. Plaque is invisible, sticky, harmful bacteria constantly forming on your teeth.*

*Luckily, there is Colgate Tartar Control toothpaste. Not only does Colgate fight ugly tartar build-up, brushing with it also helps remove harmful plaque. This is one toothpaste that really works hard to help keep your teeth clean.*

*No wonder Colgate Tartar Control is the Wise Choice. Considering what tartar and plaque can do to your teeth, would it be wise for you to use anything less?*

### The Wise Choice

"Colgate has been shown to be an effective decay-preventive dentifrice that can be of significant value when used in a conscientiously applied program of oral hygiene and regular professional care. Colgate Tartar Control has been shown to reduce the formation of tartar above the gum line, but has not been shown to have a therapeutic effect on periodontal diseases."—Council on Dental Therapeutics-American Dental Association. © 1989 Colgate-Palmolive Co.

**Figure 8.2.** Pat Morita as the "Colgate Wisdom Tooth"

tions among Asian Americans. In one study of product- and advertising-related talk at home and with friends, Chinese Americans had the least word-of-mouth communication among four American ethnic groups. The one exception was that they talked more about products and brands with which they were satisfied (Lee et al., 1999a). The community network in Asian America is invaluable in securing positive recommendations for brands or companies.

Gateways to the Asian community networks are the celebrations of culture-based events in Asian America. There are many special events on the Asian American calendar, but they vary across countries of origin and religion. Some of the most important holidays are the Lunar New Year, Cherry Blossom, Penitencia in Filipino neighborhoods, the Dragon Boat Festival, and Mid-Autumn celebrations. Some of these events are included in promotions and Web sites sponsored by cities wishing to highlight their Asian American residents. Also, many nonprofit organizations develop and supply services for newcomers to Asian American communities. Korean Baptist churches provide everything from housing assistance to legal advice, doctor referrals, and Korean-speaking translators. Asian American professional and business directories are other venues that "define" the extent of Asian American community networks.

## Ethnic Media Targeting Asian Americans

Cultural background also influences how its members use media. Several studies have indicated that Asian Americans, as well as different country-of-origin groups within Asian America, differ from other American subcultures in their patterns of media behavior (Delener & Neelankavil, 1990; Lee & Tse, 1994). This section of the chapter describes the media options for Asian Americans, whereas the following one highlights media behaviors among Asian Americans. The availability of targeted media—ethnic-oriented media both in English and in native languages (called in-language media)—has a major impact on media behaviors. Asian immigrants who have lived for less than 10 years in the United States prefer to patronize businesses that advertise in their native language (Wong, 1997, p. 49). Wherever ethnic media exist, they are not only a conduit to foreign-born Asian Americans but also "competition" for mainstream media in capturing the scarce amount of time Asian Americans spend with any media at all.

Asian Americans are more culturally isolated from mainstream America than African and Hispanic Americans. These ethnic groups have more visibility in mainstream media and popular culture and share more cultural values with Anglo Americans. African and Hispanic Americans also have a longer history of attention from mainstream marketers in ethnic and mainstream media (Bowen & Schmid, 1997; Taylor & Stern, 1997; Taylor et al., 1995).

Ethnic-oriented media have two major roles as "cultural institutions" in an ethnic community: to help newcomers learn and adapt to the cultural values and norms of a new country and to assist in retaining ethnic heritage and ties to a country of origin in the new environment (L. Lee, 1996; Shim, 1997). In ethnic communities, all media play more diverse roles in addressing their audiences' needs. In Asian America, many entrepreneurs have developed a patchwork of media vehicles in English and native languages to satisfy the needs for social interaction, cultural learning, personal identity, information, and entertainment (Taylor, 1999). They reach both urban and suburban Asian Americans, as well as most of the major country-of-origin groups among Asian Americans. As early as 1993, there were approximately 35 to 40 radio broadcasters in New York who rented "unused portions of other stations' FM channels" (called *sideband radio*) and ran programming in Asian languages (Wynter, 1993a). Sideband radio supposedly reaches 40% of the Filipino American population in New York in the Tagalog language. *Filipinas* magazine reports its reach as 10,100 Filipinos in the San Francisco Bay Area (Wong, 1997, p. 63).

The geographic concentration of Asian Americans creates an economic bonus for marketers. Because a large majority of Asian Americans live in locations such as California, New York, Hawaii, Texas, and Chicago, companies can avoid national media and make smaller buys in local markets (Wiesendanger, 1993). The advertising costs for local, ethnically targeted, in-language media range from $50 to $500 for a newspaper ad or a 30-second radio or TV spot. These prices are extremely low compared to English-language media, where a 30-second spot during prime time can cost $350,000 or more for the same number of exposures.

Even with the same number of impressions, in-language media still have the advantage of reaching individual consumers who cannot be reached in any English-language medium. A good example is the Chinese and Chinese American market in San Francisco. The prime-time Chinese-language evening news has an average 61 share for Monday to Friday, whereas all other TV stations combined produce only a 21 share (Gitlin, 1998). As another example, in 1993 one could buy 210,000 impressions in New York through a Chinese cable program for only $350 (Wiesendanger, 1993). Even the U.S. Commerce Department reports that over 82% of Chinese, Korean, and Vietnamese Americans prefer to communicate and use media in their own languages (Gitlin, 1998). In-language media are not just a preferred source for newcomers (Delener & Neelankavil,

1990; Lee & Tse, 1994). One more advantage is that tentative evidence suggests that brand or company associations made in native languages result in higher liking of those brands (Schmitt & Zhang, 1998).

There are nevertheless some important drawbacks to the use of in-language, Asian-targeted media. Circulation figures for Asian-language newspapers and ratings for Asian-language television programs are not always audited (Kang & Lee, 1999). The media planner's job is more complicated because he or she must analyze what circulation and audience numbers to believe, as well as decide how to optimize limited dollars to meet reach and frequency goals. Today there are hundreds of traditional and nontraditional media vehicles in Asian native languages. The media include in-language newspapers, magazines, television, radio, the Internet, and newsletters and local bulletins.

Kang and Lee, a major Asian American communication and marketing agency, has a Web site that includes an "Asian Media Reference Guide" to assist planners (www.asianmediaguide.com). This site presents a comprehensive list of ethnic media targeting Asian Americans and then breaks their availability down by ethnic group, medium, and vehicle. Other agencies have also produced helpful resources for companies wishing to reach Asian American consumers. The Asian Media Planning Source lists 340 nationwide publications that reach Asian Americans (Mandese, 1995). Together, these sources provide a good start for gathering information about circulation, audience size, rates, closing dates, and contacts. Unfortunately, the data are mostly provided by the media themselves and are not audited.

The preference among Asian Americans for ethnic newspapers over other media has long been reported (Delener & Neelankavil, 1990; Paskowski, 1986). Asian Americans report reading newspapers and spending more time with this medium as their dominant information source. It is impossible to know if the important role of newspapers in reaching Asian Americans is due to their high literacy rates or the fact that Asian American newspapers have been the only in-language medium available to these consumers until recently. Chinese community newspapers have long histories in cities like New York, San Francisco, and Los Angeles; *India Abroad* has been around for over 25 years. The monopoly of newspapers as in-language media is rapidly declining as electronic media outlets and Internet usage rise ("The Rise," 1995; Kang & Lee, 1999; Wiesendanger, 1993). Radio and television will become essential to the Asian media mix when full digitalization arrives. And because over 67% of Asian American households are predicted to be online in 2000, Web advertising and communications are also critical ("AsianAvenue.com," 1999).

In-language media provide Asian Americans with a sense of community, a way to keep abreast of news from their countries of origin, and a source of information relevant to their needs. Yet another reason for the popularity of in-language newspapers has been that many of the larger dailies are supported by parent companies from the country of origin. Some examples are the *Yomiuri America* and the *Nihon Keizai Shimbun,* Japanese newspapers. Many other in-language local newspapers, typically free weeklies, build circulation by providing a combination of U.S. news, local community news, and home country information.

Several magazines emerged during the 1990s to target Asian Americans, including *A Magazine* in New York, *Face* and *Yolk* from California, *Niko* of Texas, and Toronto-based *Typhoon.* All are vying for the lucrative spending power of Asian Americans across North America (Beam, 1995). The magazines vary in their emphasis on different points of interest, ranging from fashion to news and entertainment. Newer magazines such as *Onward* often target the children of immigrants, whereas older vehicles such as *India Abroad* are favored by their parents (Mehta, 1994b). As more competition enters the magazine market, more magazines targeting Asian Americans are specializing in narrower targets such as Japanese or Chinese Americans.

As noted earlier, in-language television and radio are rapidly gaining in popularity with Asian American consumers. Their programs tend to include a combination of satellite news reports or entertainment programs and locally produced news and entertainment shows. Most U.S. cities with large Asian American populations offer 24-hour multicultural television programming. In San Francisco, long-established KTSF provides news, information, and entertainment to more than 1 million Asian Americans in the area (Kang & Lee, 1999). KTSF varies in-language programs throughout the day, thus reaching Asian American ethnic groups such as Chinese, Filipinos, Vietnamese, and Koreans. Their rates range from $35 to $350 for a 30-second spot. The station has the potential to reach 2.75 million households in northern California. Other popular stations include KIKU in Hawaii and WMBC in New York. Aside from these stations focused on Asian Americans in general, there are a growing number of cable companies offering home country programming as options for their customers. Cable networks such as TVAsia, Eye on Asia, and Vision of Asia are available for local subscription in major cities. The number of in-language radio stations is expected to boom after digitalization of the medium.

Nontraditional media such as the Internet are bringing yet another alternative to the mix for reaching Asian American consumers. The Web site

AsianAvenue.com provides information about careers, money, college, and wellness, as well as chat rooms that discuss topics such as how Asian Americans are portrayed in the media ("AsianAvenue.com," 1999). With online penetration at over two thirds of Asian Americans households, the power of the Web is an excellent way for companies to build loyal relationships with affluent Asian American consumers. Video rentals are also a popular medium with Asian Americans due to strong film and television programming industries in Asia.

Direct marketing is an excellent medium for reaching Asian Americans and specific country-of-origin groups in Asian America. Some trade publications have reported that Asian Americans are one of the most difficult ethnic groups to reach, but direct marketers have a variety of general market media and lists available for targeting Asian Americans in English (Mummert, 1995). For example, there are a number of specialty lists for reaching Asian Indian Americans (Mogelonsky, 1995a). Good sources for mailing lists are the professional organizations among country-of-origin groups (Wynter, 1998a).

Asian Americans are only beginning to be wooed by marketers with in-language direct mail and telemarketing. In-language databases are scarce, and some Asian Americans do not use credit cards, a prime measure of a target's ability to pay (Mummert, 1995). However, given the potential growth in Asian American population and spending power, it is almost certain that marketers will find ways to overcome current obstacles.

Last but not least are the ubiquitous yellow-page directories listing Asian American professionals and businesses. They are mostly distributed free and tend to be country-of-origin specific: for example, the *Houston Korean Journal, China Press Weekly,* and *Chinese Yellow Pages* in Houston, the *Indian American* (a weekly) in San Antonio, *Rafu Shimpo* or *Nikkei West* in California (for Japanese Americans), *Orange County Weekly* (for Vietnamese Americans), and the national Chinese newspaper *World Journal*. Often these newspapers are published in both English and a native language (Shermach, 1994). Advertisers in these directories are drawn from local community networks and mainstream firms wishing to reach members of the Asian American communities they represent. They are excellent media for business-to-business marketing.

---

## Asian American Use of Mainstream and Ethnic Media

A major impediment to making effective media choices in reaching Asian American consumers is the absence of Simmons, Nielsen, or Information Resources, Inc. (IRI) data for Asian American audiences. Several practitioners believe that until there are television networks targeting Asian Americans there will not be the impetus or financing to collect this information (Lee et al., 1999a; Teinowitz, 1998). There is also tremendous fragmentation in Asian American media, creating barriers to economies of scale in media purchases.

Sometimes the effectiveness of media buys in reaching Asian Americans is apparent even though exposure rates are not measurable. Geffen Records ran commercials during *Flames,* a program available on cable from the Filipino Channel. The program appealed to Filipinos in the same age demographic as the general market program *Beverly Hills, 90210.* They found that 80% to 90% of their subscribers watched it every day and often had the channel on for over 6 hours per day. For the 2 weeks the ads ran, sales shot up; then they settled down again after the commercials stopped appearing (Teinowitz, 1998).

Asian Americans have low consumption of all media types—electronic, broadcast, and print. Several companies with experience in the market claim that they are too busy "getting educated" or "running small businesses." Table 8.9 highlights the inaccessibility of Asian Americans due to low media usage as compared to that of three other ethnic groups in Houston, Texas. As indicated in the table, Chinese Americans spent less than 2 hours a week with English-language television, less than 1 hour with Chinese-language television, less than 1 hour with Chinese radio, about 2 hours reading either Chinese or English newspapers, and less than 2 hours a week with magazines in either language.

In the same study, about 19% of Chinese Americans in Houston indicated that newspapers were their main source of information in 1994. Television was close behind with 18% of respondents in the study, and magazines had 16% of this audience, radio 14%, word of mouth 11%, Web sites 8%, and niche publications another 8% ("Practicing Politics," 1999). Chinese Americans in Houston also reported less usage of nontraditional media. They were more likely to buy from companies sponsoring ethnic festivals than to order from catalogs or telemarketers (Lee et al., 1999a). The implication of data like these is that marketers should minimize media expenditures, increase the hiring of Asian American sales personnel, and invest in direct marketing to opinion leaders within Asian American community networks.

Buying Asian-oriented and in-language media is the most efficient way to maximize advertising dollars in the Asian American market, even though the media themselves are fragmented by language and geographic location. In-language television networks in a few American cities, as well as cable channels, video rentals, and newspapers, are outpacing English-language, ethnic-oriented print media targeting Asian Americans.

**TABLE 8.9**  Media Usage of Chinese, Anglo, African, and Mexican Americans in
Houston, Texas

| Medium | Average Scores[a] | | | |
|---|---|---|---|---|
| | Anglo Americans | African Americans | Chinese Americans | Hispanic Americans |
| Watching English TV | 3.9 | 4.3 | 3.1 | 3.6 |
| Listening to English radio | 3.6 | 4.1 | 2.6 | 3.8 |
| Reading English newspapers | 2.5 | 2.5 | 2.0 | 2.5 |
| Reading English magazines | 2.1 | 2.6 | 2.0 | 2.5 |
| Watching Chinese/Spanish TV | N/A | N/A | 1.6 | 3.6 |
| Listening to Chinese/Spanish radio | N/A | N/A | N/A | 3.9 |
| Reading Chinese/Spanish newspapers | N/A | N/A | 2.0 | 1.9 |
| Reading Chinese/Spanish magazines | N/A | N/A | 1.6 | 2.1 |

SOURCE: Lee, La Ferle, and Tharp (1999a).
a. Scale: 1 = less than 30 minutes; 2 = 30 to 59 minutes; 3 = 1 hour to 1 hour and 59 minutes; 4 = 2 hours to 2 hours and 59 minutes; 5 = 3 hours to 3 hours and 59 minutes; 6 = 4 hours or more.

At the same time, it would be a mistake to ignore mainstream media in a mix of vehicles reaching the total Asian American market. Selective buying of mainstream media in a limited number of cities, in addition to exposure in Asian-oriented media in both English and native languages in those same locations, can deliver high reach. A combination of magazines such as *Masala, Onward,* or *Hum,* which appeal to second-generation Indian Americans, and newspapers such as *India Abroad,* favored by their immigrant parents, is needed to reach immigrants as well as acculturated Asian Americans.

English-language television is the "window on America" for new immigrants, even though they may not speak or understand English well. At the same time, messages in mainstream media do not always resonate with Asian American values. For example, first-generation Asian Americans were baffled by an

AT&T commercial with the theme and music for "Girls Just Wanna Have Fun." They asked, "Where are the husbands? Is it a failed marriage?" (Teinowitz, 1998, p. S19). Given the little time Asian Americans spend with media and the multitude of choices they have, it is especially important to break through with culturally compatible messages.

## The Marketplace as Social Network and Expression of Values

A recent poll of Asian American consumers pointed to four important attributes that were the basis of their purchase decisions. They were, in order from most to least important, quality, price for value received, service provided, and convenience. These criteria confirm no major differences between the preferences of Asian and other American consumers. They also support the proposition that Asian American consumers do not require significantly different marketing communication messages (Wong, 1997, p. 46). At the same time, they express a strong need to continue Asian traditions and values. There are several ways in which marketing programs can be adapted to create more culturally compatible relationships with Asian American consumers.

First, many foreign-born consumers are not familiar with American brand names. Tactics that build brand recognition are essential before moving Asian American consumers toward brand preference and brand loyalty. Developing this kind of relationship with Asian Americans means that marketers must first become extended members of Asian American social and professional community networks. J. C. Penney built traffic among Asian American consumers by adding well-known Asian brands and a line of cosmetics from Minnesota designed especially for Asian women (Crawford, 1998).

Sears measures its success with Asian American shoppers by their responses to promotions keyed to important Asian American holidays. For example, during the Moon Festival one year they invited Chinese and Vietnamese customers in Los Angeles to bring in coupons and receive traditional items such as moon cakes and lanterns. The promotion was supported by radio and print advertisements. Sales figures for affected stores went up 28% to 30% (Teinowitz, 1998). Tailored promotions such as these position mainstream companies as participants in traditions important to Asian American consumers.

Second, shopping is a favorite leisure activity for many Asian Americans. Retailers must create fun and informative atmospheres that meet the needs of

276 MARKETING AND CONSUMER IDENTITY

Asian American shoppers. Asian American consumers respond more positively to deference and a "soft sell" from salespersons. National retail stores in ethnic communities should consider hiring personnel who speak and understand the native languages of the country-of-origin groups who live near their stores. Even more important when selling services instead of products is building an association with leaders in the community. For example, Mony Life uses only bilingual salespersons to sell insurance and investment products in the Hindi communities of New Jersey (Louis, 1999). Too much informality can also get marketers in trouble in Asian America, where the assumption that because we share interests we are "friends" is not compatible with Asian definitions of friendship or mutual obligation. A good example of fitting into the cultural environment of consumers is the soft-sell ad in Figure 8.3, which was directed to the large number of immigrants from Hong Kong in the mid-1990s.

A third consideration is the unique focus of Asian American consumer identity around the family rather than the individual. Asian American spending of over $1 billion on long distance is double the amount of Hispanic households and three to four times that of the general market (Berkowitz, 1997). Favorite possessions of Indian Americans showed their owners' emphasis on family and culture and were not serving as expressions of individual identity or style (Mehta & Belk, 1991). Emphasis on how a product can increase a consumer's individual freedom may seem self-centered and inconsiderate of others in an Asian American family. And although many Asian Americans are proud of their cultural heritage, they also question why marketers single them out for special treatment (Lev, 1991).

Asian American consumers have been described as less venturesome and as preferring well-known and Asian-owned firms (Applegate, 1991; Burton, 1993; Delener & Neelankavil, 1990; Lee & Tse, 1994; O'Hare et al., 1994). The role of multiple family members in what may be considered individual purchase decisions must be taken into consideration in the design of communication messages and marketing programs. In cities like San Francisco, bankers adapt their marketing programs for each branch, using the languages of the country-of-origin population in each surrounding neighborhood (Wiesendanger, 1993). Some banks use "family banking" products for Asian American clients that pool the entire family's balances when calculating balance-related charges (Wiesendanger, 1993).

A fourth major difference between Asian and other American consumers is the emphasis they place on both belonging and achievement. Affluent Asian American consumers distinguish themselves with luxury goods and high-status brands. They buy signature clothing and jewelry, imported automobiles, fine li-

**Figure 8.3.** Cultural Relevance: "Please Stay to the Right"

quor, global travel, and so on. "When buying American, they prefer old, estab-lished and well-known brands, but new products and services have a good chance if they quickly establish a good reputation for quality and value" (Wong, 1997, p. 40). Over 50% of Crown Royal whisky sales in California come from Korean and Korean American consumers, drinking 20 bottles for each one con-sumed in the general market there. Case sales drop if prices charged do not rep-resent good value or if the brand is not promoted in media that are consumed by Korean Americans (Teinowitz, 1998; Zhang & Gelb, 1996). Citibank commis-sioned a unique Swarovski crystal dragon, symbol of power and beauty among several Asian American country-of-origin groups, to use as a gift for consumers opening accounts over a certain amount (Crawford, 1998).

The Asian American definition of success is framed in material terms (Lee, 1999). This is seen in their high consumption of product categories with strong links to values such as belonging and education. Status brands are very appeal-ing to Asian American consumers. A luxury car dealer in Buena Park, Califor-nia, claims that 30% to 35% of their business is from Asian American small busi-ness owners. Their customers typically buy an "inexpensive Mercedes for their children and a top-of-the-line one for the business" (Rivera, 1997, p. 40). San Francisco dealers claim that 85% of luxury car sales in the area are to com-puter/electronics professionals from Silicon Valley (Rivera, 1997). Direct mar-keters may find these consumers accessible via current databases, for the most affluent Asian American consumers are more likely than other consumers to own three or more different credit cards.

An innovative use of promotions in Asian America has been the use of schol-arships by Met Life. Their Scholar Program targets South Asian Americans. Press releases were made to vehicles such as the *India Tribune* in New York, and brochures were distributed at branches and special events and by direct mail. They received over 7,000 entry requests, making this an excellent example of us-ing the Asian American community network and showing emphasis on educa-tion and achievement (Crawford, 1998).

Asian Americans share a strong preference for buying from Asian Ameri-can-owned companies or brands. In Houston, 70% of Vietnamese Americans with bank accounts use Vietnamese-owned banks (brochure of the San Ko Asian Bank, 1997). At the same time, Asian American consumers can be activists. At least one in four consumers would boycott a company accused of racial discrimi-nation, and one of three would sign petitions in response.

A small but growing portion of business in Asian America is coming from cross-ethnic promotions. Asian-owned stores in African American neighborhoods have begun selling the soul foods of Sylvia Woods Enterprises, and Puerto Rican chicken farmers are finding that Chinese stores sell lots of chicken feet in Chinese areas. Corina's from Athens, Ohio, sells ethnically flavored dog treats. Their flavors include Mongolian beef, Korean barbecue, chicken taco, and chicken parmesan (Morse, 1999; Thomas, 1998).

Names as well as numbers and colors often have particular significance among Asians and Asian Americans. These symbolic associations can be positive or negative. For example, the number 7 supposedly brings good luck in several Chinese languages. The number 8 means prosperity, and 2 and 8 together mean easy prosperity. When Chinese consumers in San Francisco received a coupon offering $28 off their next phone bill, they couldn't believe that the coupon was real; to them, it sounded like a get-rich-quick scam (Boyd, 1994). Pronunciation of the number 3 sounds like the word for "life" in Cantonese, and the number 4 sounds like the word for "death" in Japanese (it was the "kiss of death" for the Volvo 244DL). In Korean and Chinese cultures, the number 9 is associated with longevity and the number 10 (or 1) with something guaranteed or assured. The area code of San Gabriel Valley is 818 or "prosperity guaranteed prosperity" (Berfield, 1999; Wong, 1997, pp. 122-124).

Red stands for joy and happiness among the Chinese and Japanese, purple is associated with heaven and the emperor, green is associated with health and growth, yellow with the earth, and black with guilt, evil, death, and the direction north. White is a universal funeral color throughout the world, at the same time as it stands for purity, innocence, and the direction west (Wong, 1997, pp. 125-126). The symbolic meanings of numbers, names, and colors survive Asian Americans' growing use of English. Understanding these possible meanings to Asian American consumers is another way to express cultural sensitivity.

As noted earlier, first- and second-generation as well as urban and suburban Asian Americans have very different lifestyles and values. One marketer has used these differences to define three consumer segments in the Asian Indian American market. The first group consists of early immigrants who are affluent and now nearing retirement. The second group consists of immigrants who are younger and who came to the United States at a later date but who have also become affluent. Another difference between these two groups is the roles of their wives. Members of the second wave of Indian immigrants are married to highly educated women who are employed outside the home. The third group is made up of mostly relatives of the earlier immigrants. They are often less well educated and are more likely to run small businesses such as motels and convenience stores (Mogelonsky, 1995a). Early immigrants are affluent and now nearing retirement.

The high ownership of businesses in Asian America is a major opportunity for business-to-business selling. A Chinese proverb predicts, "There is no prospect in working for others." One source reports that ethnic Chinese and Indian immigrants run almost 25% of the high-tech companies started in Silicon Valley since 1980 (Thurm, 1999). Asian Indian retailers pool resources and form associations that allow them to buy in bulk and sell at lower prices (Mogelonsky, 1995a). Asian American businesses also take advantage of Small Business Administration programs giving preference to minority-owned firms in selling to government entities (Sharpe, 1997). Cultural associations are not only helping new immigrants assimilate in Silicon Valley but also serving as a major source of business for those who join them. Monte Jade is a Chinese organization that has been accused of reverse discrimination, but 20% of its members are not of Chinese descent (Takahashi, 1998).

To summarize, designing marketing programs that fit "the Asian way of life" means hiring ethnic personnel, using ethnic-language media, generating word-of-mouth communication through community leaders, and improving postpurchase service (Lee, La Ferle, & Tharp, 1999b).

One of the most valuable sources of information about Asian American consumers is the growing number of Asian American-targeted communications, research, and marketing companies. Some of these specialists are Kang and Lee, Imada Wong, Adland, Intertrend, L3, Lee Liu and Tong, Iwatsu, and Asian and Hispanic Marketing Communications Research. Ethnic specialists and general market agencies represent the top spenders in the Asian American market: MCI, AT&T, Anheuser-Busch, Cathay Pacific Airlines, Aladdin Hotel and Casino, CIGNA, Hyundai, Miller Brewing, Martell's Cognac, Steinway and Sons, Samsung Electronics, Thai Airways, Charles Schwab, DHL Worldwide Express, Chivas Regal, New York Life, Encyclopedia Britannica, Office Depot, and Southern California Toyota Dealers. With current buying power of over $225 billion, spending in product categories such as long distance at over $1 billion, and overindexing on many other high-cost products and services, Asian American consumers are a "marketer's dream" come true if companies can master the subtleties of their behavior (Wong, 1997, p. 24).

## SUMMARY

Asian America includes peoples from different countries of origin, religions, races, and ethnic identities. It is divided across lines formed by foreign- versus native-born individuals, high versus low economic and educational backgrounds, and immigrants versus later generations. A unifying value is the legacy of Confucianism, which gives many Asian Americans a strong commitment to family, hierarchy, and community. Over time and generations, most Asian Americans blend into mainstream America, but they often retain pride in their heritage and can be chameleonlike, balancing both cultures as required, depending on the situation.

Communication preferences of Asian Americans are distinctive. Their high-context background makes them give more attention than the American mainstream to relationships between communicators and to saving face over direct messages. Their insider bias is expressed by a preference for word-of-mouth sources of information, in-language media, and Asian-owned firms. Their time with media is the least of any American ethnic group, making nontraditional media a superior investment for reaching them. As consumers, they place importance on value received, and they use well-known brand names as a surrogate measure of product quality. Some Asian American consumers read symbolic meanings into particular colors, names, and numbers. Support for community events, education, and localized promotions and communications presents opportunities for cultural partnerships between Asian American consumers and marketers.

# CHAPTER 9

# Multicultural Markets and Marketing

## Future Directions

In February 1999, several network television stations broadcast a story about the copy on California billboards for a fitness studio. The billboards stated that when aliens land on earth, they will "eat the fat ones first." Media discussions centered on the appropriateness of this reference to overweight Americans, estimated as 40% of adult Americans in 2000. Pundits asked, "Would they dare say, 'They'll eat Gay people first'? Or 'They'll eat Blacks first'?"

The answer in 1999, of course, was no! Gay Americans are at the cusp of having their political and civil rights recognized. Racial comments can make their authors liable to civil, even criminal lawsuits for slander. Fifty years ago, if the ad's statement had referred to African Americans, it would have been legal. Today, this kind of disparagement of African or Gay Americans is unacceptable to most Americans, no matter what their own sexual orientation or racial or ethnic origin. Beyond "political correctness," it is simply unacceptable treatment of other members of our cultural mosaic. Is it possible that sometime in the future it will be considered slanderous, even illegal, to disparage the overweight?

The idea that subculture communities move from outsider status to membership in our cultural mosaic over time is not a new concept (Kotkin, 1992; Ungar, 1995; Waters, 1990b; Zweigenhaft & Domhoff, 1998). The focus in the first part of this chapter is on how different levels of acceptance into mainstream America affect subculture consumer needs and identities. A descriptive model of how subculture group and individual member identities have evolved is presented. Later sections explore the potential for partnerships with other evolving subcultures in American and global cultural mosaics. New ethnic, disability, age, and regional subcultures are outlined, along with their potential to influence consumer identity in the American cultural mosaic. The last section of the chapter highlights the growing number of multicultural societies in other countries as possible venues for multicultural marketing.

## A MODEL OF THE EVOLUTION OF CONSUMER SUBCULTURES IN THE UNITED STATES

Future opportunities for multicultural marketing in the United States depend on partnerships with consumers either from new subcultures or from broader economic and cultural roles within current consumer subcultures. In the long term, extending marketing programs on the basis of compatible values to consumers outside the American market is also a path for organizational growth. To evaluate the viability of other consumer subcultures in the United States, we first review how the Gay, African American, U.S. Latino, and Asian American subcultures have moved from outsider status to full membership in the American cultural mosaic.[1]

The acceptance of other racial and ethnic groups as part of the American mainstream could be the inevitable effect of assimilation into the mainstream by an increasingly diverse population. However, as noted in Chapter 1, American mainstream beliefs and values are as changed by the accommodation of new subcultures as members of subcultures are by their own process of acculturation (Alba, 1990; Schouten, 1991; Twitchell, 1996; Turow, 1997a; Waters, 1990b). Therefore, neither assimilation nor acculturation adequately explains the movement of subcultures from outsiders to insiders in the United States.

American mainstream beliefs have always centered on equality before the law and equality of economic opportunity. When Jewish, Irish, and Italian immigrants first came to this country in large numbers, they were not considered "White" or "equal" to other Americans. Less than a century later, most of their descendants are unaware that there was a time when they were not "White." African Americans, U.S. Latinos, and women spent the 20th century pressing for recognition of their civil rights. In two centuries, we have evolved from a society in which the values of White European males determined the rules of law and economic life to a society in which different racial, religious, and ethnic groups, both sexes, and some alternative sexual orientations are considered, if not always equal, at least part of mainstream society.

Table 9.1 shows the perspectives of individuals and their subcultures (as represented by community issues) at different points in the transition from outsider to insider status in the United States. The attitudes of mainstream Americans toward members of a particular subculture are also presented as changing over time (Zweigenhaft & Domhoff, 1998). This model proposes five phases in the movement of American subcultures to full membership in mainstream America. It describes the issues important to individual subculture members, mainstream Americans, and leaders in mainstream and subculture communities as "outsiders" become accepted members of the American mainstream.

In the earliest phase, immigrants and other persons whose ethnic origin or values place them outside mainstream America accept their status as outsiders. They do not see themselves as members of American mainstream society, even though they may aspire to an "American dream" (Boyce, 1997; Dholakia & Levy, 1987; Holland & Gentry, 1999). Though individuals recognize their similarities to other persons from the same country-of-origin group or alternative lifestyle, there is little community pressure to express this group identity. As consumers, individuals are focused on basic economic survival, which is more difficult given their outsider status. Likewise, mainstream Americans see members of the subculture as "not belonging" at this time.

The next phase reflects a growing recognition by a majority of the subculture that their best chances for achieving economic goals related to the "American dream" come from aligning themselves with other members of their subculture and learning how to "fit in" (Lee & Tse, 1994; Penaloza, 1994). At this point, their leaders begin to speak out about discrimination or misrepresentation by mainstream Americans (Zweigenhaft & Domhoff, 1998, p. 190). Individuals may find themselves "between two cultures," wanting the benefits of membership in the mainstream but identifying with others who share their heritage or experiences (Stayman & Deshpande, 1989; Tuan, 1998; Williams & Qualls, 1989). Members of the mainstream may view these persons as a threat to their own values and positions of privilege within American economic and cultural life.

Over time, the voices of community among outside subcultures become more forceful and focused on achieving full political and economic participation in

**TABLE 9.1** Evolution of Consumer Subcultures in the United States

| | Phase I | Phase II | Phase III | Phase IV | Phase V |
|---|---|---|---|---|---|
| Central theme | Outsider status | Community formation | Political, economic participation | Representation within U.S. popular culture | Membership in the cultural mosaic |
| Subculture group status | Outside mainstream America | Discrimination by members of American mainstream | Recognition of political rights by mainstream | Increasing subculture share in economic/cultural life | Sharing own version of "American dream," part of cultural mosaic |
| Mainstream view of group members | "They don't belong" | "They are a threat to us" | "They want special privileges" | "They are equal but different" | "We are all 'equal but different', members of an American mosaic culture" |
| Individual self-perceptions | "I am not like other Americans" | "I have common goals with other subculture members" | "I want to be treated fairly as part of the mainstream" | "I am a unique combination of self and group values" | Personal values reflect "American dream" and mosaic of values |
| Symbolism of individual choices for time and money | "I am different" | "I am the same as this group" | "I deserve to belong too" | "I am a mix of me and them" | "I am an individual with a unique mix of values from the American mosaic" |

286

the American mainstream (Bauer & Cunningham, 1970; Cloud, 1999; Klor de Alva, 1997; Nelson & Tienda, 1997; Ungar, 1995). Mainstream Americans may feel threatened by this pressure and believe that the outsiders are requesting special, undeserved privileges. Individual consumer choices of how to spend time and money assume importance as symbols of consumers' dual identities. Though the goal of economic success still drives behavior overall, expressing a common identity with people from the same group becomes important too. Several authors refer to this as "balancing between two cultures" (Stayman & Deshpande, 1989; Williams & Qualls, 1989; Wysocki, 1997). Consumers respond positively to marketers who recognize their subculture, its values, and its contributions to American life (Holland & Gentry, 1999).

Ironically, two contradictory patterns influence consumer needs and identities during this transition stage. On the one hand, ethnicity or sexual orientation becomes less directly correlated with consumer preferences. Social identity becomes "Americanized," meaning that the self is self-constructed rather than determined by origins, that it changes according to situation, and that it is made up of multiple aspects of a person's social roles. At the same time, being a member of that subculture is an important source of the individual's perception of his or her unique place in the cultural mosaic.

The fourth phase in the evolution of consumer subcultures comes upon recognition by mainstream Americans of the civic and political equality of subculture members. In this phase, mainstream America accepts the viability of the distinctive cultural beliefs and practices of these groups in our cultural mosaic as "separate but equal," at least in principle. For individual consumers, ethnic or subcultural pride is further integrated into a multifaceted self. Community issues are focused on winning legal rights, addressing lingering economic inequalities, and seeking better representation of the subculture in American popular culture.

The last phase of the model recognizes the permeability of mainstream American values (Hammond & Morrison, 1996; Ray, 1997). As the mainstream accommodates members whose values are in conflict with those of other mainstreamers, alternative value systems are added to the mix, and mainstream values evolve in the process. Individuals see their subculture membership as just one expression of how they differ from other members of the mainstream. Personal values of individuals reflect a mix of (sometimes conflicting) cultural value systems, just as mainstream values themselves adjust when newer groups are incorporated into the "salad bowl."

Having achieved the "American dream" is one measure of full membership in the American mainstream. Economic affluence, one part of the "American dream," is symbolized by having a good job or career, owning a home, and/or being able to retire (Boyce, 1997; Nahm, 1997). However, each subculture group has its own version of the "American dream" (Dholakia & Levy, 1987; O'Hare, 1992b; Stein, 1996). Success can also mean representation in American popular culture, as measured by successful members of a subculture in entertainment, business, sports, the professions, civic life, public service, and education.

This model of the evolution of consumer subcultures in the United States will not be easy to test empirically. Few research studies place consumption attitudes and preferences in a cultural framework, and even fewer compare findings across multiple subcultures in the United States (Englis & Solomon, 1995; Gannon & Associates, 1994; Hirschman, 1985; McCracken, 1986; Mick & Buhl, 1992; Rook, 1985; Tharp & Scott, 1990; Twitchell, 1996; Williamson, 1986). Our understanding of the cultural roles of products and how consumers express cultural identities is also in its infancy (Fournier, 1998; Hirschman & Thompson, 1997; Kellner, 1995b; Oswald, 1999; Wattanasuwan, 1998). Still, the patterns of moving from outsider status to participation in the reformulation of American mainstream values, the awakening of group identity, the symbolism of consumer needs, and the formation of consumer identities have been similar for African Americans, U.S. Latinos, Gays and Lesbians, and Asian Americans.

The highly prized value of individualism in American cultural values means that individuals from collectivistic subcultures (Native Americans, for example) must meld their beliefs with more individualistic values or will remain outside the mosaic. Arab Americans include Christians and Moslems, yet until recently Christian Arab Americans have been more successful than their Moslem brethren in melding their ethnic values with those of the mainstream (Asuad, 1974; El-Badry, 1994). The point is that not *all* American subcultures exert influence over our multicultural values system in 2000.

Returning to the future place of overweight and obese Americans, why do we treat them as outsiders? Of primary significance is the invisibility of the overweight within American popular culture (Agins, 1996; Faber, Christenson, DeZwaan, & Mitchell, 1995). Media and marketing institutions can open access to group representation in popular culture venues such as film, television, music, games, and popular reading and imagery. They are gatekeepers in choosing to represent different subcultures in America, a critical role in multicultural societies. The presence of more overweight people in popular media could make them more included in our visual mosaic of Americans.

The question for marketers is whether they might find potential consumers among people belonging to subcultures outside our contemporary American cultural mosaic. Subcultures have unique communication styles and media preferences, distinctive value systems and beliefs, and particular demographic characteristics. Some subcultures may be moving toward or already part of mainstream America, but their size has not been sufficient to warrant special marketing efforts. Yet another possibility is that a group of like-minded or like-behaved individuals (e.g., the overweight or other lifestyle segments) share some but not all of the characteristics of a subculture. The next section of this chapter focuses on groups of Americans who may be candidates for multicultural marketing on the basis of values shared with a particular organization.

# EVOLVING CONSUMER SUBCULTURES IN THE UNITED STATES

In this section, a number of ethnic, cohort, and other groups are briefly profiled. With the exception of age cohorts, these social identities of American consumers have not yet drawn significant marketer attention.[2] Nevertheless, these groups could be future partners of organizations with compatible values. Where possible, the demographic, geographic, core values, media habits, media availability, and marketing preferences of each group are outlined.

## Other Ethnic Groups in the United States

### Native Americans

Over 2 million Native Americans in 555 tribes were recognized by the Bureau of Indian Affairs in 1998. The 10 largest tribes are Cherokee, Navajo, Chippewa, Sioux, Choctaw, Pueblo, Apache, Iroquois, Lumbewe, and Creek. Over one half of this population live west of the Mississippi River, and about 780,000 live on reservations. Alaska's native population is over 50% Eskimo, about 36% American Indian, and 12% Aleut (U.S. Bureau of the Census, 1993g). Table 9.2 shows size, regions, and states where Native Americans (and other ethnic groups) are most populous. The table mentions major events and specialized media for targeting Native Americans. Native Americans constitute 3% of all minorities in the United States, but they own only 1.7% of all minority

**TABLE 9.2** Profiles of Ethnic Americans

| Ethnic Group | Estimated U.S. Population | Regional Concentrations | Important Dates/Events | Significant Media |
|---|---|---|---|---|
| Native Americans | 2,000,000 | SW, NW, and Midwestern U.S.; OK, CA, AZ, NM, AL, WA | Powwows, rodeos | Reservation/ tribe news, local radio, Internet |
| Irish Americans | 40,000,000 | | March 17 New York City | Irish America Magazine |
| Italian Americans | 26,000,000 | NYC, NY; Boston; PA, NJ; NE & Mid-Atlantic U.S.; San Francisco, New Orleans, Chicago | St. Anthony/ Gabriel neigh-borhood festi-vals, San Gennaro (Sept.), Italian Heritage Month (Oct.) | Il Progreso Italo-Americano; Ambassador |
| Jewish Americans | 6,000,000 | NYC, NY; NE and N U.S.; Los Angeles, CA; Miami, FL; NJ | Rosh Hashanah | Community newsletters |
| Arab Americans | 870,000 to 3,000,000 | CA, NY, MI, NJ, PA, TX, VA, MA, OH | Ramadan | Arab-Net-TV, American Arab Directory, radio |
| German Americans | 50,000,000 | PA, TX | Oktoberfest | |
| English Americans | 50,000,000 | NE and S U.S. | | |
| Greek Americans | 1,130,000 | NYC; Boston; NE U.S.; Chi-cago; Detroit; Midwestern U.S.; CA, FL | Greek Indepen-dence, Easter, New Year's | 27 newspapers, 14 in Greek; radio, CTN |
| Iranian Americans | 650,000 | Los Angeles | | Community media in "Teheran-geles" |

SOURCES: Mogelonsky (1997), O'Hare (1998), Reese (1997), Sandor (1994b).

businesses. Seventy-five percent of their 600,000 households are family house-holds, with a large percentage headed by females. In Arizona, they represent 5.6% of the population but own only 0.45% of Arizona companies.

As many as one in three Native Americans on reservations is unemployed. Although this is a young and growing population, one of every five Native American homes lacks both telephone and indoor toilet. There is tremendous variation in Native American incomes, from the Pequot tribe, with proceeds exceeding $1 million a day from their gambling ventures, to the 30% of all Native Americans who live below the poverty level (U.S. Bureau of the Census, 1993g; Van Biema, 1994, 1995).

Native American rituals, traditions, beliefs, and worldviews are more like those of other immigrants to the United States than those of the founding fathers and their descendants (Trosper, 1992). Strong collectivism and beliefs that human beings are subject to nature's rules contrast sharply with the mainstream American commitment to individualism and a belief that humans rule nature. Native American traditions often place value on skills that may not be needed for survival today but that have continuing symbolic meaning. Their holistic views of human beings and nature lead to an emphasis on the present; several tribes do not have verb tenses for the future. Taking care of elders and measuring success by inner happiness are other important beliefs (Green, 1993).

The most important issue among leaders in Native American communities is how to keep traditions alive yet relevant to the contemporary lives of their tribes (Van Biema, 1994). Many native languages have been lost, even while others are being revived (Thompson, 1998). Land has a special significance to Native Americans and has constantly been an issue of conflict with U.S. citizens and institutions (Council on Interracial Books, 1977). Many tribes value "doing" over being. Powwows are held in many locations throughout the year. They appeal to the growing population of middle-class Native Americans, over half of whom now live in urban areas (Fixico, 1985). The pickup truck is "the 20th-century horse" among Indians and is an essential part of the material culture of modern Native Americans. Also very popular are the sporting events, especially rodeos, that they travel far to attend (Trafzer, 1985).

There has been increasing ethnic pride among Native Americans. Positive images in popular movies like *Dances With Wolves* and *Smoke Signals* also reinforce Native American identity. There continues to be a strong need to tell Native American stories; the oral tradition is maintained by visual and oral media with images that combat centuries of what they believe has been one-sided representation and misrepresentation in mainstream American culture (Koehl &

Van Boven, 1996). The writer-director of *Smoke Signals* summarized contemporary Native American life most realistically: "Sure we have different specific cultural customs, but we also read Stephen King and watch *ER* like everyone else" (Ressner, 1998, p. 69).

Most of the stereotypes about Native Americans come from non-Native American authors. Scenes sprinkled throughout school textbooks, children's stories and other literature, cartoons, movies, and television feature "painted, whooping, and feathered Indians closing in on forts, maliciously attacking 'peaceful' settlers, drunk, incompetent or childlike" (Byler, 1973, pp. 6-7). Images such as the "Indian maiden in deerskin" or the "cigar store Indian" and symbols such as tomahawks and teepees have been used to sell products as varied as baking powder, sports teams, cigarettes, butter, and alcohol. As a sign of changing times, descendants of Crazy Horse recently sued the parties making and distributing Crazy Horse malt liquor for using the name without permission (Cowen, 1997).

## Italian Americans

The 1990 census counted about 15 million people who called themselves "Italian American." If all Americans of Italian descent were included, the Italian American population would top 40 million; some say 1 of every 10 Americans has Italian blood (Krase, 1994). The current figure is accepted as near 26 million, with 90% of those in 11 states around the Mid-Atlantic and New England. In 1980, about half of those identifying as Italian American were second generation and thus still in touch with the immigrant experience. Subculture identity declines for third-generation Italian Americans, the most likely group to marry persons of other ancestry (Alba, 1985).

There is a strong concentration of Italian Americans in the Mid-Atlantic states; in fact, over 44% of all Italian Americans live there, though only 17% of the total American population lives in the area. Over 62% live in large cities such as New York, Philadelphia, Newark, Boston, New Orleans, San Francisco, and Chicago. At least 15% of the populations of New York, New Jersey, Connecticut, Rhode Island, and Massachusetts are Italian American. Italian Americans report "hearing and seeing" their neighbors as a positive quality of their neighborhoods. Though most Italians have adopted American lifestyles, their social contacts often remain within the Italian American community (Hirschman, 1985).

Italian values place the extended family at the center of social life, followed by friends and godparents, then acquaintances ("people to be polite to") and strangers ("people to be wary of") (Alba, 1985; Battistella, 1989; Krase & DeSena, 1994; Rolle, 1980). The majority of Italian Americans are Roman Catholic (70%), but Italian American families are smaller than those of other Catholic groups and the American average. Food is the "symbol of life" and is not to be wasted or eaten in a hurry. This importance is reflected in the emphasis placed on food quality and freshness of ingredients. Self-reliance, maintaining good credit, and education remain important among Italian Americans (Sowell, 1981). Several organizations represent Italian Americans, including Sons of Italy, the National Italian American Foundation (www.niaf.org), the Columbus Club, and the Cultural Italian American Organization (CIAO). Publications such as the *Italian Quarterly, Italian Americana,* and *Italica* target Italian Americans.

Many Italian Americans continue to feel that they are disparaged by images in the mass media. Programs like HBO's *The Sopranos* represent a small minority of people with Cosa Nostra heritage as if they represented all Italian Americans. Media studies report that negative portrayals of Italian American characters outnumber positive images two to one. One of six Italian American media characters is involved in some illegal activity, only one in seven is in a high-status job, and only one in six is a woman (Caso, 1984). To Italians, being Italian American is about "warmth, family orientation, hard work, doing things well, wonderful food" (Del Guidice, 1993). Successful Italian Americans like Mario Cuomo, Lee Iococca, John Travolta, Geraldine Ferraro, and Tony Bennett are excellent endorsers for brands wishing to attract the attention of Italian Americans.

### Jewish Americans

Jewish Americans constitute 2.3% of the population, or about 6 million Americans. Given their relatively small numbers, their accomplishments and influence are all the more impressive. They are the most affluent American ethnic group, with per capita incomes almost twice those of non-Jews. Over the past 30 years, Jews have constituted 20% of top civil servants and 40% of partners in major law firms ("American Survey," 1996). Well over 60% of Jewish Americans graduate from college (Singer, 1995).

Although there are Jewish Americans in every state, the North and Northeast have the largest populations. New York has over 1,450,000 Jewish Americans,

13% of the metropolitan population. Other large Jewish populations can be found in Los Angeles, Philadelphia, Chicago, Boston, and Miami (Thau, 1994). Recent migrations to the South and West are changing Jewish demographics (Wartzman, 1999a).

Rituals are an important part of Jewish religious traditions. There are three major branches of the Jewish religion, but even many "secular" Jews follow the ancient traditions of circumcisions, bar/bat mitzvahs, and marriage ceremonies under the chuppa with tallis and prayer shawls. Most Jewish Americans identify as Jewish. Whether this is an ethnic or religious identity is not always clear to them or to others (Hirschman, 1981, 1985). There are few differences in Jewish and WASP lifestyles when income and education are similar. One stockbroker said his policy was to "dress British, think Yiddish" (Hirschman, 1981).

Education is stressed in Jewish families. Community, too, is central to economic and social life. The importance of being Jewish and marrying Jewish is a frequent theme, as is involvement in arts and community organizations. Nevertheless, the population is declining as more Jews marry non-Jews and have small families. Paradoxically, a number of young Jews are becoming more religious. And many non-Jews (over two thirds of 6 million kosher product consumers) like the quality of kosher goods (Solomon, 1996, pp. 490-491). Manischewitz, long the preferred supplier for kosher dishes, underwent a makeover in 1999 to make its products "more inviting" (Shaw, 1999). A number of Internet sites and retail and financial businesses target Jewish consumers with appeals to community cohesiveness and ethnic pride (see, e.g., the Web site of the American Jewish Historical Society, www.ajhs.org; see also Auerbach, 1997).

### Irish Americans

On March 17 each year, many "Irish Americans" celebrate their ethnic heritage (Krafft, 1993; Reese, 1997). For most of them, it is a "symbolic identity," defined more as "feeling ethnic" rather than "being ethnic," for few Americans of Irish heritage speak the language or know Irish values (Alba, 1990). The U.S. Bureau of the Census (1993e) estimates that almost 40 million people, or 16% of the U.S. population, claims Irish ancestry (Spiegler, 1998). Though Irish Americans have spread throughout all regions of the country, they are overrepresented in New Jersey, Pennsylvania, and Ohio. Boston is the Irish American capital, with 33% of the total population there.

As individuals discover their Irish heritage, they may adopt symbolic gestures such as "old" Irish pronunciation of English, "wearin o' the green," and celebration of religious holidays (Auerbach, 1999). A recent *Irish American* magazine article suggested that the Irish were important in settling the West and that many "cowboy" ballads, like "Streets of Laredo," were originally Irish poetry (Meade, 1998). Contrary to their representations in the media, the Irish are not alcoholics (they have the lowest consumption and highest abstinence rates in Europe) or religiously obsessed.

Irish pride can be a strong appeal to a large number of Americans and a growing number of new Irish immigrants (Hout & Goldstein, 1994; Reese, 1997). "White ethnics spend more on adventurous vacations, look for specials, and are more likely than average Americans to use coupons" (Reese, 1997, p. 51). The *Irish Voice* and *Irish Echo* are newspapers with established ties in the Irish American community.

## Arab Americans

There are between 2 and 3 million Arab Americans, according to some sources ("Banks Offer Credit Cards," 1989). The U.S. Census Bureau (cited in El-Badry, 1994) says that about 900,000 people list an Arab country among their top two ancestries. Arab Americans include Christian Arabs as well as Moslems, Armenians, and Turks. The majority are of Lebanese, Syrian, or Palestinian origins. There are about 500,000 Armenian Americans. Their communities are concentrated in 11 states: California, New York, Michigan, Massachusetts, Rhode Island, New Jersey, Pennsylvania, Virginia, Texas, Ohio, and Illinois. Detroit counted over 70,000 Arab Americans in 1975. Currently, 36% of Arab Americans live in Detroit, New York, Los Angeles-Long Beach, Washington, D.C., Chicago, Boston, Anaheim, Bergen, Houston, and Cleveland (Asuad, 1974; El-Badry, 1994).

Overall, Arab Americans are more affluent, younger, and better educated than other Americans are. Because more than one in four Arab Americans are involved in either retailing or the health professions, they offer many business-to-business marketing opportunities (El-Badry, 1994; Zogby, 1990). About 90% of immigrants before 1940 were Christian Arabs from Syria and Lebanon. Post-World War II immigrants come from all over the Arab world and are more likely to be Muslim.

Arab Americans also complain about their images in mainstream media. By one count, 148 of 168 appearances of Arabs in movies were negative (Mahoney, 1996). Some Arab Americans believe they must suppress speaking or looking Arabic (Asfahani, 1996). Despite those fears, at least one in three Arab Americans 5 to 17 years of age speaks a language other than English at home (Zogby, 1992). Marine Midland Bank recognizes the ethnic pride of Arab and Armenian Americans by offering an "Armenian Express" and affinity MasterCard. Acts of discrimination against Arab Americans have prompted the establishment of several Arab American interest groups such as the American-Arab Anti-Discrimination Committee.

## Euro-Americans

A number of "ethnic Whites" from Greece, Germany, France, Belgium, the United Kingdom, Switzerland, eastern Europe, and Scandinavia cannot be included in other categories. Some of these are new immigrants, but most have been here for generations. Americans of European ancestry include over 200 million Americans and are the most assimilated and successful immigrants (Athens, 1997). Because the period of largest immigration from Europe was several generations ago, few of their descendants see themselves as "ethnic" (Reese, 1997). Symbolic ethnic activities include participation in events such as local Oktoberfest celebrations, food and decorating preferences, and adherence to mainstream American values (Alba, 1990).

The 1980 U.S. census estimated the following percentages of U.S.-born Whites among the national population: 22% of Irish ancestry, 26.7% English, 26.5% German, 7.3% French/French Canadian, 6.5% Italian, 5.3% Scottish, 4.3% Polish, and 3.4% Dutch; for a point of comparison, Native Americans make up 2.8% of the population (cited in Alba, 1990, p. 33). At least half of Euro-Americans eat special foods from their ethnic backgrounds, and a smaller number participate in ethnic festivals.

Some scholars foresee the development of a Euro-American identity. Richard Alba (1990) argued that this is due to the need for White Americans to find a place in the American mosaic and a growing self-consciousness about ethnic identity. He suggested that one form of ethnic identity (e.g., Irish or Italian or German American) is being displaced by another one, the European ancestry of the "original" immigrants. Non-European immigrants are beginning to share the privileges long held by White Americans of European ancestry. The mass media have influenced the decline of non-English languages in the home among European-origin Americans. They have frequently married outside their European ethnic background. Thus, the Euro-American identity creates solidarity in the face of newer immigrants fighting for resources.

In the Sladkus International study of non-Hispanic ethnic Whites, many differences across these groups were observed. In 1994, only 4 million Euro-Americans were actually "foreign born." When you add them to the second- and third-generation European Americans who maintain close ties with their heritage, "the market becomes significant" (Reese, 1997, p. 51).

Euro-Americans have been found to be more likely than others to take a cruise or rent a car. The same study suggests that they do not prefer organized tours and that they have high interest in casino gambling. Security is important to these consumers for many different products. Euro-Americans are also described as very brand loyal and most likely to use coupons. Word of mouth within the subculture community is important in reaching new immigrants: "To win one, you must win them all" (Reese, 1997, p. 54).

## Age Cohorts

Several age-groups share the central characteristics of subculture groups in America: unique demographic and geographic patterns, distinctive communication patterns and core values, and particular marketplace behaviors (Meredith & Schewe, 1994; Phillips, 1996). Younger generations of Americans tend to be more individualistic and less willing to conform than Mature Americans. The youngest groups have a different sense of time from Boomers and Senior Citizens; they are more accustomed to multitasking than older persons. They are more accepting of diversity and differences, both because they have more experience as members of a diverse cohort and because they assume less power distance and more equality with other Americans. Baby Boomers come closest to having values that mirror the contemporary mainstream—but then they turned mainstream society on its head when they were younger.

Age-groups also differ in their preferred styles of communication. Younger groups prefer visual to verbal communication, postmodern designs, and MTV-style narratives without direct story lines. Most significant is that younger Americans use high-context communication with minimal verbal content.

Many other sources have detailed the behavioral preferences and demographic characteristics of Baby Boomers, Generation X, Generation Y, teens, and children as consumers (Beck, 1998; Cropper & Speaker, 1999; Davis & Bukoff, 1999; Meredith & Schewe, 1994; Mitchell, 1996; Moschis, 1996; Phillips, 1996; Ritchie, 1995; Smith & Clurman, 1997). The following sections briefly review these characteristics of each age cohort, but the emphasis is on their values and issues that affect consumer identity. Child consumers are not discussed; their consumer needs are less driven by cultural values and social identities than the needs of older consumers.


## Baby Boomers

Being the largest age-group in American history, Baby Boomers have rewritten American lifestyles in every stage of their lives. Over 78 million people were born between 1946 and 1964. Some demographers distinguish two Boomer groups, those born between 1946 and 1954 and those born between 1955 and 1964.

Having basked in the spotlight of American popular culture for all their lives, Baby Boomers seem self-absorbed to other Americans. Their childhoods were spent in economic prosperity, and they received unprecedented access to educational opportunities. Experience has always had higher value to them than possessions; it also cultivates their taste for nostalgia (Goldman, 1994). They were the first group to see work as an experience in personal development. The Baby Boomer definition of the "American dream" is "being true to yourself" and "staying healthy" (Edmondson, 1997b). Of all age-groups, middle-aged Boomers spend the most for books, cosmetics, new cars/trucks, entertainment, restaurant meals, women's clothes, and nonbusiness computers (Braus, 1995; Russell, 1995).

Baby Boomers don't want to act or look old. Having personified "youth culture" and then having made it a mainstream ideal, Boomers now find themselves consuming almost anything that promises to slow or reverse the aging process (Braus, 1995). Today, for the first time in their lives, Baby Boomers see media images full of people other than themselves (Heath, 1996). Marketers are trying to redefine American ideals of beauty to include the aging Boomers (Darling, 1994). A major conflict is between Boomer desires to look good and to be comfortable. Rockport had to reposition comfort as "sensible" rather than "necessary" for older consumers before Boomers could see themselves in its clothes and shoes (Cox & McAuliffe, 1998). Reality has set in as middle-aged Baby Boomers face serious illnesses and the death or caretaking of their own parents.

Baby Boomers invented the "generation gap" with their parents, members of the Mature Market. The value differences still exist, though Boomers have become more conservative on issues such as crime and such as government being the solution to social ills. Boomers still support women's issues and civil rights for African Americans and U.S. Latinos. They continue to question authority, though now it's the leaders they question rather than institutions themselves (Mitchell, 1996). And their egos still tell them they are savvier than younger consumers (Ware, 1999). An interesting question will be whether "mainstream" values diverge from those of the Baby Boomers as Boomers age—as occurred for their parents, members of the Mature Market.

## Generation X

Generation X (people born between 1965 and 1976) is of particular interest to marketers because these consumers are now forming households and families (Mogelonsky, 1996b). They are a smaller age cohort (44 million persons) than the Baby Boomers or Generation Y, but on the whole they are better educated. More Gen X'ers live in more dual-income households than older age cohorts. They are also more racially and ethnically diverse than any Americans who came before them (Zill & Robinson, 1995). Their concept of family includes nontraditional households like friends living together and single parents (Davis & Bukoff, 1999).

The defining events in the lives of Generation X are frequently cited as their latchkey and divorced- or single-parent household experiences while growing up. As adults, they see hard work as a necessity but are not willing to sacrifice family life for uncertain rewards (Smith & Clurman, 1997). More than any other age group, they are insecure about the future: "Live for today, tomorrow is uncertain." This skepticism shows in their caution about making commitments (Holtz, 1995). Most interesting is that their heroes, if they have any, tend to be their parents (Ritchie, 1995). Their "American dream" is to be the boss; they are the most entrepreneurial age cohort.

The attitudes and habits of Generation X are likely to pose challenges to the organizations that attempt to reach them. Typical X'ers have negative attitudes toward advertising, yet high exposure to media. They are more likely to zip and zap commercials than other consumers. At the same time, they like to try new products; see high-tech products like computers, beepers, and fax machines as necessities; and appreciate and respond to customized marketing efforts. They spend over $125 billion on goods and services each year. And, like all other subcultures, they don't like to be portrayed as homogeneous. They hate the label *Gen X* that the rest of us use (Janoff, 1996).

Members of Generation X spend a lot of time with virtually all media and more with magazines and radio than either older or younger consumers. They do not use media in the same ways as older consumers. For example, they see television more as a source of entertainment than of product information; they use the Internet for product information. Having helped their working parents, many of these people are experienced consumers with strong preferences. Their high exposure to media has also made them cynical about marketers' promises. They were the pioneers in use of cable, video, and the Internet

## Generation Y Consumers, College Students, and Teenagers

These three groups are discussed together in 2000 because the terms refer to the same age cohort. In 10 years, however, Generation Y will retain its cohort values, but new college students and teenagers may have different ones. Generation Y, also known as the "Echo Boomers," includes persons born in 1977 to 1994; there are approximately 70 million people in this age cohort. This large age-group and its spending of over $168 billion a year are attracting a large number of companies using a broad array of integrated marketing communications and niche media (Cropper & Speaker, 1999; King, 1999). Their high levels of discretionary spending express preferences and habits that companies believe will drive their future consumer behavior (Cooper, 1990; Goff, 1999; McNeal, 1992; Merrill, 1999; Mitchell, 1997; Power, 1991). They influence their friends' and parents' purchases and in turn are influenced by trendsetters within their cohort, journalists, and other cultural leaders on the basis of personality or achievements. Being part of the most multicultural generation in American history has made them more tolerant than older Americans (Stapinski, 1999b).

These consumers' comfort with technology and preference for interactive media present opportunities to customize communications, to close transactions via e-commerce Web sites, and to build ongoing relationships (Goff, 1999). Personal computers have been part of their lives since they can remember. Less concerned about privacy issues and more interested in promotional incentives than other consumers, they are major purchasers of computers, travel, books, video games, music, and electronics over the Internet (Goff, 1999).

Generation Y lives in media-saturated worlds, from cafeterias and classrooms at school to the long hours they put in on the Internet. Peak television viewing occurs among 10- to 13-year-olds. These groups spend large amounts of time with radio and, as they get older, magazines. They pay more attention to advertising in these media than other consumers. Direct marketers are using consumer clubs and e-businesses are developing Internet communities to get the Echo Boomers' attention, deliver incentives, and reinforce loyalty.

Teenagers are important consumers today, spending over $90 billion per year (Goff, 1999). The teenage cohort (ages 13-19) is the largest it has been since the Baby Boomers were teens (Beck, 1998). By 2010, there will be over 30 million teenagers, about 12% of the total population. These teens are more diverse, affluent, and accustomed to nontraditional families than their elders are. Education is important to them, as it offers the promise of a more secure future. Extreme sports and risk taking are activities that appeal to their need for adventure and "testing the limits."

Teenagers use consumption and media to communicate with others and to try on identities (Begley, 2000; Clemetson, 2000; Ritson & Elliott, 1999). One aspect of teenage life stays the same from one generation to the next: the importance of identity issues. Finding and testing a sense of self remain the most important influences on teen habits and preferences. Four areas of conflict that summarize the teenage search for self are autonomy versus belonging, rebellion versus conformity, idealism versus pragmatism, and narcissism versus intimacy (Solomon, 1996). Media images are input for conversations with others as well as the source for ideas about who and how to be (Ritson & Elliott, 1999).

Many companies find it difficult to reach teen consumers. Not only do they spend a lot of time at school and work, they spend the most time surfing the Internet of any age group. Their Web-surfing behavior has also influenced the way they consume other media. They zip and zap television and videos; they subscribe to magazines and like them but do not renew. There are a variety of teen magazines with which girls bond (*Teen, Seventeen, Jump, YM, CosmoGirl*), but boys prefer sport and game magazines that reflect their hobbies. To better understand teen media preferences and to spot upcoming trends, several companies are combining magazines with catalogs for immediate direct marketing feedback. They also hire "trendspotters" from different teen groups to bridge the generation gap (Merrill, 1999).

The college market represents a lifestyle segment of Generation Y consumers who spend more than $45 billion on discretionary purchases each year (Swenson, 1996, p. 68). Today's 15-million-plus college students are more concerned about being well off financially and having status, power, and authority than their elders (Swenson, 1996, pp. 67-82). They have seen jobs disappear in the old economy and e-businesses invent opportunities for new careers. Most students balance responsibilities as employee and student in this rapidly changing environment. They are job and career driven as a result of the economic upheavals they have experienced growing up. Their religious interests include more alternative outlets than those of their parents, but a large percentage of teens, college students, and Generation Y are active in community organizations (Begley, 2000; Clemetson, 2000; Leland, 2000).

From experience, college students have become sophisticated consumers, skeptical of marketers, fluent in popular culture arts, and heavy users of a variety of media (Zollo, 1999). They see no conflict in commercializing the campus, even approving corporate sponsors for particular classes or events (Tannenbaum, 2000). These sometimes-contradictory values drive the preferences and behaviors of many college students.

## The Disabled as a Subculture

Disabled Americans are another subculture group viewed as outside the American mainstream and popular culture (Braithwaite, 1994). The disabled population includes people who have either physiological disabilities (hearing, speech, sight, extremity, or other physical disabilities) or mental disabilities (autism, depression, schizophrenia, retardation, or other mental diseases) and for whom survival requires distinctive behaviors and lifestyles.

Different sources have different estimates of the number of disabled Americans. The figure of 49 million physically and mentally disabled people in the United States, about 20% of the total population, is most often cited (Smolowe, 1995). One source counted more than 30 million Americans aged 21 to 64 with a physical or mental disability in 1998 (Koss-Feder, 1999). Another source repeated the number of disabled persons as 49 million and then added that there are 24 million severely disabled (Carr-Ruffino, 1996, pp. 421-456). Six percent of the disabled are believed to be under age 15, 60% are aged 15 to 64, and 34% are over 65 years of age.

Some well-known characters with disabilities have not helped create a positive presence for the disabled in media. One example is Mr. Magoo, whose recent movie was boycotted by the National Federation of the Blind (Bannon, 1997). Some critics have described the disabled as "media's monster" due to their frequent presence in horror films. Seven stereotypes have defined disabled images in the media: pitiable; "supercrip"; sinister, evil, and criminal; better off dead; maladjusted—his own worst enemy; a burden; and unable to live a successful life (Bogdan et al., 1982).

Key concerns in understanding disabled consumers are the time of onset and the severity of the disability. The particular functions that are impaired, as well as the severity, duration, and status of the disability, affect a disabled person's ability to adapt, to find psychological support, and to express emotions. Christopher Reeve ("Superman") experienced a spinal cord injury as an adult; his experience of disability and hopes for a cure differ significantly from those of persons born paraplegic. Several sources estimate that 20 million Americans have some form of hearing trouble (Sandor, 1994a). Only 2 million Americans lost their hearing before they learned to speak and understand speech—the definition of deafness.

Today, the disabled are expressing growing political pressure and are demanding more visibility in American popular life. They are organizing their own interest groups and pressing for equal time to erase their invisibility and dispel stereotypes of dependence, need, and charity. Disabled athletes like Dennis Oehler are becoming paid endorsers (Dunkel, 1995). A significant event for the disabled in their attempts to join mainstream society has been the passage of the Americans With Disabilities Act (ADA) in 1990. Though it appeared to increase the costs of doing business for small businesses and governments, it has provided improved access for Americans with disabilities. The cost of making the workplace more accessible has been estimated at $223 per disabled person. Some of the hostility about the costs of implementing ADA rules was due to confusion over who is and is not disabled. In 1998, two thirds of disabled Americans remained unemployed, and many of the 7 million with severe impairments were still not in the workplace (Smolowe, 1995).

Other aspects of the lives of disabled Americans reflect their increased cultural pride and identity as a community with shared interests, if not shared values. Many disabled persons are chafing at the labels *handicapped* and even *disabled*. These terms do not describe how people see themselves. In Internet discussion groups, they prefer the label *persons with disabilities* to *disabled* (Carr-Ruffino, 1996, pp. 421-456). Some terms used by other Americans to refer to disabled persons have included *physically challenged, retard, moron, insane, crazy, deaf and dumb, crippled,* and *lame*. None of these is acceptable to groups representing disabled persons today. Some activists among the deaf even favor teaching sign language over English as a way to recognize the uniqueness of deaf culture (Dolnick, 1993).

Marketers are discovering the loyalty and purchasing power of disabled consumers (Reedy, 1995). In 1992, the U.S. Census Bureau (cited in Mergenhagen, 1997) reported that Americans with disabilities were in control of $175 billion in discretionary income. Persons who were unemployed and disabled received over $109 billion in public and private assistance. Barbie introduced Becky, "with her own pink and purple wheelchair," in 1997 (Lewin, 1995). Fodor publishes a guide for vacations in the United States for travelers with disabilities (Murphy, 1997). There is a new magazine targeting the disabled who have only physical impairments. J. C. Penney has a line of Velcro-fitted clothing (Grover, 1995). There is also an opportunity to reach both the elderly and disabled where there is a crossover need for rehabilitation, a $2 billion market (Rosenbaum, 1991). Recent ads by Budweiser, Nissan, Levis', Target, Kmart, Eddie Bauer, Microsoft, Visa, McDonald's, and Citibank have included disabled models (Moog, 1990; Nelson, 1994). A new watchdog for images of the disabled is the *Disability Rag. On a Roll* is a talk radio show aimed at disabled Americans, and *Enable* magazine offers features such as guides to accessible summer camps and stories about wheelchair athletes (Burnett & Paul, 1996).

Marketing to the disabled consumer is in its infancy. Little is known about the demographic profile of the disabled, other than estimates of the number of persons with disabilities and of their incomes at over $700 billion. Though marketing programs targeting the disabled may be nothing more than a public relations effort for some firms, increasing the visibility of disabled consumers may bring their loyalty to future marketing efforts. As the age of users has decreased, some companies have been redesigning the wheelchair to make it more "hip" (Henderson, 1995b). Catalogs and online shopping offer convenience and wider selections of specialty merchandise. Surprisingly, many products originally designed for disabled consumers are being sought by others—good design appeals to everyone (Fost, 1998).

Even though disabled consumers have been invisible in both society and the media, pioneers in marketing to them are reaping the rewards of their loyalty. An example of their increasing visibility in media is the advertisement for Microsoft shown in Figure 9.1. An early pioneer in marketing to the disabled was Holly the Phone-In Supermarket in Toronto, a delivery service for disabled customers. The company estimated about 7% of Toronto's population was disabled and that they spent more than $300 million a year on groceries (Sutter, 1991). It is worthwhile to remember that one in three Americans will have a disability at some point in his or her adult life (Williams, 2000). The new buzzword among pioneers in marketing to the disabled is *handicapitalism* (Harris-Prager, 1999)!

The mentally disabled tend to be older than average Americans and more likely to live in the South. Only 18% of the mentally retarded and 23% of mentally ill disabled Americans are working (Mergenhagen, 1997). The mentally disabled constitute a particularly vulnerable group among persons with disabilities. They were recently the targets of a credit card company's offers of credit,

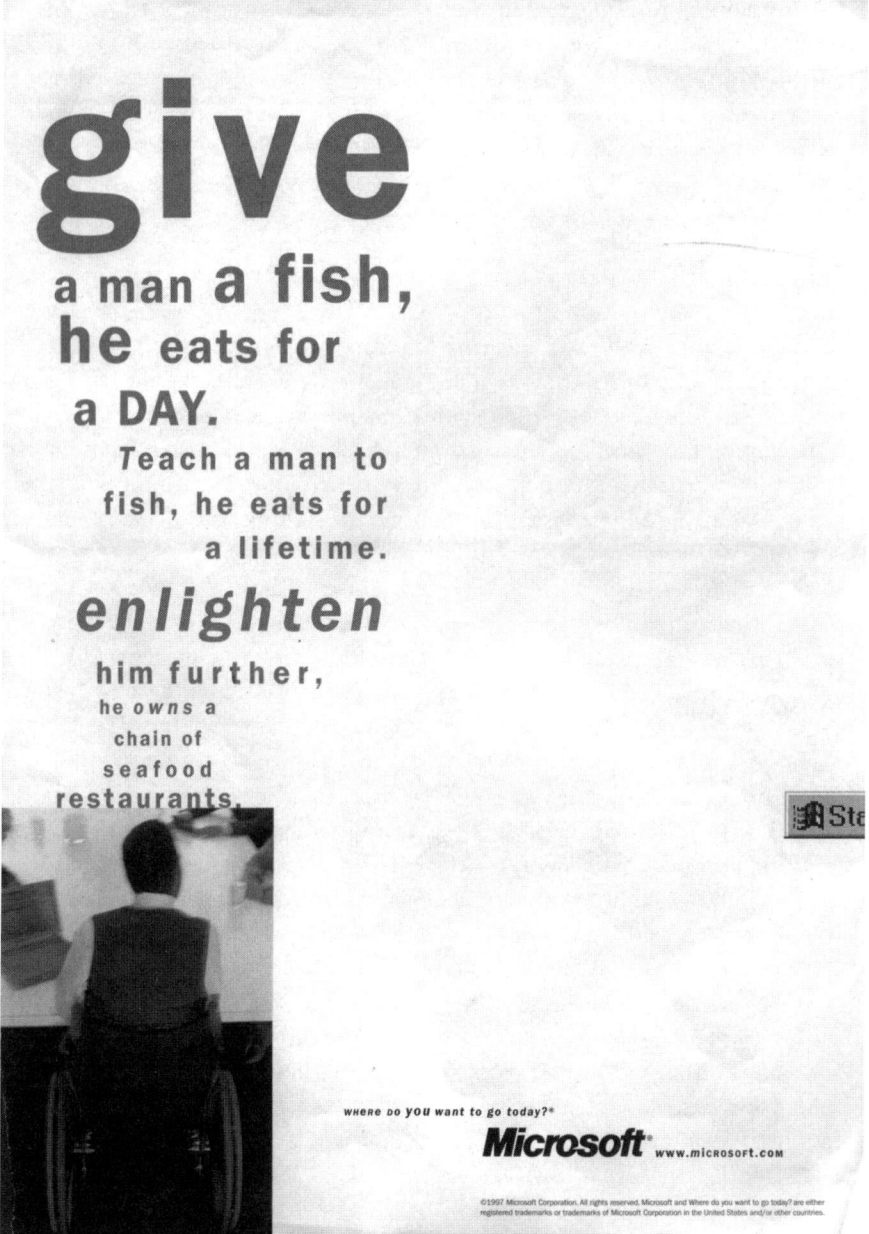

**Figure 9.1.** Microsoft Advertisement Using Disabled Actor

with disastrous results for their independence. The firm targeted the 887,000
mentally disabled adults who lived on their own. Retarded consumers began
quickly accumulating debts without the ability to pay them back. Niche marketing without a company's commitment to shared values of its target quickly attracted critics from many corners (Cahill, 1998).

## Regional Subcultures

Many factors threaten to erase the differences that have long been the source
of regional pride for Americans in particular geographic areas. An explosion in
media, the global economy, and sophisticated communication and transportation technologies have eroded isolation and distance, the roots of regional subcultures in the United States. The plugged-in, media-saturated American no longer faces climate and geography as barriers to learning and adopting a uniform
American identity.

Nevertheless, regional identities continue to flourish among residents of
many American cities, states, and regions. Undoubtedly, one of the reasons regional identities persevere is the appeal of regional mythologies that individuals
can add to other sources in building social identity. Local heroes, historical
events, prominent industries, and even media images present tangible icons that
encompass a region's values. In the past, these unique characteristics led to different lifestyles, economic opportunities, and demographics.

Today, residents can express membership in a regional subculture by their
consumption patterns and lifestyles. The values embedded in regional myths
and institutions are like the value systems of different cultures. The pace of life
in southern states reflects a different view of time from that prevailing in New
York or New England (Reed, 1993). Californians are more egalitarian with
regard to male and female roles than Midwesterners. Power distance is greater in
the South than in the Midwest and in New York more than in Chicago. Texans
and people from the Pacific Northwest vary in how they see humans and nature. New Englanders have adopted a lower-context style of communication than Southerners. American individuality is at its most visible in California lifestyles, whereas New Englanders and Southerners are collectivistic by
comparison.

Marketers have taken two approaches to regional subcultures. One strategy
assumes that regional pride is decreasing but that differences in market preferences still vary across locations. Collecting data about what residents think, do,

and believe identifies the patterns in different regions (Mitchell, 1995; Piirto, 1991b). The ability to collect massive amounts of data on consumers' needs and wants, lifestyles, hobbies, opinions, beliefs, purchases, and so on and to crunch them into distinctive groups has been enhanced by the ever-increasing computing power of market analysts. Claritas, CACI, Simmons, and Experian compete on their abilities to derive distinct geographic and lifestyle segments among American consumers. For example, Claritas announced in 1999 that the 40 clusters that they identified in the 1970s have splintered into 62 distinctive "lifestyle types" (cited in Weiss, 1999). The authors called these groups America's "modern tribes" but stated that they no longer cluster around "neighborhood type" or the regional loyalties that, according to them, are decreasing. The segments are distinctive along dimensions such as what product categories they buy, how they spend leisure time, and what brands they like.

The second approach uses regional mythologies and their values to connect with consumers who live in a particular place (Gentry, Tansuhaj, Manzer, & John, 1988; Kahle, 1986). The lingering influence of regional values can be a marker of consumer identities and loyalties there. Residents of different American locations have evolved unique views of themselves over time and history. Newcomers to these areas buy into the regional myths also, creating a new source of identity for themselves. A look into two well-known subcultures provides insight into how regional culture, its values and myths, affects consumer needs and identities.

Texas has long been known by its distinctive mythology, climate, icons, and heroes: cowboys, oil wealth, heroes at the Alamo, wide-open spaces, country-western music, the JFK assassination, high school football, big hair, cowboy boots and hats, southern hospitality, small towns, hot weather, a peculiar "twang" and slow way of talking, barbeques, cactus, braggadocio and one-upmanship, hunting and guns, cattle and ranches, pickup trucks and horses. In popular culture, these characteristics have appeared so frequently that this is what "foreigners" picture when imagining the "typical" Texan or lifestyles in Texas (O'Connor, 1986; Turner, 1996). These stereotypes do represent some pervasive Texas beliefs: "Bigger is better," "Traditions are important," "Texans are risk takers—do or die," "Be proud of where you came from," and "Don't judge people by how they dress or talk."

Although these images and characteristics of Texans obscure the true diversity of 20 million people and their lifestyles, they persist in the imaginations of all of us. Proudly, Texans think, "Texas is not so much a state as it is a state of mind." That state pride is what several companies tap into when they use "Texas values." Several years ago, Miller appealed to Texans' sense of hospitality and invited the whole state to a party. Coca-Cola invented a mythical place called Coca-Cola, Texas (Deveny, 1993; Schwartz, 1989; Stuart, 1992). Check out the print ad for Absolut vodka in Figure 9.2, which displays a "Texas" worldview about "bigger" being better!

New Yorkers also abound in regional pride, tradition, and well-known icons and customs. New York City has been the prototype of the American melting pot, so it is logical that the city serves as a magnet for all kinds of people seeking a fresh start in life. The crowding together of all these individualists and ethnic groups has also given them the reputation for being more open-minded and sophisticated than other Americans are. Because New York is an international center for trade and the arts, New Yorkers seem to know about and adopt new trends before the rest of us. New York has the reputation of being an environment that fosters anything and everything avant garde. Given that New Yorkers have a head start on the rest of us, it is easy for them to believe that the city is the birthplace of everything important in American cultural life.

People who have never visited New York learn about it from popular culture (Plotch, 1992; Salins, 1988). Terms for New York addresses symbolize "the best" in a variety of endeavors: Wall Street (finance), Madison Avenue (advertising), the Fashion District (designers), Fifth Avenue (retailing), Lincoln Center (the performing arts), the Upper East Side (design and decor), Fifty-Seventh Street (art), and Carnegie Hall (musicians). Media images often portray New Yorkers as living luxurious lives and enjoying the best and widest available choice of whatever is on sale in America. Visitors comment on how rude and unfriendly New Yorkers seem, even while they soak up the culture and arts, stare up at New York skyscrapers with awe, and enter subways with fear.

Hidden behind these stereotypes, images, and myths, New Yorkers have a number of core beliefs: self-sufficiency, self-reliance, and self-fulfillment; hard work and entrepreneurial drive; tolerance of differences; and preference for a fast pace of life and urban vitality. They have a love-hate relationship with the diversity in their environment: It is a daily irritant but a source of variety for food and entertainment. Marketing to New Yorkers means recognizing the pride they have in their city and its history. At the same time, New Yorkers see themselves as a group only when they are placed in comparison to the rest of Americans. They are staunch individualists with powerful ethnic identities. Regional pride does not translate into a "New York" consumer identity as it does for Texans.

**Figure 9.2.** Advertisement Illustrating a Texas Worldview: "Bigger Is Better"

## MARKETING OPPORTUNITIES IN MULTICULTURAL
## SETTINGS OUTSIDE THE UNITED STATES

The premise of *The Global Me*, by G. Pascal Zachary, is that "new cosmopolitans," Zachary's name for people fluent in more than one culture, are "driving a revolution in human identity" in many nations (2000a). Zachary asserted that "the more one looks at individuals, companies and nations embracing diversity, the clearer it becomes that mongrelization suits the times. Cultural mixing spurs creativity and innovation. Money follows the mongrel" (quoted in "How Hybridity Is," 2000, p. A22; see also Zachary, 2000a). The author's premise is that being fluent in more than one culture gives individuals "roots" enough to honor and keep their best traditions but "wings" enough to redefine themselves in times of rapid change. Whether or not persons with multiple identities transform their countries into multicultural societies or express those identities in marketplace preferences is the issue that concerns multicultural marketers.

The "hyphen" is what has made Americans and the American sense of self unique. Few other nations share such strong beliefs in recognizing and valuing ethnic identity as part of mainstream society. Although there are a growing number of countries with populations of mixed ethnicity, age, race, and sexual orientation, many continue to treat immigrants, their offspring, and other persons outside the mainstream as if they were not full members of society. It takes more than a diverse population to make a multicultural society, one where there is acceptance of multiple cultural value systems (Zachary, 2000b).

Countries with long histories of discrimination (e.g., South Africa) cannot evolve into societies with multiple value systems overnight. It will take generations, just as it has in the United States, to "merge" national identity with disparate ethnic identities. European countries such as Germany, France, or the United Kingdom continue to resist recognizing foreign ethnic groups (Turks, Algerians, and West Indians) as citizens with equal rights (Modood & Werbner, 1997). Countries with one or two significant ethnic minorities frequently divide themselves into separate cultural zones, such as the French- and English-speaking areas of Canada.

Other examples of multiethnic but not multicultural societies are the countries created in Africa and Asia along colonial but not ethnic or tribal lines. There are also places such as Ireland and Northern Ireland, Israel and Palestine, India and Pakistan, or Serbia and Croatia where hatreds are fostered by continuing instability and long histories of ethnic violence. In Latin American countries like Mexico, Peru, and Ecuador, people accept their dual Native-European heritage in theory, but that does not give both cultures equal access to social, political, and economic success. A preference for European values and heritage is evident in the choice of persons and institutions that control resources in these countries.

Over time, increased ethnic diversity will furnish a demographic foundation for forming multicultural societies in many of these countries. However, the American concept of self is another precondition for multicultural marketing. The idea that we can make and remake ourselves with the tools of how we spend time and money, independent of our ethnic origins, is behind the concept of consumer identity. How we spend time and money symbolizes who we are, who we want to be, and how we want to be seen (Elliott & Wattanasuwan, 1998). Our values underlie our product, service, and communication choices and communicate who we are to others. Without the malleable self, the marketplace can meet consumer needs to perform particular functions or can express our individual styles, but it does not serve as a cultural medium expressing our values and social identities.

The global economy is transporting American-style consumption to other countries and cultures (Sorrell, 1999; Weiss, 2000). Because young people are the first to adopt new marketplace preferences, age differences are more likely than ethnic origins to delineate value differences that are expressed by media and marketplace choices in other countries. The "Yuppie" lifestyle exists in many countries today, and its practitioners share similar values, such as consumption's importance in expressing identity, aspirations for upward mobility, and adoption of new ideas, new media, new products, and new behaviors. Institutions such as the Internet are just speeding up the process whereby consumption patterns are becoming more alike across cultures (Matathia & Salzman, 1999; Walker, 1996). The nation-state has become less meaningful as multinational organizations have come to reign almost with impunity over economic life (Barber, 1995). Brands and organizations provide the lingua franca of values in this increasingly global marketplace (Weber & Stalk, 1999).

The number of countries with multicultural populations may be increasing, but many organizations are trying to design global strategies that minimize cultural differences (Alden, Steenkamp, & Batra, 1999; Banerjee, 1994; Griffin, McArthur, Yamaki, & Hidalgo, 1998; Jeannet, 2000; Wehling, 1998). In several recent cases, companies have failed to realize how easily consumers in one country learn about the firm's marketing communications in other markets. Budweiser offended Native Americans by its portrayal of them drinking in beer commercials in the United Kingdom (Parker-Pope, 1996). Ford faced negative publicity in several countries when word got out that it had "whited out" the faces of Black workers from the United Kingdom in a company brochure for Polish workers. Ford claimed that it had done so because of the different racial population of its workers in Poland. Another faux pas was Colgate's use of Black men in an ad in Australia that joked that the brand gives "the white man the protection the black man has naturally" (Parker-Pope, 1996). Using the icons of one subculture group when marketing to others can be a dangerous tactic in a multicultural but global society. Global enterprises must recognize the roles they play as cultural media in consumer lives. By implication, if their core values are at odds with values in a foreign market, consumers will feel exploited by their targeted marketing focus.

The above examples illustrate a continuing need to be sensitive to different standards of ethics and taste. A good idea is to "assume you have a multiethnic client base these days. We're in a global marketplace. Ads like those are totally naive and offensive" (Parker-Pope, 1996, p. B5). Commercial enterprises have been increasingly accepted as cultural institutions for teaching values in America (Bulkeley, 1997). As this role is replicated in other countries, more scrutiny of marketers' values is inevitable (Dreyfuss, 1999; Sherry, 1993). On a more positive note, the skills required of multicultural marketers—a role as cultural and economic institution in consumers' lives—are the same skills required for long-term success in global markets (Jeannet, 2000; Wilkinson & Cheng, 1999).

## SUMMARY

The American environment provides a continual cast of outsider and insider groups as mainstream values evolve over time and new groups are accepted into membership. At different stages in the movement from outsider to mainstream participant, individuals and the subculture groups to which they belong have different self-perceptions and relationships to members of the mainstream. Consumer identities are particularly in flux throughout this process, making it difficult for marketers to predict consumer preferences on the basis of consumer ethnicity. For these reasons, symbolic group associations and values reflect consumer identity more faithfully than ethnic origin or other consumer characteristics.

The first section of this chapter described the process whereby subcultures become part of mainstream American society over time. The different perspectives of insider and outsider groups, as well as those of individuals, point to changes in the nature of consumer identity among subculture members at different points in time. By understanding these changes in identity and symbolic needs, marketers can adjust their own strategies for building relationships with subculture communities over time.

The next section of the chapter briefly reviewed the opportunities for marketing to subcultures that have not been discussed earlier in the book. Several ethnic groups have received little attention as targets for mainstream organizations to date. Native Americans remain on the periphery of American culture and popular imagery. Their collectivism and oneness with nature place their values at odds with the mainstream. Nevertheless, many Native Americans respond positively to organizations that reach them in specialized media and contemporary rituals. A large number of Americans of Irish, Jewish, and Italian origin celebrate their "symbolic" ethnic identity by foods they consume and the rituals they preserve. The values of most European-origin Americans are similar to those of the mainstream. Arab Americans retain their ethnic identity and close family relationships but also express more "symbolic" than value-based identities.

In addition to ethnic groups, some other groups of Americans exhibit the characteristics of subcultures. Disabled consumers often have distinct product or market needs and are reached by niche media and different styles of communication. They value brands and organizations that support the issues important to their community. Also, residents of some regions in the United States have characteristics of subcultures. Examples were given of values, self-perceptions, and views of the rest of the world that Texans and New Yorkers have. Texans have evolved a "Texas" consumer identity, whereas New Yorkers have not.

The last section of the chapter explored the possibility of consumer subcultures in other countries. Although the number of multiethnic countries is increasing in many parts of the world, many of these localities do not accept multiple value systems as part of their mainstream attitudes. Another difference is whether the malleable "American self" has been exported along with American brands and styles of consumption. Inevitably, however, marketers will find consumers in these foreign environments with values that are compatible with their own.

## Notes

1. The Mature Market is excluded from the model. Many of its members began life in the mainstream, only to discover their values were no longer synonymous with those of

the mainstream as its values changed over time. Being old in a youth-oriented society makes one as marginal as being overweight in a society obsessed with being thin.

2. For marketing information about particular age cohorts, see Beck, (1998), Cropper and Speaker (1999), Davis and Bukoff (1999), Meredith and Schewe (1994), Mitchell (1996), Moschis (1996), Phillips (1996), Ritchie (1995), and Smith and Clurman (1997).

# References

Below, the bolded acronyms in parentheses following particular references denote that the reference concerns one of the specialized markets discussed in Chapters 4 through 8 of this book: Mature Americans **(MA),** U.S. Latinos **(USL),** African Americans **(AfA),** Gay Americans **(GA),** or Asian Americans **(AsA).**

Aaker, J. (1997). Dimensions of brand personality. *Journal of Marketing Research, 34,* 347-357.

Access Worldwide Communications, Inc. (1999, Spring). *Culture Markets Report, 1.* **(USL)**

Adler, J., & Padgett, T. (1995, October 23). Selena country. *Newsweek,* pp. 76, 78-84. **(USL)**

After demographic shift, Atlanta mall restyles itself as a black shopping center. (1992, February 26). *Wall Street Journal,* p. B1. **(AfA)**

Agins, T. (1985, March 15). To Hispanics in U.S., a bodega, or grocery, is a vital part of life. *Wall Street Journal,* pp. A-1, A-17. **(USL)**

Agins, T. (1996, December 3). "Real" women get a new magazine sized for them. *Wall Street Journal,* p. B8.

Ajzen, I., & Fishbein, M. (1980). *Understanding attitudes and predicting social behavior.* Englewood Cliffs, NJ: Prentice Hall.

Alba, R. D. (1985). *Italian Americans: Into the twilight of ethnicity.* Englewood Cliffs, NJ: Prentice Hall.

Alba, R. D. (1990). *Ethnic identity: The transformation of white America.* New Haven, CT: Yale University Press. **(AfA)**

Albaum, G., Strandskov, J., & Duerr, E. (1994). *International marketing and export management* (2nd ed.). Reading, MA: Addison-Wesley.

Albonetti, J. G., & Dominguez, L. V. (1989, February-March). Major influences on consumer-goods' marketers' decision to target U.S. Hispanics. *Journal of Advertising Research, 29,* 9-21. **(USL)**

Alden, D. L., Steenkamp, J.-B. E. M., & Batra, R. (1999, January). Brand positioning through advertising in Asia, North America, and Europe: The role of global consumer culture. *Journal of Marketing, 63,* 75-87.

Alexander, K. (1998, December 30). Hip-hop magazine gets fiery start, good and bad. *USA Today,* p. B1. **(AfA)**

Alexander, K. L. (2000, February 10). Placing BET on the Net site part of CEO's plan to expand. *Money,* p. 3B. **(AfA)**

Alsop, R. (1999a, December 30). Are gay people more affluent than others? *Wall Street Journal,* pp. B1-B3. **(GA)**

Alsop, R. (1999b, June 29). But brewers employ in-your-mug approach. *Wall Street Journal,* p. B1. **(GA)**

Alsop, R. (1999c, June 29). Cracking the gay market code: How marketers plant subtle symbols in ads. *Wall Street Journal,* pp. B1-B4. **(GA)**

Alsop, R. (1999d, October 10). In marketing to gays, lesbians are often left out. *Wall Street Journal,* pp. B1, B4. **(GA)**

Alsop, R. (1999e, September 28). London, Paris are burning to lure gay travelers in new campaigns. *Wall Street Journal,* p. B10. **(GA)**

Althen, G. (1988). *American ways: A guide for foreigners in the United States.* Yarmouth, ME: Intercultural Press.

Altman, D. (1987). *The homosexualization of America: The Americanization of the homosexual.* New York: St. Martin's. **(GA)**

Alwitt, L. F., & Donley, T. D. (1996). *The poor consumer: Adjusting the balance of exchange.* Thousand Oaks, CA: Sage. **(AfA)**

Alwitt, L., Qualls, W. J., & Williams, J. D. (1996, May). *The susceptibility of vulnerable populations to persuasive marketing communications.* Paper presented at the annual Marketing and Public Policy Conference, Washington, DC. **(AfA)**

American Account Planning Group. (1997). Frequently asked questions. www.digipress.net/apg/faq.html#1

The American character. (1999, March 5). *Wall Street Journal,* p. A14.

American survey. (1996, March 2). *Economist,* p. 28.

Ansberry, C. (2000, January 1). Older and wiser. *Wall Street Journal,* p. R57. **(MA)**

Applegate, J. (1991, April 29). Tips for tapping the Asian-American market. *San Francisco Chronicle,* p. B5. **(AsA)**

Arce, C. (1994, April). *InfoSource's Hispanic assimilation segmentation.* Paper presented at the New Americas Advertising Forum, University of Texas at Austin. **(USL)**

Asfahani, M. (1996, December 2). Time to look and listen. *Newsweek,* p. 18.

AsianAvenue.com. (1999, November 29). *PR News, 55,* 1. **(AsA)**

Astroff, R. J. (1988-1989). Spanish gold: Stereotypes, ideology, and the construction of a U.S. Latino market. *Howard Journal of Communications, 1*(4), 155-173. **(USL)**

Asuad, B. C. (Ed.). (1974). *Arabic speaking communities in American cities.* New York: Center for Migration Studies.

Athens, L. (1997). A model for successful adaptation: The case of Greek immigrants in the South. *Migration World Magazine, 25*(1-2), 14-17.

Auerbach, J. G. (1997, September 11). Charity case: Jewish loan societies rethink the tradition of helping all comers. *Wall Street Journal,* pp. A1, A6.

Auerbach, J. G. (1999, January 22). The name's the same but the stress is on the other syllable. *Wall Street Journal,* pp. A1, A6.

Ayres, I., & Siegelman, P. (1995). Race and gender discrimination in bargaining. *American Economic Review, 85,* 304-321. **(AfA)**

Baker, S., & Judge, P. (1996, October 17). Where IBM goes, others may follow. *Business Week,* p. 39. **(GA)**

Banerjee, A. (1994, April 18). Global campaigns don't work; multinationals do. *Advertising Age,* p. 23.

Bank, D. (1999, September 28). On the Web, gay sites start to click. *Wall Street Journal,* pp. B1-B6. **(GA)**

Banks offer credit cards that target ethnic groups. (1989). *Capital District Business Review, 15*(48), 20.

Bannon, L. (1997, July 31). The vision thing: Mr. Magoo watches U.S. cultural history and struggles to adapt. *Wall Street Journal,* pp. A1, A8.

Barber, B. R. (1995). *Jihad vs. McWorld.* New York: Times Books.

Barbero, J.-M. (1993, Spring). Latin America: Cultures in the communication media. *Journal of Communication, 43,* pp. 18-30. **(USL)**

Batra, R., Myers, J. G., & Aaker, D. A. (1996). *Advertising management* (5th ed.). Englewood Cliffs, NJ: Prentice Hall.

Battistella, G. (1989). *Italian Americans in the 80's.* New York: Center for Migration Studies.

Bauer, R. A., & Cunningham, S. M. (1970, April). The Negro market. *Journal of Advertising Research, 10,* 3-13. **(AfA)**

Bauer, R. A., Cunningham, S. M., & Wortzel, L. H. (1965, July). The marketing dilemma of Negroes. *Journal of Marketing,* pp. 1-6. **(AfA)**

Beam, C. (1995). Asian-American titles take off. *Folio: The Magazine for Magazine Management, 24*(10), 27. **(AsA)**

Bean, R., & Crane, R. D. (1996). Marriage and family therapy research with ethnic minorities: Current status. *American Journal of Family Therapy, 24*(1), 3-8. **(AsA)**

Beard, F. K. (1994). Conflict in the integrated marketing communications task group. In E. Thorson (Ed.), *Proceedings of the 1994 American Academy of Advertising Conference* (pp. 21-31). Columbia: University of Missouri-Columbia.

Beatty, S. G. (1997, April 25). VW is not steering clear of "Ellen" episode. *Wall Street Journal*, pp. B1, B4. **(GA)**

Beatty, S. G. (1998, March 13). Volkswagen says notice Beetle—sort of. *Wall Street Journal*, p. B6.

Beck, M. (1990, April 23). Going for the gold. *Newsweek*, p. 74. **(MA)**

Beck, M. (1998, February 3). The next big population bulge: Generation Y shows its might. *Wall Street Journal*, p. B1.

Beck, M., Glick, D., Gordon, J., & Picker, L. (1991, November 11). School days for seniors. *Newsweek*, pp. 60, 62, 65. **(MA)**

Begley, S. (1995a, November 13). Nature plus nurture. *Newsweek*, p. 72. **(GA)**

Begley, S. (1995b, February 13). Three is not enough. *Newsweek*, pp. 67-68. **(AfA)**

Begley, S. (2000, May 8). A world of their own. *Newsweek*, pp. 53-56.

Belk, R. W. (1988, September). Possessions and the extended self. *Journal of Consumer Research, 15,* 139-168.

Bennett, M. J., & Stewart, E. C. (1991). *American cultural patterns.* Yarmouth, MA: Intercultural Press.

Bennett, P. D. (1988). *Marketing.* New York: McGraw-Hill.

Bennett, P. D., & Kassarjian, H. H. (1972). *Consumer behavior.* Englewood Cliffs, NJ: Prentice Hall. **(AfA)**

Berfield, S. (1999, November 22). Hong Kong plans a numbers game. *Business Week,* p. 6. **(AsA)**

Berger, W. (1992, April). Play fair in housing. *Real Estate Today,* pp. 15-19. **(AfA)**

Berkowitz, H. (1997). Cornering a market. In S. Biagi & M. Kern-Foxworth (Eds.), *Facing difference: Race, gender, and the mass media* (pp. 218-220). Thousand Oaks, CA: Pine Forge.

Berman, G. L. (1994). The future of Hispanic marketing. *Directo: Direct Marketing Association Council for Hispanic Marketing Newsletter.* **(USL)**

Berry, J. (1980). Acculturation as varieties of adaptation. In A. Padilla (Ed.), *Acculturation: Theory, models and some new findings* (pp. 9-25). Boulder, CO: Westview. **(AsA)**

Berry, J. W., & Annis, R. (1986). Multiculturalism and psychology in plural societies. In L. H. Ekstrand (Ed.), *Ethnic minorities and immigrants in a cross-cultural perspective* (pp. 35-51). Berwyn, Sweden: Swets North American. **(USL)**

Berry, V. T. (1996). Introduction: Racialism and the media. In V. T. Berry & C. L. Manning-Miller (Eds.), *Mediated messages and African-American culture.* Thousand Oaks, CA: Sage. **(AfA)**

Bessen, J. (1994, September-October). Riding the marketing information wave. *Harvard Business Review,* pp. 150-160.

Best, R. J. (1997). *Market-based management: Strategies for growing customer value and profitability.* Englewood Cliffs, NJ: Prentice Hall.

Black athletes dominate top performer "Q" slots. (1988, October 31). *Jet,* p. 48. **(AfA)**

Black spending. (1999, February 23). *USA Today,* p. B1. **(AfA)**

Blacks again dominate top marketing Q-ratings. (1989, May 22). *Jet,* p. 50. **(AfA)**

Blodau, M. (1999, December). Attractive airwaves. *Hispanic Business,* pp. 68, 72. **(USL)**

Blumenfeld, W. J. (1988). *Looking at gay and lesbian life.* New York: Philosophical Library. **(GA)**

Bogdan, R., et al. (1982, Fall). The disabled: Media's monster. *Social Policy, 13.*

Bosma, H. A., Graafsma, T. L. G., Grotevant, H. D., & de Levita, D. J. (Eds.). (1994). *Identity and development: An interdisciplinary approach.* Thousand Oaks, CA: Sage.

Bowen, L., & Schmid, J. (1997). Minority presence and portrayal in mainstream magazine advertising: An update. *Journalism and Mass Communication Quarterly, 74*(1), 134-146. **(AsA)**

Bower, J. L., & Christensen, C. M. (1995, January-February). Disruptive technologies: Catching the wave. *Harvard Business Review,* pp. 43-53.

Bowes, J. E. (1996). Out of the closet and into the marketplace: Meeting basic needs in the gay community. In D. L. Wardlow (Ed.), *Gays, lesbians, and consumer behavior: Theory, practice, and research issues in marketing.* New York: Harrington Park. **(GA)**

Boyce, J. N. (1997, October 7). Nonwhites wake to "American dream." *Wall Street Journal,* pp. A2, A14.

Boyd, M. (1994). Incentive marketing: Asian dawn. *Incentive Magazine.* **(AsA)**

Boykin, W. A. (1983). The academic performance of Afro-American children. In J. T. Spence (Ed.), *Achievement and achievement motives: Psychological and sociological approaches* (pp. 321-371). San Francisco: W. H. Freeman. **(AfA)**

Braithwaite, D. O. (1994). Viewing persons with disabilities as a culture. In L. A. Samovar & R. E. Porter (Eds.), *Intercultural communication: A reader* (7th ed., pp. 148-154). Belmont, CA: Wadsworth.

Branch, S. (1996, September 9). Profits at the altar. *Fortune,* pp. 120-126. **(AfA)**

Brandes, W. (1995, February 15). Black-oriented radio zeroes in on narrowly defined audiences. *Wall Street Journal,* p. B-8. **(AfA)**

Braus, P. (1993, June). What does "Hispanic" mean? *American Demographics, 15,* 46-49. **(USL)**

Braus, P. (1995, February). Boomers against gravity. *American Demographics, 17,* 50-57.

Brazil, J. (1998, December). You talkin' to me? *American Demographics, 20,* 54-59. **(MA)**

British Account Planning Group. (1997). Introducing ourselves and frequently asked questions. www.easynet.co.uk/apg/intro.html

Brody, E. W. (1990). *Communication tomorrow: New audiences, new technologies, new media.* Westport, CN: Praeger.

Bromley, E. (1992). How to teach the language of the largest target market without speaking Spanish. In L. L. Reid (Ed.), *Proceedings of the 1992 Conference of the American Academy of Advertising* (pp. 68-71). Athens: University of Georgia Press. **(USL)**

Brown, A. (1990, June). Coors cools Hispania. *Marketing and Media Decisions,* p. 30. **(USL)**

Brown, C. (1997). Changing the face of the magazine industry. In S. Biagi & S. Kern-Foxworth (Eds.), *Facing differences: Race, gender, and mass media* (pp. 154-160). Thousand Oaks, CA: Pine Forge. **(AfA)**

Brown, H. D. (1994). *Principles of language learning and teaching.* Englewood Cliffs, NJ: Prentice Hall. **(AsA)**

Brownlee, L. L. (1996, June 24). Marketing and media: Motorola gets signal on blacks' pager use. *Wall Street Journal,* p. B6. **(AfA)**

Bulkeley, W. M. (1997, September 15). Channel One taps principals as promoters. *Wall Street Journal,* pp. B-1, B-6.

Bullock, H. A. (1961a, May/June). Consumer motivations in black and white: I. *Harvard Business Review, 39,* 89-104. **(AfA)**

Bullock, H. A. (1961b, July/August). Consumer motivations in black and white: II. *Harvard Business Review, 39,* 110-124. **(AfA)**

Burnett, J. J. (1991, October/November). Examining the media habits of the affluent elderly. *Journal of Advertising Research, 31,* 33-41. **(MA)**

Burnett, J. J., & Paul, P. (1996, Fall). Assessing the media habits and needs of the mobility-disabled consumer. *Journal of Advertising, 25,* 47-59.

Burnett, J. J., & Wilkes, R. E. (1986). An appraisal of the senior citizen market. *Journal of Retail Banking, 7*(4), 57-64. **(MA)**

Burton, J. (1993, January 21). Targeting Asians: Agencies in U.S. tailor messages to new immigrants. *Far Eastern Economic Review,* pp. 40-55. **(AsA)**

Bush, V. J. (1993, May 21). Homeboys Inc. chips in to help inner-city teenagers. *Wall Street Journal,* p. B2. **(AfA)**

Byler, M. G. (1973). *American Indian authors for young readers: A selected bibliography.* New York: Association on American Indian Affairs.

Cab company wary of blacks faces sanction. (1995, February 2). *New York Times,* p. A16. **(AfA)**

Caggiano, C. (1997). Brand new. *Inc., 19*(5), 48-53.

Cahill, J. B. (1998, November 10). Charged up: Credit cards invade a new market niche: The mentally disabled. *Wall Street Journal,* pp. A-1, A-6.

Campanelli, M. (1991, May). The African American market. *Sales and Marketing Management,* p. 75. **(AfA)**

Campbell, A. (1971). *White attitudes toward black people.* Ann Arbor: University of Michigan, Institute for Social Research. **(AfA)**

Carino, B. V. (1996). Filipino Americans: Many and varied. In S. Pedraza & R. G. Rumbaut (Eds.), *Origins and destinies: Immigration, race and ethnicity in America* (pp. 293-301). Belmont, CA: Wadsworth. **(AsA)**

Carlson, R., & Goldman, B. (1994). *FastForward.* New York: HarperBusiness.

Carmichael, S., & Hamilton, C. V. (1967). *Black power: The politics of liberation in America.* New York: Vintage. **(AfA)**

Carr-Ruffino, N. (1996). *Managing diversity: People skills for a multicultural workplace.* Cincinnati, OH: South-Western. **(GA, MA, USL, AfA, AsA)**

Caso, A. (1984). *Mass media vs. the Italian Americans.* Brookline Village, MA: Branden.

Castaneda, L. (1997, April 7). African American financial index available on Web. *San Francisco Chronicle,* p. B1. **(AfA)**

Castaneda, R., & Spinner, J. (1997, October 10). Teens awarded $1 million in Bauer case. *Washington Post,* p. A1. **(AfA)**

Chambers, V., Figueroa, A., Weingert, P., & Weingarden, J. (1999, July 12). Hispanics are hot and making history. *Newsweek,* pp. 53-58. **(USL)**

Chappell, K. (1995, November). How the new generation changed black and white America. *Ebony,* pp. 190-194. **(AfA)**

Chase, B. (1997). Gay economy lures dollars of major advertisers. In S. Biagi & M. Kern-Foxworth (Eds.), *Facing differences: Race, gender, and mass media* (pp. 179-181). Thousand Oaks, CA: Pine Forge. **(GA)**

Church, G. J. (1997, December 8). Thinking big. *Time,* pp. B11, B27, B28.

Cintron, I. (1991, May 20). The world of commercials seems not to include Asia. *Newsday,* p. 33. **(AsA)**

Cisneros, H. (1997, April). *Keynote speech.* Talk given at First Hispanic Observatory, Bromley Aguilar & Associates, San Antonio, TX. **(USL)**

Claritas. (1998). Data Mart on America [Unpublished, subscriber-only database]. www.claritas.com

Cleland, K. (1998, November 16). Multicultural marketing. *Advertising Age,* pp. S26-S27. **(AfA)**

Clemetson, L. (2000, May 8). Color my world. *Newsweek,* pp. 70-74.

Cloud, J. (1998, July 20). Trans across America. *Time,* pp. 48-49. **(GA)**

Cloud, J. (1999, June 14). The pioneer: Harvey Milk. *Time,* pp. 183-186. **(GA)**

Cobo-Hanlon, L. (1999, November). My child is gay, que hago? *Latina,* pp. 122-125. **(GA)**

Cohen, G. (1994). Age related problems in the use of proper names in communication. In M. L. Hummert, J. M. Niesmann, & J. F. Nussbaum (Eds.), *Interpersonal communication in older adulthood: Interdisciplinary theory and research* (pp. 40-57). Thousand Oaks, CA: Sage. **(MA)**

Cole, C. A., & Balasubramanian, S. K. (1993, June). Age differences in consumers' search for information: Public policy implications. *Journal of Consumer Research, 20,* 157-169. **(MA)**

Collette, J. (1999, December). The desktop translator. *T.H.E. Journal,* pp. 54-55.

Collier, M. J. (1994). *Cultural identity and intercultural communication.* In L. A. Samovar & R. E. Porter (Eds.), *Intercultural communication: A reader* (pp. 36-44). Belmont, CA: Wadsworth.

Collins, G. (1994, July 7). A product's campaign seeks to remove the remaining stigma surrounding a once-taboo issue. *New York Times,* p. D18. **(MA)**

Collins, J. C., & Porras, J. I. (1994). *Built to last: Successful habits of visionary companies.* New York: HarperBusiness.

Conlin, M. (1999, December 27). Hey, what about us? *Business Week,* pp. 52-55.

Cooper, H. (1990, September). Children as customers. *American Demographics, 12,* 36-39.

Cose, E. (1995, February 13). One drop of blood history. *Newsweek,* pp. 70-72. **(AfA)**

Cose, E. (1997, March 17). The black Gen X nobody knows. *Newsweek,* p. 62. **(AfA)**

Cose, E. (2000, January 1). Our new look: The colors of race. *Newsweek,* pp. 28-36. **(AfA)**

Costa, J. A. (1996). Foreword. In D. L. Wardlow (Ed.), *Gays, lesbians, and consumer behavior: Theory, practice, and research issues in marketing* (pp. xvii-xx). New York: Harrington Park. **(GA)**

Council on Interracial Books for Children. (1977). Textbooks and Native Americans. In Council on Interracial Books for Children (Eds.), *Stereotypes, distortions and omissions in U.S. history textbooks.* New York: Author.

Cowen, M. (1997, December). The Sioux's last stand. *George,* p. 44.

Cox, E., & McAuliffe, C. (1998, July 13). When magic happens [Special planning section]. *Adweek,* p. 31.

Cox, M. (1994, March 1). New magazines cater to people with HIV. *Wall Street Journal,* p. B1. **(GA)**

Crawford, N. (1998, January). It's culture, not color. *PROMO Magazine,* pp. 47-50, 132. **(AsA)**

Crockett, R. O. (1998, October 5). Invisible—and loving it. *Business Week,* pp. 124-128. **(AfA)**

Crockett, R. O. (2000, February 7). Attention must be paid: The African American Web community is swelling—and underserved. *Business Week E.Biz,* p. EB16. **(AfA)**

Cropper, J., & Speaker, P. (1999, September). The Echo Boom comes of age. *American Demographics, 21.* www.demographics.com

Cross, R. H. (1992, October). The five degrees of customer bonding. *Direct Marketing,* pp. 33-35, 58.

Cross, W. E. (1971). The Negro-to-black conversion experience: Toward a psychology of black liberation. *Black World, 20*(9), 13-27. **(AfA)**

Cruse, H. (1967). *The crisis of Negro intellectuals.* New York: Morrow. **(AfA)**

Cundiff, E. W., & Still, R. R. (1964). *Basic marketing: Concepts, environment and decisions.* Englewood Cliffs, NJ: Prentice Hall.

Cyr, D. (1994, July). Cutting across ethnic lines. *Catalog Age.*

Darley, W. K., & Williams, J. D. (2000). Methodological issues in ethnic minority research: Changing consumer demographics and implications. In C. P. Rao (Ed.), *Marketing and multicultural diversity.* New York: Quorum. **(AfA)**

Darling, L. (1994, January 24). As customers age, new notion of beauty emerges. *New York Times,* pp. B1, B5.

Darnay, A. J. (Ed.). (1998). *Economic indicators handbook* (4th ed.). Detroit, MI: Gale Research.

Dates, J. (1990). Advertising. In J. L. Dates & W. Barlow (Eds.), *Split image: African Americans in the mass media.* Washington, DC: Howard University Press. **(AfA)**

Dates, J. L., & Pease, E. C. (1994). Warping the world: Media's mangled images of race. *Media Studies Journal, 8*(3), 89-95. **(AfA)**

D'Augelli, A. (1994). Lesbian and gay male development: Steps toward an analysis of lesbians' and gay men's lives. In B. Greene & G. Herek (Eds.), *Lesbian and gay psychology: Theory, research, and clinical applications* (pp. 118-132). Thousand Oaks, CA: Sage. **(GA)**

David, A. (1997, July 14). Shopping smart. *People,* p. 37.

David, F. J. (1991). *Who is black? One nation's definition.* University Park: Pennsylvania State University Press. **(AfA)**

Davidson, D. K. (1995, September 11). Targeting is innocent until it exploits the vulnerable. *Marketing News, 29,* 10.

Davis, A., & Bukoff, A. (1999, September). Generation X. *American Demographics, 21.* www.demographics.com

Davis, S. (1994, May 3). Fashions that fit. *Hartford Courant,* p. D-1. (**AfA**)

de la Garza, M. F.-O., Newcomb, M. D., & Myers, H. F. (1995). A multidimensional measure of cultural identity for Latino and Latina adolescents. In A. M. Padilla (Ed.), *Hispanic psychology: Critical issues in theory and research* (pp. 26-42). Thousand Oaks, CA: Sage. (**USL**)

de Mooij, M. (1998). *Global marketing and advertising: Understanding cultural paradoxes.* Thousand Oaks, CA: Sage. (**USL, AsA**)

Del Guidice, L. (1993). *Studies in Italian Amercian folklore.* Provo: Utah State University Press.

Delener, N., & Neelankavil, J. P. (1990, June/July). Informational sources and media usage: A comparison between Asian and Hispanic subcultures. *Journal of Advertising Research, 30,* 45-52. (**USL, AsA**)

Deloitte & Touche. (1990). *The African American market.* Unpublished internal document.

Dennis, E. E. (1994). Racial naming. *Media Studies Journal, 8*(3), 105-111. (**AfA**)

Deshpande, R., Hoyer, W. D., & Donthu, N. (1986). The intensity of ethnic affiliation: A study of the sociology of Hispanic consumption. *Journal of Consumer Research, 13,* 214-220. (**USL**)

Deshpande, R., & Stayman, D. M. (1994, February). A tale of two cities: Distinctiveness theory and advertising effectiveness. *Journal of Marketing Research, 31,* 57-64. (**USL**)

Deveny, K. (1993, September 22). What is a Texas consumer, anyway? *Wall Street Journal,* pp. T1, T3-T4.

Devos, G. (1975). Ethnic pluralism: Conflict and accommodation. In G. Devos & L. Romanucci-Ross (Eds.), *Ethnic identity: Cultural continuities and change* (pp. 69-81). Palo Alto, CA: Mayfield. (**AfA**)

Dholakia, R. R., & Levy, S. (1987). The consumer dream in the United States: Aspirations and achievement in a changing environment. *Journal of Macromarketing, 7*(2), 41-51.

Dirke, L. (1991, January 9). Racial stereotypes found to persist among whites. *Austin American Statesman,* p. A4. (**AfA**)

DMB&B. (1997). *The New World Teen Study: Wave II. An Hispanic perspective.* Unpublished agency document. (**USL**)

Dollard, J. (1937). *Caste and class in a small southern town.* New Haven, CT: Yale University Press. (**AfA**)

Dolnick, E. (1993, September). Deafness as culture. *Atlantic Monthly,* pp. 37-40, 43, 46-48, 50-53.

Domenech Rodriguez, M. M., Slater, M. D., & Beauvais, F. (1997). Beer advertising to Latino youth: The effects of Spanish vs. English-language targeting. In S. Biagi & M. Kern-Foxworth (Eds.), *Facing difference: Race, gender, and mass media* (pp. 205-211). Thousand Oaks, CA: Pine Forge. (**USL**)

Donnelly Marketing. (1988, May). Marketers don't understand seniors. *Mature Market Report,* p. 2. (**MA**)

Donnerstein, E., Donnerstein, M., & Koch, C. (1975). Racial discrimination in apartment rentals: A replication. *Journal of Social Psychology, 96,* 37-38. **(AfA)**

Donovan, R. J., & Leivers, S. (1993). Using paid advertising to modify racial stereotype beliefs. *Public Opinion Quarterly, 57,* 205-218.

Doss, Y. C. (1998, June 5). The gag comes off. Www.fronteramag.com/issu4/features/gag.html

Dougherty, T. (1999, December). More steady growth. *Hispanic Business,* pp. 56, 58, 60. **(USL)**

Drake, S. C., & Cayton, H. (1962). *Black metropolis.* New York: Harper & Row. **(AfA)**

Dreyfuss, R. (1999, February). America, the brand. *Mother Jones,* pp. 44-57.

DRI/McGraw-Hill. (1995, February). *Hispanic consumer market growth to 2010.* New York: Univision Holdings. **(USL)**

Druckerman, P. (2000, February 9). Web site aims to attract Latin American teens. *Wall Street Journal,* p. A22. **(USL)**

Drug store chain says ads not anti-black. (1997, February 24). Reuters. **(AfA)**

Drummond, K. T. (1995, September 25). Not in Kansas anymore. *Time,* pp. 54-55. **(GA)**

Dubin, M. (1990, August 12). An uneasy coexistence for blacks and Asians in city. *Philadelphia Inquirer,* p. 1C. **(AfA)**

Dubin, M., & Clark, R. (1990, August 8). Shop owner in slaying is released. *Philadelphia Inquirer,* p. 1B. **(AfA)**

DuBois, W. E. B. (1907). *Souls of black folk.* Chicago: A. C. McLurg. **(AfA)**

Duff, C. (1993, March 3). You, too, could be a model for catalogs. *Wall Street Journal,* p. V1. **(AfA)**

Duff, C. (1995, September 28). Profiling the aged: Fat cats or hungry victims? *Wall Street Journal,* pp. B1, B8. **(MA)**

Dunkel, T. (1995, January 23). Disabled athletes begin to enter arena of paid endorsement. *Wall Street Journal,* pp. A1, A7.

Dunn, S. W., & Lorimar, E. S. (1979). *International advertising and marketing.* Columbus, OH: Grid.

Dychtwald, K. (1989, February). Marketing toward the year 2000. *Marketing Communication, 14,* 20-24. **(MA)**

Early, G. (1995, July-August). Understanding Afrocentrism. *Civilization,* pp. 31-39. **(AfA)**

Edmondson, B. (1996, November). Black America in 2001. *American Demographics, 18,* 14-15. **(AfA)**

Edmondson, B. (1997a, February). Asian Americans in 2001. *American Demographics, 19,* 16-17. **(AsA)**

Edmondson, B. (1997b, January). Boomer dreams. *American Demographics, 19,* 27-28.

Edwards, C. (1996, December 22). Targeting minority customers makes sense. *Valley Morning Star,* p. E2. **(AfA)**

El-Badry, S. (1994, January). The Arab American market. *American Demographics, 16,* 22-30.

Elliott, R., & Wattanasuwan, K. (1998, May). Brands as symbolic resources for the construction of identity. *International Journal of Advertising,* p. 131.

Elliott, S. (1994a, June 9). A sharper view of gay consumers. *New York Times,* pp. D1, D19. **(GA)**

Elliott, S. (1994b, April 14). This weekend, a business expo will show the breadth of new interest in gay consumers. *New York Times,* p. 18. **(GA)**

Ellis, J. E. (1988, March 14). The black middle-class. *Business Week,* pp. 62-70. **(AfA)**

Ellis, J. (1999, December). That sound—the sound of advertising being allowed in—is the sound of the future being born. *Fast Company,* pp. 368-372.

Ellis, S., McCullough, J., Wallendorf, M., & Tan, C. T. (1985). Cultural values and behavior: Chineseness within geographic boundaries. *Advances in Consumer Research, 12,* 126-128. **(AsA)**

Englis, B. G., & Solomon, M. R. (1993, February). *Where perception meets reality: The social construction of lifestyles.* Paper presented at the Advertising and Consumer Psychology Conference.

Englis, B. G., & Solomon, M. R. (1995). To be and not to be: Lifestyle imagery, reference groups, and the clustering of America. *Journal of Advertising, 24*(1), 13-28.

Entman, R. M. (1994, Summer). African Americans according to TV news. *Media Studies Journal, 8*(3), 29-38. **(AfA)**

Escobar, G. (1999, January 9). Ratio of immigrants highest in 70 years. *Austin American Statesman,* p. A22.

Espiritu, Y. L. (1992). *Asian American panethnicity: Bridging institutions and identities.* Philadelphia: Temple University Press. **(AsA)**

Exeter, T. (1990, June). How big will the older market be? *American Demographics, 12,* 30-34. **(MA)**

Faber, R. J., Christenson, G. A., DeZwaan, M., & Mitchell, J. (1995). Two forms of compulsive consumption: Comorbidity of compulsive buying and binge eating. *Journal of Consumer Research, 22,* 296-304.

Faber, R. J., & O'Guinn, T. C. (1991, April). *Does translating language translate to more effective advertising? Hispanic viewers' perceptions of English versus Spanish language ads.* Paper presented at the American Academy of Advertising Conference, Reno, NV. **(USL)**

Faber, R. J., O'Guinn, T. C., & McCarty, J. A. (1987, Summer). Ethnicity, acculturation, and the importance of product attributes. *Psychology and Marketing, 4,* 121-134. **(USL)**

Fairchild, H. H. (1985). Black, Negro or Afro-American? The differences are crucial. *Journal of Black Studies, 16,* 47-55. **(AfA)**

Farley, C. J. (1999, February 8). Hip-hop nation. *Time,* pp. 54-64. **(AfA)**

Feldman, L. P., & Star, A. D. (1968). Racial factors in shopping behavior. In K. Cox & B. Enis (Eds.), *A new measure of responsibility for marketing* (pp. 216-225). Chicago: American Marketing Association. **(AfA)**

Feuer, J. (1988, August 15). Signs of the times: Hispanic outdoor advertising. *Adweek,* p. 20. **(USL)**

Figueroa, A., Clemetson, L., Weingart, P., Hayden, T., & Brand, M. (1999, July 12). Generation Ñ. *Newsweek,* pp. 58-63.

Fire starters. (1999, December). *Fast Company,* p. 386.

First event helps Sum Basho rock Vancouver. (1999-2000, Winter). *Imprint,* p. 16. **(AsA)**

Fish, J. (1995, November/December). Mixed blood. *Psychology Today,* pp. 55-61, 76, 80. **(AfA)**

Fisher, C. (1993, February 15). Poll: Hispanics stick to brands. *Advertising Age,* p. 6. **(USL)**

Fisher, C. (1995, January 23). Younger Hispanics get the word. *Advertising Age,* pp. 29, 37. **(USL)**

Fisher, C. (1996, September). Black, hip, and primed to shop. *American Demographics, 18,* 52-59. **(AfA)**

Fitch, E. (1987, February 9). Marketing to Hispanics. *Advertising Age,* pp. 52-53. **(USL)**

Fixico, M. (1985). The road to middle class Indian America. In C. E. Trafzer (Ed.), *America's Indian identity: Today's changing perspectives* (pp. 50-63). San Diego, CA: San Diego State University, Department of American Indian Studies.

Fizdale, R. (1992, Summer). Integrated communications: The whole picture. *Advertiser,* pp. 1-3.

Flores, B. A. (1994). *Chiquita's cocoon.* New York: Villard. **(USL)**

Fong, C., & Yung, J. (1995-1996). In search of the right spouse: Interracial marriage among Chinese and Japanese Americans. *Amerasia Journal, 21*(3), 77-98. **(AsA)**

Fortini-Campbell, L. (1992). *Hitting the sweet spot.* Chicago: Copy Workshop.

Fost, D. (1998, February). The fun factor: Marketing recreation to the disabled. *American Demographics, 20,* 54-60.

Fournier, S. (1998, March). Consumers and their brands: Developing relationship theory in consumer research. *Journal of Consumer Research, 24,* 343-360.

Francher, J. S. (1973). "It's the Pepsi generation. . . ." Accelerated aging and the television commercial. *International Journal of Aging and Human Development, 4,* 245-255. **(MA)**

Frank, T. (1999, July). Brand you: Better selling through anthropology. *Harper's Magazine,* pp. 74-79.

Frazier, E. F. (1957). *The black bourgeoisie.* New York: Free Press. **(AfA)**

Freedman, A. M. (1991, July 1). Malt advertising that touts firepower comes under attack by U.S. officials. *Wall Street Journal,* p. B1. **(AfA)**

Freedman, A. M. (1992, May 11). Marketing: Heileman tries a new name for strong malt. *Wall Street Journal,* p. B1. **(AfA)**

Freitas, A., Kaiser, S., & Hammidi, T. (1996). Communities, commodities, cultural space, and style. In D. L. Wardlow (Ed.), *Gays, lesbians, and consumer behavior: Theory, practice, and research issues in marketing* (pp. 83-107). New York: Harrington Park. **(GA)**

Frey, W. H. (1998, June). The diversity myth. *American Demographics, 20,* 39-43. **(AsA)**

Furman, P. (1985, October). The new wrinkle in casting. *Madison Avenue, 27,* 66-67. **(MA)**

Futterman, M., & Nugest, M. (1997, September 25). Shopper charges Bloomingdale's with bias and assault in search. *Star-Ledger,* p. 33. **(AfA)**

Gabler, N. (1998). *Life, the movie: How entertainment conquered reality.* New York: Knopf.

Gannon, M. J., & Associates. (1994). *Understanding global cultures: Metaphorical journeys through 17 countries.* Thousand Oaks, CA: Sage.

Gans, J. E., & Shook, K. L. (1994). *Policy compendium of tobacco, alcohol, and other harmful substances.* Chicago: American Medical Association. **(AfA)**

Garnets, L. D., & Kimmel, D. C. (1991). Lesbian and gay male dimensions in the psychological study of human diversity. In J. D. Goodchilds (Ed.), *Psychological perspectives on human diversity* (pp. 160-180). Washington, DC: American Psychological Association. **(GA)**

Gates, D. (1992, March 23). Apartheid, American style. *Newsweek,* p. 61. **(AfA)**

Gegax, T. T. (1997, May 26). Fast-food fast tracker: LaVan Hawkins thrives by tweaking a formula. *Newsweek,* p. 57. **(AfA)**

Gensch, D. H., & Staelin, R. (1972). The appeal of buying black. *Journal of Marketing Research, 9,* 141-148. **(AfA)**

Gentry, J. W., Tansuhaj, P., Manzer, L. L, & John, J. (1988). Do geographic subcultures vary culturally? *Advances in Consumer Research, 15,* 411-417.

Gergen, K., & Gibbs, M. S. (1966). *Role playing and modifying the self-concept.* Paper presented at the annual meeting of the Eastern Psychological Association. **(AsA)**

Gettone, V. (1981). Negative label. *Association of Black Psychologists' Newsletter, 12*(2), 3-11. **(AfA)**

Gibson, D. P. (1978). *$70 billion in the black: America's black consumers.* New York: Macmillan. **(AfA)**

Giles, H., Bourhis, R. Y., & Taylor, D. (1977). Towards a theory of language in ethnic group relations. In H. Giles & R. St. Clair (Eds.), *Language, ethnicity and intergroup relations* (pp. 307-348). London: Academic Press. **(AfA)**

Giles, H., & Coupland, N. (1991). *Language: Contexts and consequences.* Pacific Grove, CA: Brooks/Cole. **(AfA)**

Gill, M. S. (1998, March). Never say never-never land. *Out,* pp. 70-74, 113. **(GA)**

Ginsburg, J. (1999, December 20). Xtreme retailing. *Business Week,* 120-128.

Gitlin, S. (1998). Asian prime time. *Brandweek, 39*(1), 17. **(AsA)**

Glenn, E. N. (1983). Split household, small producer and dual wage earner: An analysis of Chinese-American family strategies. *Journal of Marriage and Family, 45,* 35-45. **(AsA)**

Goff, L. (1999, August). Don't miss the bus. *American Demographics, 21,* 48-54.

Golden, D. (2000, February 17). Casting a net: Web site that unites blacks is big ambition of Henry Louis Gates. *Wall Street Journal,* pp. A1, A8. **(AfA)**

Goldman, K. (1993a, June 4). Atlanta tavern says Budweiser was racially insensitive on ad. *Wall Street Journal,* p. B12. **(AfA)**

Goldman, K. (1993b, August 30). Burger King retains private eye. *Wall Street Journal,* p. B5. **(AfA)**

Goldman, K. (1993c, September 20). Seniors get little respect on Madison Ave. *Wall Street Journal,* p. B6. **(MA)**

Goldman, K. (1994, May 5). Ben & Jerry's seeks sales boost with a radical dose of nostalgia. *Wall Street Journal,* p. B7.

Goldsmith, J. (1996, September 13). Ad sales lag behind boom in Hispanic TV. *Wall Street Journal,* p. B5. **(USL)**

Goldsmith, R. E., White, J. D., & Stith, M. T. (1987, Summer). Values of middle-class blacks and whites: A replication and extension. *Psychology and Marketing, 4,* 135-144. **(AfA)**

Gollub, J. (1989, June). Six ways to age. *American Demographics, 11,* 19-23. **(MA)**

Goodson, S. R., & Shaver, M. A. (1994). Hispanic marketing: National advertiser spending patterns and media choices. *Journalism Quarterly, 71,* 191-198. **(USL)**

Gordon, M. M. (1964). *Assimilation in American life: The role of race, religion, and national origins.* New York: Oxford University Press.

Gore, A. (1998, March 31). The genetic moral code. *Advocate,* p. 9.

Graves, S. B. (1996). Diversity on television. In T. M. Macbeth (Ed.), *Tuning in to young viewers: Social science perspective on television* (pp. 61-86). Thousand Oaks, CA: Sage. **(AsA)**

Gray, V. (1997). Going after our dollars. *Black Enterprise, 27*(12), 68-78. **(AfA)**

Greeley, A. M., & Sheatsley, P. B. (1971). Attitudes toward racial integration. *Scientific American, 195,* 35-39. **(AfA)**

Green, C. L. (1999). Ethnic evaluations of advertising: Interaction effects of strength of ethnic identification, media placement, and degree of racial composition. *Journal of Advertising, 28*(1), 49-64. **(AfA)**

Green, M. (1991). *Invisible people: The depiction of minorities in magazine ads and catalogs.* New York: Department of Consumer Affairs. **(AfA)**

Green, M. K. (1993). Images of Native Americans in advertising: Some moral issues. *Journal of Business Ethics, 12,* 323-330.

Green, W. E. (1980, November 10). Reaching out: Firms seek to tighten links with Hispanics as buyers and workers. *Wall Street Journal,* pp. A1, A14. **(USL)**

Greene, B. (1994). Lesbian and gay sexual orientations: Implications for clinical training, practice, and research. In B. Greene & G. Herek (Eds.), *Lesbian and gay psychology: Theory, research and clinical applications* (pp. 1-25). Thousand Oaks, CA: Sage. **(GA)**

Greene, B. (Ed.). (1997a). *Ethnic and cultural diversity among lesbians and gay men.* Thousand Oaks, CA: Sage. **(GA)**

Greene, B. (1997b). Ethnic minority lesbians and gay men: Mental health and treatment issues. In B. Greene (Ed.), *Ethnic and cultural diversity among lesbians and gay men* (pp. 216-239). Thousand Oaks, CA: Sage. **(GA)**

Greene, M. G., Adelman, R. D., Rizzo, C., & Friedmann, E. (1994). Patients' presentation of self. In M. L. Hummert, J. M. Wiemann, & J. F. Nussbaum (Eds.), *Interpersonal communication in older adulthood: Interdisciplinary theory and research* (pp. 226-250). Thousand Oaks, CA: Sage. **(MA)**

Greer, W. H., & Cobb, P. M. (1968). *Black rage.* New York: Basic Books. **(AfA)**

Griffin, T., McArthur, D., Yamaki, T., & Hidalgo, P. (1998, May). The A,B,Cs of advertising management: Perceptions and practices of managers in Chile, Japan, and the United States. *International Journal of Advertising, 17,* 169-187.

Grimes, A. (1999, December 31). More elders find having roommates improves their lives. *Wall Street Journal,* p. B1. **(MA)**

Grover, R. (1995, May 15). A stop on the dial for the disabled. *Business Week,* p. 8.

Grover, R. (1998, December 14). Must-see TV for left-handed men under 30. *Business Week,* p. 104.

Grunwald, H. (2000, January 1). A world without a country? *Wall Street Journal,* p. R44.

Gudykunst, W. B. (1994). *Bridging differences: Effective intergroup communication* (2nd ed.). Thousand Oaks, CA: Sage.

Gudykunst, W. B., & Ting-Toomey, S. (1988). *Culture and interpersonal communication.* Thousand Oaks, CA: Sage.

Gutierrez, E. (1996, June). Beyond gay: A new generation of homosexuals claim to be happy not being gay. *Genre,* pp. 51-53. **(GA)**

Ha, T. H. (1970). *Maxims and proverbs of old Korea.* Seoul, Korea: Yonsei University Press.

Hagerty, V. (1999, December). Clicking online. *Hispanic Business,* pp. 60, 62, 64. **(USL)**

Hall, E. T. (1959). *The silent language.* New York: Doubleday.

Hall, E. T. (1976). *Beyond culture.* New York: Doubleday.

Hall, E. T. (1984). *The dance of life.* Garden City, NY: Doubleday.

Hamamoto, D. Y. (1992). Kindred spirits: The contemporary Asian American family on television. *Amerasia Journal, 18*(2), 35-53. **(AsA)**

Hamers, J., & Blanc, M. (1989). *Bilinguality and bilingualism.* Cambridge, UK: University of Cambridge Press. **(AsA)**

Hammond, J., & Morrison, J. (1996). *The stuff Americans are made of.* New York: Macmillan. **(MA)**

Hample, S. (1995, January-February). Fear of commitment. *Marketing Tools, 6,* 8-10.

Hardy, Q. (1997, April 24). School of thought: The unbearable whiteness of being. *Wall Street Journal,* pp. A1, A12.

Hare, N. (1970). *The black Anglo-Saxons.* New York: Collier. **(AfA)**

Harper, P. A. (1999, January 18). Financial commitments emerge that target minorities. Associated Press Newswire. **(AfA)**

Harre, R. (1989). Language games and texts of identity. In J. Shotter & K. J. Gergen (Eds.), *Texts of identity* (pp. 20-35). Newbury Park, CA: Sage. **(AfA)**

Harris, G. (1994). International advertising standardization: What do the multinationals actually standardize? *Journal of International Marketing, 2*(4), 13-30.

Harris, N. (1997, August 10). Eric Miller is no soda jerk. *Business Week,* p. 28. **(AfA)**

Harris-Prager, J. (1999, December 15). People with disabilities are next consumer niche. *Wall Street Journal,* pp. B1, B6.

Hatchett, D. (1988, October 15). What's going on between blacks and Koreans? *New York Voice.* **(AfA)**

Haubegger, C. (1999, July 12). Latino America. *Newsweek,* pp. 48-53. **(USL)**

Hawkins, C. (1993, June 28). Denny's: The stain that isn't coming out. *Business Week,* pp. 98-99. **(AfA)**

Heath, R. P. (1996, November). What tickles our funny bones. *American Demographics, 18,* 49-52.

Hecht, M. L., Collier, M. J., & Ribeau, S. A. (1993). *African American communication: Ethnic identity and cultural interpretation.* Newbury Park, CA: Sage. **(AfA)**

Hecht, M. L., & Ribeau, S. (1987). Afro-American identity labels and communicative effectiveness. *Journal of Language and Social Psychology, 6,* 319-326. **(AfA)**

Hecht, M. L., & Ribeau, S. (1991). Sociocultural roots of ethnic identity: A look at black America. *Journal of Black Studies, 21,* 501-513. **(AfA)**

Hecht, M. L., Ribeau, S., & Alberts, J. K. (1989). An Afro-American perspective on interethnic commmunication. *International Journal of Intercultural Relations, 14,* 31-55. **(AfA)**

Heines, V. (1999, December). Bridging the digital divide. *Hispanic Business,* p. 16. **(USL)**

Henderson, A. B. (1995a, November 15). Chrysler backs "hoop dreams" to court blacks. *Wall Street Journal,* p. B1. **(AfA)**

Henderson, A. B. (1995b, September 28). Rolling revolution: The wheelchair turns hip as new generation of user demands style. *Wall Street Journal,* pp. A1, A13.

Herek, G. (1994). Assessing heterosexuals' attitudes toward lesbians and gay men. In B. Greene & G. Herek (Eds.), *Lesbian and gay psychology: Theory, research, and clinical applications* (pp. 206-228). Thousand Oaks, CA: Sage. **(GA)**

Hernandez, S. A., & Kaufman, C. J. (1990, March). Marketing research in Hispanic barrios: A guide to survey research. *Marketing Research,* pp. 11-27. **(USL)**

Heubusch, K. (1997, April). Switching for a cause. *American Demographics, 19,* 26-27.

Hilger, M. T., & English, W. D. (1978). Consumer alienation from the marketplace. In R. S. Franz, R. M. Hopkins, & A. G. Toma (Eds.), *Proceedings of 1978 Southern Marketing Association* (pp. 78-83). Lafayette: University of Southwestern Louisiana Press. **(USL)**

Hills, G. E., Granbois, D. H., & Patterson, J. M. (1973, April). Black consumer perceptions of food store attributes. *Journal of Marketing, 37,* 47-57. **(AfA)**

Hirsch, J. S. (1995, November 9). New credit cards base appeals on sexual orientation and race. *Wall Street Journal,* pp. B1, B9. **(GA)**

Hirschman, E. (1981, Summer). American Jewish ethnicity: Its relationship to some selected aspects of consumer behavior. *Journal of Marketing, 45,* 102-110.

Hirschman, E. C. (1985, September). Primitive aspects of consumption in modern American society. *Journal of Consumer Research, 12,* 142-154.

Hirschman, E. C., & Thompson, C. J. (1997). Why media matter: Toward a richer understanding of consumers' relationships with advertising and mass media. *Journal of Advertising, 26*(1), 43-60.

Hispanic Market Connections, Inc. (1995). Language segmentation: A tested research tool for the Hispanic market. *Hispanic Market Report, 2*(1), 2. **(USL)**

Hispanic Market Connections, Inc. (1996). Explaining cultural differences: Some common themes among Hispanics. *Hispanic Market Report, 3*(2), 2. **(USL)**

Hispanic marketing wins new converts. (1988, February 8). *Adweek,* pp. 30, 32. **(USL)**

Hispanic oriented ads lose in the translation. (1986, February 23). *Austin American Statesman,* p. B6. **(USL)**

Hitch, P. (1983). Social identity and the half-Asian child. In G. Breakwell (Ed.), *Threatened identities* (pp. 107-127). New York: John Wiley. **(AsA)**

Hobbs, F. B. (1996). *Sixty-five plus in the United States.* Washington, DC: U.S. Bureau of the Census. **(MA)**

Hoeffel, J. (1994, August). A new twist on Hispanic television. *American Demographics, 16,* 16-17, 20. **(USL)**

Hof, R. D., Browder, S., & Elstrom, P. (1997, May 4). Special report: Internet communities. *Business Week,* pp. 64-67, 70, 74, 76, 80.

Hoffman, D. L., Novak, T. P., & Venkatesh, A. (1997, November). *Diversity on the Internet: The relationship of race to access and usage.* Working paper, Aspen Institute's Forum on Diversity and the Media, Queenstown, MD. **(AfA)**

Hofman, J. E. (1985). Arabs and Jews, blacks and whites: Identity and group relations. *Journal of Multilingual and Multicultural Development, 6,* 217-237. **(AfA)**

Hofstede, G. H. (1984). *Culture's consequences: International differences in work-related values.* Beverly Hills, CA: Sage. **(USL)**

Hofstede, G. (1997). *Cultures and organizations: Software of the mind.* New York: McGraw-Hill. **(AfA)**

Holland, J., & Gentry, J. W. (1999, April 1). Ethnic consumer reaction to targeted marketing: A theory of intercultural accommodation. *Journal of Advertising, 28,* 65-84.

Holstein, W. J. (1990, May 14). The stateless corporation. *Business Week,* pp. 98-106.

Holtz, G. T. (1995). *Welcome to the jungle: The why behind Generation X.* New York: St. Martin's.

Home boys. (1990, April 2). *Jet,* p. 19. **(AfA)**

Hope, L., & Klonoff, E. A. (1996). *African American acculturation: Deconstructing race and reviving culture.* Thousand Oaks, CA: Sage. **(AfA)**

Horovitz, B. (1994, May 3). Marketing. *Los Angeles Times,* p. 1. **(AfA)**

Hout, M., & Goldstein, J. R. (1994, February). How 4.5 million Irish immigrants became 40 million Irish Americans: Demographic and subjective aspects of the ethnic composition of white Americans. *American Sociological Review, 59,* 64-82.

How hybridity is yielding a new sense of identity. (2000, June 29). *Wall Street Journal,* p. A22.

HSN to debut television shopping program. (1994, July 21). *Business Wire.* **(AfA)**

Hughes, M., & Demo, D. H. (1989). Self-perception of black Americans: Self-esteem and personal efficacy. *American Journal of Sociology, 95,* 132-159. **(AfA)**

Hughes, R. (1993). *Culture of complaint: The fraying of America.* New York: Oxford University Press.

Hume, S. (1983, November 7). Stars are lacking luster as ad presenters. *Advertising Age,* p. 3. **(AfA)**

Hummert, M. L. (1994). Stereotypes of the elderly and patronizing speech. In M. L. Hummert, J. M. Wiemann, & J. F. Nussbaum (Eds.), *Interpersonal communication in older adulthood: Interdisciplinary theory and research* (pp. 162-184). Thousand Oaks, CA: Sage. **(MA)**

Hwang, S. L. (1999, April 21). Light brigades: Tobacco companies enlist the bar owner to push their goods. *Wall Street Journal,* pp. A1-A6.

Hyman, H. H., & Sheatsley, P. B. (1956). Attitudes toward desegregation. *Scientific American, 195,* 35-39. **(AfA)**

Hyman, H. H., & Sheatsley, P. B. (1964). Attitudes toward desegregation. *Scientific American, 211,* 16-23. **(AfA)**

Indicators of the century. (1999, December 31). *Time,* p. 20.

Jackson, J. S., & Gurin, G. (1987). *National survey of black Americans, 1978-1980.* Ann Arbor, MI: Inter-University Consortium for Political and Social Research, Institute for Social Research. (**AfA**)

Jacob, R. (1993, November 15). Overseas Indians: Make it big. *Fortune,* pp. 168-174. (**AsA**)

Jacobson, M. F., & Mazur, L. A. (1995). *Marketing madness.* Boulder, CO: Westview.

Jandt, F. E. (1995). *Intercultural communication: An introduction.* Thousand Oaks, CA: Sage. (**AfA, GA**)

Janoff, J. B. (1996, April 24). A Gen-X Rip Van Winkle. *Newsweek,* p. 10.

Jay, K., & Young, A. (1979). *The gay report: Lesbians and gay men speak out about sexual experiences and lifestyles.* New York: Summit. (**GA**)

Jaynes, G. D., & Williams, R. M. (Eds.). (1989). *A common destiny: Blacks and American society.* Washington, DC: National Academy Press. (**AfA**)

Jeannet, J.-P. (2000). *Managing with a global mindset.* London: Financial Times/Prentice Hall.

Jenkins, A. H. (1982). *The psychology of the Afro-American.* New York: Pergamon. (**AfA**)

Jewell, K. S. (1985). Will the real black, Afro-American, mixed, colored, Negro, please stand up? Impact of the black social movement twenty years later. *Journal of Black Studies, 16,* 57-75. (**AfA**)

Johnson, B. M. (1993a, February 15). The great Hispanic hope—for advertisers. *Business Week,* p. 122. (**USL**)

Johnson, B. (1993b, January 18). Special report: Marketing to gays and lesbians. *Advertising Age,* pp. 29-37. (**GA**)

Johnson, D. A., Porter, R., & Mateljan, P. (1991). Racial discrimination in apartment rentals. *Journal of Applied Social Psychology, 1,* 364-377. (**AfA**)

Jones, D. A. (1996). Discrimination against same-sex couples in hotel reservation policies. In D. L. Wardlow (Ed.), *Gays, lesbians, and consumer behavior: Theory, practice, and research issues in marketing* (pp. 153-159). New York: Harrington Park. (**GA**)

Judge, P. C. (1997, May 12). Is the Net redefining our identity? *Business Week,* pp. 100-102.

Kahan, H., & Mulryan, D. (1995, May). Out of the closet. *American Demographics, 17,* 40-43, 46-47. (**GA**)

Kahle, L. R. (1986, April). The nine nations of North America and the value basis of geographic segmentation. *Journal of Marketing, 50,* 37-47.

Kang & Lee. (1999, December). Asian American market. www.kanglee.com (**AsA**)

Kanner, B. (1994, April 11). On Madison Avenue: An extremely hard sell, black ads go mainstream. *New York,* pp. 12-13. (**AfA**)

Kates, S. M. (1998). *Twenty million new customers: Understanding gay men's consumer behavior.* New York: Harrington Park. (**GA**)

Kates, S. M. (1999, April 1). Making the ad perfectly queer: Marketing "normality" to the gay men's community? *Journal of Advertising,* pp. 25-45. (**GA**)

Katz, I. (1970). Experimental studies of Negro-white relationships. In L. Berkowitz (Ed.), *Advances in experimental social psychology* (Vol. 5). New York: Academic Press. (**AfA**)

Katz, M. (1996, November 18). Cable market wide open: Growing population is underserved in major metros. *Broadcasting and Cable,* pp. 54-56. (**USL**)

Kaufman, J. (2000, January 1). The omnipresent persuaders. *Wall Street Journal,* p. R26.

Kellner, D. (1995a). Cultural studies, multiculturalism and media culture. In G. Dines & J. M. Humez (Eds.), *Gender, race and class in media: A text-reader.* Thousand Oaks, CA: Sage.

Kellner, D. (1995b). *Media culture.* London: Routledge.

Kerin, R. (1979, Winter). Black model appearance and product evaluation. *Journal of Communication, 29,* 123-128. (**AfA**)

Kern-Foxworth, M. (1994). *Aunt Jemima, Uncle Ben, and Rastus: Blacks in advertising, yesterday, today, and tomorrow.* Westport, CT: Praeger. (**AfA**)

Kibria, N. (1997). The construction of "Asian American": Reflection on intermarriage and ethnic identity among second-generation Chinese and Korean Americans. *Ethnic and Racial Studies, 20,* 513-544. (**AsA**)

Kim, J. B. (1995, January 25). Brand loyalty wavers; private label gains. *Advertising Age,* p. 38. (**USL**)

King, S. R. (1999, August 28). Where does Generation Y go shopping? 70 million young shoppers without a thing to wear. *New York Times,* p. C-1.

Kitzinger, C. (1995). *Social constructionism: Implications for lesbian and gay psychology.* New York: Oxford University Press. (**GA**)

Kizilbash, A. H., & Garman, E. T. (1975-1976). Grocery retailing in Spanish neighborhoods. *Journal of Retailing, 51,* 15-21, 87. (**USL**)

Klein, M. (1998, March). Gays and the arts. *American Demographics, 20,* 33. (**GA**)

Klor de Alva, J. J. (1997). The invention of ethnic origins and the negotiation of Latino identity, 1969-1981. In M. Romero, P. Hondagneu-Sotelo, & V. Ortiz (Eds.), *Challenging fronteras* (pp. 55-79). New York: Routledge. (**USL**)

Kluckhohn, F., & Strodtbeck, F. L. (1960). *Variations in value orientations.* Westport, CT: Greenwood.

Kochman, T. (1981). *Black and white styles in conflict.* Chicago: University of Chicago Press. (**AfA**)

Koehl, C., & Van Boven, S. (1996, January 8). Taking on a stereotype. *Newsweek,* p. 8.

Kolbert, E. (1993, April 5). TV viewing and selling, by race. *New York Times,* p. D7. (**AfA**)

Konrad, W., & DeGeorge, G. (1989, April 3). U.S. companies go for the gray. *Business Week,* pp. 64-65, 67. (**MA**)

Korzenny, F. (1997, February). Study finds Spanish ads more effective. *Quirk's Marketing Research Review.* (**USL**)

Korzenny, F., McClure, J., & Rzttki, B. (1990). Ethnicity, communication, and drugs. *Journal of Drug Issues, 20,* 87-98.

Koslow, S., Shamdasani, P. N., & Touchstone, E. E. (1994, March). Exploring language effects in ethnic advertising: A sociolinguistics perspective. *Journal of Consumer Research, 20,* 575-585. (**USL**)

Koss-Feder, L. (1999, January 25). Able to work. *Time,* p. 82.

Kotkin, J. (1992). *Tribes: How race, religion and identity determine success in the new global economy.* New York: Random House.

Kotler, P. (1967). *Marketing management: Analysis, planning, and control.* Englewood Cliffs, NJ: Prentice Hall.

Kotler, P. (1990). *Principles of marketing* (3rd ed.). Englewood Cliffs, NJ: Prentice Hall.

Krafft, S. (1993, March). Listening to America's Irish echo. *American Demographics, 15,* 11-12.

Krase, J. (1994). *Italian Americans in a multicultural society.* New York: Forum Italicum.

Krase, J., & DeSena, J. N. (1994). *Italian Americans in a multicultural society.* Stony Brook, NY: Forum Italicum.

Kunda, D. (1994a, April 29). *Hispanic values and advertising.* Paper presented at the New Americas Advertising Forum, Department of Advertising, University of Texas at Austin. **(USL)**

Kunda, D. (1994b, April). *Strategic synergies between Anglo and Hispanic markets: Can they exist?* Paper presented at the New Americas Advertising Forum, Austin, TX. **(USL)**

Lach, J. (1999, February). The color of money. *American Demographics, 21,* 59-60. **(AfA)**

Lambert, Z. V. (1979, Winter). An investigation of older consumers' unmet needs and wants at the retail level. *Journal of Retailing, 55,* 35-57. **(MA)**

Lampe, P. E. (1982). Ethnic labels: Naming or name calling? *Ethnic and Racial Studies, 5,* 542-548. **(AfA)**

Larkey, L. K., & Hecht, M. L. (1991). *A comparative study of African American and Euroamerican ethnic identity.* Paper presented at the International Conference for Language and Social Psychology, Santa Barbara, CA. **(AfA)**

Lawe, S., Hawkins, S. A., & Craik, F. I. M. (1998, September 1). Repetition-induced belief in the elderly: Rehabilitating age-related memory deficits. *Journal of Consumer Research, 25,* 91-108. **(MA)**

Lazar, W. (1994). *Handbook for marketing and advertising: New trends in the American marketplace.* New York: Lexington.

Lee, C. H. (1996). *Elderly consumers' attitudes toward cybermarketing.* Unpublished master's thesis, University of Texas at Austin. **(MA)**

Lee, J. F. J. (1992). *Asian Americans: Oral histories of first to fourth generation Americans from China, the Philippines, Japan, India, the Pacific Islands, Vietnam and Cambodia.* New York: Free Press. **(AsA)**

Lee, K. W. (1999). The rise of the neo-Mandarins. *A Magazine,* pp. 22-23. **(AsA)**

Lee, L. (1996, December 24). New immigrants get crash course in consumerism. *Wall Street Journal,* p. B1. **(USL)**

Lee, P. (1991, January 1). Asian-Americans decry stereotypes in TV ads. *Los Angeles Times,* p. 6. **(AsA)**

Lee, R. A. (1997, January). The youth bias in advertising. *American Demographics,* pp. 46-50. **(MA)**

Lee, S. M. (1998). *Asian Americans: Diverse and growing* (Population Bulletin). Washington, DC: Population Reference Bureau, Inc. **(AsA)**

Lee, W. (1993). Acculturation and advertising communication strategies: A cross-cultural comparison of Chinese and Americans. *Psychology and Marketing, 10,* 381-397. **(AsA)**

Lee, W., & Callcott, M. F. (1992). *A comparative study of billboard advertising in Anglo and ethnic minority neighborhoods.* Paper presented at the American Academy of Advertising, San Antonio, TX. **(AfA)**

Lee, W.-N., La Ferle, C., & Tharp, M. (1998). *Culture of origin and the road to consumer acculturation: Rethinking our approach.* Unpublished manuscript.

Lee, W.-N., La Ferle, C., & Tharp, M. (1999a). *Ethnic influences on communication patterns: Word-of-mouth, traditional and non-traditional media usage.* Unpublished manuscript. **(AfA)**

Lee, W.-N., La Ferle, C., & Tharp, M. (1999b). *Ethnic marketing communication: A case of two cultures.* Unpublished manuscript. **(AsA)**

Lee, W.-N., Tharp, M., & La Ferle, C. (1999). Unpublished database.

Lee, W., & Tse, D. (1994, March). Changing media consumption in a new home: Acculturation patterns among Hong Kong immigrants to Canada. *Journal of Advertising, 23,* 57-70. **(AsA)**

Leigh, J. H., & Gabel, T. G. (1992). Symbolic interactionism: Its effects on consumer behavior and implications for marketing strategy. *Journal of Consumer Marketing, 9*(1), 27-38.

Leiss, W., Kline, S., & Jhally, S. (1986). *Social communication in advertising: Persons, products and images of well-being.* Toronto: Methuen.

Leland, J. (2000, May 8). Searching for a holy spirit. *Newsweek,* pp. 61-65.

Leland, J., & Samuels, A. (1997, March 17). The new generation gap. *Newsweek,* pp. 51-60. **(AfA)**

Leslie, C. (1995, February 13). The loving generation. *Newsweek,* p. 72.

Less myth, more research: Success in minority markets. (1984, May 25). *Marketing News, 17,* 32-33.

Lev, M. (1991, January 14). Asian-Americans' tastes are surveyed by marketers. *New York Times,* p. 11. **(AsA)**

Levine, D. S. (1995, July 21). Mainstream advertisers start to discover gay market. *San Francisco Business Times,* p. 5. **(GA)**

Levitt, T. (1983, May/June). The globalization of markets. *Harvard Business Review,* pp. 92-102.

Lewin, T. F. (1995, November 29). Smarter and socially sensitive. *New York Times,* p. A15.

Licata, W., & Biswas, A. (1993). Representation, roles, and occupational status of Black models in television advertisements. *Journalism Quarterly, 7,* 868-882. **(AfA)**

Lipman, J. (1991a, December 31). Ads aimed at older Americans may be too old for audience. *Wall Street Journal,* p. B4. **(MA)**

Lipman, J. (1991b, September 4). Celebrity pitchmen are popular again. *Wall Street Journal,* p. B5. **(AfA)**

Locke, D. C. (1992). *Increasing multicultural understanding: A comprehensive model.* Thousand Oaks, CA: Sage. **(AsA)**

Longman, D., & Pruden, H. O. (1972). Alienation from the marketplace: A study in black, brown, and white. *Journal of Marketing, 36,* 616-619. **(AfA, USL)**

Lonial, S. C., & Raju, P. S. (1993). The decision process and media-related interactions of the elderly: A synthesis of findings. *Review of Marketing,* pp. 277-312. **(MA)**

Louis, M. (1999, October 12). Help wanted: Gujarati speakers to sell insurance. *Wall Street Journal,* pp. B1-B16. **(AsA)**

Lowe, F. H. (1994, April 13). Cosmetics firms court blacks: Hot sales bring competition for fashion fair. *Chicago Sun-Times,* p. 65. **(AfA)**

Lucas, S. (1999, October 11). For us, forever. *Advertising Age,* pp. M94-M98. **(AfA)**

Lukenbill, G. (1995). *Untold millions: Positioning your business for the gay and lesbian consumer revolution.* New York: Harper Business. **(GA)**

Mabry, M. (1989, August 14). A long way from "Aunt Jemima." *Newsweek,* pp. 34-35. **(AfA)**

Mahoney, R. (1996, October 31). Arab Americans try to shake off "terrorist" image. *Reuters World Service.*

Majors, R. E. (1994). Discovering gay culture in America. In L. A. Samovar & R. E. Porter (Eds.), *Intercultural communication: A reader* (7th ed., pp. 165-172). Belmont, CA: Wadsworth. **(GA)**

Mandese, J. (1995, August 9). Directory helps map Asian-American media. *Advertising Age, 66,* p. 34. **(AsA)**

Marable, M. (1994). Reconciling race and reality. *Media Studies Journal, 8*(3), 11-18. **(AfA)**

Marin, G., & Marin, B. V. (1991). *Research with Hispanic populations.* Newbury Park, CA: Sage. **(USL)**

Marin, R. (1997-1998, December 29-January 5). Lick me, flog me, buy me! *Newsweek,* p. 85. **(GA)**

Market Segment Research, Inc. (1993). *The 1993 MSR minority market report.* Coral Gables, FL: Author.

Market Segment Research, Inc. (1994). *Minority market report and database.* Coral Gables, FL: Author.

Market Segment Research, Inc. (1996). *Minority market report and database.* Coral Gables, FL: Author.

*Market Share Reporter.* (1993). Detroit: Gale Research.

Marriott, M. (1995, July 31). Cybersoul not found. *Newsweek,* pp. 62-64. **(AfA)**

Martin, D., & Levine, M. (1991). Reaching consumers in the 1990's: The rise of micro-marketing. *Soap-Cosmetics-Chemical Specialties* [Information Access Company], *67*(5), 42.

Martindale, C. (1997). Only in glimpses: Portrayal of America's largest minority groups by the *New York Times.* In S. Biagi & M. Kern-Foxworth (Eds.), *Facing difference: Race, gender, and the mass media* (pp. 89-95). Thousand Oaks, CA: Pine Forge. **(AsA)**

Matathia, I., & Salzman, M. (1999). *Next: Trends for the near future.* New York: Overlook.

Mathews, J. (1992, June 1). From closet to mainstream. *Newsweek,* p. 62. **(GA)**

Matsuoka, J. K. (1990). Differential acculturation among Vietnamese refugees. *Social Work, 35,* 602-633. **(AsA)**

Mayer, A. J., Joyce, T., Simons, P. E., & Cook, W. J. (1977, February 28). The graying of America. *Newsweek,* pp. 50-52, 55-58, 63-64. **(MA)**

McAdoo, H. P. (1992). Upward mobility and parenting in middle-income black families. In A. K. H. Burlew, W. C. Banks, H. P. McAdoo, & D. A. ya Azibo (Eds.), *African American psychology: Theory, research, and practice* (pp. 63-86). Newbury Park, CA: Sage. **(AfA)**

McAdoo, H. P. (Ed.). (1993). *Family ethnicity: Strength in diversity.* Newbury Park, CA: Sage. **(AsA)**

McAllister, L. (1993, July). Ethnic customs influence how ethnic-Americans gift. *Gifts and Decorative Accessories,* pp. 52-53, 77-79.

McAllister, M. P. (1996). *The commercialization of American culture.* Thousand Oaks, CA: Sage.

McCarroll, T. (1993). It's a mass market no more. *Time, 142*(21), 80-81.

McCarthy, E. J. (1960). *Basic marketing: A managerial approach.* Homewood, IL: Richard D. Irwin.

McConahay, J. B. (1986). Modern racism, ambivalence, and the modern racism scale. In J. F. Dovidio & S. L. Gaertner (Eds.), *Prejudice, discrimination, and racism* (pp. 91-124). New York: Academic Press.

McConahay, J. B., Hardee, B., & Batts, V. (1981). Has racism declined in America? *Journal of Conflict Resolution, 25,* 563-579. **(AfA)**

McCracken, G. (1986, June). Culture and consumption: A theoretical account of the structure and movement of the cultural meaning of consumer goods. *Journal of Consumer Research, 13,* 71-83.

McGann, A., & Russell, J. T. (1988). *Advertising media* (2nd ed.). Homewood, IL: Richard D. Irwin.

McGinn, D. (1998, November 23). The new Ford. *Newsweek,* p. 56.

McGuire, W. J., McGuire, C. V., Child, P., & Fujioka, T. (1978). Salience of ethnicity in the spontaneous self-concept as a function of one's ethnic distinctiveness in the social environment. *Journal of Personality and Social Psychology, 36,* 511-520.

McLaughlin, R. (1999). African Americans. *Target Marketing, 22*(3), 100-101. **(AfA)**

McManus, J. (1998, December). Tapped in, tapped out. *American Demographics, 20,* 6.

McNeal, J. U. (1992). *Kids as customers: A handbook of marketing to children.* New York: Lexington.

McNeill, J. (1988). *Taking a chance on God: Liberating theology for gays, lesbians, and their lovers, families, and friends.* Boston: Beacon. **(GA)**

McShane, L. (1998, March 27). Fashion designer rebuts racism allegations on Net. *Philadelphia Inquirer,* p. D1. **(AfA)**

Meade, D. (1998, March-April). Celtic cowboys, poets and musicians. *Irish America,* pp. 85-88.

Media kit. (1996). *Advocate.* **(GA)**

Mehta, R., & Belk, R. W. (1991). Artifacts, identity, and transition: Favorite possessions of Indians and Indian immigrants to the United States. *Journal of Consumer Research, 17,* 398-411. **(AsA)**

Mehta, S. (1994a, August 23). Big companies heighten their pitch to minority firms. *Wall Street Journal,* p. B-2.

Mehta, S. N. (1994b, July 26). New magazines target U.S.-born ethnic minorities. *Wall Street Journal,* p. B-2. **(AsA)**

Melcher, R. (1997, May 19). United colors of Miller. *Business Week,* p. 96. **(USL, AfA, AsA)**

Meredith, G., & Schewe, C. (1994, December). The power of cohorts. *American Demographics, 16,* 22-27.

Mergenhagen, P. (1997, July). Enabling disabled workers. *American Demographics, 19,* 36-42.

Merrill, C. (1999, October). Keeping up with teens. *American Demographics, 21,* 27.

Meyer, M. (1994). *The politics and poetics of camp.* London: Routledge. **(GA)**

Meyer, T. P. (1990, March). Advertising to Hispanics: A research agenda for the next decade. In P. A. Stout (Ed.), *Proceedings of 1990 Conference of the American Academy of Advertising* (pp. 157-162). Austin: University of Texas, College of Communication. **(USL)**

Mick, D. G., & Buhl, C. (1992). A meaning-based model of advertising experiences. *Journal of Consumer Research, 19,* 317-338.

Miller, B. (1997, March). The quest for lifelong learning. *American Demographics, 19,* 20, 22. **(MA)**

Miller, C. (1993, December 6). Xers know they're a target market, and they hate that. *Marketing News, 27,* 15.

Miller, C. (1994, May 23). Cadillac promo targets African-Americans. *Marketing News,* p. 12. **(AfA)**

Milliones, J. (1980). Construction of a black consciousness measure: Psycho-therapeutic implications. *Psychotherapy: Theory, Research and Practice, 17,* 175-182. **(AfA)**

Min, P. G. (1995). *Asian Americans.* Thousand Oaks, CA: Sage. **(AsA)**

Mitchell, S. (1995, February). Birds of a feather. *American Demographics, 17,* 40-48.

Mitchell, S. (1996, August). Are Boomers their parents? *American Demographics, 18,* 40-45.

Mitchell, S. (1997). *Generation X: The young adult market.* Ithaca, NY: New Strategist.

Modood, T., & Werbner, P. (Eds.). (1997). *The politics of multiculturalism in the New Europe: Racism, identity and community.* London: Zed.

Mogelonsky, M. (1995a, August). Asian-Indian Americans. *American Demographics, 17,* 32-39. **(AsA)**

Mogelonsky, M. (1995b, October). First language comes first. *American Demographics, 17,* 21.

Mogelonsky, M. (1996a, September). Aficionados de cerveza. *American Demographics, 18,* 8. **(USL, AfA)**

Mogelonsky, M. (1996b, May). The rocky road to adulthood. *American Demographics, 18,* 26-35, 56.

Mogelonsky, M. (1997, March). Natural(ized) Americans. *American Demographics, 19,* 45-49.

Mogelonsky, M. (1998, December). Meet the inner city shopper. *American Demographics, 20,* 38. **(AfA)**

Montero, D. (1980). *Japanese Americans: Changing patterns of ethnic affiliation over three generations.* Boulder, CO: Westview. **(AsA)**

Moog, C. (1990). *Are they selling her lips? Advertising and identity.* New York: William Morrow.

Moore, D., Williams, J. D., & Qualls, W. J. (1996). Target marketing of tobacco and alcohol related products to ethnic minority groups in the U.S. *Ethnicity and Disease, 6*(1&2), 83-98. **(AfA)**

Morgan, C., & Levy, D. (1993). *Segmenting the mature market.* Chicago: Probus. **(MA)**

Morganthau, T. (1992, April 6). Losing ground. *Newsweek,* pp. 20-23. **(AfA)**

Morganthau, T. (1995, February 13). What color is black? *Newsweek,* pp. 62-65. **(AfA)**

Morrison, T., Conaway, W. H., & Border, G. A. (1995). *Kiss, bow or shake hands: How to do business in sixty countries.* New York: Adams Media. **(AsA)**

Morrow, H. (1988, August 29). Among Hispanics, phone surveys may be preferable to doing door-to-door interviews. *Marketing News,* pp. 23, 26. **(USL)**

Morse, D. (1999, February 19). Just sell it: Where gang members are shoe salesmen. *Wall Street Journal,* pp. A1, A6. **(AsA)**

Moschis, G. P. (1988, November 21). Survey: Age is not good indicator of consumer need. *Marketing News,* p. 6. **(MA)**

Moschis, G. P. (1992). *Marketing to older consumers.* Westport, CT: Quorum. **(MA)**

Moschis, G. (1994). *Marketing strategies for the mature market.* Westport, CT: Quorum. **(MA)**

Moschis, G. P. (1996, September). Life stages of the mature market. *American Demographics,* pp. 44-50. **(MA)**

Moyerman, D. R., & Forman, B. D. (1992). Acculturation and adjustment: A meta-analytic study. *Hispanic Journal of Behavioral Sciences, 14,* 163-200. **(USL)**

Mueller, B. (1996). *International advertising: Communicating across cultures.* Belmont, CA: Wadsworth. **(AsA)**

Mueller, M. L., & Schement, J. R. (1996). Universal service from the bottom up: A study of telephone penetration in Camden, New Jersey. *Information Society, 12,* 273-292. **(AfA)**

Muhammad, T. K. (1996, December). B.E. readers are cyber-ready. *Black Enterprise,* p. 39. **(AfA)**

Mulhern, F. J., Williams, J. D., & Leone, R. P. (1998). Variability of brand price elasticities across retail stores: Ethnicity, income and brand determinants. *Journal of Retailing, 74,* 427-446.

Mulryan/Nash. (1997). *1997 Gay press report.* New York: Author. **(GA)**

Mummert, H. (1995). Reaching ethnic markets. *Target Marketing News, 18*(11). **(AsA)**

Murphy, K. (1997, March 31). Barriers drop for the disabled. *Business Week,* p. 99.

Myers, S. L., & Chan, T. (1995). Racial discrimination in housing markets, accounting for credit risk. *Social Science Quarterly, 76,* 543-561. **(AfA)**

Myrdal, G. (1944). *An American dilemma: The Negro problem and modern democracy.* New York: Harper & Row. **(AfA)**

Nagourney, A. (1999, October 31). Tribalism: In politics, ethnic posturing isn't simple anymore. *New York Times,* p. WK4.

Nahm, H. Y. (1997). An AsiAm dream. *Transpacific,* p. 112. **(AsA)**

Narisetti, R. (1997, January 15). Too many choices: P&G, seeing shoppers were being confused, overhauls marketing. *Wall Street Journal,* pp. A1, A8.

Narisetti, R. (1998, November 11). New and improved: Pieces of the puzzle—Ad experts talk about how their business will be transformed by technology. *Wall Street Journal,* p. S4.

Natale, R. (1997). The Latin factor: Hollywood plugs into a burgeoning and profitable ethnic market. In S. Biagi & M. Kern-Foxworth (Eds.), *Facing difference: Race, gender, and mass media* (pp. 216-218). Thousand Oaks, CA: Pine Forge. **(USL)**

National Register Publishing Company. (2000). *Standard directory of advertising agencies.* Skokie, IL: Author.

Nelson, C., & Tienda, M. (1997). The structuring of Hispanic ethnicity: Historical and contemporary perspectives. In M. Romero, P. Hondagneu-Sotelo, & V. Ortiz (Eds.), *Challenging fronteras* (pp. 7-29). New York: Routledge. **(USL)**

Nelson, J. (1994). *The disabled, the media and the information age.* Westport, CN: Greenwood.

Ness, T. E., & Stith, M. T. (1984). Middle-class values in blacks and whites. In R. E. Pitts & A. G. Woodside (Eds.), *Personal values and consumer psychology* (pp. 231-237). Lexington, MA: Lexington. **(AfA)**

New survey reveals 5 lifestyle segments of ages 18-49 black women. (1984, August 21). *Marketing News, 17,* 6. **(AfA)**

Nielsen Media Research. (2000, March). *Audited circulation.* New York: A. C. Nielsen Co.

1980 Media expenditures. (1981, January 5). *Advertising Age,* pp. 10-56.

Nobles, W. W. (1980). Extended self: Rethinking the so-called Negro self-concept. In R. L. Jones (Ed.), *Black psychology* (2nd ed.). New York: Harper & Row. **(AfA)**

Nordholm, M. (1998, December). The future of Spanish-language radio. *Hispanic Business,* p. 62. **(USL)**

Novak, D. L., & Hoffman, T. P. (1998, April 17). Bridging the racial divide on the Internet. *Science, 280,* 390. **(AfA)**

Nuiry, O. E. (1996, July). Ban the bandito! *Hispanic,* pp. 26-32. **(USL)**

O'Barr, W. M. (1994). *Culture and the ad: Exploring otherness in the world of advertising.* Boulder, CO: Westview. **(AfA)**

Oberg, K. (1960). Culture shock: Adjustment to new cultural environments. *Practical Anthropology, 7,* 177-182. **(AsA)**

O'Brien, D. J., & Fugita, S. S. (1991). *The Japanese American experience.* Bloomington: Indiana University Press. **(AsA)**

Ocamb, K. (1998, March 31). Someone's in the desert with Dinah. *Advocate,* p. 39-40. **(GA)**

O'Connor, R. F. (1986). *Texas myths.* Austin: Texas Commission for the Humanities.

O'Donnell, J. (1994, April 17). Cadillac targeting new groups: Division making pitches to female and black buyers. *Plain Dealer,* p. 1F. **(AfA)**

O'Guinn, T. C., Faber, R. J., & Imperia, G. (1986). Subcultural influences on family decision making. *Psychology and Marketing, 3,* 305-317. **(USL)**

O'Hare, W. P. (1992a). In the black in the '90's. *Beyond the Rating Magazine.* **(AfA)**

O'Hare, W. (1992b, January). Reaching for the dream. *American Demographics, 14,* 25. **(AsA)**

O'Hare, W. (1998, April). Managing multiple-race data. *American Demographics, 20,* 42-47.

O'Hare, W., & Felt, C. (1991). *Asian Americans: America's fastest growing minority group.* Washington, DC: Population Reference Bureau. **(AsA)**

O'Hare, W. P., & Frey, W. H. (1992, September). Booming, suburban, and black. *American Demographics, 14,* 30-38. **(AfA)**

O'Hare, W. P., Frey, W. H., & Fost, D. (1994, May). Asians in the suburbs. *American Demographics, 16,* 33-38. **(AsA)**

Okazawa-Rey, M., & Wong, M. (1997). Organizing in communities of color: Addressing interethnic conflicts. *Social Justice, 24*(1), 24. **(AfA, AsA)**

Oliver, J. A. (1992, April). To reach minorities, try busting myths. *American Demographics,* pp. 14-15.

The 100 largest U.S. multinationals. (1980, July 7). *Forbes,* p. 102.

The 100 largest U.S. multinationals. (1990, July 23). *Forbes,* p. 362.

The 100 largest U.S. multinationals. (1995, July 17). *Forbes,* p. 274.

Ono, Y. (1994, September 16). Marketing and media: Aunt Jemima brand hires Gladys Knight. *Wall Street Journal,* p. B3. **(AfA)**

Ostruff, J. (1989). *Successful marketing to the 50+ consumer.* Englewood Cliffs, NJ: Prentice Hall. **(MA)**

Oswald, L. R. (1999, March). Culture swapping: Consumption and the ethnogenesis of middle-class Haitian immigrants. *Journal of Consumer Research, 25,* 303-318. **(AfA)**

Outdoor cigarette and alcohol advertising is targeted toward the minority populations. (1991, May-June). *National Medical Association News,* pp. 1-2. **(AfA)**

PA files complaint against Avis. (1997, October 20). *Philadelphia Inquirer,* p. R4. **(AfA)**

Padilla, B. (1999, April). Projective techniques: Do they work in the Hispanic market? *Quirk's Marketing Research Review,* pp. 30-34. **(USL)**

Padilla, F. (Ed.). (1994). *Handbook of Hispanic cultures in the United States: Sociology.* Houston, TX: Arte Publico. **(USL)**

Painton, P. (1993, April 26). The shrinking ten percent. *Time,* pp. 27-29. **(GA)**

Palomo, J. R. (1996, February 18). Seeds of African culture sown in life, literature, language. *Austin American Statesman,* p. A1. **(AfA)**

Park, I. H., & Cho, L.-J. (1995). Confucianism and the Korean family. *Journal of Comparative Family Studies, 26*(1), 117-135. **(AsA)**

Parker-Pope, T. (1996, July 16). British Budweiser ads rankle. *Wall Street Journal,* pp. B-1, B-5.

Paskowski, M. (1986, October). Trailblazing in Asian America. *Marketing and Media Decisions,* pp. 74-80. **(AsA)**

Patterson, G. A. (1995, May 31). Target "micromarkets" its way to success; No 2 stores are alike. *Wall Street Journal,* pp. A1-A9.

Paulin, G. D. (1998, March). A growing market: Expenditures by Hispanic consumers. *Monthly Labor Review,* pp. 3-20. **(USL)**

Penaloza, L. (1994, June). Atravesando fronteras/border crossings: A critical ethnographic exploration of the consumer acculturation of Mexican immigrants. *Journal of Consumer Research, 21,* 32-54. **(USL)**

Penaloza, L. (1996). We're here, we're queer, and we're going shopping! A critical perspective on the accommodation of gays and lesbians in the U.S. marketplace. In D. L. Wardlow (Ed.), *Gays, lesbians, and consumer behavior: Theory, practice, and research issues in marketing* (pp. 9-41). New York: Harrington Park. **(GA)**

Penaloza, L. N., & Gilly, M. C. (1986, Winter). The Hispanic family: Consumer research issues. *Psychology and Marketing, 3,* 291-303. **(USL)**

Penaloza, L., & Gilly, M. C. (1999, July). Marketer acculturation: The changer and the changed. *Journal of Marketing, 63,* 84-106. **(USL, AfA)**

Peplau, L., Cochran, S., & Mays, V. (1997). A national survey of the intimate relationships of African American lesbians and gay men. In B. Greene (Ed.), *Ethnic and cultural diversity among lesbians and gay men* (pp. 11-38). Thousand Oaks, CA: Sage. **(GA)**

Peppers, D., & Rogers, M. (1993). *The one to one future.* New York: Doubleday.

Pepsi marketers faced rebuffs in the field and in home office. (1997, September 5). *Wall Street Journal,* p. B1. **(AfA)**

Petersen, A. (1999, December 6). Logging in: Lost in the maze. *Wall Street Journal,* p. R6. **(MA)**

Petersen, A., & Rose, M. (2000, January 14). Database of a merged AOL brings cheers and chills. *Wall Street Journal,* p. B6.

Petrecca, L., & Arndorfer, J. B. (1998, March 2). Insurer places gay-themed ads in mainstream media. *Advertising Age,* p. 12. **(GA)**

Petrof, J. V. (1963, Fall). The effect of student boycotts upon the purchasing habits of Negro families in Atlanta, Georgia. *Phylon,* pp. 266-270. **(AfA)**

Petrof, J. V. (1967, Fall). Consumer strategy for Negro retailers. *Journal of Retailing, 43,* 30-38. **(AfA)**

Petrozzello, D. (1996, November 18). Hispanic radio formats going strong. *Broadcasting and Cable, 126,* 60-62. **(USL)**

Petzinger, T. (2000, January 1). So long, supply and demand. *Wall Street Journal,* p. R31.

Phillips, M. M. (1996, August 13). Selling by evoking what defines a generation. *Wall Street Journal,* pp. B1, B7. **(MA)**

Piirto, R. (1991a). *Beyond mind games: The marketing power of psychographics.* Ithaca, NY: American Demographics Books. **(USL)**

Piirto, R. (1991b, December). Geodemographics: You are where you live. *American Demographics, 13,* 52-57.

Pine, B. J., Peppers, D., & Rogers, M. (1995, March-April). Do you want to keep your customers forever? *Harvard Business Review,* p. 103.

Pinkney, A. (1969). *Black Americans.* Englewood Cliffs, NJ: Prentice Hall. **(AfA)**

Pitts, L. (1998, February 13). Motown still has a lesson for African-Americans. *Fort Worth Star-Telegram*, p. 9. **(AfA)**

Plotch, B. (1992). *New York walks*. New York: Henry Holt.

Poniewozik, J. (1999, October 25). TV's coming-out. *Time*, pp. 116-117. **(GA)**

Portes, A., & MacLeod, D. (1996, July). What shall I call myself? Hispanic identity formation in the second generation. *Ethnic and Racial Studies, 19*, 523-548. **(USL)**

Positive images may help elderly. (1999, November 2). *Dallas Morning News*, p. 3A. **(MA)**

Potgieter, C. (1997). From apartheid to Mandela's constitution. In B. Greene (Ed.), *Ethnic and cultural diversity among lesbians and gay men* (pp. 88-116). Thousand Oaks, CA: Sage. **(GA)**

Power, C. (1991, September 9). Getting 'em while they're young. *Business Week*, pp. 94-95.

Power, C. (1993, Annual Special Issue). How to get closer to your customers. *Business Week/Enterprise*, pp. 42-45.

Practicing politics: Where is your political locus? (1999, June-July). *A Magazine*, p. 10. **(AsA)**

Pruden, H. O., & Longman, D. S. (1972, July). Race, alienation, and consumerism. *Journal of Marketing, 36*, pp. 58-63. **(USL)**

Putnam, R. D. (1995, December). Tuning in, tuning out: The strange disappearance of social capital in America. *Political Science and Politics, 28*, 664-683.

Quandary over one term to cover myriad people. (1994, November 8). *Wall Street Journal*, p. B-1. **(USL)**

Ragaza, A. (1999, February 8). I don't count as "diversity." *Newsweek*, p. 13. **(AsA)**

Ramirez, M. (1984). Assessing and understanding biculturalism-multiculturalism in Mexican-American adults. In J. L. Martinez & R. H. Mendoza (Eds.), *Chicano psychology* (2nd ed., pp. 77-94). Orlando, FL: Academic Press. **(USL, AfA)**

Ramirez, M., & Castaneda, A. (1974). *Cultural democracy, bicognitive development and education*. New York: Academic Press. **(USL, AfA)**

Randazzo, S. (1995). *The myth-makers*. Chicago: Probus.

Rapp, S., & Collins, T. (1988). *Maxi-marketing: The new direction in advertising, promotion, and marketing strategy*. New York: McGraw-Hill.

Ray, P. H. (1997, February). The emerging culture. *American Demographics, 19*, 28-32.

Reed, J. S. (1993). *My tears spoiled my aim and other reflections on Southern culture*. Orlando, FL: Harcourt Brace.

Reed, V. M. (1991, Winter-Spring). Civil rights legislation and the housing status of black Americans: Evidence from fair housing audits and segregation indices. *Review of Black Political Economy*, pp. 29-42. **(AfA)**

Reedy, J. (1995). *Marketing to consumers with disabilities*. Chicago: Probus.

Reese, S. (1997, March). When whites aren't a mass market. *American Demographics, 19*, 51-54.

Reflections in black: The African-American greeting card market. (1994). *Greetings Magazine, 8*(5), 17. **(AfA)**

Reid, I. S., Stagmaier, J., & Reid, C. C. (1986). Research design used to describe and explain black consumer behavior. In R. E. Pitts (Ed.), *Cultural and subcultural influences.* Chicago: American Marketing Association. **(AfA)**

Reilly, P. (1996, January 2). Spate of magazines bet on black readers. *Wall Street Journal,* p. B-6. **(AfA)**

Reitman, V. (1992, June 15). Black newspaper group threatens a boycott of P&G. *Wall Street Journal,* p. B1. **(AfA)**

Ressner, J. (1998, June 29). They've gotta have it. *Time,* p. 69.

Retailers target ethnic consumers. (1991, September 30). *Advertising Age,* p. 50. **(AfA)**

Reyes, S. (1994, August 4). Ethnic stereotypes have formidable staying power. *Corpus Christi Caller-Times,* p. A11. **(USL)**

Ribeau, S. A., Baldwin, J. R., & Hecht, M. L. (1994). An African-American communication perspective. In L. A. Samovar & R. E. Porter (Eds.), *Intercultural communication: A reader* (pp. 140-147). Belmont, CA: Wadsworth. **(AfA)**

The rise of radio in the Asian-American market. (1995, August 28). *Brandweek, 36,* 2. **(AsA)**

Ritchie, K. (1995). *Marketing to generation X.* New York: Lexington.

Ritson, M., & Elliott, R. (1999). The social uses of advertising: An ethnographic study of adolescent advertising audiences. *Journal of Consumer Research, 26,* 260-277.

Rittenberg, T., & Parthasarathy, M. (1997, Fall). Ethical implications of target market selection. *Journal of Macromarketing, 17,* 49-64.

Rivera, E. (1997). Prototypes of the Asian century. *Transpacific,* 40-109. **(AsA)**

Roberts, J. L. (1999, January 4). Fraying nets. *Newsweek,* p. 66.

Robertson, T. S., Zielinski, J., & Ward, S. (1984). *Consumer behavior.* Glenview, IL: Scott, Foresman. **(AfA)**

Robinson, P. A., & Rao, C. P. (1986). A critical review and reassessment of black consumer behavioral research. In *Proceedings: Southwestern Marketing Association Conference* (pp. 9-13). **(AfA)**

A robust economy bolsters purchasing power. (1998, December). *Hispanic Business,* p. 60. **(USL)**

Rodriguez, G. (1997, May 4). The rising language of Latino media: English. *Los Angeles Times,* p. M1. **(USL)**

Rodriguez, V. (1990, January 16). Charting Latino listeners. *Dallas Morning News,* pp. 5C-6C. **(USL)**

Rokeach, M. (1973). *The nature of human values.* New York: Free Press.

Rolle, A. (1980). *The Italian Americans.* London: Free Press.

Romney, L. (1999, June 22). A Latino Internet revolution. *Los Angeles Times,* pp. A1, A25. **(USL)**

Rook, D. (1985). The ritual dimension of consumer behavior. *Journal of Consumer Research, 12,* 251-264.

Rosenbaum, S. (1991, July). Rehab products aimed at elderly and disabled. *Health Industry Today,* p. 8. **(MA)**

Rosenthal, E. M. (1979, June 4). Emerging local TV sales changing market's shape. *Television/Radio Age, 26,* 37-39, 82.

Roslow, P., & Nicholls, J. A. F. (1996, May-June). Targeting the Hispanic market: Comparative persuasion of TV commercials in Spanish and English. *Journal of Advertising Research, 36*(3), 67-77. **(USL)**

Rossman, M. L. (1994). *Multicultural marketing: Selling to a diverse America.* New York: American Marketing Association.

Rudd, N. A. (1996). Appearance and self-presentation research in gay consumer cultures: Issues and impact. In D. L. Wardlow (Ed.), *Gays, lesbians, and consumer behavior: Theory, practice, and research issues in marketing.* New York: Harrington Park. **(GA)**

Rueschenberg, E. J., & Buriel, R. (1995). Mexican American family functioning and acculturation. In A. M. Padilla (Ed.), *Hispanic psychology* (pp. 15-25). Thousand Oaks, CA: Sage. **(USL)**

Russell, C. (1995, December). The Baby Boom turns 50. *American Demographics, 17,* 22-33.

Russell, C. (1997, July). The ungraying of America. *American Demographics, 19,* 12-15. **(MA)**

Russell, J. (1999, December). Tuning in to the stock market. *Hispanic Business,* pp. 52, 54. **(USL)**

Ryan, N. (1991, June 9). Marketing to black consumers: Brand companies going after piece of $250 billion pie. *Chicago Tribune,* p. 6. **(AfA)**

Saegert, J., & Deiter, D. P. (1980). *Response rates to mail questionnaires in an ethnic minority population.* Unpublished working paper, Center for Studies in Business, Economics, and Human Resources, University of Texas at San Antonio. **(USL)**

Saegert, J., Hoover, R. J., & Tharp Hilger, M. (1985). Characteristics of Mexican American consumers. *Journal of Consumer Research, 12*(1), 104-109. **(USL)**

Sakamoto, A., & Furuichi, S. (1997). Wages among white and Japanese-American male workers. *Research in Stratification and Mobility, 15,* 177-206. **(AsA)**

Salholz, E., & Glick, D. (1993, June 21). The power and the pride. *Newsweek,* pp. 54-60. **(GA)**

Salins, P. (1988). *New York unbound.* New York: Basil Blackwell.

Samovar, L. A., & Porter, R. E. (1991). *Communication between cultures.* Belmont, CA: Wadsworth. **(USL)**

Sampson, W. A., & Milam, V. (1975, December). The intraracial attitudes of the black middle class: Have they changed? *Social Problems.* **(AfA)**

San Francisco tells pizza shops to hold the excuses. (1996, July 14). *New York Times,* p. A22. **(AfA)**

Sandberg, J., & Weber, T. E. (1997, April 8). WebTV finds a following among net-surfing seniors. *Wall Street Journal,* pp. B1, B4. **(MA)**

Sanders, A. L. (1999, November 29). Unmarried with children. *Time,* p. 114.

Sanders, J. M., & Nee, V. (1996). Immigrant self-employment: The family as social capital and the value of human capital. *American Sociological Review, 61,* 231-249. **(AsA)**

Sandor, G. (1994a, November). Hearing a new market. *American Demographics, 16,* 48-55.

Sandor. G. (1994b, June). The "Other" Americans. *American Demographics, 16,* 36-44.

Saporito, B. (1999, November 15). Wrestling with your conscience. *Time,* pp. 71-74.

Sasao, T., & Sue, S. (1993). Toward a culturally anchored ecological framework of research in ethnic-cultural communities. *American Journal of Community Psychology, 21,* 705-726. **(AfA)**

Saveri, G. (1995, May 29). The importance of being solvent. *Business Week,* p. 38. **(GA)**

Scenic America. (1989). *Billboards in Baltimore: A blight on beauty and a scourge on health in our city.* Washington, DC: American Medical Association. **(AfA)**

Schement, J. R. (1997, October). *Thorough Americans: Minorities and the new media.* Paper presented at the Aspen Institute Conference, Aspen, CO. **(AfA)**

Schewe, C. D. (1990, June). Get in position for the older market. *American Demographics, 12,* 38-41, 61, 63. **(MA)**

Schiller, Z. (1989, August 28). Stalking the new consumer. *Business Week,* pp. 54-58, 62.

Schlesinger, A. M. (1992). *The disuniting of America: Reflections on a multicultural society.* New York: W. W. Norton.

Schlinger, M. J., & Plummer, J. (1972, May). Advertising in black and white. *Journal of Marketing Research, 9,* 149-153. **(AfA)**

Schmid, J. (1995), Ethnic niche catalogs. *Target Marketing, 18*(11), 18. **(AsA)**

Schmitt, B. H., & Zhang, S. (1998, September). Language structure and categorization: A study of classifiers in consumer cognition, judgment, and choice. *Journal of Consumer Research, 25,* 108-120. **(AsA)**

Schonfeld, E. (1998, September 28). The customized, digitized, have-it-your-way economy. *Fortune,* pp. 115-124.

Schooler, C., & Basil, M. D. (1989, May). *Alcohol and cigarette advertising on billboards: Targeting with social cues.* Paper presented at the annual meeting of the International Communication Association, Dublin, Ireland. **(AfA)**

Schouten, J. (1991). Selves in transition: Symbolic consumption in personal rites of passage and identity construction. *Journal of Consumer Research, 17,* 412-425.

Schultz, D. E., & Barnes, B. E. (1995). *Strategic advertising campaigns.* Lincolnwood, IL: NTC Business.

Schultz, D. E., Tannenbaum, S. I., & Lauterborn, R. E. (1994). *Integrated marketing communications: Pulling it together and making it work.* Lincolnwood, IL: NTC Business.

Schwartz, J. (1989, June). Longnecks and longhorns. *American Demographics, 11,* 46.

Schwarz, B. (1995, May). The diversity myth: America's leading export. *Atlantic Monthly,* pp. 57-58, 60-62, 64-67.

Scott, B. M., Denniston, R. W., & Magruder, K. M. (1992). Alcohol advertising in the African American community. *Journal of Drug Issues, 22,* 455-469. **(AfA)**

Sears, T. J. (1990). *Growing up gay in the South.* New York: Haworth. **(GA)**

Seelye, H. N., & Seelye-James, A. (1996). *Culture clash: Managing in a multicultural world.* Lincolnwood, IL: NTC Publishing Group.

Sharpe, R. (1997, September 9). Asian-Americans gain sharply in big program of affirmative action. *Wall Street Journal,* pp. A-1, A-8. **(AsA)**

Shaw, J. (1999, November 8). Manischewitz leavens its image. *Fortune,* p. 48.

Shaw-Taylor, Y., & Benokraitis, N. V. (1995). The presentation of minorities in marriage and family textbooks. *Teaching Sociology, 23*(2), 22-135. **(AsA)**

Shepard, S. (1997, August 3). The race issue: More than a "black and white thing"? *Austin American-Statesman*, pp. J1, J6. (**AfA**)

Shergill, S. (1993). The changing U.S. media and marketing environment: Implications for media advertising expenditures in the 1990s. *International Journal of Advertising, 12,* 95-115.

Shermach, K. (1994, January 17). Yellow pages publishers find niches among ethnic groups. *Marketing News,* p. 5. (**AsA**)

Sherry, J. F., Jr. (1993). Cultural propriety in a global marketplace. In A. F. Firat, N. Dholakia, & R. P. Bagozzi (Eds.), *Philosophical and radical thought in marketing* (pp. 179-191). Lexington, MA: D. C. Heath.

Shim, J. C. (1997). The importance of ethnic newspapers to U.S. newcomers. In S. Biagi & M. Kern-Foxworth (Eds.), *Facing difference: Race, gender, and the mass media* (pp. 250-255). Thousand Oaks, CA: Pine Forge. (**AsA**)

Shimp, T. A., & Sharma, S. (1987). Consumer ethnocentrism: Construction and validation of the CETSCALE. *Journal of Marketing Research, 24,* 280-289. (**AfA**)

Shinagawa, L. H., & Pang, G. Y. (1996). Asian American panethnicity and intermarriage. *Amerasia Journal, 22*(2), 127-152. (**AsA**)

Shopping for a cause. (1999, December). *Fast Company,* p. 446.

Shorris, E. (1992). *Latinos: A biography of the people.* New York: W. W. Norton. (**USL**)

Sigelman, L., & Welch, S. (1984). Race, gender and opinion toward black and female presidential candidates. *Public Opinion Quarterly, 48,* 467-475. (**AfA**)

Simons, J. (1998, Dec. 10). Even amid boom times, some insecurities die hard. *Wall Street Journal,* p. A-10. (**AfA**)

Simpson, J. C. (1991, December 23). Tidings of black pride and joy. *Time,* p. 81. (**AfA**)

Sing a song of selling. (1999, May 24). *Business Week,* pp. 66-68. (**MA**)

Singer, D. (1995). *American Jewish year book.* New York: American Jewish Committee.

Sirgy, M. J. (1982). Self concept in consumer behavior: A critical review. *Journal of Consumer Research, 9,* 287-300.

Sissors, J. Z., & Summarek, J. (1987). *Media planning* (2nd ed.). Lincolnwood, IL: NTC Business Books.

Skriloff, L. (1997, February 17). Out of the box: A diverse Netizenry. *Brandweek,* pp. 17-18. (**AfA**)

Smith, J. (1990, August 3). Hate crime rising, says report. *Philadelphia Tribune,* p. 1B. (**AfA**)

Smith, J. W., & Clurman, A. (1997). *Rocking the ages: The Yankelovich report on generational marketing.* New York: HarperBusiness.

Smith, K. L. (1998). *How advertisers use the World Wide Web to reach niche markets.* Unpublished master's thesis, University of Texas at Austin. (**GA**)

Smith, L. E., & Millham, J. (1979). Sex role stereotypes among dyads: An assessment of intimacy, gender, and race. *Journal of Black Psychology, 6,* 1-6. (**AfA**)

Smith, T. W., & Dempsey, G. N. (1983). The polls: Ethnic social distance and prejudice. *Public Opinion Quarterly, 47,* 584-600. (**AfA**)

Smitherman, G. (1984). Black language as power. In C. Kramarae, M. Schulz, & W. M. O'Barr (Eds.), *Language and power* (pp. 101-115). Beverly Hills, CA: Sage. (**AfA**)

Smolowe, J. (1995, July 31). Noble aims, mixed results. *Time,* pp. 54-55.

Snider, J. H. (1992, November-December). Shopping in the information age. *Futurist,* pp. 14-18.

Snyder, R., Freeman, J. E., & Condray, S. E. (1991). Magazine ad portrayal of blacks: Gender and readership effects. In M. Lynn & J. Jackson (Eds.), *Proceedings of the Society for Consumer Psychology* (pp. 81-87). Washington, DC: American Psychological Association. **(AfA)**

Solomon, C., & Johnson, R. (1995, August 30). Hispanic buying power lures Texas marketers. *Wall Street Journal: Texas Journal,* p. T-1. **(USL)**

Solomon, J. (1988). *The signs of our times.* Los Angeles: Jeremy P. Tarcher.

Solomon, M. R. (1988). Building up and breaking down: The impact of cultural sorting on symbolic consumption. *Research in Consumer Behavior, 3,* 325-351.

Solomon, M. (1996). *Consumer behavior: Buying, having, and being* (3rd ed.). Englewood Cliffs, NJ: Prentice Hall.

Solzhenitsyn, A. I. (1974). *The Gulag archipelago, 1918-1956: An experiment in literary investigation.* New York: Harper & Row.

Sorrell, M. (1999, September). Whatever happened to globalization? *Fast Company,* pp. 231-236.

Soruco, G. R. (1990a, April). *Hispanic consumer behavior and the development of advertising copy: The advantages of qualitative research techniques.* Paper presented at the annual meeting of the American Academy of Advertising, Orlando, FL. **(USL)**

Soruco, G. R. (1990b). *Sampling and non-sampling errors in Hispanic population telephone surveys.* Unpublished manuscript. **(USL)**

Sowell, T. (1981). *Ethnic America.* New York: Basic Books.

Spanning the world. (1999, July 26). *Forbes,* pp. 202-204.

Spiegler, M. (1998, July). The Cocktail Nation. *American Demographics, 20,* 40.

Spigner, C. (1994). Race, gender, and the status quo: Asian and African American relations in a Hollywood film. *Explorations in Ethnic Studies, 17*(1), 89-101. **(AsA)**

Standard Rate and Data Service. (1999). *Hispanic Media and Market Source* (Vol. 11, No. 1). Wilmette, IL: Author. **(USL)**

Stankevich, D. (1998, July). Marketing to Hispanics. *Discount Merchandiser, 38,* 35-45. **(USL)**

Stapinski, H. (1999a, July). Generacion Latino. *American Demographics, 21.* www.demographics.com **(USL)**

Stapinski, H. (1999b, February). Y not love? *American Demographics, 21,* 62-68.

Stayman, D. M., & Deshpande, R. (1989). Situational ethnicity and consumer behavior. *Journal of Consumer Research, 16,* 361-371. **(USL, AsA)**

Stearns, J. M., Unger, L. S., & Luebkeman, S. G. (1987). The portrayal of blacks in magazine and television advertising. In S. P. Douglas & M. R. Solomon (Eds.), *AMA Educators' Proceedings.* Chicago: American Marketing Association. **(AfA)**

Stein, H. (1996, December 24). The American dream. *Wall Street Journal,* p. A8.

Steinhauer, J. (1997, July 2). A minority market with major sales. *New York Times,* pp. C1, C3. **(USL)**

Sterngold, J. (1998, December 29). A racial divide widens on network TV. *New York Times,* p. 1. **(AfA)**

Stevens, N. (1982). The effectiveness of time-compressed television advertisements with older adults. *Journal of Advertising, 11*(4), 48-55. (**MA**)

Stewart, D. W., & Rice, R. (1995). Integrated marketing: New technologies, non-traditional media, and non-media promotion in the marketing of alcoholic beverages. In S. E. Martin (Ed.), *The effects of the mass media on the use and abuse of alcohol* (Research Monograph). Washington, DC: National Institute of Alcohol Abuse and Alcoholism. (**AfA**)

Stewart, E. C., & Bennett, M. J. (1991). *American cultural patterns: A cross-cultural perspective* (Rev. ed.). Yarmouth, ME: Intercultural Press.

Stewart, T. A. (1991, December 16). Gay in corporate America: What's it like and how business attitudes are changing. *Fortune,* pp. 42-46, 50, 54, 56. (**GA**)

Stipp, D. (1999, July 19). Hell no, we won't go! Surprising demographic trends raise a tough question: Will the elderly live so long that society can't cope? *Fortune,* pp. 102-108. (**MA**)

Stith, M. T. (1984). Middle-class values in Blacks and Whites. In R. E. Pitts & A. G. Woodside (Eds.), *Personal values and consumer psychology,* (pp. 231-237). Lexington, MA: Lexington Books.

Stone, B. (2000, January 10). Cyber-Santa's sleigh ride. *Newsweek,* p. 40.

Strauss, W., & Howe, N. (1991). *Generations: The history of America's future, 1584-2069.* New York: William Morrow.

Stuart, E. (1992, March 2). Coca-Cola hires GSD&M. *New York Times,* p. C10.

Sturdivant, F. D. (1969). Business and the Mexican-American community. *California Management Review, 11,* 73-80. (**USL**)

Subervi, F. (1994, July). *La chispa.* Paper presented at the University of Texas, College of Communication Workshop for Tichenor Media, Inc. Managers, Austin, TX. (**USL**)

Subervi-Velez, F. (1986, January). The mass media and ethnic assimilation and pluralism: A review and research proposal with special focus on Hispanics. *Communication Research, 13,* 71-96. (**USL**)

Sumner, G. A. (1906). *Folkways.* New York: Ginn. (**AfA**)

Survey measures blacks' media, product ad preferences. (1981, August 21). *Marketing News,* p. 6. (**AfA**)

Sutter, S. (1991, December 16). Holly calls on the handicapped: May be a first. *Marketing,* p. 3.

Swayne, L. E., & Greco, A. J. (1987). The portrayal of older Americans in television commercials. *Journal of Advertising, 16*(1), 47-54. (**MA**)

Swenson, C. A. (1996). *Selling to a segmented market: The lifestyle approach.* Lincolnwood, IL: NTC Business Books.

Szybillo, G. J., & Jacoby, J. (1974). Effects of different levels of integration on advertising preference and intention to purchse. *Journal of Applied Psychology, 59,* 274-280. (**AfA**)

Taeuber, C. (1993). *Sixty-five plus in America.* Washington, DC: U.S. Bureau of the Census. (**MA**)

Tajfel, H. (1981). *Human categories and social groups.* Cambridge, UK: Cambridge University Press. (**AfA**)

Tajfel, H. (Ed.). (1982). *Social identity and intergroup relations.* Cambridge, UK: Cambridge University Press. **(AfA)**

Takahashi, D. (1998, March 18). Ethnic networks help immigrants rise in Silicon Valley. *Wall Street Journal,* pp. B1-B6. **(AsA)**

Takaki, R. (1993). *A different mirror: A history of multicultural America.* Boston: Back Bay. **(AfA, AsA, USL)**

Tan, A. (1989). *The Joy Luck Club.* New York: G. P. Putnam.

Tannen, D. (1990). *You just don't understand: Women and men in conversation.* New York: Ballantine.

Tannenbaum, J. A. (2000, January 31). Marketers on campus: A new bag of tricks. *Wall Street Journal,* pp. B1, B8.

Taylor, C. R., & Lee, J. Y. (1994). Not in Vogue: Portrayals of Asian Americans in magazine advertising. *Journal of Public Policy and Marketing, 13,* 239-245. **(AsA)**

Taylor, C. R., Lee, J. Y, & Stern, B. B. (1995). Portrayals of African, Hispanic, and Asian Americans in magazine advertising. *American Behavioral Scientist, 38,* 608-621. **(AfA, USL, AsA)**

Taylor, C. R., & Stern, B. B. (1997). Asian Americans: Television advertising and the "model minority" stereotype. *Journal of Advertising, 26*(2), 47-61. **(AsA)**

Taylor, D. G., Sheatsley, P. B., & Greeley, A. M. (1978). Attitudes toward racial integration. *Scientific American, 238,* 42-49. **(AfA)**

Taylor, E. G. (1999). *A cross-media study of audience choice: The influence of traits, needs, and attitudes on individual selection of "media repertoires."* Unpublished doctoral dissertation, University of Texas at Austin. **(AsA)**

Teinowitz, I. (1998, November 16). Multicultural marketing. *Advertising Age,* pp. S1-S23. **(AfA)**

Tejada, C. (1996, November 27). HFS orders its Avis unit to end pact with franchisee accused of racial bias. *Wall Street Journal,* p. B1. **(AfA)**

Tejada, C. (1999, October 5). With new deal, a radio giant grows larger. *Wall Street Journal,* p. B1.

Television Digest. (1982). *Cable and station coverage atlas.* New York: A. C. Nielsen.

Tepper, K. (1994). The role of labeling processes in elderly consumers' responses to age segmentation cues. *Journal of Consumer Research, 20,* 503-519. **(MA)**

Terpstra, V., & Sarathy, R. (1997). *International marketing* (7th ed.). Ft. Worth, TX: Dryden.

Tharp, M., & Scott, L. M. (1990, Fall). The role of marketing processes in creating cultural meaning. *Journal of Macromarketing, 10,* 67-80.

Tharp, M., & Villarreal de Silva, R. (1998, May). *Questioning the construct of U.S. Hispanic ethnic identity.* Paper presented at the 1998 International Trade and Finance Assocation Meetings, Atlantic City, NJ. **(USL)**

Tharp, M., & Villarreal de Silva, R. (1999, May). *Psychographic, universal and culture-specific values: Implications for marketing to Hispanics.* Paper presented at the 1999 International Trade and Finance Association Meetings, Casablanca, Morocco. **(USL)**

Thau, R. (1994, June). The new Jewish exodus. *American Demographics, 16,* 10-11.

Thernstrom, A., & Thernstrom, S. (1997). *America in black and white: One nation, indivisible.* New York: Simon & Schuster. **(AfA)**

Thomas, C. W., & Thomas, S. W. (1971). Something borrowed, something black. In C. W. Thomas (Ed.), *Boys no more.* Beverly Hills, CA: Glencoe. **(AfA)**

Thomas, P. (1998, April 21). Minority businesses increase cross-ethnic marketing. *Wall Street Journal,* p. B2. **(AsA)**

Thomas, P. (2000, January 12). Immigrant entrepreneurs slip from top. *Wall Street Journal,* p. A2. **(AsA)**

Thomas, V., & Wolfe, D. B. (1995, May). Why won't television grow up? *American Demographics, 17,* 24-31. **(MA)**

Thompson, C. (1998, July 12). Lost tongues, lost spirits. *Austin American-Statesman,* pp. C1, C8.

Thompson, L. (1995, June 12). Search for a gay gene. *Time,* pp. 60-61. **(GA)**

Thurm, S. (1999, June 24). Asian immigrants are reshaping Silicon Valley. *Wall Street Journal,* p. B6. **(AsA)**

Tilove, J. (1998, November 8). Jefferson's new legacy makes blood the real U.S. melting pot. *Newark Star-Ledger,* p. 53. **(AfA)**

Tolley, B. S., & Goett, J. J. (1971, April). Reactions to blacks in newspapers. *Journal of Advertising Research, 11,* 11-17. **(AfA)**

Top five most trusted sources for company and product information. (1998). *Minority Markets Alert, 10*(12), p. 6. **(AfA)**

Torres, J. (1999, October). Invisible ink? *Hispanic,* pp. 23-31. **(USL)**

Toyota ad: Unlike your last boyfriend, it goes to work in the morning. (1999, January 25). *Jet,* p. 68. **(AfA)**

Trafzer, C. E. (1985). The twentieth century horse: The role of the pickup truck in Indian country. In C. E. Trafzer (Ed.), *America's Indian identity: Today's changing perspectives* (pp. 28-37). San Diego, CA: San Diego State University, Department of American Indian Studies.

Treas, J. (1995, May). Older Americans in the 1990s and beyond. *Population Bulletin, 50*(2), 2-43. **(MA)**

Trompenaars, F., & Hampden-Turner, C. (1998). *Riding the waves of culture: Understanding diversity in global business* (2nd ed.). New York: McGraw-Hill. **(AsA)**

Trosper, R. L. (1992). Mind sets and economic development on Indian reservations. In S. Cornell & J. P. Kalt (Eds.), *What can tribes do? Strategies and institutions in American Indian economic development* (pp. 302-328). Berkeley: University of California Press.

Tseng, L. P. D., & Stern, B. L. (1996). Cultural differences in information obtainment for financial decisions—east versus west. *Journal of Euro-Marketing, 5*(1), 37.

Tsiantar, D., & Miller, A. (1991, April 1). Dipping into granny's wallet. *Newsweek,* p. 43. **(MA)**

Tuaca targets lesbians. (1995, August 14). *Marketing News,* p. 6. **(GA)**

Tuan, M. (1998). *Forever foreigners or honorary whites? The Asian ethnic experience today.* New Brunswick, NJ: Rutgers University Press. **(AsA)**

Tucker, M. (1995). *The representation of elderly persons in prime time television advertising.* Master's thesis, School of Mass Communications, University of South Florida at Tampa. **(MA)**

Tuller, D. (1994, June 10). Gays, lesbians listed as 6% of population. *San Francisco Chronicle*, p. A3. **(GA)**

Turner, J. C. (1987). *Rediscovering the social group*. London: Basil Blackwell. **(AfA)**

Turner, R. M. (1996). *Texas traditions: The culture of the Lone Star state*. Toronto: Little, Brown.

Turow, J. (1997a). *Breaking up America: Advertisers and the new media world*. Chicago: University of Chicago Press.

Turow, J. (1997b). The dark side of target marketing. *American Demographics, 19*, 51-54.

Twitchell, J. B. (1996). *Adcult USA: The triumph of advertising in American culture*. New York: Columbia University Press.

U.S. Attorney General. (1997, May 14). 7 Asian American and white Syracuse University students attacked at Denny's restaurant after they were denied service. News release.

U.S. average household spending by consumer households. (1998). *Minority Markets Alert, 10*(7), 8. **(AfA)**

U.S. balance of payments accounts. (1997, June). *Survey of Current Business, 78*, 6.

U.S. Bureau of Statistics. (1995). *Statistical abstract of the United States*. Washington, DC: Government Printing Office.

U.S. Bureau of the Census. (1961). *U.S. census of population* (PC (1)-1A). Washington, DC: Author.

U.S. Bureau of the Census. (1990). 1990 decennial census of population and housing characteristics. www.census.gov/main/www/cen1990.html

U.S. Bureau of the Census. (1992). *1990 census of population: General population characteristics*. Washington, DC: Author.

U.S. Bureau of the Census. (1993a). *1990 census of population: Social and economic characteristics*. Washington, DC: Author.

U.S. Bureau of the Census. (1993b). *Population projections of the United States by age, sex, race, and Hispanic origin: 1993 to 2050* (Current Population Reports, P25-1104). Washington, DC: Author.

U.S. Bureau of the Census. (1993c). *We the American . . . Asians*. Washington, DC: Author. **(AsA)**

U.S. Bureau of the Census. (1993d). *We the American . . . Blacks*. Washington, DC: Author. **(AfA)**

U.S. Bureau of the Census. (1993e). *We the American . . . foreign born*. Washington, DC: Author.

U.S. Bureau of the Census. (1993f, November). *We the American . . . Hispanics*. Washington, DC: Author. **(USL)**

U.S. Bureau of the Census. (1993g). *We . . . the First Americans*. Washington, DC: Author.

U.S. Bureau of the Census. (1994a). *1993 statistical abstract of the United States* (114th ed.). Washington, DC: Author.

U.S. Bureau of the Census. (1994b). Population estimates for states by race and Hispanic origin: 1993. www.census.gov/population/estimates/state

U.S. Bureau of the Census. (1995). *The nation's Asian and Pacific Islander population—1994* (Statistical Brief). Washington, DC: Author.

U.S. Bureau of the Census. (1996, February). Population projections of the United States by age, sex, race, and Hispanic origin: 1995 to 2050 (Current Population Reports P25-1130). www.census.gov/prod/1/pop/p25-1130/p251130b.pdf

U.S. Bureau of the Census. (1997a). *Hispanic population of the United States* (Current Population Survey). Washington, DC: Author. **(USL)**

U.S. Bureau of the Census. (1997b). Selected characteristics of the population by race: March 1997. Www.bls.census.gov/cps/pub/1997/int_race.htm **(AfA)**

U.S. Bureau of the Census. (1998a). *Money income in the United States: 1997.* Washington, DC: Author.

U.S. Bureau of the Census (1998b). *National population projections.* www.census.gov/population/projections/nation/nas/npas9600.txt.

U.S. Bureau of the Census. (1998c). Population statistics. Www.census.gov/population/statab/ccdb/ccdb305.txt

U.S. Bureau of the Census. (1998d). *Poverty in the United States: 1997.* Washington, DC: Author.

U.S. Bureau of the Census. (1998e). Resident population: Selected characteristics and projections. www.census.gov/statab/freq/98s0012.txt

U.S. Bureau of the Census. (1999a, January 26). 1990 population by city and by state. www.census.gov

U.S. Bureau of the Census. (1999b). Population estimates for counties by race and Hispanic origin: July 1, 1998. Www.census.gov/population/estimates/county/crh/crhca98.txt

U.S. Bureau of the Census. (1999c). Population estimates for states by race and Hispanic origin: July 1, 1998. www.census.gov/population/estimates/state/srh/srhus98.txt

U.S. Bureau of the Census (1999d, January 30). Population projections. www.census.gov/population/projections/

U.S. Bureau of the Census. (1999e). Selected characteristics of the population, by sex and race: March 1998. www.census.gov/population/socdemo/race/api98/table02.txt

U.S. Bureau of the Census. (1999f). States ranked by Asian and Pacific Islander population in 1998. www.census.gov/population/estimates/state/rank/strnktb4.txt

U.S. Bureau of the Census. (1999g, February 9). Table 1.1. March 1997 CPS: Age by race—ethnicity: Both sexes—values. Www.census.gov/population/socdemo/hispanic/cps97/tab01-1.txt

U.S. Bureau of the Census. (2000). Population Estimates Program, Population Division. www.census.gov/population/www/estimates/ popest.html.

Underhill, P. (1996, April). Seniors in stores. *American Demographics, 18,* 44-48. **(MA)**

Ungar, S. J. (1995). *Fresh blood: The new American immigrants.* New York: Simon & Schuster. **(USL, AsA)**

Ursic, A. C., Ursic, M. L., & Ursic, V. L. (1986, June). A longitudinal study of the use of the elderly in magazine advertising. *Journal of Consumer Research, 13,* 131-133. **(MA)**

Vaillancourt, M. (1997). Big Crow's first stand: Descendant of Crazy Horse goes public to keep legendary warrior's name off high-octane beer. In S. Biagi &

M. Kern-Foxworth (Eds.), *Facing difference: Race, gender, and mass media* (pp. 212-214). Thousand Oaks, CA: Pine Forge.

Valdes, M. I., & Sesane, M. H. (1995). *Hispanic market handbook.* New York: Gale Research. **(USL)**

Valencia, H. (1983, June 24). Snafus persist in marketing to Hispanics. *Marketing News,* p. 3. **(USL)**

Valencia, H. (1985). Developing an index to measure "Hispanicness." In E. C. Hirschman & M. B. Holbrook (Eds.), *Advances in consumer research* (Vol. 12, pp. 118-121). Provo, UT: Advances in Consumer Research. **(USL)**

Valencia, H. (1989). Hispanic values and subcultural research. *Journal of the Academy of Marketing Science, 17,* 23-29. **(USL)**

Van Biema, D. (1994, October 31). Native American treasures. *Time,* pp. 73-74.

Van Biema, D. (1995, September 18). Bury my heart in committee. *Time,* pp. 48-51.

Vargas, R. (1996). Families celebrate the Day of the Dead. *Hispanic, 9*(11), 72-73. **(USL)**

Veciana-Suarez, A. (1990). *Hispanic media: Impact and influence.* Washington, DC: Media Institute. **(USL)**

Vincenti, L. (1998, July 6). For merchants, inner cities offer golden opportunity. *Home Furnishing Network, 72,* 1. **(AfA)**

Vitucci, J. D. (1999, December). Hispanic purchasing power remains strong. *Hispanic Business,* p. 72. **(USL)**

Wagner, J., & Soberon-Ferrer, H. (1990). The effect of ethnicity on selected household expenditures. *Social Science Journal, 27,* 181-198. **(AfA)**

Walker, C. (1996, September). The global middle class. *American Demographics, 18,* 40-46.

Walker, C., & Moses, E. (1996, September). The age of self-navigation. *American Demographics, 18,* 36-44. **(AfA)**

Walker, M. M., & Macklin, M. C. (1992, July-August). The use of role modeling in targeting advertising to grandparents. *Journal of Advertising Research, 32,* 37-43. **(MA)**

Wallendorf, M., & Nelson, D. (1986). An archaeological examination of ethnic differences in body care rituals. *Psychology and Marketing, 3,* 273-289. **(USL)**

Wallendorf, M., & Reilly, M. D. (1983). Ethnic migration, assimilation and consumption. *Journal of Consumer Research, 10,* 293-302. **(USL)**

Wallich, P. (1999, November). Future tech: Who needs Berlitz? *Discover,* p. 55.

Walters, A. S., & Curran, M.-C. (1996). "Excuse me, sir. May I help you and your boyfriend?" Salespersons' differential treatment of homosexual and straight customers. In D. L. Wardlow (Ed.), *Gays, lesbians, and consumer behavior: Theory, practice, and research issues in marketing* (pp. 144-145). New York: Harrington Park. **(GA)**

Walters, J. M. (1992). *The division of labor in same sex households: The role of gender in housework.* Unpublished master's thesis, University of Texas at Austin. **(GA)**

Wang, L. L. (1998). Race, class, citizenship, and extra-territoriality: Asian Americans and the 1996 campaign finance scandal. *Amerasia Journal, 24*(1), 1-21. **(AsA)**

Wang, N. (1998). From tennis rackets to tinted contacts. *A Magazine,* 33-34, 76. **(AsA)**

Ward, L. B. (1994, July 12). Small business working for Glory, Ohio firm pioneering market for African-American foods. *Cincinnati Enquirer,* p. D1. **(AfA)**

Ware, R. (1999, September). Over 50: Demanding and in demand. *American Demographics, 21.* www.demographics.com **(MA)**

Warren, S. (1995, October 25). Business owners cautiously begin targeting pitches to gay market. *Wall Street Journal,* pp. T1, T4. **(GA)**

Wartzman, R. (1995, December 7). Houston turns out to be the capital of the egg roll. *Wall Street Journal,* pp. A1, A9.

Wartzman, R. (1999a, April 27). Exacting practice makes near-perfect for California esrogs. *Wall Street Journal,* pp. A1, A8.

Wartzman, R. (1999b, June 3). Read their lips: When you translate Got Milk? what do you have? *Wall Street Journal,* pp. A1, A8. **(USL)**

Wartzman, R., & Flint, J. (2000, February 25). Nielsen ratings spark a battle over just who speaks Spanish. *Wall Street Journal,* pp. B1-B4. **(USL)**

Waters, M. C. (1990b). *Ethnic options: Choosing identities in America.* Berkeley: University of California Press. **(USL)**

Wattanasuwan, R. E. K. (1998, May). Brands as symbolic resources for the construction of identity. *International Journal of Advertising, 17,* 131-150.

Web marketers beginning to focus on minority audience. (1997, February 28). *Interactive Marketing News,* pp. 4, 9. **(AfA)**

Weber, A. M., & Stalk, G. (1999, February-March). Fast pack 1999. *Fast Company,* pp. 134-150.

Webster, C. (1992, September-October). The effects of Hispanic subcultural identification on information search behavior. *Journal of Advertising Research, 32,* 54-62. **(USL)**

Webster, C. (1994). Effects of Hispanic ethnic identification on marital roles in the purchase decision process. *Journal of Consumer Research, 21,* 319-331. **(USL)**

Webster, N. C. (1994, May 30). Playing to gay segment opens doors for marketers. *Advertising Age,* p. 1. **(GA)**

Wehling, R. L. (1998, January). Even at P&G, only three brands make truly global grade so far. *Advertising Age International,* 8.

Weinstein, B. (1994, May). Ethnic marketing: The new numbers game. *Profiles,* pp. 51-54.

Weisend, T. (1997). Stonewalled: Advertisers are ignoring the homosexual community. In S. Biagi & M. Kern-Foxworth (Eds.), *Facing difference: Race, gender, and mass media* (pp. 214-216). Thousand Oaks, CA: Pine Forge. **(GA)**

Weiss, M. J. (1999, October). Parallel universe. *American Demographics, 21,* 58-63.

Weiss, M. J. (2000, March-April). The beautiful and the demmed: You are what you buy—where you live. *Utne Reader,* pp. 54-59.

Weiss, M. S. (1973). Division and unity: Social process in a Chinese-American community. In S. Stanley & N. N. Wagner (Eds.), *Asian Americans: Psychological perspectives.* Ben Lomond, CA: Science and Behavior Books. **(AsA)**

Weissman, R. X. (1998, December). The kids are all right—they're just a little converged. *American Demographics, 20,* 30-32.

Westerman, M. (1989, March). Death of the Frito bandito. *American Demographics, 11,* 28-32. **(USL)**

Whipple, T. W., & Neidell, L. A. (1971). Black and white perceptions of competing stores. *Journal of Retailing, 47*(4), 5-20. **(AfA)**

White, C. L., & Burke, P. J. (1987). Ethnic role identity among black and white college students: An interactionist approach. *Sociological Perspectives, 30,* 310-331. **(AfA)**

White, J. B. (2000, January 1). The company we'll keep. *Wall Street Journal,* p. R36.

Whittler, T. E. (1989). Viewers' processing of actor's race and message claims in advertising stimuli. *Psychology and Marketing, 6,* 287-309. **(AfA)**

Whittler, T. E. (1991). The effects of actor's race in commercial advertising: Review and extension. *Journal of Advertising, 20*(1), 54-60. **(AfA)**

Whittler, T. E., Calantone, R. J., & Young, M. R. (1991). Strength of ethnic affiliation: Examining black identification with black culture. *Journal of Social Psychology, 131,* 461-467. **(AfA)**

Wickham, D. (1999, January 19). Minority radio gets passed over, wrongly. *USA Today,* p. 17A. **(AfA)**

Wiesendanger, B. (1993). Asian-Americans: The three biggest myths. *Sales and Marketing Management, 145*(11), 86-88. **(AsA)**

Wildstrom, S. H. (2000, January 10). On the Web, it's 1984. *Business Week,* p. 28.

Wilkes, R. E., & Valencia, H. (1989). Hispanics and blacks in television commercials. *Journal of Advertising, 18*(1), 19-25. **(USL)**

Wilkinson, I. F., & Cheng, C. (1999, January 1). Perspectives: Multicultural marketing in Australia: Synergy in diversity. *Journal of International Marketing, 7*(3), 106-125.

Williams, G. (1991). *Teens as consumers: A survey of attitudes and behaviors.* Unpublished master's thesis, University of Texas at Austin. **(AfA)**

Williams, J. D. (1987). Examining the effectiveness of celebrity advertising to minorities: Entertainers vs. athletes. In R. L. King (Ed.), *Minority marketing: Issues and prospects. Proceedings of the Academy of Marketing Science Conference* (pp. 107-111). Charleston, SC: Academy of Marketing Science. **(AfA)**

Williams, J. D. (1989a). African and European roots of multi-culturalism in the consumer behavior of American blacks. In D. T. Tan & J. N. Sheth (Eds.), *Historical perspectives in consumer research: National and international perspectives.* Singapore: ACR. **(AfA)**

Williams, J. D. (1989b). Ebonics and advertising to the black consumer: A need for research to analyze language and communication styles in a linguistic perspective. In J. M. Hawes & J. Thanopoulos (Eds.), *Developments in marketing science: Vol. 13. Proceedings of the Thirteenth Annual Conference of the Academy of Marketing Science* (pp. 637-642). Orlando, FL: Academy of Marketing Science. **(AfA)**

Williams, J. (2000, March 20). The new workforce. *Business Week,* pp. 64-74.

Williams, J. D., & Grantham, K. D. (1999). Racial and ethnic identity in the marketplace: An examination of nonverbal and peripheral cues. *Advances in Consumer Research, 26,* 451-454. **(AfA)**

Williams, J. D., & Qualls, W. J. (1989). Middle-class black consumers and intensity of ethnic identification. *Psychology and Marketing, 6,* 263-286. **(AfA)**

Williams, J., Qualls, W., & Grier, S. (1995, Fall). Racially exclusive real estate advertising: Public policy implication for fair housing practices. *Journal of Public Policy and Marketing, 14,* 225-244. **(AfA)**

Williams, J. D., & Snuggs, T. (1996, October). *Survey of attitudes toward customer service in retail stores: The role of race.* Paper presented at the Multicultural Marketing Conference, Virginia Beach, VA. (**AfA**)

Williams, N. (1990). *The Mexican American family: Tradition and change.* Dixon Hills, NY: General Hall. (**USL**)

Williamson, J. (1986). *Consuming passions: The dynamics of popular culture.* London: Marion Boyars.

Willis, M. G. (1992). Learning styles of African American children: A review of the literature and interventions. In A. K. H. Burlew, W. C. Banks, H. P. McAdoo, & D. A. ya Azibo (Eds.), *African American psychology: Theory, research, and practice* (pp. 63-86). Newbury Park, CA: Sage.

Wilson, C. C., & Gutierrez, F. (1995). *Race, multiculturalism, and the media: From mass to class communication* (2nd ed.). Thousand Oaks, CA: Sage. (**USL**)

Wilson, G. L. (1980). Sticks and stones and racial slurs do hurt: The word nigger is what's not allowed. In Racism and Sexism Resource Center for Education (Eds.), *Children, race and racism: How race awareness develops interracial books for children.* New York: Racism and Sexism Resource Center for Education. (**AfA**)

Winter, A. D. (1975). *The gay press of the United States: A history of the gay community and its publications.* Unpublished master's thesis, University of Texas at Austin. (**GA**)

Wolfe, D. B. (1990). *Serving the ageless market.* New York: McGraw-Hill. (**MA**)

Wolk, M. (1992, June 21). Mainstream marketers treat gay publications with respect. *Houston Chronicle,* pp. 2-3. (**GA**)

Wonder, J., & Donovan, P. (1984). *Whole brain thinking,* p.268. New York: Ballantine Books.

Wong, A. M. (1997). *Target: The U.S. Asian market.* Palos Verdes, CA: Pacific Heritage. (**AsA**)

Woods, G. B. (1995a). *Advertising and marketing to the new majority.* Belmont, CA: Wadsworth. (**AfA**)

Woods, G. B. (1995b). The role of ethnic advertising agencies. In S. Biagi & M. Kern-Foxworth (Eds.), *Facing difference: Race, gender, and mass media.* Thousand Oaks, CA: Pine Forge.

Woodson, C. G. (1933). *The miseducation of the Negro.* Washington, DC: Associate Publishers. (**AfA**)

Woodward, K. L., & Johnson, P. (1995, December 11). The advent of Kwanzaa. *Newsweek,* p. 88. (**AfA**)

Wrigley ads to focus on minority health. (1997, June 4). *Wall Street Journal,* p. B1. (**AfA**)

Wu, D. T. L. (1997). *Asian Pacific Americans in the workplace.* Walnut Creek, CA: Altamira. (**AsA**)

Wynter, L. E. (1993a). Business and race. *Wall Street Journal,* B1. (**AsA**)

Wynter, L. E. (1993b, November 24). Minorities play the hero in more TV ads as clients discover multicultural sells. *Wall Street Journal,* pp. B1, B7. (**AfA**)

Wynter, L. E. (1993c, October 26). Stores have different ideas on African style. *Wall Street Journal,* p. B1. (**AfA**)

Wynter, L. E. (1994, September 7). An untapped market of 11 million homes. *Wall Street Journal,* p. B1. **(AfA)**

Wynter, L. E. (1995, November 8). Odds and ends. *Wall Street Journal,* p. B1. **(USL)**

Wynter, L. E. (1996a, February 7). Advocates try to tie diversity to profit. *Wall Street Journal,* p. B1. **(AfA)**

Wynter, L. E. (1996b, July 3). Cosmetics firms find women blur color lines. *Wall Street Journal,* p. B1. **(AfA)**

Wynter, L. E. (1996c, September 13). Groups want census to expand race choices. *Wall Street Journal,* p. B1. **(AfA)**

Wynter, L. E. (1997a, September 3). Blacks and Hispanics gain spending clout. *Wall Street Journal,* p. B1. **(USL, AfA)**

Wynter, L. E. (1997b, July 2). J C Penney launches Diahann Carroll line. *Wall Street Journal,* p .B1. **(AfA)**

Wynter, L. E. (1998a, June 10). Film distributor tries to crack Asian market. *Wall Street Journal,* p. B1. **(AsA)**

Wynter, L. E. (1998b, August 5). Marketers rely on gospel to inspire black buying. *Wall Street Journal,* p. B1. **(AfA)**

Wynter, L. E. (1998c, October 7). "Urban" sportswear goes mainstream. *Wall Street Journal,* p. B1. **(AfA)**

Wynter, L. E. (1999a, April 7). Daytime TV viewership isn't divided by race. *Wall Street Journal,* p. B1. **(AfA)**

Wynter, L. E. (1999b, October 6). For black dot-coms, A new band of angels. *Wall Street Journal,* p. B1. **(AfA)**

Wynter, L. E. (1999c, September 8). Networks need to find a better balance with minority roles. *Wall Street Journal,* p. B1. **(AfA)**

Wynter, L. E. (1999d, February 3). Samplers and getaways help push black books. *Wall Street Journal,* p. B1. **(AfA)**

Wysocki, B. (1997, May 12). Elite U.S. immigrants straddle two cultures. *Wall Street Journal,* pp. B1, B6. **(AsA)**

Yanagisako, S. J. (1985). *Transforming the past: Tradition and kinship among Japanese Americans.* Stanford, CA: Stanford University Press. **(AsA)**

Yang, J., Gan, D., Hong, T., & Staff of *A Magazine.* (1997). *Eastern Standard Time: A guide to Asian influence on American culture, from Astro boy to Zen Buddhism.* Boston: Mariner Original. **(AsA)**

Yankelovich Partners. (1994). Yankelovich Hispanic Monitor [Electronic database]. www.yankelovich.com **(USL)**

Yankelovich Partners. (1997). Yankelovich Hispanic Monitor [Electronic database]. www.yankelovich.com **(USL)**

Yeh, C. J., & Huang, K. (1996). The collectivistic nature of ethnic identity development among Asian-American college students. *Adolescence, 31,* 645-661. **(AsA)**

Yinger, J. (1986). Measuring racial discrimination with fair housing audits: Caught in the act. *American Economic Review, 76,* 881-893. **(AfA)**

Young-chol, K. (1991). *Proverbs, East and West: An anthology of Chinese, Korean, and Japanese sayings with Western equivalents.* Elizabeth, NJ: Hollym. **(AsA)**

Yovovich, B. G. (1982, November 19). Marketing to blacks: The debate rages on. *Advertising Age,* p. M9. **(AfA)**

Zachary, G. P. (2000a). *The global me.* New York: Perseus.

Zachary, G. P. (2000b, March 28). A philosopher in red sneakers gains influence as a global guru. *Wall Street Journal,* pp. B1, B4.

Zate, M. (1998a, December). From niche to mainstream. *Hispanic Business,* pp. 50, 52, 56, 58. **(USL)**

Zate, M. (1998b, December). Hispanic ad budgets explode. *Hispanic Business,* pp. 58, 60. **(USL)**

Zbar, J. D. (1995a, January 23). Hispanic direct mail greeted by open door. *Advertising Age,* p. 39. **(USL)**

Zbar, J. D. (1995b, January 23). Wire turns hot for cable adding Hispanic homes. *Advertising Age,* p. 40.

Zbar, J. D. (1996, March 18). Special report: Marketing to Hispanics. *Advertising Age,* pp. 27-29. **(USL)**

Zbar, J. D. (1998, November 16). Multicultural marketing. *Advertising Age,* pp. S24-S25. **(AfA)**

Zhang, Y., & Gelb, B. D. (1996). Matching advertising appeals to culture: The influence of products' use conditions. *Journal of Advertising, 25*(3), 29-46. **(AsA)**

Zill, N., & Robinson, J. (1995, April). The Generation X difference. *American Demographics, 17,* 24-33.

Zinkhan, G., Qualls, W. J., & Biswas, A. (1990). The use of blacks in magazine and television advertising 1946 to 1968. *Journalism Quarterly, 67,* 547-553. **(AfA)**

Zogby, J. (1992). *Arab America today: A demographic profile of Arab Americans.* Washington, DC: Arab American Institute.

Zola, I. K. (1962-1963). Feelings about age among older people. *Journal of Gerontology, 17-18,* 65-68. **(MA)**

Zollo, P. (1999, May). Not quite the TV generation. *American Demographics, 21,* 35-36.

Zonana, V. F. (1992, Summer). Who Madison Avenue wakes up with. *Out,* pp. 40-43. **(GA)**

Zweigenhaft, R. L., & Domhoff, G. W. (1998). *Diversity in the power elite: Have women and minorities reached the top?* New Haven, CT: Yale University Press.

# Index

Aaker, D. A., 71
Aaker, J., 34
ABC, 144, 204, 230
Absolut vodka:
  Gay/Lesbian market, 24, 226
Access Worldwide Communications, Inc., 142
Account planner, 77
Acculturation, 259, 284
  Asian American, 260
  experience, 259-260
  patterns, 9
  process, 58
  See also Melting pot metaphor; Salad bowl
    metaphor
ACLU Gay and Lesbian Rights, 224
ACT-UP, 224
Adelman, R. D., 115
Adland, 280
Adler, J., 142
Adult life, experiential stages of, 99
Advertising, 12, 157
  celebrity, 156, 200
  exaggeration in, 35

  in program content, 38
  subculture communication styles in, 15
  See also specific subcultures; Spanish-lan-
    guage advertising
Advertising Age, 10
Advocate, 220, 226-227
African American advertising agencies, 196
African American brand characters, 188
African American consumers, 187-199
  atmosphere and, 195
  brand attitudes, 193
  communication sources, 193-194
  early marketing efforts to, 187-190
  preferences, 190-194
  reasonable pricing and, 194
  retail preferences, 193
  spending, 190-191
  white consumers and, 175
African American cultural values, 179-187
  African origins, 179, 183
  balancing two cultures, 185-187
  ethnic identity/labels, 183-185
  expressiveness, 261

gender roles, 261
personal identity, 261
power distance, 261
relationship to nature, 261
social networks, 261
uncertainty avoidance, 261
use of time, 261
*See also* African-origin beliefs
African American diversity, 170, 172-179
    class, 173-175
    *diaspora* and, 170
    generational, 178-179
    residence, 175-178
African American neighborhoods,
        Asian-owned businesses in, 278-279
African American population, 172
    growth, 173, 247
    projected growth, 247
African American professional organizations,
        198
African Americans, 2, 3, 15, 23, 35, 62, 73,
        211, 283, 288, 312
    absence of in mainstream media, 200
    affluent, 176-178
    Afrocentric products preference, 50
    attitude toward ethic marketing, 37
    boycotts by, 170
    civil rights struggle, 284-285
    collectivism, 179
    communication style, 261
    community networks, 199-201
    consumption decision process, 54
    cultural pride, 49
    disposable income, 172
    dominant cultural values, 261
    "double consciousness," 174-175
    education levels, 249
    ethnic identity, 41, 183-184
    ethnic market specialists, 88
    family care of elderly, 101
    household size, 172
    household types, 254
    income level, 5, 6, 172, 173
    increasing media visibility, 196
    in Mature Market, 94, 95
    label preferences, 184
    labels, 167, 184
    marketplace discrimination against,
        169-171
    media portrayals, 40
    music, 178-179, 205

poverty, 175
product usage, 44
research studies of, 74
store patronage, 44-45
style, 178
trend-setting behaviors, 134, 187, 201
*See also specific corporations*; African
    Americans, advertising/marketing to; Af-
    rican Americans, geographic dispersion
    of; African Americans, language and;
    African Americans, media usage among
African Americans, advertising/marketing to,
        187-190, 209-211
    avoiding insensitivity, 189
    biggest spenders, 190
    direct mail, 209
    Ebonics usage, 195-196
    effective, 194-199
    negative reactions, 189-190
    use of African American celebrities, 200,
        204
African Americans, geographic dispersion of,
        7, 8, 175, 176, 177. *See also specific
        U.S. states*
African Americans, language and, 184-185
    code switching, 185
    Ebonics, 185, 195
African Americans, media usage among,
        38-39, 43, 54, 201-202, 274
    billboards, 206-207
    Internet, 207-209
    magazines, 205-206, 274
    newspapers, 206, 274
    premium cable, 204
    print media, 205-206
    radio, 201, 204-205, 274
    television, 196, 201, 202-204, 274
African-origin beliefs:
    affect, 181
    communalism, 182
    expressive individualism, 182
    harmony, 181
    movement, 181
    orality, 182
    social time perspective, 182
    spirituality, 181
    versus other American subculture beliefs,
        181-182
    verve, 181
Afrocentrism, 179, 183, 185
    advertisement, 180

Age cohorts, 92, 297-302. *See also* Baby
  Boomers; Children; Generation X; Gen-
  eration Y; Mature Americans; Teenagers
Age cohort values, 108, 111
Agins, T., 139, 154, 288
Ajzen, I., 32
Alabama:
  African Americans, 177
Aladdin Hotel and Casino:
  Asian American market, 280
Alaska:
  Native Americans, 290
Alba, R. D., 41, 166, 284, 292, 293, 294, 296
Albaum, G., 61
Alberts, J. K., 184
Albonetti, J. G., 156
Alden, D. L., 311
Alexander, K., 178
Alexander, K. L., 204
Alsop, R., 220, 221, 222, 223, 231, 233, 234,
  240
Althen, G., 47, 48, 49, 139, 255, 263, 264,
  265
Altman, D., 225
Alwitt, L., 192
Alwitt, L. F., 201
American Account Planning Group, 77
American Airlines:
  Gay/Lesbian market, 226
American-Arab Anti-Discrimination Commit-
  tee, 296
American Association of Retired Persons
    (AARP), 45-46, 63-64, 102
  credit card, 64
  definition of Mature Americans, 92
  *Modern Maturity* magazine, 63, 114
  success of, 114
American corporations:
  assertive cultural role, 36
  revenues from foreign sources, 20
  use of labeling, 42
  *See also specific American corporations*
American culture, mainstream, 47-49
  acceptance of mistakes, 48
  Asian influences, 262-263
  as unique, 47
  competitiveness in, 48
  constantly improvising in, 48
  decision making in, 49
  dominant cultural values, 261
  fixing things in, 48

  Hispanization, 142-143
  impatience with time in, 48
  importance of individualism in, 47
  importance of one's job in, 48
  insistence on choice in, 48
  making dreams come true in, 48
  search for newness in everything, 48
  view of human nature in, 47
  view of nature in, 47
  *See also* Communication style, mainstream
    American; Individualistic societies
"American dream," 9, 154, 285, 288
  African American, 192
  Asian American, 46
  Baby Boomer, 298
  current immigrants' view, 50
  gay and lesbian, 222
  of economic opportunity, 50
  of home ownership, 14, 50, 288
  of material affluence, 14, 288
American Express:
  Gay/Lesbian market, 233-234
American Home Products:
  African American market, 190
American Jewish Historical Society, 294
American Negro College Fund, 199
American Psychiatric Association, 226
American Public Health Association, 207
Americans with Disabilities Act (ADA), 303
American values, mainstream:
  activity orientation, 138
  cultural lessons, 255
  family, 138
  human nature orientation, 139
  language, 138
  permeability, 287
  reformulation, 288
  religion, 138
  self-perceptions, 139
  versus Asian American values, 255
  versus U.S. Hispanic values, 138-139
  worldviews, 138
  *See also* Individualistic societies
Anheuser-Busch:
  African American market, 190
  Asian American market, 280
  Gay/Lesbian market, 231
  Latino market, 152
Annis, R., 129
Ansberry, C., 103
AOL/Time Warner merger, 21

Applegate, J., 276
Arab Americans, 288, 290, 295-296, 313
  affluence, 295
  age, 295
  discrimination against, 296
  educational attainment, 295
  ethnic pride, 296
  important dates/events, 290
  in health professions, 295
  in retail, 295
  media portrayals, 295
  significant media, 290
  2000 population figures, 290, 295
  *See also* Armenian Americans
Arbitron, 146, 205
Arce, C., 131
Arizona:
  Latinos, 135
  Mexican Americans, 128
  Native Americans, 290
Arkansas:
  Mature Americans, 97
Armenian Americans, 295
Arndorfer, J. B., 231
Asfahani, M., 295
Asia America:
  generational differences, 257-258
  role of community, 250-253
Asian American communication styles, 261,
    263-264, 281
  bilingualism, 264
  message interpretation, 263-264
  ritual interaction, 264
Asian American communities, 252. *See also*
    *specific Asian groups*
Asian American consumers, 276, 278, 280
  affluent, 276-277
  basis of purchase decisions, 275
  boycotts by, 278
  family versus individual, 276
  preference for Asian brands, 278
  preference for Asian-owned firms, 276,
    278, 281
  preference for status brands, 278, 281
  preference for well-known firms, 276
  response to salespeople, 276
  *See also specific Asian American groups*;
    Asian American marketplace
Asian American information sources:
  Asian American community network,
    264-265, 268
  credibility, 264-265, 268

Asian American marketplace:
  as social network, 275-280
Asian American-oriented media:
  cable networks, 271
  effectiveness, 273
  fragmentation, 273
  Internet, 271-272
  magazines, 271, 274
  mainstream, 274
  newspapers, 270-271, 272, 274
  print, 273
  publications, 270
  radio, 269, 271
  targeting Asian Americans, 268-272
  television, 269, 270, 271, 274-275
  *See also* Asian Americans, media usage of;
    In-language media
Asian American pan-ethnicity, 259
Asian American population:
  growth, 244, 245, 247
  projected growth, 247
  trends, 246
  U.S. immigration policy and, 244
Asian Americans, 2, 3, 4, 23, 73, 82, 166,
    243-244, 281, 288
  acculturation experience, 260, 262
  "American dream," 46
  ancestry, 248
  as "model minority," 46, 248-250, 257
  as term, 243
  chameleon behavior, 260
  children as family change agents, 247
  collectivism, 179
  consumption decision process, 54
  diversity, 53, 248-250
  dominant cultural values, 261
  education levels, 249, 250, 257-258
  entrepreneurs, 263, 280
  ethnic identity, 41
  ethnic pride, 258, 276
  extended family households, 253
  fashion designers, 263
  gender roles, 261
  generational differences, 257-258
  Generation 1.5, 247-248
  glass ceiling, 250
  group-centered behavior, 256
  holiday celebrations, 260, 275
  household types, 254
  income, 6, 248, 249, 250
  in engineering/high technology, 252
  influences on mainstream America, 262-263

in Mature Market, 95
intermarriage, 258
marriage, 260
media portrayal, 262-263
native-born versus foreign-born, 245, 247
preferences for well-known brands/companies, 254, 276
product usage by, 44
professional/business concentration, 252
relationship to nature, 261
religious differences, 256
reluctance to try new products, 76
research studies of, 74
role of family, 256-257
role switching, 260
shared immigrant experiences, 244-248
significance of colors, 279, 281
significance of numbers, 279, 281
stereotypes, 262
store patronage, 44-45
traditions, 253-258
use of time, 261
violence against, 259
*See also specific corporations*; Asian Americans, advertising/marketing to; Asian Americans, geographic dispersion of; Asian Americans, media usage of; Asian American values; Asian Indian Americans; Cambodian Americans; Chinese Americans; Filipino Americans; Hmong Americans; Japanese Americans; Korean Americans; Laotian Americans; Vietnamese Americans
Asian Americans, advertising/marketing to, 265-268, 275-276, 278, 280
cross-ethnic promotions, 278-279
culture-based events, 268, 275
direct marketing, 272
effective, 273
ethnic media, 268-272
face-to-face, 265
insider preference, 265, 281
obstacles, 265, 268, 272-273
suggestions for, 273, 280
word-of-mouth, 265, 280, 281
yellow page directories, 272
*See also* In-language media
Asian Americans, geographic dispersion of, 7, 8, 53, 250, 251, 252, 269
advertiser reach, 250
selected cities, 251
selected counties, 251

West Coast, 250
*See also specific U.S. states*
Asian Americans, media usage of, 38-39, 269, 272-275
Internet, 271-272
magazines, 269, 271, 274
newspapers, 270, 272, 274
radio, 269, 274
television, 269, 273-274
video rentals, 272
*See also* Asian American-oriented media; In-language media
Asian American values:
Confucian, 253-256, 281
cultural lessons and, 255
family, 256-257, 281
gender roles, 261
insider bias, 254, 281
manners, 253
outlook, 253
personal identity, 261
power distance, 261
relationship to nature, 261
religion, 256
social network roles, 261
social relations, 253
uncertainty avoidance, 261
use of time, 261
Asian and Hispanic Marketing Communications Research, 280
AsianAvenue.com, 272
Asian immigrants:
adjusting to American life, 258-262
as Generation 1.0, 247
businesses patronized, 268
Cambodian, 244
Chinese, 244, 280
Filipinos, 244
Indians, 244, 280
Koreans, 244
Laotian, 244
native-language media exposure, 9
Silicon Valley entrepreneurs, 280
Vietnamese, 244
*See also specific Asian groups*
Asian immigrants, geographic concentration of, 250-252
advertiser reach and, 250
Asian Indian Americans, 245, 248, 276
communities, 252
consumer segments, 279-280
Generation 1.5, 262

Generation 2.0, 262
   income, 248
   leaders, 258
   magazines, 274
   networks, 258
   newspapers, 270, 274, 278
   population trends, 246
Asian Media Planning Source, 270
Assimilation, 284
Astroff, R. J., 144
Asuad, B. C., 288, 295
AT&T:
   African American market, 27, 190, 196,
      197, 198
   Asian American market, 280
   as multicultural marketer in United States,
      23-24, 74
   commercial, 275
   Filipino market, 25
   Gay/Lesbian market, 231, 234
   Generation X market, 28
   Latino market, 26, 152, 155
Athens, L., 296
Audience measurement/research, U.S. Latino,
   149
Auerbach, J. G., 294, 295
Avon:
   African American market, 86
   Asian American market, 86
   efforts to appeal to minorities, 86
   Latino market, 86
Ayres, I., 169


Baby Boomers, 35, 43, 82, 297, 298-299, 301
   age cohort values, 111
   aging, 75
   "American dream," 298
   as grandparents, 117
   as Mature Americans, 92-93
   early versus late, 53
   generation gap and, 298
   parents of, 298, 299
   politics, 298-299
   product preferences, 298
   shared experiences, 54
   size of cohort, 298
   spending patterns, 298
Baker, S., 238
Balasubramanian, S. K., 120
Baldwin, J. R., 58

Banerjee, A., 311
Bank, D., 228
Bannon, L., 302
Barber, B. R., 311
Barbero, J.-M., 145
Barnes, B. E., 71, 78
Basil, M. D., 207
Batra, R., 71, 311
Battistella, G., 293
Batts, V., 168
Bauer, R. A., 186, 193, 287
BBDO Worldwide, 202-203
Beam, C., 271
Bean, R., 263
Beard, F. K., 71
Beatty, S. G., 15, 40, 52, 230
Beauvais, F., 74
Beck, M., 93, 108, 116, 289, 297, 301, 314
Begley, S., 165, 225, 301, 302
Belk, R. W., 34, 276
Benetton:
   Gay/Lesbian market, 226
Bennett, M. J., 40, 41, 139, 255, 263
Bennett, P. D., 62, 90, 186
Bennett, Tony, 293
Benokraitis, N. V., 263
Benson & Hedges:
   Gay/Lesbian market, 234, 235
Berfield, S., 279
Berger, W., 169
Berkowitz, H., 74, 276
Berman, G. L., 134, 149, 161
Berry, J., 247
Berry, J. W., 129
Berry, V. T., 189
Bessen, J., 13
Best, R. J., 62, 90
Bhatia, Sabeer, 263
Bilingual/crossover media, 150
Birch, 146
Bisexuals, 216, 218
Biswas, A., 200, 202
Blanc, M., 247
Black Entertainment Television (BET), 204
   magazine, 206
Blodau, M., 145
Blumenfeld, W. J., 223
Bogdan, R., 302
Border, G. A., 264
Border mentality, 57, 58-59, 61, 82, 89
   brand positioning and, 58

nurturing in company decision makers, 58
Bosma, H. A., 41
Bourhis, R. Y., 184
Bowen, L., 262, 269
Bower, J. L., 13
Bowes, J. E., 233
Boyce, J. N., 9, 50, 285, 288
Boyd, M., 279
Boykin, W. A., 179
Braithwaite, D. O., 108, 302
Branch, S., 198
Brand, M., 142
Brand "bloc" buying, 137, 139, 142
Brandes, W., 205
Brand loyalty, 61-62, 275, 297, 303
Brand management, 76
Brand managers, 76
Brand market, 61
Brand-person relationship, 33-34
Brand positioning, 58. *See also* Border
    mentality
Brand preference, 275
Brand recognition, building, 275
Braus, P., 125, 298
Brazil, J., 93, 117, 119
British Account Planning Group, 77
Broadband cable networks, 12
Brody, E. W., 70
Bromley, E., 129, 131
Browder, S., 79
Brown, A., 78, 79
Brown, C., 206
Brown, H. D., 259, 260
Brownlee, L. L., 191, 192, 206
Budweiser, Native Americans and, 311
Buhl, C., 288
Bukoff, A., 289, 297, 299, 314
Bulkeley, W. M., 312
Bullock, H. A., 186
Bureau of Indian Affairs, 289
Burger King:
    African American market, 190, 198-199,
        204
    Latino market, 59
Buriel, R., 132
Burke, P. J., 183, 184
Burnett, J. J., 114, 304
Burrell, Tom, 192
Burrell Communications, 196
Burton, J., 265, 276
Bush, V. J., 196

*Business Week,* 220
Byler, M. G., 292

CACI, 307
Caggiano, C., 70
Cadillac:
    African American market, 195
Cahill, J. B., 306
Calantone, R. J., 183
California:
    African Americans, 7, 8, 177
    African Americans (Los Angeles), 176
    African Americans (Oakland), 176
    Arab Americans, 290
    Arab Americans (Anaheim), 295
    Arab Americans (Los Angeles-Long
        Beach), 295
    Armenian Americans, 295
    Asian Americans 7, 8, 53, 251, 252, 269
    Asian Americans (Los Angeles), 250, 251
    Asian Americans (San Francisco), 250,
        251, 276
    Asian Americans (San Jose), 251
    Central Americans, U.S., 128
    Filipinos (San Francisco Bay Area), 269
    Greek Americans, 290
    Iranian Americans (Los Angeles), 290
    Italian Americans (San Francisco), 290
    Jewish Americans (Los Angeles), 290, 294
    Korean Americans, 278
    Latinos, 5, 7, 8, 53, 134, 135
    Latinos (Fresno), 133, 135
    Latinos (Los Angeles), 133, 134, 135
    Latinos (Los Angeles County), 134
    Latinos (San Diego), 135
    Latinos (San Francisco, 133, 135
    Mature Americans, 7, 8, 96, 97, 120
    Mature Americans (Los Angeles), 98
    Mature Americans (San Diego), 98
    Mature Americans (San Francisco), 98
    Mexican Americans, 128
    Mexican Americans (Fresno), 133
    Mexican Americans (Los Angeles), 127,
        133
    Mexican Americans (San Francisco), 133
    Native Americans, 290
    Puerto Rican Americans, 128
    Salvadoran Americans (Los Angeles), 133
    Salvadoran Americans (San Francisco), 133
    South Americans, U.S., 128

White Americans, 7
California Milk Processors Board, 134
Callcott, M. F., 207
Cambodian Americans, 245, 248
Campanelli, M., 199, 206, 209, 210
Campbell, A., 168
Carino, B. V., 245
Carlson, R., 13
Carmichael, S., 184
Carnival Cruise Lines, 143
Carr-Ruffino, N., 70, 103, 132, 137, 139, 143, 167, 175, 182, 183, 184, 185, 302, 303
Caso, A., 293
Castaneda, A., 187
Castaneda, L., 208
Castaneda, R., 171
Cathay Pacific Airlines:
Asian American market, 280
Cayton, H., 174
CBS, 11, 144, 204
targeting older viewers, 112
Central Americans, U.S., 127, 128, 133, 162.
See also specific U.S. states
Chambers, V., 142
Chan, T., 169
Chang, Michael:
in advertisement, 265, 266
Chappell, K., 187
Charity event sponsorships, 12, 42, 156, 210
Charles Schwab:
Asian American market, 280
Charlie the Tuna, 33
Chase, B., 233
Cheng, C., 73, 312
Chevrolet, 10
Chevron:
foreign revenue, 20
Child, P., 49
Children:
as consumers, 297
Coca-Cola advertising to, 15, 16
Chinese Americans, 1, 243, 245, 248
attitude toward ethic marketing, 37
communities, 252
income, 248
intermarriage, 259
leaders, 258
media portrayals, 40
media usage, 54, 269, 273, 274
networks, 258
population trends, 246

self-labeling, 259
See also specific corporations
Chisholm-Mingo Group, 196
Chivas Regal:
Asian American market, 280
Cho, L.-J., 253
Cho, Margaret, 263
Choices, consumer:
abundance of, 70
Christensen, C. M., 13
Christenson, G. A., 288
Chrysler:
African American market, 196, 204
Chu, James, 263
Church, G. J., 19
CIGNA:
Asian American market, 280
Cintron, I., 262
Cisneros, H., 39
Citibank:
Asian American market, 278
Citicorp:
foreign revenue, 20
Civil Rights movement, 169
Claritas, 133, 307
Clark, R., 169
Cleland, K., 207
Clemetson, L., 142, 301, 302
Cloud, J., 214, 220, 287
Clurman, A., 54, 289, 297, 299, 314
CNN, 19, 112
Spanish-language news, 150
Cobb, P. M., 174
Cobo-Hanlon, L., 216, 221
Coca-Cola, 15
advertising, 15, 16, 17, 18
African American market, 15, 18, 190
Latino market, 15, 16
Cochran, S., 221
Cohen, G., 114
Cole, C. A., 120
Colgate-Palmolive:
African American market, 190
Australian Blacks and, 312
Latino market, 152, 155, 160
Collectivistic societies, 21-22, 288. See also High-context cultures
Collette, J., 12
Collier, M. J., 46, 58, 90, 183, 185, 200, 201
Collins, G., 117
Collins, J. C., 36, 62

Collins, T., 33
Colorado:
  Latinos, 135
  Mexican Americans, 128
Columbia House, 21
Columbus Club, 293
Communication style, mainstream American,
  49
Communication styles, subculture:
  in advertising, 15
  *See also specific consumer subcultures*
Community United Against Violence, 224
CompareNet, 79
Competition:
  global basis, 15, 19-21
Computer bulletin boards, 12
Conaway, W. H., 264
Condray, S. E., 200, 201
Congressional Black Caucus Foundation, 198
Conlin, M., 19, 21
Consumer clubs, 12
Consumer dialogue, 77-80. *See also* Contact
  points
Consumer identities, 290
  as subcultures, 49-54
  brand images, 70
  brand/store choices, 71
  constant change, 79, 312
  frequency of product/brand purchases, 71
  influences on purchases, 80
  in multicultural America, 51
  product images, 70
  products/services, 59
  product usage, 71
  situational, 74
  usage occasion, 71
  *See also specific subcultures*; Social iden-
    tity
Consumer loyalty, 75
  advertising language usage, 32
  changes, 32-33
  corporate civic policies, 32
  corporate environmental policies, 32
  corporate human rights policies, 32
  to Apple Computer, 70
Consumers:
  adapting to multicultural society, 32
  media repertoire, 39
  valuing, 23-24
  *See also specific consumer subcultures*;
    Consumer subcultures

Consumer subcultures, 2, 21, 289
  as demographically/behaviorally distin-
    guishable, 52
  consumer identities as, 49-54
  consumption decision processes, 54
  distinctive media usage patterns, 54
  diversity, 53
  dominant cultural values, 261
  geographic concentration, 53-54
  growing importance, 35
  identification with specific, 49
  sensitivity to marketers' broad groups,
    52-53
  underlying norms/beliefs/worldviews, 45
  values, 31
  *See also specific consumer subcultures*;
    Consumer subcultures, model of evolu-
    tion of
Consumer subcultures, model of evolution of,
  285-288
  community formation (phase 2), 285, 286
  membership in cultural mosaic (phase 5),
    286, 287
  outsider status (phase 1), 285, 286, 288
  political/economic participation (phase 3),
    285, 286, 287
  representation in U.S. popular culture
    (phase 4), 286, 287
Consumption:
  changing meaning of, 2
  social identity/values expression, 31-34
Contact points, 72, 87
  brand, 73, 78
  cultural compatibility perceptions and, 78
  organization, 73, 78
Continental Airlines:
  Gay/Lesbian market, 231
Cook, W. J., 96
Cooper, H., 300
Coors, 78-79
  African American market, 78, 199, 204
  Gay/Lesbian Market, 226
  Latino market, 78, 79
  lawsuits against, 78
Corina's, 279
Cose, E., 15, 166, 167, 178
Costa, J. A., 214, 215
Council on Interracial Books for Children,
  291
Coupland, N., 184
Cowen, M., 292

Cox, E., 298
Cox, M., 240
Craik, F. I. M., 115
Crane, R. D., 263
Crawford, N., 275, 278
Crockett, R. O., 43, 207, 208
Cropper, J., 289, 297, 300, 314
Cross, R. H., 79
Cross, W. E., 185
Crown Royal:
    Korean American market, 278
Cruse, H., 174
Cuban Americans, 75, 127, 128, 133, 149,
    151, 155, 162
    median annual income, 133
    third-generation's Spanish usage, 143
    See also specific U.S. states
Cultural compatibility:
    marketing plans and, 57, 59, 90
    programs, 61
Cultural Italian American Organization
    (CIAO), 293
Culturally compatible marketers, 74
Cultural partnership, buyer/seller, 24, 86
    versus niche marketing, 24
Cultural stress, 260
Cultural studies, 76
Cultural transmigration, 260
Culture shock, 260
Cundiff, E. W., 14, 74
Cunningham, S. M., 186, 193, 287
Cuomo, Mario, 293
Curran, M.-C., 240
Customized media, 79
Cyr, D., 35

Darley, W. K., 168
Darling, L., 298
Darnay, A. J., 19
Data sources portfolio, 13, 29
Dates, J., 188, 205
Dates, J. L., 169
D'Augelli, A., 215
David, A., 61, 79
David, F. J., 166
Davidson, D. K., 80
Davis, A., 289, 297, 299, 314
Davis, S., 190, 195, 209
DeGeorge, G., 101
Deiter, D. P., 149, 163
de la Garza, M. F.-O., 129, 130

Delener, N., 74, 76, 268, 269, 270, 276
de Levita, D. J., 41
Del Giudice, L., 293
Deloitte & Touche, 193
Del Monte:
    Latino market, 156
Demo, D. H., 183
de Mooij, M., 21, 22, 23, 47, 143, 182, 200,
    254, 255, 263, 265
Dempsey, G. N., 168
Dennis, E. E., 184
Denniston, R. W., 210
DeSena, J. N., 293
Deshpande, R., 41, 42, 49, 129, 132, 143, 161,
    260, 285, 287
Deveny, K., 308
Devos, G., 183
DeZwaan, M., 288
DHL Worldwide Express:
    Asian American market, 280
Dholakia, R. R., 285, 288
Diaspora:
    African American, 170
    ethnic Chinese, 1
Digital Queers, 224
Dignity (religious group), 223
Direct mail, 209
    African Americans and, 209
    Spanish-language, 152
Direct mail marketers, 209
    African American, 209
Dirke, L., 169
Disabled Americans, 35, 302-306, 313
    advertisers' understanding of, 302-303
    as endorsers, 303
    as political force, 303
    as print models, 304
    boycotts by, 302
    brand loyalty, 303
    labeling issues, 303
    media portrayals, 40, 302
    media stereotypes, 302
    mentally disabled segment, 304, 306
    population size, 302
    publications for, 304
    purchasing power, 303
    radio talk shows for, 304
Disney:
    Gay/Lesbian market, 240-241
Diversity, marketplace
    consumer's point of view, 70-71

U.S. population, 3
*See also specific subcultures*; Population trends, U.S.
DMB&B, 134
Dollard, J., 174
Dollar General Corporation:
  African American market, 199
Dolnick, E., 303
Domenech Rodriguez, M. M., 74
Domhoff, G. W., 284, 285
Dominguez, L. V., 156
Dominican Americans, 133, 162
Donley, T. D., 201
Donnelly Marketing, 93
Donnerstein, E., 169
Donnerstein, M., 169
Donovan, R. J., 40
Donthu, N., 41, 143, 161
Doss, Y. C., 144
Dougherty, T., 145, 152, 155
Dow Chemical:
  foreign revenue, 20
Drake, S. C., 174
Dreyfuss, R., 312
DRI/McGraw-Hill, 154
Druckerman, P., 153
Drummond, K. T., 238
Dubin, M., 169
DuBois, W. E. B., 174, 185
Duerr, E., 61
Duff, C., 101, 200
Dunkel, T., 303
Dunn, S. W., 11
Du Pont:
  foreign revenue, 20
Dychtwald, K., 112

Early, G., 179
E-commerce businesses, 12
Edmondson, B., 172, 175, 252, 298
Edwards, C., 195, 199
El-Badry, S., 74, 288, 295
El Dorado radio, 146
*Ellen* television show, "coming out" episode of, 52, 230
Elliott, R., 301, 311
Elliott, S., 218, 240
Ellis, J., 13, 75, 79, 81
Ellis, J. E., 174
Ellis, S., 187
Elstrom, P., 79

Enculturation, 60. *See also* Transmigration
Encyclopedia Britannica:
  Asian American market, 280
Engelhard Minerals:
  foreign revenue, 20
Englis, B. G., 15, 38, 49, 71, 288
English, W. D., 137
English Americans, 290, 296
  2000 population figures, 290
Entman, R. M., 169
Escobar, G., 9
Espiritu, Y. L., 259
Ethnic identity:
  as chosen, 41
  measurement, 41
  symbolic, 42
Ethnicity:
  as economic asset, 9
  as liability, 9
  social identity and, 41-42
Ethnic marketing, 72-73, 86
  danger of, 89
  ethnic group attitudes, 37
  versus mass marketing, 24
Ethnic market specialists, 88
  African American, 88
  qualifications, 88
  *See also* Market specialists
Ethnic-oriented media:
  as cultural institutions, 269
Ethnocentrism, 168
Ethnographic observations, 76
Euro-Americans, 296-297, 313
  brand loyalty, 290
  coupon use, 290
  leisure activities, 290
  1980 population figures, 296
  symbolic ethnic activities, 296
Event sponsorships, 12
Exeter, T., 94
Experian, 307
Exploiting targeted groups, 89
Exxon:
  foreign revenue, 20

Faber, R. J., 137, 142, 154, 155, 156, 288
Fairchild, H. H., 184
Family Values Boomers, 192
Farley, C. J., 178
Fax machines, 12
FCC, 204

Federal Express:
  use of all-inclusive advertising, 83
Feldman, L. P., 186
Felt, C., 245, 256
Female Americans:
  positive group image search, 10
Ferraro, Geraldine, 293
Feuer, J., 152
Figueroa, A., 142
Filipino Americans, 243, 245, 248
  communities, 252
  income, 248
  media usage, 269, 273
  population trends, 246
  *See also specific U.S. states*; AT&T
Filipino Channel, 273
Fish, J., 165
Fishbein, M., 32
Fisher, C., 149, 156, 172, 175, 176, 178, 191,
    192, 195, 202
Fitch, E., 163
Fixico, M., 291
Fizdale, R., 71, 78
Flint, J., 151
Flores, B. A., 137, 142, 144, 154
Florida:
  African Americans, 7, 8, 177
  African Americans (Miami), 176
  Asian Americans, 7, 8, 251
  Central Americans, U.S., 128
  Cuban Americans, 127, 128
  Cuban Americans (Miami), 133, 149, 151
  Greek Americans, 290
  Jewish Americans (Miami), 290, 294
  Latinos, 7, 8, 53, 134, 135
  Latinos (Miami), 133, 135
  Mature Americans, 7, 8, 53, 96, 97,
    120-121
  Mexican Americans, 127
  Puerto Rican Americans, 128
  South Americans, U.S., 128
  White Americans, 7
Focus group discussions, 76
Fodor, 303
Fong, C., 258
Ford, 79-80
  African Americans and, 190
  foreign revenue, 20
  U.K. Blacks and, 311-312
Forman, B. D., 142
Fortini-Campbell, L., 77

Fost, D., 252, 276, 304
Fournier, S., 33, 34, 288
Fox, 11, 149, 204
Francher, J. S., 102
Frank, T., 34
Frazier, E. F., 174, 186
Freedman, A. M., 210, 211
Freeman, J. E., 200, 201
Freeport-McMoRan, 78
Freitas, A., 233, 234, 240
Frey, W. H., 5, 177, 252, 276
Friedmann, E., 115
Frito Bandito, 144
Fruit of the Loom:
  use of all-inclusive advertising, 83
FUBU, 178
Fugita, S. S., 256
Fujioka, T., 49
Furman, P., 102
Furuichi, S., 248
Futterman, M., 171

Gabel, T. G., 54, 81
Gabler, N., 38
Gan, D., 263
Gannon, M. J., & Associates, 288
Gans, J. E., 207
Gap, The, 81
Garman, E. T., 139, 154
Garnets, L. D., 216
Gates, D., 173
Gay.com Network, 224
Gay communities:
  diverse, 225-226
  organizing, 213
  popularity of Halloween, 234, 238
Gay consumers:
  alternatives for companies to attract,
    233-238
  as trendsetters, 240
  companies specializing in, 239-240
  efforts to attract/retain, 241
  of fashion, 225, 240
  of fitness products, 225
  response of to marketing experiences, 231,
    233-234, 238-241
  self-perceived boundary between straight
    Americans and, 217
Gay/Lesbian Market, 2, 3, 23, 241
  access to, 213
  dangers in overtly targeting, 240-241

demographics, 217-221
difficulty in understanding, 213
direct marketing to, 228
education levels, 220-221
mainstream firms targeting, 226
media endorsement of, 226-231
opportunities for marketers, 221
research studies of, 74
segmenting, 238-240
similarities with immigrant markets, 231, 233
spending power, 220, 238-239
using Gay friendly media, 217
using Gay-owned media, 217
*See also specific corporations*; Gays and lesbians
Gay/Lesbian Market, 2, 3, 23, 241
access to, 213
dangers in overtly targeting, 240-241
demographics, 217-221
difficulty in understanding, 213
direct marketing to, 228
education levels, 220-221
mainstream firms targeting, 226
media endorsement of, 226-231
opportunities for marketers, 221
research studies of, 74
segmenting, 238-240
similarities with immigrant markets, 231, 233
spending power, 220, 238-239
using Gay friendly media, 217
using Gay-owned media, 217
*See also specific corporations*; Gays and lesbians
Gay-friendly businesses, 223
Gay Games, 231, 234
sponsors, 231
Gay-Lesbian-Straight Education Network, 226
Gay Liberation Movement, 226
Gay-oriented advertising, 235-237
encoding with "double entendres," 231
encoding with "Gayspeak," 231, 234, 236, 237
gay symbols in, 225, 234
Gay-oriented media, 226-231
books, 228
catalogs, 228
direct mail lists, 241
films, 228-229
Gayellow Pages, 228

gay-friendly business directories, 240, 241
history, 226-227
Internet, 228, 241
magazines, 227, 241
national advertising expenditures, 227
newspapers, 220, 226
print, 227-228
specialized, 229
television networks, 228, 241
television programs, 229
Gay-owned businesses, 223
Gay political organizations, 224
Gay population, size of, 217-218
Gay pride, 213
Gay rights movement, 225-226
Gay Rights parade, 226
Gays and lesbians, 213-214, 217, 241, 283, 288
acceptance by family members, 216
as hate crime victims, 226
camp style, 225
"coming out," 215, 221, 226
consumption decision process, 54
derogative labels, 216
disapproval of in Latino community, 221
identity issues, 214-217
images of in mainstream media, 229-230
in African society, 221
in Asian society, 221
in Native American culture, 221
labeling issues, 216-217
lifestyles, 217, 223, 225
meaning of terms, 218
media usage, 43
media visibility of, 40
"passing for straight," 215
personal relationships, 223
political organizations, 225
religious groups, 223
staying "in the closet," 42
stereotypes, 233
strong sense of community, 221-222
support of family members, 216
*See also* Bisexuals; Gay/Lesbian Market; Gays and lesbians, geographic locations of; Lesbian; Transgendered
Gays and lesbians, geographic locations of, 53, 218, 221-222, 223
neighborhoods, 222
suburban concentration, 218
top 25 metropolitan areas, 219

urban concentration, 218
"Gayspeak," 217, 231, 234, 236, 237, 238, 241
Gay-Straight Alliances, 226
Gay symbols, 225, 234
Geffen Records, 273
Gegax, T. T., 199
Gelb, B. D., 278
General Electric:
    foreign revenue, 20
General Motors:
    African Americans and, 190
    foreign revenue, 20
    Latino market, 152
Generation EN-YE Latinos, 142
Generation X Americans, 35, 297, 299-300
    age cohort values, 111
    "American dream," 299
    as entrepreneurs, 299
    attitude toward target marketing, 33
    cable television use, 300
    common childhood, 299
    cynicism toward advertisers, 300
    diversity, 53
    educational attainment, 299
    Internet use, 300
    media exposure, 299, 300
    media usage, 43, 299
    positive group image search, 10
    shared experiences, 54
    size of cohort, 299
    video use, 300
    World Wide Web and, 54
    See also AT&T; Snapple
Generation Y Americans, 35, 297, 299, 300
    college market, 301-302
    influences, 300
    Internet use, 300
    size of cohort, 300
    spending, 300
Gensch, D. H., 169
Gentry, J. W., 73, 285, 287, 307
Georgia:
    African Americans, 177
    African Americans (Atlanta), 176
    Mature Market, 97
Gergen, K., 260
German Americans, 42, 290, 296
    important dates/events, 290
    2000 population figures, 290
Gettone, V., 184

Gibbs, M. S., 260
Gibson, D. P., 186
Giles, H., 184
Gill, M. S., 241
Gilly, M. C., 35, 57, 59, 60, 76, 142, 154, 156, 169
Ginsburg, J., 34
Gitlin, S., 269
GLAAD, 224
Glenn, E. N., 252
Glick, D., 116, 218
Global firms:
    consumer loyalty, 33
"Global village" marketplace, 15
    increasing importance, 19
Glory Foods:
    African American market, 195
Goett, J. J., 196, 201
Goff, L., 300, 301
Golden, D., 208
Goldman, B., 13
Goldman, K., 103, 171, 190, 202, 298
Goldsmith, J., 152
Goldsmith, R. E., 174
Goldstein, J. R., 295
Gollub, J., 96, 99
Goodson, S. R., 145
Gordon, J., 116
Gordon, M. M., 9
Gore, A., 227
Goya Food Products, 64, 70, 159
    Latino market, 64, 70, 156, 159
Graafsma, T. L. G., 41
Granbois, D. H., 169
Grantham, K. D., 185, 193
Graves, S. B., 262
Gray, V., 190
Greco, A. J., 102
Greek Americans, 290, 296
    important dates/events, 290
    significant media, 290
    2000 population figures, 290
Greeley, A. M., 168, 269
Green, C. L., 183
Green, M., 83, 144, 200
Green, M. K., 291
Green, W. E., 78
Greene, B., 215, 216, 220, 221
Greene, M. G., 115
Greer, W. H., 174
Grier, S., 169, 196, 201

Griffin, T., 311
Grimes, A., 96
Grotevant, H. D., 41
Group identity:
    labeling, 42, 52
    personal identity and, 43
    self-labeling, 42
    *See also* Consumer identities; Social iden-
    tity
Group pride, marketing efforts and, 46
Grover, R., 11, 304
Grunwald, H., 19
Guamanian Americans, 248
Gudykunst, W. B., 58, 75, 90
Gulf Oil:
    foreign revenue, 20
Gurin, G., 184
Gutierrez, E., 241
Gutierrez, F., 89, 144, 152, 153, 156

Ha, T. H., 255
Hagerty, V., 153
Hall, E. T., 22, 58, 75, 90, 261
Hallmark:
    African American market, 190
Hamamoto, D. Y., 262
Hamers, J., 247
Hamilton, C. V., 184
Hammidi, T., 233, 234, 240
Hammond, J., 48, 92, 139, 182, 287
Hampden-Turner, C., 21, 47, 261, 264
Hample, S., 64
"Handicapitalism," 304
Hard-Core Traditionalists, 192
Hardee, B., 168
Hardy, Q., 10
Hare, N., 174
Harper, P. A., 198, 205
Harre, R., 184
Harris, G., 61
Harris, N., 190
Harris-Prager, J., 304
Hartford Insurance:
    Gay/Lesbian market, 230-231, 232
Hasbro:
    use of all-inclusive advertising, 83
Hatchett, D., 169
Haubegger, C., 142
Hawaii:
    Asian Americans, 251, 252, 269
    Asian Americans (Honolulu), 250, 251

Hawkins, C., 170
Hawkins, LaVan, 198-199
Hawkins, S. A., 115
Hayden, T., 142
HBO, 204
Heath, R. P., 298
Hecht, M. L., 46, 58, 90, 183, 184, 185, 200,
    201
Heftel, 145
Heines, V., 153
Henderson, A. B., 196, 304
Herek, G., 215
Hernandez, S. A., 149, 163
Heubusch, K., 61, 74
Hewlett-Packard:
    foreign revenue, 20
Hidalgo, P., 311
High-context cultures, 75
    communication styles in, 22, 48
    *See also specific subcultures*
Hilger, M. T., 137
Hills, G. E., 169
Hiram Walker:
    Gay/Lesbian market, 226, 231
Hirsch, J. S., 240
Hirschman, E., 294
Hirschman, E. C., 12, 288, 292, 294
Hispanic acculturation measures, 129-131
    Bromley Aguilar and Associates' AIGs,
        129, 131
    Market Segment Research, Inc., 129, 130
    Multidimensional Measure of Cultural
        Identity, 129, 130
    NuStats, Inc., 129, 131
    *See also* Latinos, segmenting U.S.
Hispanic & Asian Market Communications
    Research, Inc., 149
Hispanic as term, 125, 128
Hispanic Broadcasting Corporation, 145, 146
*Hispanic Business,* 147, 151
Hispanic family:
    extended family household, 136
    gender roles, 136, 137, 142, 162
    versus Anglo-American family, 136, 137
    *See also* Latinos, U.S.
Hispanic market, 128
    competitors in, 155
    largest advertisers in, 152, 155
Hispanic Market Connections, Inc., 136, 151,
    149
Hispanic marketing mistakes, 162-163

Hispanic media preferences, 150
Hispanic population, U.S., 132-135
    age, 132-133, 134
    dropout rates, 133
    education level, 133
    family income, 133
    family size, 133
    growth, 247
    median annual income, 133
    projected growth, 247
    size, 132
    *See also* Latinos, U.S.
Hispanics, U.S., 123-125, 172. *See also* His-
    panic population, U.S.; Latinos, U.S.
Hispanic teenagers:
    biculturalism, 134
    bilingualism, 134
    trend-setting behaviors, 134
Hispanic values, symbols of, 136-139,
    142-144
    activity orientation, 138
    church, 136, 137, 138
    family, 136, 137, 138, 162
    human nature orientation, 139
    self-perceptions, 139
    Spanish retention, 136, 137, 138, 143, 162
    versus mainstream American values,
        138-139
    worldviews, 138
    *See also* Hispanic culture; Latinos, U.S.
Hitch, P., 247
Hmong Americans, 248
    poverty rate, 248
Hobbs, F. B., 97
Hoeffel, J., 151
Hof, R. D., 79
Hoffman, D. L., 201, 207, 208
Hoffman, T. P., 208
Hofman, J. E., 183
Hofstede, G. H., 21, 22, 47, 143, 200, 261
Holland, J., 73, 285, 287
Holstein, W. J., 19
Holtz, G. T., 54, 299
Home Shopping Network, 204
Homophobia, 230
Homosexuality, debate over "cause" of, 225
Honda:
    African American market, 190
Hong, T., 263
Hoover, R. J., 76, 155
Hope, L., 187
Horovitz, B., 202

Hout, M., 295
Howe, N., 92
Hoyer, W. D., 41, 143, 161
Huang, K., 259
Hughes, M., 183
Hughes, R., 35
Human Rights Campaign, 224
Hume, S., 200
Hummert, M. L., 103, 104, 108
Hwang, S. L., 89
Hyman, H. H., 168
"Hyphenated Americans," 35
Hyundai:
    Asian American market, 280

IBM:
    foreign revenue, 20
Identity formation process, 42. *See also* Group
    identity
Identity markers, substitutes for permanent,
    35
IKEA:
    Gay/Lesbian market, 234, 240
Illinois:
    African Americans, 7, 8, 177
    African Americans (Chicago), 176
    Arab Americans (Chicago), 295
    Armenian Americans, 295
    Asian Americans, 7, 8, 251
    Asian Americans (Chicago), 252, 269
    Greek Americans (Chicago), 290
    Italian Americans (Chicago), 290
    Jewish Americans (Chicago), 294
    Latinos, 7, 8, 53, 134, 135
    Latinos (Chicago), 135
    Mature Americans, 7, 8, 97
    Mature Americans (Chicago), 98
    Mexican Americans, 128
    Mexican Americans (Chicago), 127
    Puerto Rican Americans, 128
    White Americans, 7
Imada Wong, 280
Imperia, G., 137, 142
In-depth interviewing, 76
Individualistic societies, 22, 288. *See also*
        Low-context cultures; Self-identity; So-
    cial identity
Indonesian Americans, 248
Information filters, buyer, 75
Information Resources, Inc. (IRI), 272-273
In-language media, 268, 269, 281

Asian, 270-271
    cable networks, 271, 273
    Chinese, 269, 270
    direct mail, 272
    drawbacks, 270
    effectiveness, 273
    Japanese, 271
    KIKU radio (Hawaii), 271
    KTSF radio (San Francisco), 271
    radio stations, 271
    telemarketing, 272
    television networks, 273
    vehicles, 270
    WMBC radio (New York), 271
Insight into consumers, 81, 82
Integrity (Gay religious group), 223
*International Herald Tribune,* 19
Internet, 10, 21, 32, 190, 311
    Asian in-language, 270
    Asian-oriented, 271-272
    cultural role, 79
    Generation X and, 300
    Generation Y and, 300
    Hispanic content, 153
    teenage consumers and, 301
    *See also* World Wide Web
Internet access, 12
    Anglo-American households, 153
    Asian American households, 153
    Hispanic households, 153
Intertrend, 280
Iococca, Lee, 293
Iowa:
    Mature Americans, 96, 97
Iranian Americans, 42, 290
    significant media, 290
    2000 population, 290
Iraqi Americans, 42
Irish Americans, 294-295, 296, 313
    ethnic pride, 295
    geographic concentrations, 294
    important dates/events, 290
    newspapers for, 295
    significant media, 290
    traditions, 294-295
    2000 population figures, 290, 294
Irish immigrants, 42, 284
Italian Americans, 292-293, 296, 313
    celebrity product endorsers, 293
    dates/events, 290
    family, 293

food, 293
    geographic concentration, 292
    media portrayal, 293
    negative stereotypes, 293
    neighborhood/community importance,
        292-293
    1990 population figures, 292
    organizations, 293
    positive group image search, 10
    publications for, 293
    religion, 293
    significant media, 290
    2000 population figures, 290
    values, 293
Italian immigrants, 42, 284
ITT:
    foreign revenue, 20
Iwatsu, 280

J. C. Penney, 174, 304
    African American market, 190, 195
    Asian American market, 275
Jackson, J. S., 184
Jacob, R., 257
Jacobson, M. F., 38
Jacoby, J., 196, 201
Jandt, F. E., 22, 47, 48, 58, 75, 90, 139, 170,
        179, 215, 216, 218, 220, 223, 225, 226,
        227, 230
Janoff, J. B., 299
Japanese Americans, 42, 243, 245, 248
    communities, 252
    intermarriage, 259
    leaders, 258
    networks, 258
    newspapers, 271
    population trends, 246
    poverty rate, 248
    self-labeling, 259
    versus Hmong Americans, 248
Jay, K., 222, 223
Jaynes, G. D., 184, 186
Jeannet, J.-P., 311, 312
Jenkins, A. H., 185
Jewell, K. S., 184
Jewish Americans, 293-294, 313
    affluence, 293
    educational attainment, 293
    geographic concentration, 293-294
    importance of community, 294
    importance of education, 294

importance of religion, 294
important dates/events, 290
intermarriage, 294
Internet sites for, 294
positive group image search, 10
rituals/traditions, 294
significant media, 290
2000 population figures, 290, 293
Jewish immigrants, 42, 284
Jhally, S., 36
John, J., 307
Johnson, B., 74
Johnson, B. M., 142
Johnson, D. A., 169
Johnson, P., 194
Johnson, R., 133
Johnson & Johnson:
Latino market, 152, 155
Jones, D. A., 240
Joyce, T., 96
Judge, P., 238
Judge, P. C., 35, 43

Kahan, H., 74, 218, 222, 233
Kahle, L. R., 307
Kaiser, S., 233, 234, 240
Kang & Lee, 270, 271, 280
Kanner, B., 187, 190
Kassarjian, H. H., 186
Kates, S. M., 225, 234, 238
Katz, I., 168
Katz, M., 149
Kaufman, C. J., 149, 163
Kaufman, J., 61, 78
Kellner, D., 34, 40, 43, 288
Kenneth Cole:
Gay/Lesbian market, 234
Kerin, R., 196, 201
Kern-Foxworth, M., 189
Khosla, Vinod, 263
Kibria, N., 258
Kim, J. B., 155
Kimmel, D. C., 216
King, S. R., 300
Kitzinger, C., 217
Kizilbash, A. H., 139, 154
Klein, M., 227
Kline, S., 36
Klonoff, E. A., 187
Klor de Alva, J. J., 287
Kluckhohn, F., 261

Kmart, 62, 116
Gay/Lesbian market, 234
Koch, C., 169
Kochman, T., 185, 186
Koehl, C., 291
Kolbert, E., 203
Konrad, W., 101
Korean-American Grocers Association, 252
Korean Americans, 243, 248
business owners, 252
communities, 252
income, 248
leaders, 258
media usage, 269
networks, 258
population trends, 246
self-labeling, 259
Korzenny, F., 153, 210
Koslow, S., 75, 143, 145
Koss-Feder, L., 302
Kotkin, J., 35, 284
Kotler, P., 14, 29, 74
Krafft, S., 294
Kraft Foods:
African American market, 199
Latino market, 152, 155
Krase, J., 292, 293
Kunda, D., 83, 139
Kwanzaa, 192, 194

Labeling issues, 42, 52
Lach, J., 176
LaFerle, C., 5, 37, 54, 193, 194, 200, 209,
268, 273, 274, 280
Lambert, Z. V., 116
Lampe, P. E., 184
Laotian Americans, 245, 248
Larkey, L. K., 183, 184
"Latino" as term, 125-126, 128
Latino culture, U.S.:
as culture of adaptation, 132
as unique, 132
interpersonal relationships, 143-144, 162
Latino immigrants:
native-language media exposure, 9
Latino media images, 144. See also Span-
ish-language media
Latinos, segmenting U.S.:
AIG I (Spanish Dominant), 131
AIG II (Bilingual/Bicultural), 131
AIG III (English Dominant), 131

American identification, 130
Deep Roots, 131
First-Borns, 131
high level of bicultural familiarity, 130
Latino identification, 130
low level of bicultural familiarity, 130
moderate Hispanic cultural identification, 130
Newcomers, 131
strong Hispanic cultural identification, 130
Transitionals, 131
Transplants, 131
weak Hispanic cultural identification, 130
Latinos, U.S., 2, 3, 23, 73, 166, 204, 208, 288
acculturation, 129-132
as challenge to marketers, 125
as important consumers, 154
brand commitment, 76
brand loyalty, 143, 155-156
building familiarity with, 156
churches, 268
civil rights struggle, 285
collectivism, 179
communication style, 261
consumption decision process, 54
diversity, 53, 124-125
dominant cultural values, 261
ethnic identity, 41
ethnic pride, 124, 129, 154
favorite music, 134
favorite television shows, 134
gender roles, 261
importance of family, 124
income level, 4-5, 6
in Mature Market, 94, 95
Internet and, 152-153
leisure time activities, 161
media portrayals, 40
media usage, 38-39, 274
origins, 127-128, 162
personal identity, 261
power distance, 261
product usage, 44
purchasing power, 133
relationship to nature, 261
research studies, 74
response to ethnic-directed marketing efforts, 143
shared values, 124-125
social relationships/organizations, 143, 261
Spanish language retention, 124, 129
store patronage, 44-45
uncertainty avoidance, 261
use of time, 261
See also specific Latino subcultures and specific corporations; Hispanic acculturation measures; Hispanic population, U.S.; Hispanics, U.S.; Latinos, geographic dispersion of U.S.; Latinos, segmenting U.S.
Latinos, geographic dispersion of U.S., 5, 7, 8, 53, 133, 134, 135. See also specific Latino subcultures and U.S. states
Lauterborn, R. E., 71
Lawe, S., 115
Lazar, W., 48
Lee, C. H., 113, 114
Lee, J. F. J., 262
Lee, J. Y., 262
Lee, K. W., 278
Lee, L., 139, 260, 265, 269
Lee, R. A., 93, 120
Lee, S. M., 250, 256
Lee, W., 207, 254, 260, 265, 268, 270, 276, 285
Lee, W.-N., 5, 37, 54, 193, 194, 200, 209, 268, 273, 274, 280
Lee Liu and Tong, 280
Leigh, J. H., 54, 81
Leiss, W., 36
Leivers, S., 40
Leland, J., 178, 179, 302
Leo Burnett, 87
Leone, R. P., 194
Lesbigay Directory at IGC, 224
Lev, M., 276
Levine, D. S., 227, 231
Levine, M., 64
Levi's:
environmental impact policy, 73
human resource policy, 73
Vice President for Ethnic Markets, 86
Levitt, T., 14, 29
Levy, D., 102
Levy, S., 285, 288
Lewin, T. F., 303
Licata, W., 202
Lifetime cable network, 112
Lin, Frank, 263
Lipman, J., 32, 108, 200
Locke, D. C., 256
Longman, D., 154

Longman, D. S., 137
Lonial, S. C., 102, 117
Lorimar, E. S., 11
Louis, M., 276
Louisiana:
    African Americans, 177
    African Americans (New Orleans), 176
    Italian Americans (New Orleans), 290
LOV (List of Values), 192
Low-context cultures:
    communication styles, 22, 48
Lowe, F. H., 195
L3, 280
Lucas, S., 178
Luebkeman, S. G., 200
Lukenbill, G., 214, 217, 218, 222, 225, 230,
    238, 239, 240


Mabry, M., 189
Macklin, M. C., 102, 112, 119
MacLeod, D., 125
Magruder, K. M., 210
Mahoney, R., 295
Majors, R. E., 58, 223
Malaysian Americans, 248
Mandese, J., 270
Manischewitz, 294
Manzer, L. L., 307
Marable, M., 170
Marin, B. V., 125
Marin, G., 125
Marin, R., 230
Marine Midland:
    Arab American market, 296
Market analysts, 307
Market boundaries, national borders irrelevant
    as, 15
Market Development, Inc., 142, 149
    Hispanic Monitor, 142
Market identification, 75
Market information:
    extensive, 80-81
    intensive, 81-82
    sources on African Americans, 199-201
Marketing:
    as economic exchange/cultural medium,
    34-37
Marketing communications planning, inte-
    grated, 71-72
Marketing decision matrix, 24
Marketing institutions:

    as cultural players, 36
Marketing messages. all-inclusive, 83-86
    companies utilizing, 83
    for U.S. general market, 84-85
Marketing mix, 14
    making tactical changes in, 86
    traditional, 59-60
Marketing opportunities, non-U.S. multicul-
    tural settings, 310-312
    cultural sensitivity and, 312
    examples of negative strategies, 311-312
Marketing planners, 76, 89
Marketing shifts:
    brand managers to market specialists, 76-77
    extensive to intensive market information,
    80-82
    long-term profitability to shared interests,
    61-64
    market segmentation to market identifica-
    tion, 74-76
    mass communication to consumer dia-
    logue/organization contact points, 77-80
    mass markets to mass choices, 70-73
    niche marketing to matrix market planning,
    64, 70
Marketing strategies:
    evolution, 14
    meeting consumers' information needs, 32
Marketing style, 70
Marketing tool kit, traditional, 72
Market management, 76-77
Market managers, 76-77
Market niches, 13
Market segmentation, 14, 15, 74-75
    decline, 13-15
    effective, 74
    philosophical basis, 13
    tactics, 14
Market Segment Research, Inc., 39, 45, 129,
    130, 149
Market segments:
    profitability, 13
    response to marketing strategies, 75
Market specialists, 76-77, 89
    qualifications, 77
    See also Ethnic market specialists
Marriott, M., 208
Martell's Cognac:
    Asian American market, 280
Martin, D., 64
Martindale, C., 262

Mary Kay:
  African American market, 86
  Asian American market, 86
  Latino market, 86
  targeting minorities, 86
Maryland:
  African Americans, 177
  African Americans (Baltimore), 176
  Mature Americans (Baltimore), 98
Massachusetts:
  Arab Americans, 290
  Arab Americans (Boston), 295
  Armenian Americans, 295
  Asian Americans, 251, 252
  Greek Americans (Boston), 290
  Irish Americans (Boston), 294
  Italian Americans (Boston), 290
  Jewish Americans (Boston), 294
  Latinos, 135
Mass marketing, 14
  decline, 13-15
  philosophical basis, 13
  versus ethnic marketing, 24
  versus niche marketing, 24
Mass markets, decline of, 13-15
Mass media, costs of:
  versus direct media/interactive media costs, 10-13
Matathia, I., 311
Mateljan, P., 169
Mathews, J., 227
Matsuda, 263
Matsuoka, J. K., 260
Matrix market planning, 64, 81
  implementing, 64
  McDonald's as example, 64, 65-66
  versus mass marketing, 64
  versus niche marketing, 64
Mattachine Society of Washington, 226
Mattel:
  African American market, 199, 204
Mature Americans, 3, 23, 91-93, 120-121, 297
  advertising preferences, 115
  age cohort values, 108, 111
  as activist consumers, 115-116
  as Baby Boomers' parents, 298, 299
  as culturally invisible, 93, 94, 98-102
  as fastest-growing subculture, 91
  as grandparents, 117
  as risk aversive consumers, 119
  "being" experiences of interest to, 119

boycotting firms, 33, 116
civic activities, 102
consumer behavior, 16-117, 119-120
continuing education program attendance, 116
cultural pride, 49
description, 93
diversity, 120
fastest-growing group of, 94-95, 120
feeling of alienation, 45
"gulag" of, 94-97
in workplace, 96
in youth-oriented society, 103-104, 108, 112
length of retirement, 96
media consumption levels, 112, 114
media portrayals, 40
meeting information needs of, 120
negative stereotypes, 93, 103, 104, 121
political strength, 102, 120
positive group image search, 10
positive stereotypes, 103, 104, 108, 121
processing of advertising, 114-115
targeting in Florida, 5
*See also* Mature Americans, media usage of; Mature Market
Mature Americans, media usage of, 54, 112-115
  books, 113
  Internet, 114
  magazines, 113, 114
  newspapers, 113, 121
  television, 112, 113
  Web TV, 114
Mature Market, 2, 35, 52, 298, 299
  AARP and, 45-46, 63-64
  advertisements targeted to, 105-107
  African Americans, 94, 95
  Asian Americans, 95
  benefit appeal to, 108, 110
  building partnerships with, 103
  communication barriers, 103
  consumption decision process, 54
  corporate courting, 117
  debate over membership in, 92-93
  ethnic composition, 95
  fear appeal to, 108, 109
  future of, 94
  gauging diversity of, 121
  gender, 94, 95
  heroes/celebrities of, 117, 120

"illderly," 96
income level, 5, 6
Native Americans, 95
race, 94, 95
research studies, 74
segments, 96
senior citizen discounts in, 108
sharing in family events, 119
size, 95
states with highest percentages, 96
states with largest numbers, 96
U.S. Latinos, 94, 95
"wellderly," 96
White Americans, 95
*See also* Mature Americans; Mature Market, age-based classification of; Mature Market, economic strength of; Mature Market, geographic dispersion of; Mature Market, values-based classification of; McDonald's
Mature Market, age-based classification of, 94, 96
"do age," 108
"feel age," 108
"interest age," 108
"look age," 108
"old old," 95, 96
"perceived age," 93, 108
problems, 96
"young old," 95, 96
Mature Market, economic strength of, 98-102, 120
disposable income, 101
home ownership, 101, 102
interest-earning assets, 101
median net worth, 101
personal wealth, 101
Mature Market, geographic dispersion of, 7, 8, 53, 96, 97-98, 120-121. *See also specific U.S. states*
Mature Market, values-based classification of, 96, 99-101
adapters, 100
ailing outgoers, 101, 116
attainers, 99-100
explorers, 100
frail recluses, 101, 116
healthy hermits, 100-101, 116
healthy indulgers, 100, 116
martyrs, 100
pragmatists, 100

preservers, 100
Mayer, A. J., 96
Mays, V., 221
Mazur, L. A., 38
McAdoo, H. P., 172, 258, 264
McAllister, L., 71
McAllister, M. P., 38
McArthur, D., 311
McAuliffe, C., 298
McCarroll, T., 32, 71
McCarthy, E. J., 14, 29, 74
McCarty, J. A., 156
McClure, J., 210
McConahay, J. B., 168
McCracken, G., 33, 35, 80, 288
McCullough, J., 187
McDonald's:
African American market, 64, 65, 69, 190, 199, 210
Latino market, 64, 65, 68, 152, 155
matrix market planning, 64-66
Mature Americans and, 64, 65, 67
niche marketing tactics, 65-66
McDonald's advertising, 67-69. *See also* McDonald's marketing strategies
McDonald's marketing strategies, 64, 65, 66. *See also* McDonald's advertising
McGann, A., 11
McGinn, D., 61
McGuire, C. V., 49
McGuire, W. J., 49
MCI:
African American market, 190
Asian American market, 280
Latino market, 152, 155
McLaughlin, R., 176
McManus, J., 36, 70, 72
McNeal, J. U., 300
McNeill, J., 223
McShane, L., 190
Meade, D., 295
Media:
as cultural player, 36
Media consumption decisions, 54. *See also specific subcultures*
Media credibility, 12
celebrity endorsement and, 12, 156, 161
Media fragmentation, 12
Media institutions/representations:
in multicultural society, 37-40
Media planning, 10, 11

Media portrayals, 37
  and knowledge of other social groups, 36, 37
  myths, 40
  symbols, 40
  *See also specific subcultures*
Media usage:
  ethnic differences in, 38-39, 54
  *See also specific consumer subcultures*
Mehta, R., 276
Mehta, S., 86
Mehta, S. N., 271
Melcher, R., 86
Melting pot metaphor, 15
  versus salad bowl metaphor, 5, 9, 29
Meredith, G., 54, 75, 92, 111, 289, 297, 314
Mergenhagen, P., 303, 304
Mergers and acquisitions, media, 21
Merrill, C., 300, 301
Metropolitan Community Church, 223
Metropolitan Life Insurance Company:
  Asian American market, 257
  Scholar Program, 278
  South Asian market, 278
Mexican American:
  as group identity, 43
  median annual income, 133
Mexican American culture, 10
  new traditions, 136
Mexican Americans, 75, 127, 128
  attitude toward ethic marketing, 37, 162
  importance of life cycle rituals, 136-137
  Spanish language usage by third-generation, 143
  *See also* Mexican Americans, geographic dispersion of
Mexican Americans, geographic dispersion of, 127, 128, 133, 149. *See also specific U.S. states*
Mexican American subculture, 10
Meyer, M., 225
Meyer, T. P., 155
Michigan:
  African Americans, 177
  African Americans (Detroit), 176
  Arab Americans, 290
  Arab Americans (Detroit), 295
  Armenian Americans, 295
  Greek Americans (Detroit), 290
  Mature Americans, 97
  Mature Americans (Detroit), 98

Mick, D. G., 288
Micro-marketing, 86
Microsoft advertisement, 304, 305
Milam, V., 174
Miller, B., 102
Miller, C., 74, 195
Miller Brewing, 86
  African American market, 190, 211
  Asian American market, 280
  Gay/Lesbian market, 231, 233, 234
Millham, J., 184
Milliones, J., 185
Min, P. G., 245, 259
Missouri:
  African Americans (Kansas City), 176
  African Americans (St. Louis), 176
  Mature Americans, 97
Mitchell, J., 288
Mitchell, S., 5, 33, 289, 297, 299, 300, 307, 314
Mobil:
  foreign revenue, 20
"Model minority," Asian Americans as, 46, 248-250, 257-258
Modems, 12
Modood, T., 310
Moffett, Jim Bob, 78
Mogelonsky, M., 150, 175, 191, 194, 262, 272, 280, 290, 299
MoneyGram:
  African American market, 190
Monte Jade, 280
Montero, D., 256
Mony Life, New Jersey Hindi community and, 276
Moog, C., 71, 304
Moore, D., 193, 210, 211
Morgan, C., 102
Morganthau, T., 166, 167, 175
Morita, Pat:
  in advertisement, 265, 267
Morrison, J., 48, 92, 139, 182, 287
Morrison, T., 264
Morrow, H., 149, 163
Morse, D., 279
Moschis, G. P., 32, 96, 100, 112, 113, 114, 116, 289, 297, 314
Moses, E., 31, 192
Moyerman, D. R., 142
MTV, 11
MTV Latino, 149

Mueller, B., 254
Mueller, M. L., 204
Muhammad, T. K., 208
Mulhern, F. J., 194
Mulryan, D., 74, 218, 222, 233
Mulryan/Nash, 227
Multicultural marketers, required skills of, 312
Multicultural marketing, 73
  ethical dilemmas, 87-89
  pioneers, 74
  tools, 42
Multicultural marketing plans/programs, 162
  cultural compatibility, 57
  implementing, 82, 88, 90
Multicultural marketplace:
  measuring success, 89
Multicultural society:
  consumer adaptation, 32
  defining, 21-23
  successful interaction, 49
Mummert, H., 272
Murphy, K., 304
Myers, H. F., 129, 130
Myers, J. G., 71
Myers, S. L., 169
Myrdal, G., 174
Myths, media use of, 40

NAACP, 198
Nagourney, A., 5
Nahm, H. Y., 260, 288
Narisetti, R., 11, 70, 79
Natale, R., 74
National Association of Black Journalists, 198
National Black MBA Association, 198
National Council of Senior Citizens, 102
National Federation of the Blind, 302
National Gay and Lesbian Task Force, 224
National Italian American Federation, 293
National Lesbian and Gay Health Association, 224
National Register Publishing Company, 196
National Urban League, 198
Native American population, 296
  growth, 247
  1998 figures, 289
  projected growth, 247
  regional concentrations, 290
  2000 figures, 290
  See also specific U.S. states; Native Americans

Native Americans, 288, 289-292, 311, 313
  beliefs/worldviews, 291
  cultural/ethnic pride, 49, 291
  gambling income, 291
  important dates/events, 290
  in Mature Market, 95
  in popular movies, 291-292
  media portrayals, 40
  pick-up trucks, 291
  positive group image search, 9-10
  poverty, 291
  rituals/traditions, 291
  significant media, 290
  sporting events, 291
  stereotypes, 292
  unemployment, 291
  view of nature, 291
  See also Native American population
Natori, Josie, 263
Naya:
  Gay/Lesbian market, 231
NBC, 144, 204
Nebraska:
  Mature Americans, 97
Nee, V., 252
Neelankavil, J. P., 74, 76, 268, 269, 270, 276
Neidell, L. A., 169
Nelson, C., 287
Nelson, D., 154
Nelson, J., 304
Ness, T. E., 174
Nevada:
  Latinos, 135
New Coke, 15
Newcomb, M. D., 129, 130
New Jersey:
  African Americans, 177
  African Americans (Newark), 176
  Arab Americans, 290
  Arab Americans (Bergen), 295
  Armenian Americans, 295
  Asian Americans, 251, 252
  Central Americans, U.S., 128
  Cuban Americans, 128
  Hindi community, 276
  Irish Americans, 294
  Italian Americans, 290
  Jewish Americans, 290
  Latinos, 135
  Mature Americans, 97
  Puerto Rican Americans, 128
  South Americans, U.S., 128

New Mexico:
  Latinos, 135
  Mexican Americans, 128
  Native Americans, 290
New York City:
  as regional subculture, 308, 313
  *See also* New York State
New York Life:
  Asian American market, 280
New York State:
  African Americans, 7, 8, 177
  African Americans (NYC), 175, 176
  Arab Americans, 290
  Arab Americans (NYC), 295
  Armenian Americans, 295
  Asian Americans, 7, 8, 251, 252, 269
  Asian Americans (NYC),, 250, 251
  Central Americans, U.S. (NYC), 128, 133
  Cuban Americans, 128
  Dominican Americans (NYC), 133
  Filipinos (NYC), 269
  Greek Americans (NYC), 290
  Italian Americans, 290
  Italian Americans (NYC), 290
  Jewish Americans, 290
  Jewish Americans (NYC), 290, 293-294
  Latinos, 7, 8, 53, 134, 135
  Latinos (NYC), 133, 134, 135
  Mature Americans, 7, 8, 96, 97
  Mature Americans (NYC), 98
  Puerto Rican Americans (NYC), 127, 128, 133
  South Americans, U.S. (NYC), 128, 133
  White Americans, 7
Nichemanship, 20, 43
Niche marketers, 61
Niche marketing, 14, 73, 306
  buyer/seller cultural partnership versus, 24
  consumer loyalty and, 33
  costs, 61
  McDonald's tactics, 65-66
  versus mass marketing, 24
Niche marketing strategies, 72-73. *See also*
    *specific niche marketing strategies*
Nicholls, J. A. F., 32, 39, 143, 145
Nielsen Media Research, 146, 147, 193, 202, 203, 272
  Hispanic Family Panel, 151
Nobles W. W., 179
Nordholm, M., 145
North Carolina:
  African Americans, 177

Mature Americans, 97
North Dakota:
  Mature Americans, 97
Norwegian Cruise Lines:
  Gay/Lesbian market, 240
Novak, D. L., 208
Novak, T. P., 201, 207, 208
Nugest, M., 171
Nuiry, O. E., 144
NuStats, Inc., 129, 131, 149

O'Barr, W. M., 40, 188
Oberg, K., 260
O'Brien, D. J., 256
Ocamb, K., 231
O'Connor, R. F., 307
O'Donnell, J., 195
Office Depot:
  Asian American market, 280
O'Guinn, T. C., 137, 142, 155, 156
O'Hare, W., 245, 256, 288, 290
O'Hare, W. P., 177, 178, 252, 276
Ohio:
  African Americans, 177
  African Americans (Cleveland), 176
  Arab Americans, 290
  Arab Americans (Cleveland), 295
  Armenian Americans, 295
  Irish Americans, 294
  Mature Americans, 97
Okazawa-Rey, M., 169
Oklahoma:
  Native Americans, 290
Old Navy, 81
Oliver, J. A., 163
Ono, Y., 188, 189
Organizations:
  becoming multicultural entities, 59
Ostruff, J., 114
Oswald, L. R., 50, 288
Overlooked Opinions, 74

Pacific Bell Ethnic Markets Group, 86
Package designs, 12
Padgett, T., 142
Padilla, B., 136
Padilla, F., 147
Painton, P., 217
Pakistani Americans, 248
Palomo, J. R., 170, 179
Pang, G. Y., 256, 258

Park, I. H., 253
Parker-Pope, T., 311, 312
Parthasarathy, M., 87
Paskowski, M., 270
Patterson, G. A., 86
Patterson, J. M., 169
Paul, P., 304
Paulin, G. D., 154
Pease, E. C., 169
Peller, Clara, 102
Penaloza, L., 58, 90, 156, 220, 233, 240, 285
Penaloza, L. N., 35, 57, 59, 60, 76, 142, 154, 156, 169
Pennsylvania:
    African Americans, 177
    African Americans (Philadelphia), 176
    Arab Americans, 290
    Armenian Americans, 295
    German Americans, 290
    Irish Americans, 294
    Italian Americans, 290
    Jewish Americans (Philadelphia), 294
    Mature Americans, 96, 97
    Mature Americans (Philadelphia), 98
Peplau, L., 221
Peppers, D., 33, 79
PepsiCo:
    African American market, 190, 198
    use of all-inclusive advertising, 83
Petersen, A., 12, 21, 114
Petrecca, L., 231
Petrof, J. V., 169
Petrozzello, D., 145
Petzinger, T., 21
Philip Morris:
    African American market, 190, 211
    foreign revenue, 20
    Gay/Lesbian market, 226, 234
Phillips, M. M., 92, 111, 117, 289, 297, 314
Picker, L., 116
Piirto, R., 132, 307
Pillsbury Doughboy, 31
Pine, B. J., 79
Pinkney, A., 173
Pitts, L., 187
Plotch, B., 308
Plummer, J., 196, 201
Pokémon, 263
Political correctness, 283
Poniewozik, J., 229
Population trends, U.S., 4
Porras, J. I., 36, 62

Porter, R., 169
Porter, R. E., 58, 75, 90, 143
Portes, A., 125
Post Yuppies, 192
Potgieter, C., 221
Power, C., 70, 300
Predicting marketplace behavior, 74-75
Price Waterhouse Coopers, 21
Proctor & Gamble, 10, 11, 86
    African American market, 190, 206
    foreign revenue, 20
    Latino market, 152, 154, 155
    Pampers database, 70
    Vice President for Ethnic Markets, 86
Product placements:
    effectiveness, 82
    in film, 12
    in media, 12
Product usage:
    ethnic differences, 44
Profitability, long-term:
    economic models, 62
Promotions:
    consumer, 12
    trade, 12
Pruden, H. O., 137, 154
Psychographic information, 81
Public relations, 12
Puerto Rican Americans, 127, 128, 133, 162
    chicken farmers, 279
    English fluency, 129
    median annual income, 133
    See also specific U. S. states
Putnam, R. D., 34

Quaker Oats:
    African American market, 190
Qualls, W., 169, 196, 201
Qualls, W. J., 49, 58, 169, 175, 192, 193, 200, 210, 211, 285, 287
Queer Nation, 224
Quintanilla, Selena, 142, 156
Qworld, 224

Race:
    as socially constructed, 165
    myth of, 165-168
    "one-drop" rule, 166
Racial prejudice, 168-170
    measuring, 168
Racial stereotypes, television-created, 169

Racial targeting, 210
Radio Unica, 145, 146
Ragaza, A., 250
Rainbow-PUSH Coalition, 198
Raju, P. S., 102, 117
Ramirez, M., 186, 187
Randazzo, S., 59, 70, 71, 79, 81
Rao, C. P., 174
Rapp, S., 33
Ray, P. H., 48, 287
Redefining markets, 21
Reed, J. S., 306
Reed, V. M., 169
Reedy, J., 303
Reese, S., 290, 294, 295, 296, 297
Reeve, Christopher, 303
Refugee Act of 1980, 244
Regional subcultures, 306-309, 313
    as modern tribes, 307
    communication styles, 306
    gender roles, 306
    lifestyles, 306
    marketing approaches to, 306-307
    pace of life, 306
    power distance, 306
    values, 306
    view of humans and nature, 306
    *See also specific U.S. states*
Reid, C. C., 174
Reid, I. S., 174
Reilly, M. D., 10, 132, 154
Reilly, P., 206
Reitman, V., 206
Relationship marketing, 72, 73
    focus, 33
    techniques, 15
Ressner, J., 292
Revlon:
    African American market, 190, 198
Reyes, S., 144
Rhode Island:
    Armenian Americans, 295
    Mature Americans, 96, 97
Ribeau, S., 184
Ribeau, S. A., 46, 58, 90, 183, 185, 200, 201
Rice, R., 210
Ritchie, K., 74, 289, 297, 299, 314
Ritson, M., 301
Rittenberg, T., 87
Rivera, E., 278
Rizzo, C., 115
Roberts, J. L., 11

Robertson, T. S., 192
Robinson, J., 299
Robinson, P. A., 174
Rockport, 298
Rodriguez, G., 149, 152
Rodriguez, V., 149, 163
Rogers, M., 33, 79
Rokeach, M., 23
Role switching, 260
    Asian American, 260
Rolle, A., 293
Romney, L., 152
Rook, D., 288
Rose, M., 12, 21
Rosenbaum, S., 304
Rosenthal, E. M., 10
Roslow, P., 32, 39, 143, 145
Rossman, M. L., 32
Rudd, N. A., 233, 240
Rueschenberg, E. J., 132
Russell, C., 120, 298
Russell, J., 145
Russell, J. T., 11
Ryan, N., 191
Rzttki, B., 210

Saab:
    Gay/Lesbian market, 233
Saegert, J., 76, 149, 155, 163
Sakamoto, A., 248
Salad bowl metaphor, 287
    appeal, 23
    versus melting pot metaphor, 5, 9, 29
Salholz, E., 218
Salins, P., 308
Salvadoran Americans, 133
Salzman, M., 311
Samovar, L. A., 58, 75, 90, 143
Sampson, W. A., 174
Samsung Electronics:
    Asian American market, 280
Samuels, A., 178, 179
Sandberg, J., 114
Sanders, A. L., 5
Sanders, J. M., 252
Sandor, G., 290, 303
Saporito, B., 63, 87
Sarathy, R., 61
Sasao, T., 168
Saveri, G., 226, 241
Scenic America, 207

Schement, J. R., 204
Schewe, C., 54, 75, 92, 111, 289, 297, 314
Schewe, C. D., 119
Schick:
    use of all-inclusive advertising, 83
Schiller, Z., 70, 86
Schlesinger, A. M., 35
Schlinger, M. J., 196, 201
Schmid, J., 262, 265, 269
Schmitt, B. H., 270
Schonfeld, E., 12, 13, 70
Schooler, C., 207
Schouten, J., 34, 284
Schultz, D. E., 71, 78
Schwab:
    Gay/Lesbian market, 231
Schwarz, B., 15
Schwartz, J., 308
Scott, B. M., 210
Scott, L. M., 70, 80, 288
Sears:
    African American market, 190, 195
    Asian American market, 275
    Latino market, 152, 155
Sears, T. J., 222
Seelye, H. N., 48, 49
Seelye-James, A., 48, 49
Self-identity, 55
    brand use, 33-34
    marketplace expression, 43
    social identity and, 40-46
Self-Navigators, 192
Semiotic analysis of meaning, 76
Sesane, M. H., 163
Shamdasani, P. N., 75, 143, 145
Shared customer values, 62
Shared interests, buyer/marketer, 62
    measures, 63
Sharma, S., 168
Sharpe, R., 280
Shaver, M. A., 145
Shaw, J., 294
Shaw-Taylor, Y., 263
Sheatsley, P. B., 168, 269
Shepard, S., 168
Shergill, S., 11
Shermach, K., 272
Sherry, J. F., Jr., 312
Shifting identity, 57
Shim, J. C., 269
Shimp, T. A., 168

Shinagawa, L. H., 256, 258
Shook, K. L., 207
Shopping:
    as Asian American leisure activity, 275-276
Shorris, E., 126
Sideband radio, 269
Siegelman, P., 169
Sigelman, L., 168
Silvia Woods Enterprises, 279
Simmons, 272, 307
Simons, J., 120, 174
Simons, P. E., 96
Simpatia, 143
Simpson, J. C., 194
Singer, D., 293
Sirgy, M. J., 34, 41, 43, 50
Sissors, J. Z., 11
Si-TV, 149
Skriloff, L., 208
Sladkus International study, 297
Slater, M. D., 74
Smith, J., 169
Smith, J. W., 54, 289, 297, 299, 314
Smith, L. E., 184
Smith, T. W., 168
Smitherman, G., 184, 185
Smolowe, J., 302, 303
Snapple:
    Generation X market, 70
Snider, J. H., 79
Snuggs, T., 169, 171, 193
Snyder, R., 200, 201
Soberon-Ferrer, H., 167, 187
Social identity:
    age and, 50, 51, 54, 58
    Americanization of, 287
    biology/race and, 50, 51, 54, 58
    culture and, 50
    disability and, 51, 58
    education and, 50
    ethnicity and, 51, 54, 58
    family life cycle stage and, 50
    gender and, 51, 54, 58
    geography and, 50, 51, 54, 58
    occupation and, 50
    self-identity and, 40-46
    sexual orientation and, 50, 51, 54, 58
    social class and, 50
    social interaction and, 46
    See also Consumer identities
Social identity/consumer choice model, 46

Socialization agents, American, 34
  media as, 34
Social selves, multiple, 42
Solomon, C., 133
Solomon, J., 70, 71
Solomon, M., 294, 301
Solomon, M. R., 15, 38, 49, 70, 71, 75, 288
Solzhenitsyn, A. I., 94
Sons of Italy, 293
Sorrell, M., 311
Soruco, G. R., 149, 163
South Americans, U.S., 127, 128, 133, 162.
  *See also specific U.S. states*
South Carolina:
  African Americans, 177
South Dakota:
  Mature Americans, 97
Southern California Toyota Dealers:
  Asian American market, 280
Sowell, T., 293
Spanish Broadcasting System-SBS, 145, 146
Spanish-language advertising, 137, 140, 141,
      145, 149, 151, 154, 160
  billboards, 152
  direct mail, 152
  Hispanicized, 155
  print ads, 158
  radio, 145, 152
Spanish-language media, 150
  cable television, 146
  Chicago-based, 146, 148
  growth, 145
  Los Angeles-based, 146, 147, 148
  magazines, 146-147, 150
  Miami-based, 146, 147, 148
  newspapers, 145, 146, 147, 148, 150, 151
  New York-based, 146, 147, 148
  radio, 145, 146, 148, 149, 150
  San Antonio-based, 146, 148
  television, 145, 146, 148, 149, 150
  yellow pages directories, 152
Spanish-language usage, 136, 137, 138, 143
  symbolic value, 143
Speaker, P., 289, 297, 300, 314
Spiegler, M., 294
Spigner, C., 262
Spinner, J., 171
Spokesperson icons, assigning human quali-
      ties to, 33. *See also specific spokesper-
      son icons*
Sprint:

African American market, 190
Staelin, R., 169
Staff of A Magazine, 263
Stagmaier, J., 174
Stalk, G., 311
Standard Oil-CA:
  foreign revenue, 20
Stankevich, D., 155
Stapinski, H., 142, 300
Star, A. D., 186
Station Index, 151
Stayman, D. M., 41, 42, 49, 129, 132, 161,
      260, 285, 287
Stearns, J. M., 200
Steenkamp, J.-B. E. M., 311
Stein, H., 288
Steinhauer, J., 155
Steinway and Sons:
  Asian American market, 280
Stereotyping, media, 36
Stern, B. B., 250, 257, 258, 262, 269
Sterngold, J., 204
Stevens, N., 115
Stewart, D. W., 210
Stewart, E. C., 40, 41, 139, 255, 263
Stewart, T. A., 214, 226
Still, R. R., 14, 74
Stipp, D., 94
Stith, M. T., 174
Stone, B., 12
Store patronage, ethnic differences in, 44-45
Strandskov, J., 61
Strategy Research International, 149, 150
Strauss, W., 92
Strodtbeck, F. L., 261
Stuart, E., 308
Sturdivant, F. D., 154
Subcultures, consumer. *See* Consumer subcul-
      tures
Subervi, F., 132
Subervi-Velez, F., 42
Suburu:
  Gay/Lesbian market, 234
Sue, S., 168
Sui, Anna, 263
Summarek, J., 11
Sumner, G. A., 168
Sumo wrestling, 263
Sutter, S., 304
Swayne, L. E., 102
Swenson, C. A., 301

Symbols, media use of, 40
Szybillo, G. J., 196, 201

Taeuber, C., 5, 91, 94, 101
Tajfel, H., 184
Takahashi, D., 263, 280
Takaki, R., 245, 258, 259
Tam, Vivienne, 263
Tamagotchi, 263
Tan, A., 253, 263
Tan, C. T., 187
Tannen, D., 58
Tannenbaum, J. A., 302
Tannenbaum, S. I., 71
Tansuhaj, R., 307
Target marketing, 13
Target (store), 86
    greeters, 116
Taylor, C. R., 250, 257, 258, 262, 269
Taylor, D., 184
Taylor, D. G., 168, 269
Taylor, E. G., 39, 269
Technologies, convergence of new, 13
Technology, media cost changes and, 10-13
Teenage consumers, 297, 301
    advertisers' difficulty reaching, 301
    areas of conflict, 301
    as trendspotters, 301
    as Web surfers, 301
    cohort size, 301
    education and, 301
    magazines, 301
    research studies of, 74
Teinowitz, I., 5, 50, 76, 88, 167, 273, 275,
    278
Tejada, C., 13, 170
Telemundo Network, 146, 148, 149, 150
Television, interactive, 10
Television advertising:
    major network, 10, 11
Television Digest, 11
Tennessee:
    African Americans (Memphis), 176
Tepper, K., 108
Terpstra, V., 61
Texaco:
    foreign revenue, 20
Texas:
    African Americans, 7, 8, 177
    African Americans (Dallas), 176
    African Americans (Houston), 176, 274

Arab Americans, 290
Arab Americans (Houston), 295
Armenian Americans, 295
Asian Americans, 7, 8, 251, 252, 269
    as regional subculture, 307-308, 309,
        313
Chinese Americans (Houston), 274
German Americans, 290
Latinos, 5, 7, 8, 53, 134, 135
Latinos (Brownsville), 135
Latinos (Dallas-Fort Worth), 135
Latinos (El Paso), 135
Latinos (Houston), 135, 274
Latinos (McAllen), 135
Latinos (San Antonio), 133, 135
Mature Americans, 7, 8, 96, 97
Mature Americans (Houston), 98
Mature Americans (San Antonio), 98
Mexican Americans, 128
Mexican Americans (Houston), 127
Mexican Americans (San Antonio), 127,
    133, 149
Vietnamese Americans (Houston), 278
White Americans, 7
White Americans (Houston), 274
Thai Airways:
    Asian American market, 280
Thai Americans, 248
Tharp, M., 5, 37, 42, 54, 70, 80, 129, 132,
    193, 194, 200, 209, 268, 273, 274, 280,
    288
Tharp Hilger, M., 76, 155
Thau, R., 294
Thomas, C. W., 185
Thomas, P., 248, 279
Thomas, S. W., 185
Thomas, V., 112
Thompson, C., 291
Thompson, C. J., 12, 288
Thompson, L., 225
Thurm, S., 263, 280
Tichenor, 145, 146
Tienda, M., 287
"Tiger Woods phenomenon," 168
Tilove, J., 166
Time magazine, 19
Ting-Toomey, S., 58, 75, 90
Tokenism, 53
Tolley, B. S., 196, 201
Tonka:
    use of all-inclusive advertising, 83
Torres, J., 144, 151

Touchstone, E. E., 75, 143, 145
Toyota:
    African American market, 190, 199, 204
    Latino market, 152, 155
Trafzer, C. E., 291
Transgendered, 218, 220
Transmigration, 57, 59-60, 82, 86, 89. *See also* Enculturation
Travolta, John, 293
Treas, J., 103
Trompenaars, F., 21, 47, 261, 264
Trosper, R. L., 291
Tse, D., 254, 265, 268, 270, 276, 285
Tsiantar, D.,
Tuan, M., 257, 258, 259, 264, 285
Tucker, M., 102
Tuller, D., 218
Turner, J. C., 184
Turner, R. M., 307
Turner Broadcasting, 21
Turow, J., 35, 36, 57, 70, 75, 86, 87, 284
Twitchell, J. B., 35, 38, 54, 80, 284, 288

U.S. Attorney General, 170
U.S. Bureau of Statistics, 172
U.S. Bureau of the Census, 4, 5, 6, 7, 8, 50,, 95, 96, 98, 127, 128, 129, 133, 135, 172, 173, 177, 219, 241, 245, 246, 247, 248, 249, 251, 254, 289, 291, 294, 295, 303
    categories of Asians/Pacific Islanders, 248
    classification of U.S. Hispanics, 126, 127-128
    definition of Mature American, 92
    recognition of racial diversity, 167
U.S. Census, 88
    1980, 296
    1990, 91, 132, 245
    1970, 245
    2000, 167
U.S. Department of Commerce, 269
U.S. Department of Justice, 226
U.S. Department of Labor:
    definition of Mature American, 92
U.S. Supreme Court, 166
Underhill, P., 116, 120
Ungar, S. J., 124, 245, 257, 284, 287
Unger, L. S., 200
United Negro College Fund, 198
Univision Network, 146, 147, 148, 150, 151, 153
UniWorld, 196

UPN, 204
Urban legends, 190
Urban marketing techniques, 134
Ursic, A. C., 102
Ursic, M. L., 102
Ursic, V. L., 102
USAir:
    use of all-inclusive advertising, 83

Vaillancourt, M., 74
Valdes, M. I., 163
Valencia, H., 83, 86, 129, 137, 139, 142, 163, 187, 193, 194, 200
VALS-2, 192
Values:
    mainstream, 2
    subcultural, 2
Value systems, multiple, 2
    in multicultural society, 31
Van Biema, D., 291
Van Boven, S., 292
Vargas, R., 136
VCRs, 19
Veciana-Suarez, A., 147, 148
Venkatesh, A., 201, 207, 208
Videos, rental, 12
Vietnamese Americans, 243, 245, 248
    communities, 252
    in agriculture, 252
    income, 248
    in fishing, 252
    in personal services, 252
    leaders, 258
    media usage, 269
    networks, 258
    population trends, 246
    self-labeling, 259
    using Vietnamese-owned banks, 278
Villarreal, R., 42, 129, 132
Vincenti, L., 175
Virgin Atlantic Airways:
    Gay/Lesbian market, 226
Virginia:
    African Americans, 177
    African Americans (Norfolk-Virginia Beach-Newport News), 176
    African Americans (Richmond), 175
    Arab Americans, 290
    Armenian Americans, 295
    Asian Americans, 251
    Mature Market, 97

Vitucci, J. D., 133

Wagner, J., 167, 187
Walker, C., 31, 192, 311
Walker, M. M., 102, 112, 119
Wallendorf, M., 10, 132, 154, 187
Wallich, P., 12
Wal-Mart, 62, 116
    advertising with disabled Americans, 40
    multicultural marketing, 87
Walters, A. S., 240
Walters, J. M., 223
Wang, L. L., 262
Wang, N., 265
Ward, L. B., 195
Ward, S., 192
Ware, R., 299
Warner Brothers, 11
Warren, S., 240
Wartzman, R., 5, 134, 151, 294
Washington, D.C.:
    African Americans, 176
    Arab Americans, 295
    Latinos, 135
Washington State:
    Asian Americans, 251, 252
    Asian Americans (Seattle), 250
    Mexican Americans, 128
    Native Americans, 290
Waters, M., 132
Waters, M. C., 41, 42, 284
Wattanasuwan, K., 311
Wattanasuwan, R. E. K., 34, 288
WB, 204
Weber, A. M., 311
Weber, T. E., 114
Web sites, 12
Webster, C., 74, 76, 139
Webster, N. C., 40, 137
Webster's Dictionary, 187
Wehling, R. L., 311
Weingarden, J., 142
Weingert, P., 142
Weinstein, B., 53
Weisend, T., 74
Weiss, M. J., 307, 311
Weiss, M. S., 245
Weissman, R. X., 39
Welch, S., 168
Wells Fargo Bank:
    Chinese American market, 70

San Francisco's Chinese Americans and, 70
Wendy's, 102
Werbner, P., 310
Westerman, M., 144, 163
Western Union:
    African American market, 190
West Virginia:
    Mature Americans, 96, 97
Whipple, T. W., 169
White, C. L., 183, 184
White, J. B., 13, 14, 29
White, J. D., 174
White American population:
    growth, 247
    projected growth, 247
White Americans, 7, 35, 296
    attitude toward ethic marketing, 37
    education levels, 249
    ethnic identity, 41
    household types, 254
    income, 6, 249
    in Mature Market, 95
    males, 9
    media usage, 38-39
    product usage, 44
    store patronage, 44-45
    See also specific U.S. states; Euro-Ameri-
      cans
Whittler, T. E., 86, 183, 201
Wickham, D., 205
Wiesedanger, B., 76, 269, 270, 276
Wildstrom, S. H., 87
Wilkes, R. E., 83, 86, 114, 193, 194, 200
Wilkinson, I. F., 73, 312
Williams, G., 200
Williams, J. D., 49, 58, 168, 169, 171, 174,
    175, 285, 185, 192, 193, 194, 195, 200,
    210, 211, 287
Williams, J., 169, 196, 201, 304
Williams, N., 136, 137
Williams, R. M., 184, 186
Williamson, J., 288
Willis, M. G., 182
Wilson, C. C., 89, 144, 152, 153, 156
Wilson, G. L., 189
Winter, A. D., 230
Wisconsin:
    African Americans (Milwaukee), 176
Wolfe, D. B., 96, 99, 108, 111, 112, 115,
    119
Wolk, M., 238

Women:
  civil rights struggle, 285
Wong, A. M., 252, 253, 259, 264, 265, 268, 269, 275, 278, 279, 280
Wong, M., 169
Woods, G. B., 32, 196
Woodson, C. G., 174
Woodward, K. L., 194
Word of mouth:
  as mature Americans' information source, 114
World Wide Web, 12, 79, 152
  Generation X and, 54
  Mature Americans and, 114
  *See also* Internet; Internet access
Wortzel, L. H., 186, 193
Wrigley:
  African American market, 198, 210
Wu, D. T. L., 247, 257
Wynter, L. E., 76, 83, 86, 152, 167, 173, 174, 178, 190, 191, 195, 198, 202, 206, 208, 209, 269, 272
Wysocki, B., 257, 258, 259, 263, 287

Xerox:
  use of all-inclusive advertising, 83

Yamaki, T., 311
Yanagisako, S. J., 260

Yang, Andrew, 263
Yang, J., 263
Yankelovich Hispanic Monitor, 155
Yankelovich Monitor Survey, 220
Yankelovich Partners, 146, 150
Yankelovich study, 218
Yeh, C. J., 259
Yinger, J., 169
Young, A., 222, 223
Young, M. R., 183
Young and Rubicam, 87
Young-chol, K., 255
Youth-oriented society, Mature Americans in, 103-104, 108, 112
Yovovich, B. G., 186
Yung, J., 258

Zachary, G. P., 310
Zate, M., 147, 152
Zbar, J. D., 32, 149, 152, 154, 191
Zhang, S., 270
Zhang, Y., 278
Zielinski, J., 192
Zill, N., 299
Zinkhan, G., 200
Zogby, J., 295, 296
Zola, I. K., 108
Zollo, P., 302
Zonana, V. F., 238
Zweigenhaft, R. L., 284, 285

# About the Authors

ERNEST W. BROMLEY joined Sosa & Associates in 1981. He is now Chairman/CEO of the renamed multimillion-dollar advertising agency Bromley Communications and its staff of 135 employees. Bromley Communications is owned 49% by the Macmanus Group, on whose Group Operations Committee he serves. He was instrumental in developing the agency's research and Hispanic marketing approach, Acculturation Influence Groups (AIGs). This principle of segmenting Hispanic consumers into levels of language and culture comfort zones was a breakthrough concept in the early 1980s but is now widely accepted by the industry. Such innovative thinking has built the agency into the leading Hispanic marketing communications company, empowering clients such as Procter & Gamble, Burger King, Coca-Cola, and Western Union, in the changing American marketplace. Prior to joining the agency, Bromley taught economics at the University of Texas at San Antonio. He has a BA in political science and an MBA from the University of Texas at San Antonio. His current duties involve development and execution of the agency's vision and its outstanding products and services. He also works closely with account teams in developing sound marketing strategies for clients. He serves on a number of advisory boards and is an active community and civic leader.

SATOMI FURUICHI is Postdoctoral Fellow at the Center for Social Work Research at the University of Texas at Austin. She taught courses in Asian Americans at the University of Texas at Austin while in the graduate program there. She received her MA and PhD in Sociology from the University of Texas at Austin and her BA in Sociology from Austin College in Sherman, Texas. Dr. Furuichi's research interests include racial stratification, inequality, and comparative history of Japanese immigration to the United States and Brazil. She has presented her work at sociological association meetings and has been published in Research in Social Stratification and Mobility.

CARRIE LA FERLE is Assistant Professor in the Department of Advertising at Michigan State University. She received her BA in sociology from the University of Western Ontario, her MA in advertising from Michigan State University, and her PhD in advertising from the University of Texas at Austin. Her research interests include issues related to cross-cultural communication, cross media promotion, role socialization, and the influence of emotion in advertising. She has presented her work both domestically and internationally, and her work has been published in journals such as the *Journal of Current Issues and Research in Advertising,* the *International Journal of Advertising,* and the *Journal of Advertising Research.* Prior to her career in academia, she obtained industry-related experience in Canada, the United States, and Japan.

WEI-NA LEE is Associate Professor of Advertising and Executive Director of the Office of Survey Research at the University of Texas at Austin. She received her PhD in communication and her MS in advertising from the University of Illinois at Urbana-Champaign. Her MA in journalism is from the University of Wisconsin—Madison. She was a visiting professor at DDB Needham, Chicago, and at D'Arcy Masius Benton and Bowles in New York. Her research interests concern cross-cultural consumer behavior, with an emphasis on ethnic identity in a multicultural environment. Her research articles have appeared in *Journal of Advertising, Journal of Advertising Research, International Journal of Advertising, Journal of Business Research,* and *Psychology and Marketing,* among others. She is a Research Fellow of the American Academy of Advertising and the recipient of several research awards.

MARYE C. THARP is Associate Professor in the Department of Advertising at the University of Texas at Austin. She received her PhD, MBA, and BBA in marketing and her BA in Spanish and French, all from the University of Texas at

Austin. Previously she was an Associate Professor of Marketing at the University of Texas at San Antonio. Her research interests involve multicultural and international advertising and marketing. Her publications include books on international and multicultural marketing and articles appearing in the *Journal of Macromarketing, International Journal of Advertising, Journalism Quarterly, Journal of Global Marketing, Journal of Inter-American Studies and World Affairs, Columbia Journal of World Business,* and *Journal of Consumer Research,* among others. She has been a visiting lecturer and Fulbright scholar at the Universidad Autonoma de San Luis Potosi, the Universidad de las Américas, and the Instituto Tecnológico de Estudios Superiores de Monterrey in México, the Universidad del Pacífico in Peru, and the University of Kent at Canterbury in England. She is also active as consultant for private and public enterprises in the United States and other countries.

JEROME D. WILLIAMS is Associate Professor of Marketing at Penn State University. He also has taught marketing as a visiting professor at the Wharton School of the University of Pennsylvania, the University of Michigan, the National University of Singapore, Nanyang Technological University in Singapore, Chinese University of Hong Kong, the University of Auckland in New Zealand, and the University of the West Indies in Jamaica. He earned his PhD in business administration with a minor in social psychology from the University of Colorado, his MS in industrial administration from Union College, and his BA in English from the University of Pennsylvania. His research interests cover a number of areas in the business-to-business and consumer marketing domains, with emphasis on ethnic minority marketing. He has been an expert witness on consumer response to advertising strategies and has been interviewed extensively in the national media as part of the debate on the ethics of target marketing, particularly the targeting of alcohol and tobacco products to ethnic minority consumers. He sits on the Executive Board of the Society for Consumer Psychology of the American Psychological Association. He also is a member of the American Marketing Association, Association for Consumer Research, American Academy of Advertising, Academy of Marketing Science, National Economic Association, American Psychological Society, and International Society for Quality of Life Studies.